EDWARD VI

EDWARD VI

THE LOST KING
OF ENGLAND

CHRIS SKIDMORE

ST. MARTIN'S PRESS ✹ NEW YORK

To my parents.

www.stmartins.com

Library of Congress Cataloging-in-Publication Data

Skidmore, Chris, 1981–
    Edward VI : the lost King of England / Chris Skidmore.—1st U.S. ed.
        p. cm.
    Includes bibliographical references and index.
    ISBN-13: 978-0-312-35142-7
    ISBN-10: 0-312-35142-9
    1. Edward VI, King of England, 1537–1553. 2. Great Britain—Kings and rulers—Biography. 3. Great Britain—History—Edward VI, 1547–1553. 4. Great Britain—Court and courtiers—History—16th century. I. Title.

DA345 .S55 2007
942.05'3092—dc22
[B]
                                         2007030740

First published in Great Britain by Weidenfeld & Nicolson,
an imprint of The Orion Publishing Group Ltd

First U.S. Edition: November 2007

10 9 8 7 6 5 4 3 2 1

CONTENTS

List of Illustrations   vii

Acknowledgements   ix

Biographies   xi

Chronology   xvii

Tables of Genealogy   xix

Introduction   1

1. Marriages, Birth and Death   10

2. Last Will and Testament   40

3. A Second Josiah   55

4. Milder Climates   68

5. The Downfall of the Lord Admiral   97

6. Commotion Time   112

7. Coup d'Etat   135

8. Uncertain Times   156

9. Hidden Conspiracies   183

10. The Destruction of the Duke   205

11. An Emerging King   227

12. Promise Unfulfilled   243

13. Nemesis   263

Select Bibliography   290

Notes   299

Index   333

LIST OF ILLUSTRATIONS

Endpapers: The Coronation procession of King Edward VI. (Bridgeman Art Library: Society of Antiquaries)

1. 'No painting ever boasted greater': Hans Holbein's mural of Henry VIII. (2006 HM Queen Elizabeth II)
2. The image of royal supremacy. (Bridgeman Art Library: Thyssen-Bornemisza Collection, Madrid)
3. The reality. (Bridgeman Art Library: Society of Antiquaries)
4. Jane Seymour. (Bridgeman Art Library: Kunsthistorisches Museum, Vienna)
5. 'Little one, emulate thy father and be the heir of his virtue'. (AKG London: National Gallery of Art, Washington DC, Andrew Mellon Collection)
6. Henry was a devoted father to his son. (2006 HM Queen Elizabeth II)
7. Edward's early childhood was one of carefree abandon. (AKG London: Kunstmuseum, Basel)
8. Henry Howard, Earl of Surrey. (National Portrait Gallery)
9. Edward at Ashridge House. (2006 HM Queen Elizabeth II)
10. Sir John Cheke. (Getty Images)
11. Allegory of Edward's reign. (National Portrait Gallery)
12. Henry VIII's last will and testament. (National Archives)
13. William Paget, Henry VIII's private secretary. (National Portrait Gallery)
14. Edward Seymour, Duke of Somerset and Edward's uncle: portrait by Hans Holbein. (Bridgeman Art Library: Trustees of the Weston Park Foundation)
15. Edward's signature. (Bridgeman Art Library)
16. Edward on the cusp of manhood. (AKG London: Louvre, Paris)
17. Princess Mary, Edward's elder half-sister. (National Portrait Gallery)

18. A teenage Princess Elizabeth, Edward's half-sister. (2006 HM Queen Elizabeth II)

19. Katherine Parr, Henry VIII's sixth wife. (National Portrait Gallery)

20. Sir Thomas Seymour, Somerset's younger brother. (National Portrait Gallery)

21. Thomas Cranmer, Archbishop of Canterbury. (Bridgeman Art Library: Lambeth Palace)

22. An allegory of Edward's reign, from John Foxe's *Acts and Monuments*, 1570. (Bridgeman Art Library)

23. John Dudley, later Duke of Northumberland. (W&N Archive)

24. Thomas Wriothesley, Earl of Southampton. (Private Collection)

25. A woodcut from Foxe's *Acts and Monuments* showing Hugh Latimer preaching. (Bridgeman Art Library)

26. A seventeenth-century woodcut of the Duke of Somerset's execution on Tower Hill. (W&N Archive)

27. The frontispiece of the controversial 1549 Book of Common Prayer. (Bridgeman Art Library)

28. Edward VI opening Parliament in March 1553. (2006 HM Queen Elizabeth II)

29. Edward's 'devise for the succession'. (Inner Temple, Library)

30. Lady Jane Grey, Edward's ill-fated cousin. (Bridgeman Art Library)

ACKNOWLEDGEMENTS

When writing this book, two maxims always remained at the back of my mind. George Orwell's words, 'All writers are vain, selfish and lazy, and at the very bottom of their motives lies a mystery', constantly resounded in my head, though in some hope of reprieve, I always clung to Jane Austen's dictum that 'I have been a selfish being all my life, in practice, not in principle'. Indeed, I feel that I have been incredibly selfish in writing this book. From the first moment I was introduced to Edward VI's reign at the age of sixteen, I was already hooked; it seemed this dramatic burst of history had gone ignored for too long, overshadowed by Henry VIII and Elizabeth, yet Edward's was a reign of supreme importance, not only for understanding the progress of the English Reformation, but also the essential politics of the age. It has been a joy to research and write this book; I certainly do not deserve to have written it. Above all, I realize that none of this would have been possible without the kind support of many friends – they know who they are – along the way.

There are a few mentions I would still like to add. I would like to thank Robert Lacey for his unstinting support for the project – not only teaching me how to write but pointing me in entirely the right direction for where I wanted to be going. Jonathan Pegg, my agent, never lost faith in the book when I nearly had; Ian Drury and Penny Gardiner at Weidenfeld have turned it into something marvellous, far beyond what I thought achievable. Caroline Cambridge helped to kick-start everything, though I am indebted beyond measure to Hannah Hockey, who not only managed to get things off the ground for me, but lived with the burden of myself and Edward VI for more than an entire year. I will always be grateful for her dedicated support.

My supervisor Steven Gunn has been both a model of scholarship and patience that I will always attempt to emulate. Tracey Sowerby and Paul Cavill kindly read through early drafts of chapters, whilst James Carlyle and Clare Rodaway helped translate Edward's essays. My tutor Christopher Haigh helped fuel my interest in Edward, which was initially ignited by Elizabeth Thorne – I could never have asked for better teachers. Lastly, I would like to thank my parents for decades of their support and encouragement, for which this book is deservedly dedicated to them.

BIOGRAPHIES

Henry Fitzalan, Earl of Arundel Traditionally viewed as a Catholic and conservative nobleman, Arundel was involved in the 1549 coup that engineered Somerset's downfall, though he quickly grew dissatisfied with the direction of events as Dudley gained the upper hand over Wriothesley, and was eventually removed from the council. Arundel then allied with Somerset in a bid to remove Dudley in a bizarre assassination plot. Exiled from court and heavily fined for his part in the scheme, Arundel was restored to favour when Dudley realized he was unable to do without his support. Arundel's revenge came shortly afterwards when his rallying speech announcing his defection to Mary's cause prompted Mary to be proclaimed in London by the council.

Kat Ashley Elizabeth's loose-tongued gentlewoman, whose revelations about the princess's behaviour with Sir Thomas Seymour cost her her job.

John Cheke Edward's tutor, whose reforming religious outlook heavily influenced the king's own faith.

Richard Cox Edward's almoner and tutor alongside John Cheke.

Thomas Cranmer Archbishop of Canterbury and Edward's godfather. Hailed as the architect of the English Reformation, Cranmer dictated the pace of religious reform during Edward's reign in an attempt to placate both Protestants and Catholics.

John Dudley, Viscount Lisle, Earl of Warwick and Duke of Northumberland The son of a traitor, Dudley managed to climb the ranks of Henry's court as an accomplished horseman and soldier. Having grown increasingly dissatisfied with Somerset's leadership, Dudley's ruthless suppression of Kett's rebellion was followed shortly by his seminal role in organizing the October 1549 coup. A political chameleon, Dudley finally sided with the reformers and Protestants once he realized where Edward's true feelings lay. Having managed to gain control of the Privy Chamber, Dudley became President of the Council. His careful manipulation of Edward allowed the king to believe that he was increasingly grasping the reins of power. Dudley nevertheless retained control until the last, and having acquiesced with Edward's decision to place Lady Jane Grey upon the throne, went to his death upon the scaffold recanting both his former life and his Protestant faith.

Barnaby Fitzpatrick School friend and close confidant of Edward, whose letters to him whilst in France reveal the close intimacy and affection between them.

Stephen Gardiner Bishop of Westminster and a powerful voice on Henry's council, Gardiner found himself cold-shouldered when left out of Henry's will and consequently isolated for the rest of Edward's reign. A staunch critic of the Edwardian Reformation, he opposed the new Prayer Book, which resulted in his imprisonment in the Tower, where he remained for the duration of Edward's reign.

John Gates Gentleman of the Privy Chamber and supporter of Dudley, who ended his life on the scaffold with his master.

Lady Jane Grey Protestant bluestocking daughter of the Duke of Suffolk who, having been named by Edward as an heir to the throne, was promptly married off to Dudley's son, Guildford. When Edward's condition deteriorated, his decision to appoint her as his heir apparent propelled Jane to the throne on 10 July 1553. Queen for nine days, she was deserted by her own nobility in favour of Mary, and was forced to abdicate. Imprisoned in the Tower, she was executed upon the scaffold the following year.

Henry Grey, Marquess of Dorset and Duke of Suffolk Wealthy magnate who blundered first into supporting Sir Thomas Seymour's schemes before becoming a supporter of Dudley. As father of Lady Jane Grey, his hopes of founding a new royal dynasty upon Edward's death were dashed within days, when support for his daughter's reign collapsed.

William Herbert, Earl of Pembroke Gentleman of Henry's Privy Chamber who became one of the most powerful members of the nobility due to his military strength. His decision to support Dudley in the October 1549 coup doomed Somerset's protectorate. Herbert was consequently rewarded with lavish grants of lands and titles. Considered by observers to be one of the three most important members of the council, alongside Dudley and Northampton.

Robert Kett   Norfolk gentry landowner whose surprising decision to lead a camp of thousands of rebels into Norwich resulted in the eponymous rebellion during the 'commotion time', eventually claiming some six thousand rebel lives.

Hugh Latimer   Protestant preacher whose inflammatory sermons set the tone for reform at court.

Richard Morison   Polemicist under Henry VIII and later Imperial ambassador under Edward.

William Paget   Private Secretary of Henry VIII and close confidant of Edward Seymour. Paget was instrumental in ensuring that Seymour was appointed Lord Protector, though growing increasingly dissatisfied with Seymour's rule, Paget eventually deserted his ally in return for a peerage. Permanently tainted by his association with Seymour, Paget was later arrested and heavily fined when an attempted assassination plot against Dudley backfired.

Thomas Palmer   Close supporter of Dudley, whose evidence enabled the Duke of Somerset to be framed for attempted murder. Palmer later followed Dudley to the scaffold for his part in supporting Queen Jane.

Katherine Parr   Henry VIII's sixth wife, who shared her enthusiasm for learning with Edward and Elizabeth. She began an affair with Sir Thomas Seymour almost immediately after Henry's death, and married him shortly afterwards. She fell out publicly with the Duchess of Somerset. She became pregnant in 1548 and gave birth to a child, Mary, in September that year, but she died a few days later, probably of puerperal fever.

William Parr, Marquess of Northampton   Katherine Parr's brother, whose support for Dudley gained him influence and power on the council.

Edward Seymour, Earl of Hertford and Duke of Somerset   Edward's maternal uncle through his sister Jane, his military prowess allowed him to rise quickly to prominence during the fading years of Henry's reign. Upon Henry's death he became Protector of the Realm, having been granted unprecedented powers through which to exercise his authority. Both a reformer and liberal in his social attitudes. His leniency towards the rebels of the 1549 commotions ultimately proved to be his downfall, engineered in a coup planned by Dudley and Wriothesley. He was rehabilitated to power the following year. Somerset's manipulation of his popularity and relentless scheming against Dudley resulted in his final humiliation and execution.

Thomas Seymour, 1st Baron Seymour   Edward's younger uncle, Seymour lived in the shadow of his elder brother, bitter at his success and disappointed that he had not been afforded a share of it. Appointed Lord Admiral, Seymour began an affair with and then married Queen Katherine Parr within months of Henry's death. Katherine's pregnancy did not prevent Seymour from extending his dalliances towards Elizabeth, though when his wife died shortly after childbirth, Seymour was left isolated. Having struggled to persuade Edward to appoint him Governor of the Realm, he plotted to kidnap the king and in all probability engineer civil war. Discovered entering Edward's chamber late at night, Seymour was found guilty of treason and executed in March 1549.

Anne Stanhope, Duchess of Somerset   Somerset's haughty wife, whose public falling out with Katherine Parr helped contribute to the growing enmity between the Seymour brothers. Universally unpopular for her pride and lavish lifestyle, she remained a strong influence upon her husband's Protestant attitudes.

Sir Michael Stanhope   The Duchess of Somerset's brother; Head of the Privy Chamber under Somerset, he was later executed for his part in Somerset's conspiracy.

Henry Howard, Earl of Surrey   Brash and arrogant son of the Duke of Norfolk, whose use of the royal arms and attempts to gain control of Edward during the dying days of Henry's reign resulted in his execution.

William Thomas   Clerk to the Council, whose secret correspondence with Edward over policy suggests that Edward may have been more in control of government matters than previously thought. Thomas's friendship with Dudley, however, suggests that the entire relationship may have been contrived for Dudley's own benefit in order to keep Edward in check.

Elizabeth Tudor   Edward's stepsister from Henry VIII's marriage to Anne Boleyn. Despite an embarrassing interlude with his uncle, Thomas Seymour, she remained on good terms with her younger brother, sharing a similar Protestant outlook no doubt fostered by the tutors they shared, Roger Ascham and Jean Belmain.

Mary Tudor   Edward's elder stepsister. The daughter of Henry VIII and Katherine of Aragon, she remained firmly committed to the Catholic faith. Her defiance of the Edwardian Reformation made her household a touchstone for Catholic resistance. Held in deep suspicion by the council, her confrontations with Edward over her right to hear mass marked a nadir in their relationship. Excluded from the succession under Edward's final will, Mary's surprising victory over Northumberland and Queen Jane was largely due to a groundswell of popular support, and might justifiably be counted as one of the few successful rebellions of English history. Mary's 'annus mirabilis' was the high point of a reign largely beset by failure. Her marriage to Philip II was greeted with xenophobic hostility, whilst her desire to return England to Rome was rounded upon by Protestant polemicists, whose influence in creating the portrait of 'bloody Mary' remains in strong currency to this day.

Thomas Wriothesley, Earl of Southampton   Lord Chancellor under Henry VIII, he was responsible for the Earl of Surrey's downfall and execution. An important conservative, he was brought down by Somerset in his attempt to be made Protector. Later a key plotter in the October 1549 coup, Wriothesley seemed likely to take charge of the council, but was outmanoeuvred by Dudley who forced his eventual disgrace, leading to his possible suicide.

Imperial Ambassadors
Jehan Scheyfve
Van der Delft
Simon Renard

French Ambassadors
Odet de Selve
Boisdauphin
Maréchal St André
Francois de Scepeaux, Maréchal de Vieilleville

CHRONOLOGY

30 May 1536	Henry marries Jane Seymour
12 October 1537	Edward VI born
24 October 1537	Jane Seymour dies
30 December 1546	Henry makes his final will and testament
13 January 1547	Earl of Surrey tried and convicted for treason
28 January 1547	Henry VIII dies
31 January 1547	Edward Seymour elected Protector
20 February 1547	Edward's coronation
5 March 1547	Thomas Wriothesley resigns his post as Chancellor
10 September 1547	Battle of Pinkie
19 March 1549	Sir Thomas Seymour executed
9 June 1549	New Book of Common Prayer comes into use
10 June 1549	Western 'Prayer Book' rebellion begins at Sampford Courtenay, Devon
2 July 1549	Exeter besieged
8 July 1549	Kett's rebellion, Norfolk, begins
6 August 1549	Siege at Exeter lifted
27 August 1549	Kett's forces defeated by Dudley's troops
5 October 1549	Somerset issues proclamation announcing conspiracy against him
7 October 1549	Somerset flees to Windsor with Edward
8 October 1549	Dudley and the council issue proclamation denouncing Somerset
11 October 1549	Somerset arrested
January 1550	Wriothesley and Arundel arrested
2 February 1550	Dudley appointed Lord Great Master and Lord President of the Council
6 February 1550	Somerset released from the Tower
2 May 1550	Joan Bocher burned at the stake for heresy

7 May 1550	Somerset readmitted to the council
2 July 1550	Mary's planned escape foiled
30 July 1550	Wriothesley dies
17 March 1551	Edward confronts Mary over her continued hearing of the mass
16? April 1551	Attempt to assassinate Dudley foiled
8 May 1551	Proclamation issued announcing debasement of the coinage
7 July 1551	Outbreak of sweating sickness ravages London
23 August 1551	Mary's household officers arrested for disobedience
11 October 1551	Dudley created Duke of Northumberland
16 October 1551	Somerset arrested
1 December 1551	Somerset tried and convicted of felony
22 January 1552	Somerset executed
15 July 1552	Edward leaves London for his first summer progress
1 November 1552	Second Book of Common Prayer introduced
1 March 1553	Edward opens Parliament
11 April 1553	Edward moves to Greenwich on account of deteriorating illness
21 May 1553	Lady Jane Grey married to Dudley's son, Guildford
21 June 1553	Edward's 'Devise' approved
4 July 1553	Mary secretly travels towards Norfolk
6 July 1553	Edward dies
10 July 1553	Jane proclaimed Queen
19 July 1553	Mary proclaimed Queen
21 July 1553	Dudley arrested
8 August 1553	Edward buried
18 August 1553	Dudley tried and convicted of treason
22 August 1553	Dudley executed

TABLES OF GENEALOGY

1. The Tudors
2. The Seymours
3. The Dudleys
4. The Howards

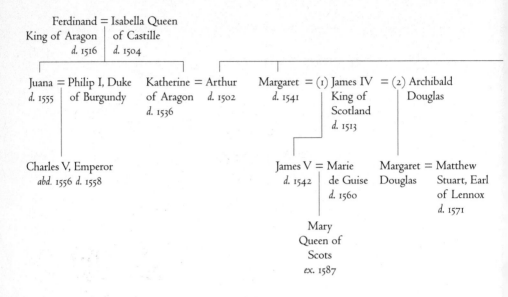

Ferdinand = Isabella Queen
King of Aragon | of Castille
d. 1516 | d. 1504

Juana = Philip I, Duke   Katherine = Arthur   Margaret = (1) James IV = (2) Archibald
d. 1555 | of Burgundy   of Aragon d. 1502 d. 1541 | King of | Douglas
   d. 1536   Scotland
                    d. 1513

Charles V, Emperor   James V = Marie   Margaret = Matthew
abd. 1556 d. 1558   d. 1542 | de Guise Douglas Stuart, Earl
                           d. 1560   of Lennox
                                       d. 1571

                               Mary
                           Queen of
                            Scots
                            ex. 1587

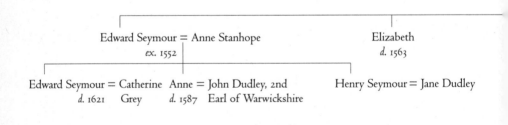

Edward Seymour = Anne Stanhope   Elizabeth
ex. 1552 | d. 1563

Edward Seymour = Catherine Anne = John Dudley, 2nd   Henry Seymour = Jane Dudley
d. 1621 | Grey   d. 1587 Earl of Warwickshire

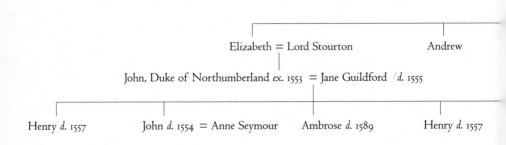

Elizabeth = Lord Stourton   Andrew

John, Duke of Northumberland ex. 1553 = Jane Guildford d. 1555

Henry d. 1557   John d. 1554 = Anne Seymour   Ambrose d. 1589   Henry d. 1557

TUDOR FAMILY TREE
✢

Henry VII *d.* 1509 = Elizabeth of York *d.* 1503

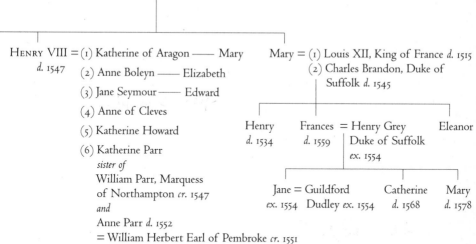

HENRY VIII = (1) Katherine of Aragon ——— Mary
d. 1547 (2) Anne Boleyn ——— Elizabeth
(3) Jane Seymour ——— Edward
(4) Anne of Cleves
(5) Katherine Howard
(6) Katherine Parr
sister of
William Parr, Marquess
of Northampton *cr.* 1547
and
Anne Parr *d.* 1552
= William Herbert Earl of Pembroke *cr.* 1551

Mary = (1) Louis XII, King of France *d.* 1515
(2) Charles Brandon, Duke of
Suffolk *d.* 1545

Henry   Frances = Henry Grey   Eleanor
d. 1534   *d.* 1559   Duke of Suffolk
ex. 1554

Jane = Guildford   Catherine   Mary
ex. 1554 Dudley *ex.* 1554   *d.* 1568   *d.* 1578

SEYMOUR FAMILY TREE
✢

Sir John Seymour = Margery Wentworth
d. 1536

Jane = Henry VIII   Thomas = Katherine Parr   Henry   John   Dorothy etc
ex. 1549 | *d.* 1548

Edward VI *d.* 1553   Mary *d.* 1550?

DUDLEY FAMILY TREE
✢

Edmund Dudley = Anne Windsor
ex. 1510

Jerome   Simon

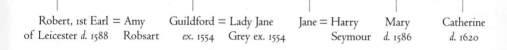

Robert, 1st Earl = Amy   Guildford = Lady Jane   Jane = Harry   Mary   Catherine
of Leicester *d.* 1588   Robsart   *ex.* 1554   Grey *ex.* 1554   Seymour   *d.* 1586   *d.* 1620

HOWARD FAMILY TREE
✣

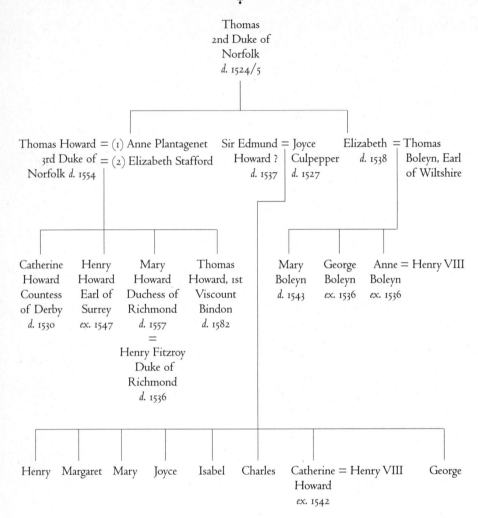

Thomas
2nd Duke of
Norfolk
d. 1524/5

Thomas Howard = (1) Anne Plantagenet   Sir Edmund = Joyce   Elizabeth = Thomas
3rd Duke of = (2) Elizabeth Stafford   Howard ?   Culpepper   *d.* 1538   Boleyn, Earl
Norfolk *d.* 1554   *d.* 1537   *d.* 1527   of Wiltshire

Catherine   Henry   Mary   Thomas   Mary   George   Anne = Henry VIII
Howard   Howard   Howard   Howard, 1st   Boleyn   Boleyn   Boleyn
Countess   Earl of   Duchess of Viscount   *d.* 1543 *ex.* 1536 *ex.* 1536
of Derby   Surrey   Richmond   Bindon
d. 1530   *ex.* 1547 *d.* 1557   *d.* 1582
                        =
                        Henry Fitzroy
                        Duke of
                        Richmond
                        d. 1536

Henry   Margaret   Mary   Joyce   Isabel   Charles   Catherine = Henry VIII   George
                                                     Howard
                                                     ex. 1542

INTRODUCTION

'We have a Prince! Can any man, that dare vouch himself to be a right English man, hear this, and feel not within himself such a wonderful force, an inerrable strength of gladness; can his body be born in England, and here his heart not leap for joy; can there lie any vein so far, so hid in a corner, but it shall feel the blood heated, now much lighter to run ... even as though it were a carrier of this good news?' *Richard Morison, on the news of Edward's birth, 1537.*[1]

There exists in the Royal Collection a painting called *The Family of Henry VIII*. Painted around 1545 by an unknown artist, Henry sits on his throne beneath the royal canopy and the marbled columns of Whitehall Palace; to his left his deceased wife, Jane Seymour, kneels, whilst to his right his sole male child and heir, Edward, stands. In the wings of the chamber, noticeably detached from this scene of family life, are Henry's two other daughters, Mary and Elizabeth, both proclaimed illegitimate in the complicated marital history of their father's reign. The message being portrayed is clear: nearing the end of his life, Henry saw the future of the Tudor dynasty in the hands of his son, the soon to be proclaimed Edward VI. Katherine of Aragon and Anne Boleyn had been painted out of history; Henry's only rightful queen was Jane, the matriarch of this dynasty. When he died two years later, it was his will that he be buried next to Jane, and a monument was to be erected above them with carved effigies of them 'as if sweetly sleeping'. Of all his wives, only she had dutifully provided him with the only thing that mattered: a precious son, Edward. Henry joined her in the grave assured that he had secured his dynasty with the male heir he had craved for so long.

When Edward was born on Friday, 12 October 1537, Henry's twenty-seven-year wait for an heir had come to an end. Such was the excitement that the Tower guards shot off two thousand rounds of ammunition to compete with the pealing of the church bells that sounded in London throughout the day. Bonfires were lit and impromptu street parties began, fuelled by the free wine and beer generously provided by the merchants of the Hanseatic League.

Nine years later, when Edward succeeded his father, the proclamations of 'Long live King Edward' following the news of Henry's death, spread with joyous enthusiasm. Much had changed since that ecstatic day when Edward's birth had first been announced. Henry's deteriorating health and ballooning weight had left him with a volatile temper likely to flare up upon the slightest provocation. And as his descent into middle age brought with it the disasters of his failed marriages to Anne of Cleves – the 'Flanders Mare' – and the adulterous Katherine Howard, Henry had lashed out at those closest to him as he searched for scapegoats. His first minister and chief adviser, Thomas Cromwell, had been sent to the block leaving Henry rudderless, his failing judgement steering him into costly wars with Scotland and France, subsuming the country's wealth and leaving it teetering upon the point of bankruptcy.

Cromwell, along with Thomas Cranmer, the Archbishop of Canterbury, had been one of the pivotal architects of Henry's reformation of the Church. According to one report, it was claimed that he had made a pact with Henry, promising him power beyond his wildest imagination. But this all paled in importance beside what Henry really wanted – a legitimate male heir. For it was becoming all too clear that his queen, Katherine of Aragon, fast approaching middle age, would be unable to provide him with a son. With the seductive Anne Boleyn taking the king's fancy, Henry demanded a solution fast. The answer seemed simple enough – Henry would divorce Katherine and marry Anne. Yet in taking this course, Henry literally took a leap of faith; with the Pope unwilling even to countenance annulling Henry's first marriage (upon the dubious grounds that she had already slept with his brother Arthur, to whom she had been betrothed before his untimely death) Henry was forced to break with the Roman Catholic Church. Under a series of laws that redefined the king's position, Henry became Supreme Head of his very own Church of England. Cromwell had been as good as his word: Henry now controlled not only his subjects' bodies, but also their souls.

These new powers were matched by equally radical laws to enforce them. A new statute made it treason to call the king a tyrant or heretic – punishable by death – whilst each man and woman was forced to swear an oath committing their obedience to Henry's supremacy. Those who refused to do so – including Henry's own chancellor, Thomas More – went to the block as martyrs to their Catholic faith and traitors to the king. A new climate of fear prevailed; 'What will be the end of this tragedy, God knows', one commentator recorded. Meanwhile Cromwell, in his exalted position as lay Vicegerent of the King (with greater power in the Church than even the Archbishop of Canterbury), turned his attention to fresh targets – the monasteries. In 1536, after they had been denounced as seed beds of iniquity (with commissioners allegedly discovering 'not seven but more than 700,000 deadly sins'), 372 smaller monasteries were suppressed, with the fate of the greater monasteries left hanging precariously in the balance.[2]

All this was too much for Henry's northern subjects. In desperation they rose up united in defence of their Catholic Church – under the banner of 'The five wounds of Christ' – determined to protect their devotions and convince their king to change his mind. As their numbers swelled to 30,000, the Pilgrimage of Grace, as this 'rebellion' was named, soon grew to become the greatest threat to the Tudor regime.

Henry had the victory, crushing the rising mercilessly. The rebels paid for their disobedience with their lives. With all resistance suppressed, nothing could save the remaining monasteries. Their dissolution brought to the Crown land and property worth well over £100,000 a year, making way for the greatest redistribution of land since the Norman Conquest, with large tranches being sold off to up and coming courtiers for £1.3 million. Henry, meanwhile, was careful to retain his share of the spoils, accumulating fifty-five royal palaces by the end of his reign.

With the evangelical reformers in the ascendant, new ways to ridicule the shrines and devotions that were classed as 'abuses' were found; some were broken up, exposed for the shams that they were, whilst in a macabre twist, their defenders – such as the friar William Forest – were condemned to burn in the blazing fires of their treasured relics. Destruction was followed by further reform. Ten years earlier the translator William Tyndale had been condemned as a heretic for producing the first English Bible; now, with the tables turned, bibles in English, following Tyndale's translation almost to the letter, were ordered to be placed in every church, free for all to read. But as preachers started to press too hard for further reform – particularly over the doctrine of transsubstantiation (the belief that the bread and wine transform into the body and blood of Christ during the miracle of the mass), Henry began to get cold feet, particularly since a new Catholic league made up of the

Holy Roman Empire, France and Scotland seemed poised to launch an invasion upon England.

This new mood was reflected in the passing of the Act of Six Articles, with its threat of punishment by burning for denying transubstantiation. Later, Henry withdrew further, banning all men under the rank of yeoman from reading the bibles that he had once encouraged all to read. The Reformation was over. Henry had gone so far, but this was far enough for a man who had once proudly boasted of his title 'Defender of the Faith', granted by the Pope. Though purgatory had been abandoned, prayers for the dead still remained. And though the veneration of saints' images had been discouraged, the medieval rood-lofts painted with saints' images continued to dominate parish churches in which the mass was still sung.

No one could deny that England was a very different realm to the one Henry had inherited, but as his reign drew to a close, the reformers were already looking ahead to the next – and his heir, Edward. Henry had been favourably compared to the Old Testament King Solomon, the builder of the Temple. Yet Solomon had seen his reign degenerate as lust clouded his judgement, preventing him from completing the Temple he had begun to build. Now the parallels were being drawn once more, with the young Prince Edward being compared to the eight-year-old Old Testament King Josiah, who had destroyed idols and restored the true scripture to his people.

Henry had left Edward with a golden inheritance; the prince stood on the cusp of becoming the greatest and most powerful English monarch history had witnessed. As men thought then, Edward should be recognized as a central figure in the Tudor age. Yet historians have tended to sideline him in favour of his elder sisters, Mary and Elizabeth. This is unfair, and ignores one of the most dynamic and important periods of Tudor history. Edward may have only been fifteen years old when he died, tantalizingly close to adulthood, and though his reign was just six years long, as Richard Hooker later remarked, 'He died young, but lived long. For life is an action.'[3] His reign is exciting precisely because it was so densely packed and the dramatic events that unfolded within it took place during an age of radical religious and political turmoil.

The religious reformation that took place in Edward's reign went far beyond anything Henry could ever have imagined. The Bible in English, free for all to read, the abolition of the chantries and masses for the dead, the widespread destruction of images and saints' shrines, new services in

English read by ministers forbidden from wearing traditional vestments, the abolition of the mass and the introduction of communion in both kinds revolutionized a society where religion was paramount to an understanding of human nature.

Edward's kingship was to be a new start – a new beginning that turned its back upon the cruelty and tyrannous reign of his father. Henry's harsh treason legislation was repealed; Edward's fresh, young persona was the lead for new ideas. Writers began addressing social and economic problems with greater sensitivity and there was a new impetus to aid the poor.

But the early hope and promise that a fresh start brought turned sour. Edward's reign became a time of intrigue, deceit, plotting and treason, very nearly plunging the country into civil war. The stability that the Tudors had sought to achieve came close to being torn apart. Edward's own uncle, Thomas Seymour, after failing to force Edward to agree to schemes to make him Protector, attempted to kidnap him from his own bed. The plot failed and Seymour was executed. Barely a few months later, two of the largest rebellions of the century, in which perhaps fifteen thousand rebels were to lose their lives, brought the Tudor regime to a crisis point not seen since that of the Peasants' Revolt of 1381. Edward's guardian, Edward Seymour, Duke of Somerset, was deposed in a court *coup d'état* to be replaced by his rival, John Dudley, Earl of Warwick – later to be made Duke of Northumberland. Somerset and Dudley's rivalry stemmed from a clash of personalities. Somerset was regarded as the champion of the poor and oppressed, whose petitions and grievances he listened to, much to the displeasure of his aristocratic colleagues. Dudley, on the other hand, was a master tactician and the archetypal Machiavellian politician, who was reported to have had 'such a head that he seldom went about anything but he conceived first three or four purposes beforehand'.[4] The ambitions and fierce rivalry of these two men eventually brought them both to the scaffold. Somerset was executed in January 1552 for plotting to assassinate Dudley. After wresting power from Somerset, Dudley took control of Edward and became Lord President of the Council, only to meet his end in a desperate and failed attempt to preserve Edward's Protestant legacy, as the driving force behind the nine-day reign of Lady Jane Grey as queen.

Meanwhile, no one could be certain of the direction events might take. Catholics and Protestants battled for control of the government, whilst hyper-inflation and poor harvests plunged the realm into one of its worst economic crises of the century. When the sweating sickness returned – a disease that seems to have infected only the English – men thought it was a plague from God for their sins. Yet the Reformation continued at full pace: the medieval interiors of churches were ripped out, to be replaced by wooden communion tables and whitewashed walls; saints' days were abolished, along with the cherished processions and rituals that often had defined men's world-view. The reformers did not get their way without a fight – particularly from Edward's Catholic sister Mary, who had attempted to flee the realm in protest before challenging Edward to a dramatic showdown at court. Loyalties were divided as politics and religion often competed for men's allegiance. The forces of greed, corruption and ambition – the desire for power – all appear in this extraordinary tale. Yet equally important to ask is why England did not succumb to civil war. The reigns of minors usually ended in disaster – the fate of the Princes in the Tower was all too fresh in the minds of many.

The enigma points to Edward himself. Was Edward merely a pawn in a fascinating political game, or did he represent more than has been allowed him? For Edward's historical personality is not just his own; it has become an amalgam of those early hopes, together with the legend that developed around him after his death as a 'godly imp', enhanced by the Protestant historian John Foxe. Though a child, Edward bore the ideological weight of what being king had become in the Reformation; he was now God's representative on earth, the leader of the English 'empire': only he could assure the health of men's souls. In life, his youth allowed men to ponder the future, to speculate on his coming of age. This, in part, came from his extraordinary gifts and intelligence. Edward was seen as a child prodigy – he could speak Latin and French fluently, wrote secret notes to himself in Greek to hide his thoughts from nosy courtiers and, under the guidance of his tutors, immersed himself into a scholarly world of Protestant theology and Renaissance humanism. Edward studied scripture at a phenomenal rate and built up an immense library for a child. His writings exist in voluminous quantity – over a hundred of his essays in Latin and Greek survive in the British Library, as yet still unstudied in detail. Among a vast array of topics, he wrote on the effects of war, devised reforms for council procedure and denounced the evils of the papacy in a tract that remained in print a hundred years after his death.

Historians have begun to recognize that the king's own personality increasingly came to matter during the later part of his reign.[5] In a world where the king was a child, he was expected to grow up very fast indeed. By the time Edward had turned twelve, there were already provisions in place to provide him with the training needed for the administration of the state – he took part in council debates, influenced the future religious direction of the kingdom and eventually played a crucial role in determining the direction of his succession under his chosen heir, Queen Jane.

But Edward does not just appear as the studious Protestant stalwart that he is often made out to be. The human side of his story should not be forgotten. For a child, the burden he carried was great: an orphan at nine, he was to lose his stepmother and both his uncles during his reign. What effect did this have on him? Edward's surviving journal, into which he noted the events and political torment that swirled around his court, provides us with a window into the mind of this Tudor monarch, demonstrating the daily life of the king, his court and the government around him. It is this that makes this story a unique one. Despite the pressures of office, we know that growing up he still made time for leisure. He enjoyed music, playing the lute, and increasing the number of musicians at the royal court. He also enjoyed the pastimes of his father – at the tiltyard, on the hunt or tennis court. He even acted in plays at court.

It was Edward's brilliant precociousness that kept his realm together. However, unlike the imbecile Henry VI, contemporaries knew that Edward had the ability to become an extraordinary king upon adulthood – one that might, like his role model Josiah, later punish the wicked for their sins – 'At this time,' warned one chronicler shortly after Somerset's execution, 'many . . . talked that the young King was now to be feared.'[6]

Edward's premature death cut short a life of brilliant promise. Yet the story does not end there, for in death as in life Edward's reign continued its drama. One of Edward's last surviving actions was to alter the line of succession with his own hand, disinheriting his sisters Mary and Elizabeth in favour of a new dynasty founded upon the Protestant faith – with his cousin Lady Jane Grey as his heir and England's queen. Out of fear, everyone obeyed Edward's wishes – four days after his death Jane was proclaimed queen, with orders sent for Mary's arrest. Yet Mary had escaped – fleeing to Norfolk she rounded up her supporters and proclaimed herself the nation's rightful queen. It seemed that the realm was fast gearing up for civil war.

Yet against all the odds and with the entire ruling elite against her,

Mary won through; she had been placed on the throne by her people who preferred the claim of the true daughter of Henry VIII to the daughter-in-law of Dudley, a man they regarded as a detested tyrant. Her remarkable and unexpected victory over Queen Jane would become a crucial turning point in history, and the only successful popular revolution of the entire Tudor age.

It brought an end to one of the most remarkable chapters of English history, yet Edward has often been considered only a footnote in the margins of Tudor histories all too concerned with Elizabeth or Henry VIII to take notice of the last Tudor king – for whom Henry had sacrificed so much and from whose reign Elizabeth would learn her lessons in statecraft.

Mary's reign was to mark the beginning of England's temporary return to Rome and the undoing of the efforts of Edward's. Yet as Mary's regime became notoriously unpopular after the re-introduction of harsh heresy laws, the burning of hundreds of Protestants – including Cranmer – and the loss of Calais, England's last hold on the European continent, so Edward's posthumous reputation scaled new heights. Upon Elizabeth's accession to the throne and the Protestant settlement of 1559, Edward's Protestant legacy was to remain. The hope that his short reign had promised had finally come to fruition; Edward's dream of a Protestant nation had become a reality. The Anglican Church had been transformed in his six-year reign; it is testament to this fact that it was Edward's portrait that still graced the frontispiece of the Elizabethan official 'Bishop's Bible' in 1595.

Those six years that Edward sat upon the throne are still with us today. As Diarmaid MacCulloch has written, 'the Church of England was in fact permanently shaped by the reign of Edward VI'.[7] Edward set out a vision of a Protestant nation, the idea of England as a 'godly isle', a vision later taken up again under Elizabeth. And it was in Edward's reign that the words of ceremonies so well known to us now, and which form a crucial aspect of our national culture and identity, were created. The Book of Common Prayer, first published in 1549 and revised again in 1552, brought a new tone of authority to the prose of the English language – words that act almost as a subtext to the background of the lives of generations were forged here; for example, whilst the medieval marriage service used to include the wife's promise to be 'bonner and buxom in bed and at the board', it was in Edward's reign that for the first time both partners were required to 'love, cherish and obey', and the wedding vows still spoken to this day, 'for better for worse, for richer for poorer, in sickness and in health', were first set down.

Two different strands make up Edward's reign: the personality of this Tudor king who was the most gifted of all his siblings; and the political world that sought to cope with a child as ruler. Reconstructing his own world-view from his diary and letters, I aim to contrast the personal life of the king at court with the intrigue and, at times, chaos that encircled him. Above all, I have attempted to bring out the reality of Tudor political life – that curious mix of new idealism, as the Renaissance and its political ideas found expression in government reform, and the intrigue and duplicity of factions at court.

The legacy of Edward's reign is one of the most exciting political histories of the Tudor age, from which few appeared unscathed. His untimely death cut short a life that, forged in the remarkable political circumstance of his childhood, would have left us with a very different Tudor England than that fashioned under the female monarchies of Mary and Elizabeth.

I

MARRIAGES, BIRTH AND DEATH

✥

Henry VIII never underestimated the importance of a male heir. It was a lesson he had learnt at an early age. The turn of Fortune's wheel could be cruel, as it had been when he was just ten years old. Then the sudden death of his elder brother Arthur in April 1502 propelled him into the limelight as heir to the throne; overnight, Henry's life changed drastically. He was never meant to be king, nor had he even been prepared for such a task. For the sensitive and mild-mannered young child, a career in the Church had possibly beckoned; now, as Prince of Wales and sole male heir of the Tudor dynasty, he was kept so closely guarded that a Spanish envoy remarked how he might have been a girl, locked away in his chamber and only allowed to speak when answering his father.

Arthur's death was a devastating blow for his father, Henry VII. His victory against Richard III at the battle of Bosworth Field in 1485 had seemed unequivocal, ending over half a century of civil war between the rival houses of Lancaster and York, later better known as the Wars of the Roses. Yet new claimants to the throne had sprung up, challenging his legitimacy to rule. For the next fifteen years, Henry battled for his new dynasty to be recognized by the ruling empires of Europe, marrying his eldest son Arthur off to Katherine of Aragon, the daughter of Ferdinand and Isabella, the rulers of Spain. Nevertheless, Henry had always struggled to fit in amongst his own subjects and in particular his nobility – the ruling families, around fifty in number, upon whose support the monarch was largely dependent. Raised in Brittany and France, Henry was an outsider who brought with him a new style of government from overseas, scrutinizing every payment issued from his chamber with his own hand. For all it was worth, Henry's penny-pinching ways earned him little respect and fewer friends.

With only one male heir to fall back on – and a child at that – Henry knew that the Tudor name was seriously under threat. Yet worse still was to come the following year, when his wife Queen Elizabeth died in childbirth, attempting to deliver him another precious son. The Tudor dynasty hung dangerously by the thread of his son's life: with no other male heirs, extinction of the royal line loomed close.

The effects of all this upon the forming mind of the young Henry VIII cannot possibly be overestimated, for when he came to the throne six years later, aged almost eighteen, he was determined not to make his father's mistakes. In the years leading up to his death, Henry VII had placed his nobility under heavy financial penalties and bonds for the slightest misdemeanour, much to their chagrin. Now, in an inspired move designed to bolster his own reputation, Henry agreed to have his father's chief ministers, Richard Empson and Edmund Dudley, made scapegoats, ordering that they be thrown into the Tower and executed upon dubious charges of treason. Henry came as an immediate breath of fresh air; he soon ingratiated himself with the ruling elite, sharing their passions for hawking and hunting, and recklessly joining them in dangerous jousting competitions – the sight of which would have had his father turning in his grave. But he realized that for his reign to be fully secure and his mind set at rest, a male heir was vital. Fortunately for Henry, his brother's death had resulted in him gaining a wife – Arthur's widow, Katherine of Aragon. As to her womanly duties of providing the realm's heir, she did not disappoint. On New Year's Day 1511, Queen Katherine was delivered of a boy. As the style of his newborn son and heir, also named Henry, was proclaimed, the news was welcomed with bells, bonfires and the endless salute of guns shot from the Tower.

Henry celebrated with a pilgrimage to Walsingham, before returning to Westminster for a tournament and pageant. It was the most splendid of his reign. There he was mobbed by the crowd, who for souvenirs ripped off the golden 'Hs' and 'Ks' sewn on to his doublet. In his joy, Henry did not care. Yet the celebrations proved premature: seven weeks later, the baby was dead.

In February 1516, Katherine was again delivered of a healthy child. This time the baby lived – the only problem being that the child was a girl, Mary. Though naturally disappointed, Henry remained optimistic. 'We are both young,' he told the Venetian ambassador. 'If it was a daughter this time, by the grace of God the sons will follow.' Yet they did not, and his subjects' anxiety over the succession began to reflect Henry's own: 'I pray God heartily to send us a Prince,' one courtier wrote, 'for the surety of this realm.' But it was not to be, for Katherine was destined to fail in her duties. After three miscarriages (two of them male) and two infants who had died within weeks of the birth (one male), by the end of the 1520s Henry had to face up to the inevitable. Katherine was now approaching her forties and surely reaching an age when conception was an unlikely and dangerous possibility – she would have to go. For Henry had a new lover – Katherine's maid-of-honour, Anne Boleyn – who would accept nothing less than to take her mistress's place as queen. Allure had turned to infatuation as Anne promised to provide Henry with the one thing Katherine had not: a son. But once she had replaced Katherine in Henry's affections – though not in his subjects' – she fared little better as queen, and the birth of their daughter Elizabeth, together with two miscarriages, convinced Henry that 'God did not wish to give him male children'.[1]

Besides, Anne made as many enemies as she had friends. She made the mistake of crossing Thomas Cromwell, Henry's first minister – a mistake for which she would pay heavily. As loyalties divided, splintering the court, with factions competing for the king's favour, it soon became clear to Cromwell that Anne was a more dangerous prospect than he had feared. At first, she had been the reason behind his meteoric rise at court; her thinly veiled hatred of Henry's former favourite, Cardinal Wolsey, allowing Cromwell to take Wolsey's place once he fell from grace. But Cromwell knew if he was to save his own head from eventually reaching the block, he had to seek Anne's first. After her third miscarriage, he engineered a plot to bring down the queen, accusing her of adultery with her musician, Mark Smeaton. Henry believed every charge levelled against Anne: whether there was any truth behind them, Henry probably did not care; he wanted her gone. Eleven days after Anne's execution, he had married once again.

His choice of the plain Jane Seymour as bride was in stark contrast to Anne. 'She is of middle height, and nobody thinks she is of much beauty,' the Imperial ambassador confided.[2] Quiet and obedient, she came as a refreshing change: 'She is as gentle a lady as ever I knew,' one courtier wrote. 'The King hath come out of hell into heaven.'[3]

Jane's motto, 'Bound to obey and serve', reflected her own under-standing of what needed to be done. She would be Henry's dutiful wife and subject, yet she aimed not just to be Henry's loyal queen, but to give him exactly what he wanted: a son. It was through her, she intended, that the Tudor dynasty would be reborn. Although in no doubt as to what needed to be achieved, however, Jane struggled to conceive. Henry soon grew restless. His eyes began to wander once more; meeting two young ladies, he admitted with a sigh he was 'sorry that he had not seen them before they were married'.[4]

Yet in early spring 1537 Jane knew she was pregnant. Shortly afterwards, she travelled with a no doubt overjoyed Henry, making a pilgrimage at Canterbury. Here they gave thanks to God and laid their offerings at the shrine of the English saint Thomas Becket. It was the last time Henry would make such a gesture. As the dissolution of the monasteries continued apace, such devotions were ordered to be abandoned. Within a year Becket's memory would be denounced, his shrine broken up and his bones scattered.

By April Jane's pregnancy was considered advanced enough for the news to be announced at a meeting of the Privy Council, where the need was felt to record their congratulations in the minutes. Soon the good news had spread across the country; in late May it was announced that the child had 'quickened' – kicked – sparking off further cause for celebration. Mass was celebrated in St Paul's with a thanksgiving, and the *Te Deum* was ordered to be sung in churches across the country. 'God send her good deliverance of a prince,' wrote one courtier expectantly, 'to the joy of all faithful subjects.'[5]

Henry marked his own expectation of fathering an heir by commissioning the court painter Hans Holbein the Younger to prepare a fresco for the walls of the Privy Chamber, depicting himself, Jane, his father Henry VII and his mother Elizabeth of York. The symbolism was telling, for Henry stands dominant in heroic pose, towering in front of his age-weary father. Beside them a monumental inscription set into a plinth proudly read:

> If you rejoice to see the likeness of glorious heroes, look on these, for no painting ever boasted greater. How difficult the debate, the issue, the question whether the father or son be the superior. Each of them has triumphed. The first got the better of his enemies, bore up his so-often ruined land and gave lasting peace to his people. The son, born to still greater things, turned away from the altars of that unworthy man and brings in men of integrity. The presumptuousness of popes has yielded to unerring virtue, and with Henry VIII bearing the sceptre in his hand, religion has been restored, and with him on the throne the truths of God have begun to be held in due reverence.[6]

On the other side of the monument, it was easy not to notice Jane, both diminutive and submissive. This was hardly surprising, for Henry expected his queen and soon-to-be mother to his heir to act the obedient subject. Jane played the role to perfection. She was, Henry wrote in September 1537, 'of that loving inclination and reverend conformity'. He could not leave her side since Jane, 'being a woman', might take fright in his absence, risking miscarriage.[7]

With her pregnancy in its final stage, Jane took to her chamber on 16 September. Her confinement lasted three weeks, culminating in a difficult and painful labour lasting over thirty hours.[8] Meanwhile the plague had been raging around Hampton Court, and Henry was forced to move to Esher for four days. Everybody waited anxiously. 'We look daily for a Prince,' one courtier wrote to another. 'God send what shall please him.' On Thursday 11 October a solemn procession took place at St Paul's to pray for Jane.[9]

At two o'clock in the morning of St Edward's Day, Friday 12 October, Jane gave birth to a healthy child. By eight o'clock the news had leaked out of the court. It was a son. The church bells of London began a fanatical peal that lasted throughout the day, whilst in celebration the *Te Deum* was again sung in every parish church. At St Paul's there was a solemn procession. Bonfires were lit in streets; garlands were hung from balconies, whilst fruit and wine were handed out as presents by city merchants. Eager to impress, German merchants at the Steel Yard distributed a hogshead of wine and two barrels of beer to the poor.[10] The celebrations continued well into the night as the Lord Mayor rode through the crowds, thanking the people for their rejoicing and calling on them to give thanks to God. To finish, the guards at the Tower of London fired off over two thousand rounds into the night sky.

Messengers were dispatched across the country with letters from the queen proudly announcing the news.[11] Jane urged her subjects to give thanks to God, 'but also continually pray for the long continuance and preservation of the same here in this life . . . and tranquillity of this whole realm'. Indeed, it could be said that the baby's life and the future prospects of the kingdom were one and the same.

Letters were soon shuttling across Europe, their contents running along a similar vein. 'Here be no news,' Thomas Cromwell wrote, 'but very good news . . . I have received this morning . . . it hath pleased Almighty God of his goodness, to send unto the Queen's Grace deliverance of a goodly Prince.' The announcement of the birth, another letter read, 'hath more rejoiced this realm and all true hearts ... more than anything hath done this 40 years'.[12]

Henry was at his hunting lodge in Esher when he heard. After the long wait of twenty-seven years, he finally had his heir. No record survives of the moment he first found out the news, though one suspects that musing upon the sacrifices he had made – divorce, Reformation, execution – a sense of vindication pulsed through him. Overcome with joy, he sped back to Hampton Court to choose the baby's name: Edward, after his distant royal ancestor, Edward the Confessor, whose memory happened to be celebrated that day – his saint's day.

Like an over-protective father, Henry took immediate control of the situation, commanding that every room and hall in the nursery recently built for the prince be swept and soaped down, ready for its royal occupant. The baby was then taken from Jane's arms and placed in the care of a wet nurse and other nursemaids; Jane did not make a fuss about suckling her child – for now she took her rest after an exhausting labour.

On Monday 15 October, Edward was christened in the royal chapel at Hampton Court. Preparations had begun almost immediately after the baby was born, but now Henry began to grow nervous for the child's safety. The plague had been rife in areas outside London for the past few months, centred about Croydon. Now a proclamation was hastily dispatched forbidding anyone residing in affected areas to come to court at all. This would mean that the king's own niece, Gertrude Courtenay, the Marchioness of Exeter, who had been appointed to carry the prince himself, would have been barred from the ceremony, had it not been for her own pleading.

Writing to Henry the day before, she waxed on unashamedly: Edward's birth was 'the most joyful news, and glad tidings, that came to England these many years; for which we, all your Grace's poor subjects are most bounden to give thanks to Almighty God that it hath pleased him of his great mercy so to remember Your Grace with a Prince, and us all, your poor subjects, to the great comfort, universal weal, and quietness of this your whole realm; beseeching Almighty God to send His Grace life and long ... ' And so it continues, Gertrude giving her thanks to Henry, 'as my poor heart can think', for granting her the honour of carrying Edward during the ceremony, she being 'so poor a woman to so high a room': 'Which service ... I should have been as glad to have done as any poor woman living. And much it grieveth me, that my fortune is so evil, by reason of sickness here, in Croydon, to be banished.'[13]

As Gertrude well knew, with Henry flattery got you everywhere; needless to say, she got her way. Henry had made a rare exception, but the nobility scattered across the country on their estates had already taken to their saddles to arrive at the most eagerly expected event of the decade, to glimpse a sight of the new heir to the throne. Their retinues were ordered to be scaled down to reduce the risk of infection: dukes, usually accustomed to travelling with their entourage numbering into hundreds, were allowed no more than six gentlemen, marquesses no more than five. Nevertheless, the audience that gathered in the state rooms that led from the bedchamber to the Royal Chapel was still expected to number around four hundred.

The ceremonies for the christening followed the carefully planned ordinances set down by Henry's grandmother, Lady Margaret Beaufort. These were intended to place the aura of the royal majesty on display at its most spectacular, but on this occasion they would also create exactly the right atmosphere to introduce not only the new royal family to the court, but to the nobility of the country their future king.[14]

First, at around six o'clock, the guests filed past the king and queen in the bedchamber, who sat in silence on a state pallet lifted from the floor and decorated with the royal arms, Henry in full regalia and Jane swaddled in fur and velvet. Custom, or at least Margaret, had dictated that neither would take part in the ceremony, nor be present to watch the christening. They would wait until the baby was returned to them, when they would then bless their child.

The godparents had been decided even before Edward's birth. The Duke of Norfolk, the Duke of Suffolk and Archbishop Cranmer were to stand as his godfathers, whilst his elder stepsister, the Princess Mary, was godmother.

It was not until nearly midnight that all the guests had been greeted and the procession – suitably arranged according to every varying degree of status – stood ready to depart. Headed by Gentlemen of the Privy Chamber carrying torches, the choir and the Dean began their slow walk in front of pairs of chaplains, bishops, Privy Councillors, and noblemen. Next went the great officers of state paired with foreign ambassadors. Norfolk, Suffolk and Cranmer came next, followed by various earls carrying water basins, wax tapers and a gold salt cellar, all ceremonial gifts for the prince.

There was even a part to play for the four-year-old Princess Elizabeth who, coming behind them, held a jewelled baptismal chrism. It was a heavy, somewhat cumbersome object, and as she could hardly have been expected to bear its weight alone, she herself was carried in the arms of Edward Seymour, Jane's brother.

Next Edward appeared, clothed in a delicate white gown, placed gently upon a cushion held in the arms of the beaming Gertrude, who walked beneath a canopy of a fine cloth of gold. It seems that she performed her duties well enough, albeit for one nervous moment when the Duke of Norfolk stepped in to support Edward's head, she being either unable to control the squirming child or bear his weight.

The final part of the procession was formed by the wet nurse and midwife, shielded under a canopy held up by six gentlemen. As god-mother, Princess Mary brought up the end of the procession, surrounded by ladies of her chamber carrying lighted wax tapers. Snaking through passages lined with spectators and guards, and taking precaution to avoid the draughtiest areas of the palace, the party eventually reached the Royal Chapel.

Henry had renovated Wolsey's old chapel two years before, so that it now shone with the full splendour of the Renaissance. A magnificent oak hammer-beam roof had been installed, painted blue and inlaid with stars of gold-leaf to create the effect that heaven itself, complete with trumpeting angels, was present above. The royal motto *Dieu et mon Droit* had been carved across its arches, and the arms of Henry and Jane set in plaques on either side of the door, where they can still be seen today.

For this occasion, however, a specially designed octagonal screen had been constructed around the brand new font made from silver gilt, with guards armed with spears posted over its doors; all this was deliberate, for such secrecy had been devised to enhance the sacred nature of the rite, raising the spectacle of majesty and awe of the occasion. Inside, its walls were hung with arras, cloth of gold and rich tapestries. A space had been curtained off containing a fire pan of coals, perfume and silver basins of water 'to wash the prince if need be'.

Hidden from the audience, Cranmer, cradling the baby in his arms, began the ceremony at midnight. Those sitting in the pews could see nothing, hearing only the litany of the blessing echo through the chapel until the sound of the twenty-four trumpeters heralded the Garter King-of-Arms' announcement, proclaiming the prince's new style: 'God of His Almighty and infinite grace give and grant good life and long to the right high, right excellent and noble Prince, Prince Edward, Duke of

Cornwall and Earl of Chester, most dear and most entirely beloved son to our most dread and gracious Lord, King Henry VIII.'

After a final chorus of the *Te Deum*, the procession re-formed to return the prince to his waiting parents in the state bedchamber. Though it was now well into the early hours of the morning, the blazing torches were 'so many that it seemed like day'. The king and queen gave their formal blessing; as Henry took his son in his arms tears ran down his face. No description survives of Jane's appearance. Perhaps amidst the celebrations, her quiet demeanour easily went unnoticed.[15]

As the nobles and dignitaries departed, content at the sight of the nation's new heir, elsewhere across the country the news of Edward's birth was welcomed with no less rejoicing.[16] Above all, it is the sense of relief that one detects most strongly in the celebrations. Hugh Latimer, Bishop of Worcester, gave his 'due thanks to our Lord God, God of England; for verily he hath showed himself God of England, or rather an English God'. It was the first expression of a sentiment that was to dominate Edward's life. The boy not only embodied the hopes of a nation, he was part of their salvation: since Henry had ordered the break with the Catholic Church, it was the king, Defender of the Faith, who was to bear the moral responsibility for the care of his subjects' souls. Edward's birth was a clear sign of God's favour in the new Church of England and Henry's personal reward for his decision to break with Rome. As Latimer commented, 'He hath overcome all our illness with his exceeding goodness; so that we are now more than compelled to serve him, seek his glory, promote his word.' Edward, put simply, was God's gift to the nation. This little baby, barely days old, was already being marked out for great things.[17]

Celebrations at court continued throughout the week. In his prolonged state of euphoria, Henry created six new knights and raised Jane's brother, Edward Seymour, to Earl of Hertford.[18] Yet two days after the christening, Jane fell suddenly ill. Rejoicing now turned to prayer. On Friday 19 October there was a general procession at St Paul's for 'the health of the Queen'. The Royal Chapel now filled with sorrowful courtiers praying for Jane's safety. 'If good prayers can save her,' wrote one, 'she is not like to die, for never [a] lady was so much plained with every man, rich and poor.'[19]

Henry postponed a hunting trip he had planned to mark the start of the season, but only temporarily. If Jane's condition did not improve, he remarked, he 'could not find it in his heart to tarry'. This need not be taken as a mark of insensitivity or callousness on Henry's part, who probably had no need to be reminded of the painful memories of his own mother's death in childbirth.[20] Nevertheless the doctors seemed hopeful for Jane's recovery – if she survived the night, they believed, she would be 'past danger'.

But the prognosis had come too soon. On Wednesday 23 October Jane suffered 'a natural laxe' – most likely heavy bleeding. Throughout the night and into Thursday morning, her condition worsened drastically.[21] She spent the morning with her confessor, who now prepared to give her the last rites. At eight o'clock that same evening, in a sudden change of mind Henry rushed back to her chamber. The Duke of Norfolk wrote hurriedly to Thomas Cromwell, demanding he repair to Hampton Court as fast as possible 'to comfort our good master, for as our mistress, there is no likelihood of her life, the more pity, and I fear she shall not be alive at the time ye shall read this'. That night, at around midnight, Jane died.[22]

Puerperal fever, a form of blood poisoning resulting from infection contracted by poor hygiene, has been suggested as the cause of her death, though it is more probable that Jane suffered from a massive haemorrhage as a result of parts of the torn placenta remaining in her womb.[23] Experienced midwives were trained as a matter of routine to examine the afterbirth to check that it had been completely discharged, but Jane had the misfortune to be attended by the best doctors of her age that money could buy. Yet they were academics, experts in medicine but without any practical experience of delivering a child: Cromwell later laid the blame on those about her, 'which suffered her to take great cold and to eat much things that her fantasy in sickness called for'. Jane's tragedy is that any lesser woman than a queen would probably have received better treatment.[24]

Soon rumours began to circulate of a very different story, that Jane had died as the result of a caesarean operation performed at Henry's instigation. According to one story in circulation by November 1538, Henry was present at the labour when he was told by a gentlewoman 'that one of the two must die'. Choosing his heir to be saved, he ordered the baby to be 'cut out of his mother's womb'. This prophecy was repeated elsewhere and became the subject of numerous ballads.[25] In the Vatican library, there exists a contemporary document concerning the birth that goes even further, damning Henry for having Jane's limbs purposely stretched 'for the purpose of making passage for the child' before having her womb sliced open, 'so that the child ready to be born, might be taken out ...'[26] Determined to blacken Henry's name, these charges were later repeated by the Catholic writers Nicholas Harpsfield and Nicholas Sanders. Sanders wrote in 1581 that Henry, on being asked the question by doctors whether to save the mother or child, answered that it should be the boy, 'because he could easily provide himself with other wives'. How Henry already knew the sex of the child, Sanders did not explain. Harpsfield, in his unpublished 'Treatise of Marriage', c. 1558, merely noted that Jane died 'for the safeguard of the child', but claimed somewhat incredibly that Edward was born 'as some say that adders are, by gnawing out of the mother's womb'.[27]

Is there any truth to be found in these stories? The answer, most likely, is no. The primitive nature of Tudor surgery meant that a caesarean operation would result normally in immediate death – it was not usually performed until the mother was already dead or beyond survival. But Jane had lived for another twelve days and her health initially seemed good, and she had sat patiently at her son's christening, composed and regal, for over six hours. Some commentators even looked forward to the cementing of the dynasty with a second child.[28] The rumour, however, remained compelling, a convenient accusation for Catholics to smear the dynasty with. In any case, the distinction between fact and fiction was never a priority in the curious and superstitious mind of Tudor man, where rumour could easily seem very real indeed. Henry, and in turn Edward, would never be free of its taint.

For the moment, Henry took no notice of any rumours that had begun to circulate around the court and beyond; perhaps he was unaware of them, for his grief seems to have been nothing less than genuine. Distraught, he fled to Windsor, leaving the funeral arrangements to others. There he went into seclusion, refusing to see anyone. Writing alone at his desk, he numbed the pain of loss by throwing himself into his work, replying to those who had sent their congratulations on Edward's birth. He wrote tersely to Francis I: 'Divine Providence ... hath mingled my joy with the bitterness of the death of her who brought me this happiness.'[29]

News of the queen's death provoked a sense of national mourning on a scale not previously witnessed in Tudor England. Richard Morison, pamphleteer with responsibility for government propaganda, attempted to alleviate the sorrow of his fellow Englishmen by composing a 'Comfortable Consolation, wherein the People may see how far greater causes they have to be glad for the joyful Birth of Prince Edward, than sorry for the death of Queen Jane'. This contained a fictitious seven-page speech from the queen, 'if she could speak to us', including Jane's supposedly dying wish to the nation: 'I have left you me babe . . . in his nonage, I shall think your love implied to the profit of mine heir, if you give it all to his father.' For Morison, even in death there was advantage to be had – no opportunity to pull heart strings and press obedience to the regime was to be wasted.[30]

After her body had been embalmed and her entrails removed and buried at the Royal Chapel, Jane lay in state, crowned and bejewelled and wearing a robe of gold tissue, for three weeks. On 8 November her coffin, surrounded by four white silk banners depicting the life of the Virgin Mary, left Hampton Court for Windsor. Princess Mary was again to play a central role in the ceremony, this time as chief mourner. Behind her the court followed in much the same fashion as they had paraded through Hampton Court during the joyous celebration of Edward's christening, though now they all wore black – the new fashion – rather than the traditional purple mourning garments. One extra touch was the white headdress that the ladies of her chamber wore, signifying that the queen had died in childbed. Jane was buried on 12 November 1537, with a requiem mass at Windsor and a dirge sung at St Paul's. No monument was ever erected in her memory, but a brass plaque was set above the vault. Its Latin inscription played upon the tragic irony of her emblem the Phoenix, the mythical bird whose death brought life:

> Here lieth a Phoenix, by whose death
> Another Phoenix life gave breath:
> It is to be lamented much
> The world at once never knew two such.[31]

In London, the church bells continued to ring from midday until six in the evening, though this time at a low funereal toll. Twelve hundred masses were ordered to be sung in the City by the Lord Mayor; privately, Henry requested twelve. Custom precluded the presence of husbands at their wives' funerals, though Henry may not have been in any state to attend. Cuthbert Tunstall, the Bishop of Durham, attempted to alleviate his sorrow – though God had taken his queen, Henry should not forget 'our most noble Prince, to whom God hath ordained your Majesty to be mother as well as father'.[32] The Duke of Norfolk in person urged him to think about taking a new wife, but Cromwell was already one step ahead, hot on his heels for another queen and another son to fully secure the dynasty. Within days he had sent Henry a list of suitable candidates, but was clearly taken aback with the king's less than enthusiastic response, noting that 'He has framed his mind to be indifferent to the thing'.[33]

Of all this, of course, Edward knew nothing. Later he would come to lament 'how unfortunate have I been to those of my blood, my mother I slew at my birth'; but for now, hidden away in his nursery, he was oblivious to the commotion that his entrance into the world had caused. The first few weeks of his life had been as momentous as any; for the moment, a courtier reported, he 'sucketh like a child of his puissance'.[34]

For the first six years of his life Edward, as he later mentioned in his diary, was brought up 'among the women'.[35] From birth, the Tudors handed their children over to the care of a separate household of servants, far removed from the bustle of the royal court. At its head was Margaret, Lady Bryan, the mistress of the household, but who acted more like the family nanny, a role she had performed for Edward's two elder sisters, and by now had considerable experience in the needs of royal children.

She probably liked to think that she knew what was best for them. An early surviving letter of hers to Cromwell in 1538 gives an impression of bossiness. Edward's nursery, she believed, was 'very bare for such a time ... he hath never a good jewel to set on his cape'. This was no obstacle for a woman who knew how to get her way: 'Howbeit I shall order all things for my Lord's honour the best I can,' she continued, 'so as I trust the King's grace shall be contented with all.'[36]

Reading her report, the colour must have drained from Cromwell's face. No doubt terrified that the news might find its way to Henry, he promptly transferred £5,000 (£1.5 million in today's money) into Edward's household funds. With her nursery now fully stocked, Lady Bryan happily relayed Edward's progress back to the court: he was healthy and merry, she noted, and had grown his first few teeth; three had come through whilst the fourth was just appearing. It was undoubtedly a relief to the wet nurse when, in October 1538, Sibyl Penne was appointed as his dry nurse, later becoming a favourite of Edward's, who affectionately named her 'Mother Jak'. Four 'rockers' were also employed to attend to the prince's cradle, one of whom was still receiving a pension of £10 (£2,000) fourteen years later.[37]

Far removed from the comforts of the court, and in a world where superstition and prophecies were held to be real in the minds of many, a series of alarming and unexplained incidents seemed to strike right at the heart of Edward's safety. Voodoo dolls representing Edward had been found with pins driven through their bodies, whilst rumours concerning Edward began to surface in taverns, fuelled by a strong belief in prophecy.[38] Cromwell ordered his network of spies to keep their ears to the ground. It was not long before a tinker in his pay reported a conversation that carried past the sound of clinking tankards at the Bell Inn on Tower Hill, where one John Ryan told of a prophecy that the prince 'should be as great a murderer as his father' since 'he must be a murderer by kind for he murdered his mother in his birth'.[39] When pressed to explain what he meant, Ryan stated that he had heard a prophecy from 'the best Chronicler in England' that the 'child that murdered thy mother in her womb . . . shalt have so much treason wrought in thy time more than ever thy father had'.[40] Who was the chronicler? Further examinations revealed the suspect to be Robert Fayery, a royal herald. A direct link had been traced back to the court, but further leads came to nothing.[41] Was this malicious gossip, or did Fayery know more than he was meant to have let on – perhaps the real truth behind Edward's own controversial birth? Again the evidence is tantalizing, but leads nowhere. For Henry, however, all this was alarming in the extreme: the line between rumour and magic, treason and plot, was a fine one.

Security measures were stepped up with the creation of a formal household especially for the prince. Henry personally dictated new regulations for the conduct of Edward's household.[42] The introduction to his text highlights his anxiety over the health and safety of his son for whom he considered 'there is nothing in the world so noble, just and perfect'.

The rest of the document reads much like a sermon, dictated by a king still enthralled by the thought of his own supremacy upon earth, seeking to fashion his own apostolic succession. Edward was a gift from God 'for his consolation and comfort of the whole realm' and a demonstration of 'his bottomless divine providence'. He was, as Henry affectionately termed it, 'this whole realm's most precious jewel'.

It was all the more necessary, then, that the utmost care be taken to protect the child from harm. The prince's household, sworn under oath, was to be strictly confined. A detailed check roll of every servant present, outlining their age and estate, was to be presented to Henry. Nobody under the degree of a knight was to be allowed in Edward's presence. And regardless of title, no one was to touch the prince unless they had been commanded by the king to do so. If permission was granted, any bodily contact was strictly limited to a kiss on the hand. Even then, one of the heads of the household had to be in constant attendance, watching hawkishly over the child, and before Edward offered his hand the well-wisher's kiss was to be tested with a 'reverent assay'.

Nothing must escape the closest of scrutiny. All foods for Edward's consumption – bread, meat, milk, eggs and butter – were to be first eaten in large quantity; his clothes thoroughly washed, dried, brushed and stored safely, to be tested and worn before Edward put them on. New clothes were to be washed before being aired beside the fireplace and scented with perfume, 'so that the same way his grace may have no harm or displeasure'. The improvements were soon in place, with an extra washing house and kitchen quickly built at Hampton Court to cope with the new demands.[43]

The risk of infection and disease was always a threat against which constant vigilance and protection were needed. Those bringing in wood for fires should be clean and disease-free; once finished with their task they were to depart immediately, whilst servant boys and pages were forbidden from even stepping foot into the household, since they 'without any respect go to and fro and be not wary of the dangers of infection and do often times resort into suspect places'.[44]

Despite Henry's concern, he remained an all too absent parent in Edward's life, though occasionally he paid him the odd visit, such as in May 1538 when he spent the day with Edward, 'dallying with him in his arms a long space and so holding him in a window to the sight and great comfort of all the people'. But these rare glimpses into Henry's relationship with Edward are precisely that, for seldom would the austere and stuffy atmosphere of the royal court allow for any semblance of parental responsibility.[45]

Rather it was his elder sister Mary who took it upon herself, as godmother, to visit her royal brother. Aged twenty-two, portraits show her to be a genteel young lady with fair skin and auburn hair, if not quite as attractive as her younger sister. Living in residence at Hampton Court, she was only a barge journey across the river to the prince's nursery at Richmond. Mary showed genuine interest in her little brother, paying him visits in November 1537, and again the next March, April and May. In March she had journeyed by horse, riding to Richmond on the late Queen Jane's own little saddle horse – perhaps on that occasion more than any other she realized the need for her sisterly affection to be lavished upon her motherless brother. Visits would be spent being entertained by minstrels, to whom her accounts show she gave ten shillings. Not even Edward's nannies were to be spared from her generosity. Later, in 1539 she gave his nurse five yards of yellow satin amounting to 37s 6d, and a gilt spoon to each rocker, costing 44s 0d.[46]

Contemporaries seem to have been genuinely struck by Edward's beauty, with ambassadors and courtiers queuing up to meet the young prince in the flesh. When the Spanish ambassadors were finally granted permission to visit Edward they considered him 'the prettiest child we ever saw'. A month later the Chancellor Thomas Audley thought him, 'so goodly a child of his age, so merry, so pleasant, so good and loving countenance' (although one wonders what Henry would have said if they had dared to think otherwise).[47]

Edward's was a beauty that perhaps would not appeal today. The first surviving portrait from which Edward's grey eyes stare out at us was painted by Hans Holbein when the prince was fourteen months old. White-faced with fair skin, almost to the point of transparency, Edward sits attired in clothes suited to a Tudor gentleman – a doublet of vivid red and yellow, designed to contrast with his delicate, somewhat podgy, skin beneath. But what might seem pallid or even insipid to us was the admiration of the Renaissance courtier: as a young man, Henry VIII's lily-white skin and light auburn beard drew praise from ambassadors across Europe.

Here in the painting, a few locks of Edward's fine blond hair protrude from his feathered cap held on by a ribbon tied beneath his neck. His cheeks are those of a well-fed infant, but the painting gives little sense of any childish temperament behind his stern features – instead, Edward sits oddly poised with a rattle in his left hand. Yet the rattle symbolizes more than a plaything, being held in the fashion of a sceptre. Holbein's point is clear: Edward, though barely a toddler, was heir to the throne and was expected to bear rule. He held majesty.

The recipient of the painting no doubt got the message: it was given to Henry by the painter as his New Year's Day gift in 1539.[48] But in case the point needed pressing, Richard Morison added a few lines of text beneath:

Little one, emulate thy father and be the heir of his virtue; the world contains nothing greater. Heaven and earth could scarcely produce a son whose glory would surpass that of a father. Do thou but equal the deeds of thy parent and men can ask no more. Shouldst thou surpass him, thou has outstript all, nor shall any surpass thee in ages to come.

When the painting was unveiled to the court, it was an instant success. The effect was obvious: this little prince would one day be king. John Leland, later immortalized in his famous 'itinerary' describing his travels across the country, even felt inspired to write a poem, 'On the Image of the Incomparable Prince Edward', describing how the more he looked at the painting and 'your [Edward's] delightful face and appearance, so I seem to see the form of your magnanimous father shining forth in your face'.[49]

That New Year, Edward, too, was showered with gifts. The child probably took little interest in the expensive items of gold and silver plate, such as his father's gift of a gilt standing cup with 'antique works with a man on the top', preferring instead the Earl of Essex's gift of a bell of gold with a whistle. His sisters sent more personal gifts: Mary, a coat of crimson satin embroidered with gold and pearls and with sleeves of tinsel, whilst Elizabeth went even further, sending a shirt 'of her own working'.[50]

As heir to the throne, Edward naturally attracted much attention from ambassadors, already angling for a possible marriage alliance. Generally they were pleased with what they saw.[51] But Edward did not always act the obedient child. By the beginning of 1539, Cromwell finally got his way and negotiations for Henry's fourth marriage, to Anne of Cleves, had begun. When Anne's brother, the Duke of Cleves, sent his ambassadors from Germany on a state visit, they were happily received by the king at Hampton Court. Yet what happened next was the cause of considerable embarrassment – and, at least for some, amusement.

Having been led on a guided tour of the building, the ambassadors were treated to a visit to Edward's nursery. The royal prince was brought forward in the arms of Sibyl Penne, with Lady Bryan hovering not far away. As the Germans, bearded and strangely attired, approached to get a closer look at the child, Sibyl attempted to free Edward's hand so that it might receive a kiss from the eminent dignitaries. But Edward would have none of it, and buried his face into Sibyl's shoulder, refusing to even look at his guests. Lady Bryan intervened. Attempting to coax the child out of what was becoming a difficult diplomatic situation, she used the best tactics that her long experience had taught her, 'cheering, dandeling and flattering' the little prince. It was to little avail. Edward burst into tears, and was only consoled when the Earl of Essex thrust his own bearded face into the child and played with him until Edward laughed. But as soon as the Germans approached once more, Edward dived back into the folds of Sibyl's arms, and the ambassadors, obtaining 'none other sight of my Lord Prince, for all the labour taken', withdrew disappointed.

For Essex, still a staunch Catholic, Edward's evident distaste for these Protestant foreigners was cause for celebration. 'Now, full well knowest thou,' he cried out to the prince after they had departed, 'that I am thy father's true man and thine, and these others be false knaves!'[52]

Edward was fast becoming a toddler. Paying a visit to his country nursery, the Lord Chancellor Thomas Audley reported back to Cromwell that the Hertfordshire air was doing him much good. He had grown, losing his baby fat, 'and waxeth firm and stiff'. Edward could now stand unaided and would probably be able to walk 'if they would suffer him'. Nevertheless, Audley approved of his care: 'They do yet best, considering his Grace is yet tender, that he should not strain himself, as his own courage would serve him, till he come above a year of age.' The prince was to be moved from his current residence before the winter set in, to which Audley fully agreed: 'It will be a cold house in winter, though in summer it is a good air.'[53]

For the next few years, Edward's household led an itinerant journey through some of the many smaller royal palaces and hunting lodges that Henry possessed on the outskirts of London. It was a life devoted to leisure and enjoyment. On his removal to Hunsdon around Easter 1540, Lady Bryan wrote to Cromwell informing him, as she was accustomed to, of Edward's progress: 'My Lord Prince's grace is in good health and merry ... his grace danced and played so wantonly that he could not stand still, and was as full of pretty toys as ever I saw child in my life.[54] Mary continued her visits, spoiling her brother with presents. Elizabeth was less generous, demonstrating a early habit for thrift for which she would become readily noted, but her gifts were no less thoughtful, for each year she sent her brother a cambric shirt that she had made herself.

Edward's health was the subject of close scrutiny; every waking hour of his life he was carefully monitored by doctors who swarmed around him, constantly checking his temperature and fussing over what he might or might not eat. The prince's health seemed good, with the French ambassador reporting in October 1541 that Edward was 'handsome, well-fed and remarkably tall for his age'. But that same month Edward came down with quartan fever, a form of malaria.[55]

Henry was so distraught that even his appetite suffered – he was said to be 'sad, and disinclined for feasting'. In fear that he might lose his only son, he anxiously summoned the best doctors from across the country to discover a cure. For ten days it was uncertain whether Edward would survive. His rich and luxurious diet had not helped matters. One of the doctors who had been summoned to the royal court and had examined the prince for the first time told the French ambassador that Edward was 'so gross and unhealthy that he could not believe, judging from what he could see now, that he would live long'. Despite this prediction, however, Edward threw off the illness, even though, in April 1542, doctors were still predicting him a short life.[56]

Desperate to aid his son's recovery, Henry dispatched his own personal doctor, Dr William Butts, to Edward's side. Butts visited frequently, and it was not long before his fastidious manner began to annoy the petulant prince who – confined to broths and soups – had developed a craving for meat. Edward's spirits, however, were fast picking up, and Butts finally allowed Edward to eat his coveted dish, observing diligently that though the prince had brought up one piece of 'corrupt matter', he had felt 'no disposition to vomit'. By now, fed up with Butts fussing around him, Edward had become impatient, telling the doctor – whom he had begun to call a fool and a knave – to go away. It was a clear and reassuring sign, Butts concluded, that the Prince's strengths were fully recovered and that his work there was done.[57]

Edward was allowed to return to his carefree lifestyle, residing at the royal palaces of Hunsdon, Havering and Ashridge where his household soon began to expand. There he often divided his time between visits from his sisters and playing with a select band of friends. One of these was a girl named Jane, the granddaughter of his chamberlain, Sir William Sidney; later she became Duchess of Feria, and her memoirs give us an insight into Edward's early life. She was six, younger than Edward by three months, and Edward took a shine to her; we might even describe them as childhood sweethearts. They talked, the prince 'taking particular pleasure in her conversation', read together, danced, played, 'and such like pastimes, answerable to their spirits and innocency of years'. When they played cards together and Jane lost, Edward consoled her saying, 'Now, Jane, your King is gone, I shall be good enough for you'. She remembered how the prince would call her 'my Jane'; in her adult life as duchess, looking back through the years, she never quite lost her early childhood affection for Edward: 'His inclination and natural disposition,' she recalled, 'was of great towardness to all virtuous parts and princely qualities; a marvellous sweet child, of very mild and generous condition ...'[58]

Edward was also given the chance to spend more time with his father, and in the autumn of 1543 his household was moved next to Henry's own in a neighbouring house. In December, Henry invited all three of his children to spend Christmas with him at court. The occasion marked the formal reconciliation of the king to his previously disinherited daughters, the princesses Mary and Elizabeth, which was made official in the Act of Succession passed in Parliament the following spring, when they were both restored to their places in the succession behind Edward.

In celebration Henry dined with all three of his children at Whitehall, taking the opportunity to introduce them to the court at a reception afterwards.[59] The occasion was commemorated in the painting *The Family of Henry VIII*. Painted by an unknown artist, Henry sits on his throne beneath the royal canopy and marbled columns of Whitehall Palace. Edward stands to his right and to his left kneels his wife – not his latest, Katherine Parr, whom he had married two years before, but Jane, here resurrected as his true queen, the mother of his heir and matriarch of the dynasty.

What we are seeing here is very much history as Henry, never one to make too much of a distinction between image and reality, believed it should be portrayed. He had always been keen to express his true feelings in art, like the lovers' knots with 'H' and 'A' he had ordered to be carved at St James's in celebration of his marriage to Anne Boleyn, only to be hastily gouged out three years later upon Anne's execution.

Now Katherine of Aragon and Anne Boleyn, not to mention Anne of Cleves and Katherine Howard, were to be literally painted out of memory. There, upon the richly tapestried rug, was the nuclear family – Henry, Jane, and Edward – that the king had longed for.

But it is the relationship between Henry and Edward that is of greatest importance here, for they look almost identical; Edward a miniature Henry. Unlike the women of the picture, whose averted eyes gaze vacantly away, both Henry and his heir stare directly at the viewer. Its effect is one of both power and solidarity, a reinforcement of the bond between father and son. Moreover, Henry's affection for Edward is clear, his right arm placed protectively around the boy's shoulder, a pose echoed in a remarkable cameo of the king doting upon his beloved son. Edward was very much his father's favourite child.[60]

Henry already had great plans in mind for Edward. With the death of the Scottish king James V in December 1542, three weeks after his crushing defeat by the English at Solway Moss, the crown of Scotland had passed to his baby daughter, Mary, barely a week old. Looking to unite the realms of England and Scotland, Henry sought her betrothal to Edward. The English diplomat, Sir Ralph Sadler, had seen the child in March 1543: 'It is as goodly a child as I have seen of her age', and in turn, Mary's ambassadors visited Edward at Enfield, 'greatly rejoicing to behold so goodly and towardly an imp'.[61]

Henry was assisted in his ambition by the pro-English party led by the Protestant Earl of Arran, Mary's governor. But Henry's terms were harsh. Mary was to be handed over to him within two years to learn 'the fashion and nurture of English ways': 'I look on her as my own daughter,' he added. When the ambassadors hesitated, he grew angry: 'Such a marriage is to be desired for the daughter of any king in Christendom!'[62] Despite the Scottish Parliament's instance that such a demand would be 'a right high and right great inconvenience', negotiations continued, culminating in a treaty signed at Greenwich on 1 July 1543, agreeing to both peace and marriage.

By December, however, the Scottish parliament had declared it void, renewing their traditional 'Auld alliance' with France. Henry was enraged. On 10 April 1544 he gave orders for Hertford to 'put all to fire and sword, burn Edinburgh town, so razed and defaced when you have sacked and gotten what ye can of it, as there may remain forever a perpetual memory of the vengeance of God lightened upon [them] for their falsehood and disloyalty'.[63] Determined to secure Mary's person as Edward's bride, Henry refused to countenance anything but success; the 'Rough wooing', as it was to be termed, had begun.

By summer 1544 Henry had also turned his interests to France, arriving in person at Calais to march upon Boulogne. In his absence, Henry had installed Katherine Parr as regent and Edward's uncle Edward Seymour as Lieutenant of the Kingdom. It was at this time that Henry also decided that Edward's household should be remodelled. Edward was moved to Hampton Court, where an official court was to be established around him. It was a sign that Edward, now six years old, was entering the first stage of manhood.

The event was a seminal moment in the young prince's life, and one that he did not forget to include in his diary when writing up the events of his early life. The ladies and gentlewomen of his chamber, the 'women'

Edward remembered being brought up with, were discharged, and in their place an all-male establishment was formed around the prince. The establishment of Edward's household also marked the beginning of Edward's formal education; as Edward himself noted, by 'well-learned men, who sought to bring him up in learning of tongues, of the scripture, of philosophy, and all liberal sciences'. Richard Cox was appointed his almoner and tutor, with John Cheke acting as his deputy, 'for the better instruction of a Prince, and the diligent teaching of such children as be appointed to attend upon him'.[64]

Between them, Cox and Cheke made a formidable team. Roger Ascham, Edward's calligraphy teacher, called Cox 'the best schoolmaster of our time', a feat equalled only by his reputation for discipline, for he was also considered 'the greatest beater'.[65] John Cheke was only thirty years old, but his academic record was on a par to none. Already Regius Professor of Greek at Cambridge, his fellow dons regretted having to let him go. Cheke's mission was clear – to give Edward the finest education befitting a Christian prince. He faced a heady task: 'To be masters of princes on earth,' wrote one contemporary, 'is to have the office of gods that be in heaven ... because they have, among their hands, him that afterwards ought to govern all the world.' Edward would not merely be born to rule: he was to be trained for greatness. In Henry's eyes, Edward was already the 'greatest person in Christendom', yet he had every intention that his son was to become the greatest king that walked the earth since biblical times.[66] From henceforth, Edward would be given the best education a prince could receive. At the time, Henry could hardly have realized that in setting Edward upon such a path, he would install in his son beliefs and intentions starkly different from his own, and even with the benefits of hindsight, there is little reason to suspect that this would be the outcome. Katherine Parr may have regarded Cox and Cheke as 'Christ's special advocates', but Cox had assisted in writing the King's Book, a conservative statement of doctrine, whilst for the time being Cheke was more preoccupied in reforming the pronunciation of Greek letters than in the reformation of the Church. In these perilous times, he commented, he could be 'merry on the bank's side without dangering himself on the sea'.[67]

Edward was not brought up alone, but educated amongst the sons of the nobility – the 'primroses of nobility' – of roughly his own age. The purpose of this miniature court formed around the prince was not merely to keep Edward company, but to foster the relationship between the royal heir and a nobility that would one day be expected to serve him.

Some became Edward's close friends, including Charles Brandon, Duke of Suffolk, and his brother Henry, whose doodles can still be found on Edward's school work. But Edward's closest companion and best friend was Barnaby Fitzpatrick, the son of Lord Upper Ossory, whom he later wrote to fondly and rewarded with generous gifts of money. A century later, the historian Thomas Fuller asserted that Barnaby had even acted as Edward's 'proxy for correction' and was whipped in place of Edward when the prince misbehaved by tutors not willing to incur Henry's wrath.[68]

This was a likely invention. We know from a report of Edward's progress, written by his tutor Cox in December 1544, that not even the nation's heir was able to avoid the cane. The report is also a unique insight into the methods of a royal tutor in the sixteenth century. Whilst Edward was preoccupied with his father's expedition to Boulogne, Cox decided to tailor his lessons to fit a martial theme. Learning was to be treated like a siege, with Edward set the task of conquering 'the captains of ignorance'. It was an inspired teaching method; Edward soon took to the challenge with relish and was soon able to decline nouns and verbs in Latin with ease.

Despite Fuller's assertions to the contrary, it seems that Edward had become a bit of a brat, confident that not even Cox could lay a hand on him. The tutor had other ideas. Carrying on with his metaphor, he described how there remained one captain of ignorance – Edward's stubbornness – that he named 'Captain Will' ('an ungracious fellow'). Cox tried everything, but it was of little use for Edward paid no notice. Cox despaired, until eventually his temper boiled over and he gave Edward 'such a wound that he wist [knew] not what to do'. Edward was stunned – 'Captain Will' had been vanquished; 'I never heard from him since,' Cox reported. He was sure Edward had learnt his lesson, and that no further similar punishments would be necessary.[69]

With his studies back on track, Edward's Latin grammar was improving at such a speed that he was now ready to turn his studies to the classical texts of Cato, Aesop's Fables, 'and other wholesome and godly lessons that shall be devised for him'. Reading practice took place at mass, where Edward read a passage from the proverbs of Solomon each day, learning 'to beware of strange and wanton women, to be obedient to father and mother, to be thankful to them that telleth him of his faults ...' And despite the earlier hiccup, Edward's behaviour was impeccable, Cox considering the prince 'a vessel most apt to receive all goodness and learning, witty, sharp and pleasant'.

Edward's lessons with John Cheke were more captivating, often involving visits from eminent scholars and the best minds of the day to share their experiences with the prince. Cheke encouraged the poet Walter Haddon to visit Edward and in 1545 summoned the topographer John Leland to tell the prince about his constant journeying across the country, later made famous in his *Itinerary*.[70]

There was no shortage of materials to draw upon to assist Edward's learning, for the Royal Library was stocked with maps detailing cities and sieges from across the world and even a model of the port at Dover 'made of earth set in a box of wood'. A 'great globe of the description of the world' stood in the centre of the room, whilst other curiosities brought back by travellers and ambassadors as novelty gifts for the king – an elephant's 'tooth' and 'a gripe's egg' for instance – could be found littered around Hampton Court.[71]

An inventory cataloguing the entire contents of Henry's royal palaces reveals that Edward was probably given his own study to work in; his own personal writing desk was covered in black velvet and embroidered with the letter 'E', whilst near by a cabinet filled with papers contained knives, a wooden compass, scales and weights, and a little black coffer filled with chessmen. Another desk, covered with green velvet, was filled with writing tools and instruments. Around the room – no doubt also for Edward's use – were two tables of slate framed in wood for writing upon, a two-foot rule of metal, hawk's bells, two spectacle cases (one observer later remarked how it seemed Edward suffered from poor eyesight) and an hourglass of white bone, whilst five astronomical instruments hung on the wall.

The inventory gives us a rare insight into the world of Edward's childhood, and of the toys and playthings with which the prince surrounded himself. On a set of shelves in another private study next to Edward's bedchamber, for instance, lay documents concerning his mother Jane – perhaps mementos – beside a comb case fashioned in the shape of a horse with a rider upon its back, a red box filled with 'small tools of sorcery', books and a puppet; other boxes contained chessmen, hawk's head caps and a horseman's mace of steel gilt. And hidden out of the way on the highest shelf was an enamelled glass table depicting Christ's passion, next to a spear of fine morisco work and a javelin. Beside lay a staff 'of unicorns' horns garnished with silver gilt' and two 'instruments of sorcery of silver white called spattelles'. Near by, perhaps on the floor, another box covered with embroidered crimson satin contained shirts and 'other things for young children' and, next to it, a painted box contained 'a dried dragon' – probably a type of herb – together with five song books.

Edward enjoyed music and listening to singing, particularly to metrical psalms that his groom, Thomas Sternhold, later remembered the prince ordered him to sing.[72] Edward was also taught how to play the lute by Henry's favourite musician, Philip van Wilder, with Edward writing to his father thanking him for sending 'him to me, that I may be more expert in striking the lute; herein your love appeareth to be very great'.[73] Other activities are less well documented, but entries within the inventory – gloves for hawking, a fishing rod, fencing swords, greyhounds' collars – and a portrait of Edward playing with a pet monkey, suggest that Edward enjoyed his leisure just as much as his work.

Edward's learning was greatly encouraged by his stepmother, Katherine Parr, whom Henry had married in July 1543. Katherine was an impressive and well-educated woman. She had fashioned her household into something of a humanist circle; in her widowhood, she invited reformers into her home, and her influence may be detected in the appointments of several royal tutors for Edward and the princesses. To Edward, she was his 'most dear mother' and the two corresponded frequently, Edward writing in September 1546 that 'I received so many benefits from you that my mind can hardly grasp them'.[74]

Katherine herself was a latecomer to learning, and found common cause with Edward as they both sought to improve their calligraphic hand. Here Edward considered he had the advantage. On one occasion he wrote rather priggishly to the queen:

> I perceive that you have given your attention to the Roman characters, so that my Praeceptor [Cox] could not be persuaded but that your secretary wrote them, till he observed your name written equally well. I also was much surprised. I hear too, that your highness is progressing in the Latin tongue ... Wherefore I feel no little joy, for letters are lasting; but other things that seem so perish. Literature also conduces to virtuous conduct, but ignorance thereof leads to vice. And, just as the sun is the light of the world, so is learning the light of the mind.[75]

Nevertheless, Edward could be modest when modesty was required, especially to those whose prodigious learning and capabilities he genuinely respected and admired. He wrote to his godfather, Archbishop Cranmer, that his Latin was 'more barbarous than barbarism itself' and told the Bishop of Chichester that 'if you compare my Latinity with yours, it were as if you compared clay with jewels'.[76]

But it was the ever-dominant figure of his father who left him truly awestruck. Whilst Henry had been absent on campaign in France, Edward worried whether to write, lest he disturb him with his 'boyish letters'. Eventually he summoned the courage, writing how he hoped his letter would bring Henry refreshment after his weary campaign, 'For, seeing you are a loving and kind father to me . . . I hope I shall prove to you a most dutiful son.' A week later he wrote again, this time wishing peace, 'because I should hope to visit you sooner, and because you would have rest and recreation'.

All these were no doubt genuine expressions of a son's love starved of affection by his absent father. He was anxious, he told Henry, 'to be assured that you are safe and well; for, though I have some reliance on the hearing of the ear, yet I have more confidence in my own eyes'. Henry did not reply, but wrote to Katherine instead to relay the news of his successful siege at Boulogne, adding, 'I am too busy to write more but send blessings to all my children'.[77]

When Henry finally returned from France, Edward wrote to his father overjoyed: 'I have heard that I am to visit your majesty . . . I now obtain my second wish. My first wish was, that you and your kingdom might have peace; and secondly, that I might see you. These done, I shall be happy.' There is no evidence that Henry ever bothered to reply, but in the only expression of affection he knew, he continued to lavish his son with expensive presents, which Edward gratefully acknowledged, writing: 'You have treated me so kindly, like a most loving father, and one who would wish me always to act rightly. I also thank you that you have given me great and costly gifts, as chains, rings, jewelled buttons, neck-chains, and breast-pins, and necklaces, garments, and very many other things; in which things and gifts is conspicuous your fatherly affection towards me; for, if you did not love me, you would not give me these fine gifts of jewellery.'[78]

Henry's magnificent tastes were fashioning Edward's own lifestyle. The prince had grown up surrounded by splendour and beauty; the walls of his rooms were hung with Flemish tapestries depicting classical and biblical scenes that Henry had confiscated from Cardinal Wolsey; he ate only from the finest quality cutlery, set with precious stones – even his napkins were garnished with gold and silver – whilst his books were decorated with covers of enamelled gold clasped with a ruby, and crosses and fleurs-de-lis set with diamonds and rubies, pendants of white sapphires.[79] His clothes were fashioned only from the best materials – delicate cloths of gold embroidered with silver that sparkled with pearls, emeralds, diamonds and rubies, so much so that one French observer later recalled how when Edward moved through the court, entire rooms sparkled. Even the buttons of his clothes were made from solid gold and his caps were garnished with diamonds and sapphires, but perhaps his most prized possession was a dagger of gold that he wore hung from a rope of pearls, its sheath garnished with diamonds, rubies and emeralds, with a large speckled green stone embedded in the hilt.[80]

It is probably this dagger that Edward holds in a portrait painted at Ashridge around 1546. Standing between a windowsill and an ornate classical styled column, Edward's puffed up poise is as entirely contrived as that of his father's. One can almost imagine the artist directing the prince to hold his shoulders high and breathe deeply, staring straight at the easel. To create the effect, the many layers of Edward's clothes seem too large for him, heavy and burdensome. But the symbolism of the picture rides above the implausibility of the situation, for its message is that Edward will inherit Henry's mantle as king to continue the Tudor dynasty. No more clearly is this highlighted than in the position of Edward's left hand, directing the viewer's attention to his modest but nevertheless prominent codpiece, a symbol of his increasing virility and power as he approached adolescence and adulthood. In fact, few could have realized then that within a year Edward would have taken his father's place as king.

By 1546, Edward had matured into a diligent student. Writing to Cranmer, his tutor Cox found him 'merry and in health, and of such towardness in learning, godliness, gentleness, and all honest qualities, that both you and I and all this realm ought to think him and take him for a singular gift sent of God': above all, he was 'an imp worthy of such a father'.[81] Edward even seems to have begun to enjoy his studies, writing to Cox that 'Letters are better than treasures of gold and silver'. He had learned four books of Cato by heart, and was making good use of the Bible, Aesop's Fables and the *Satellitium* of Ludovico Vives, the Tudor textbook that had formed the basis of his sisters' education and induction into courtly manners.

Edward's own letters to his tutor Cox reveal a mind obsessed with self-improvement. 'If I have not studied elegant words and phrases,' he wrote, 'I hope my negligence in this point will find excuse: for I have done my best.' Edward seems to have excelled over his peers, who perhaps felt less pressure than the prince to succeed: 'Negligent they may have been,' Edward felt the need to explain, 'I have only done my duty.'[82] This sense of duty was extreme, driven entirely by the desire – perhaps fear – not to disappoint his father whom he had promised that he should 'be tortured with stripes of ignominy if, through negligence, I should omit even the smallest particle of my duty'. Everything was done for a singular purpose: to prepare himself for the duties of kingship.

It remains difficult to get under the skin of Edward's early writings, for there is little of the personal to be found within them. Peppered with classical and biblical quotations, they were clearly intended as exercises in composition rather than expressions of personal feeling: as Edward himself told Cox, he wrote 'because it exercises my hand ... trims up my Latin style'. The letters survive mainly as copies in a presentation work in the hand of the Cambridge scholar Roger Ascham, himself a royal tutor who assisted both Edward and Elizabeth with their penmanship, and who was probably eager to present the prince as a model of humanist scholarship.[83] Neither can one be sure where Edward's words begin and those of his tutors' – eager to impress Henry with the fruits of their labours – end. In particular, it is not difficult to believe that behind Edward's urging for peace, coupled with such assertions that 'Noise and riot is an evil; therefore war is an evil. Rest is a blessing; therefore peace is a blessing', might be his tutor's voice, echoing the concerns of the council and court who had become increasingly nervous about the spiralling costs of Henry's expedition to France.

Away from his studies, Edward maintained a good relationship with both his sisters. Elizabeth may have shared some of his early lessons at Ashridge, though this is unlikely to have continued after the formal establishment of Edward's household. It was Mary's company, however, in which he 'took special content', when apart sending her presents – including a basket of artichokes – together with the occasional letter. In May 1546, hearing that she had been taken ill, he wrote to her:

Although I do not frequently write to you, my dearest sister, yet I would not have you suppose me to be ungrateful and forgetful of you. For I love you quite as well as if I had sent letters to you more frequently, and I like you even as a brother ought to like a very dear sister, who hath within herself all the embellishments of virtue and honourable station. For, in the same manner as I put on my best garments very seldom, yet these I like better than others; even so I write to you very rarely, yet I love you most.[84]

Despite being twenty years younger than Mary, Edward was determined to act the protective brother to his elder sister. Four days later he wrote to his stepmother, Queen Katherine, asking her to keep a careful eye on the princess. Worried that she needed protecting 'from all the wiles and enchantments of the evil one', he beseeched the queen to persuade her 'to attend no longer to foreign dances and merriments which do not become a most Christian princess'. How Katherine responded the records do not reveal, though the letter is a telling insight into a relationship that would become fraught in later years, when both siblings chose to place their religious belief before family loyalty, resulting in a stand-off when Mary refused to give up hearing mass despite Edward's repeated insistence. Edward's relationship with Elizabeth seems to have been less strained, with the prince determined to emulate his sister's capable learning and writings 'to my utmost power, if not to surpass, at least to equal you in . . . zeal'.[85]

Other glimpses of Edward remain as anecdote, yet they reveal the innocence of an unassuming child, unaware of the momentous changes that had taken place during his father's reign. As he passed the ruins of a monastery on a journey, he enquired what buildings had stood there. 'Religious houses, dissolved and demolished by the order of the King your Grace's father, for abuses,' came the reply. Perplexed, Edward replied: 'Could not the King my father punish the offenders and suffer so goodly buildings to stand? And put in better men, that might have inhabited and governed them?'[86] Edward's strong Protestant opinions had yet to form, and his beliefs still revolved around the Catholic religion; he attended mass, worked in rooms adorned with images of saints and even had among his possessions 'a piece of the holy cross enclosed in gold'.[87]

In August 1546 Henry decided that Edward, not quite nine years old, should perform his first official duty, receiving the French Admiral on his arrival for a state visit at Hampton Court. It was to be his first royal rite of passage and Edward's induction into the ceremonial life at court. He prepared assiduously, nervously writing to Katherine – did the Admiral understand Latin? 'For, if he does, I should wish to learn further what I may say to him.'[88] Above all, he did not want to let his father down. He had prayed to God, he told Katherine, that he would be able to satisfy his expectations.

Riding out three miles from the palace gates accompanied by two thousand horse, he dismounted at the riverside. The French Admiral, disembarking from his ship, then kissed Edward's hand before the prince returned the compliment upon both cheeks. Edward made a short speech of welcome, his first public speech. It was a success: according to the chronicler Edward Hall, Edward's 'lowly and honourable manner' impressed everyone, who 'greatly rejoiced, and much marvelled at his wit and audacity'.[89]

Edward's studies entered a new stage when he began to learn to write French in October 1546, apparently with ease, and two months later he was able to write a short letter to Elizabeth in French. But he struggled to speak the language, and when he met the French ambassador the following February, it was noticeable that Edward could speak only in Latin 'since he does not understand French yet and is only just beginning to learn it'.[90] Yet as the year came to its end, no one could doubt that the prince was excelling. For Cox, the early years of Edward's schooling had left the prince equipped with the basics to learn the tools of kingship. 'I trust the Prince's Grace will content his father's expectations hereafter,' he wrote to Henry's private secretary, William Paget. 'We suffered him hitherto to grow up according to his own wish.'[91]

2

LAST WILL AND TESTAMENT

Meanwhile, the final year of Henry's life was one of desperate uncertainty. The king, in control to the last, had become capricious, his instability heightened by the continuous pain from varicose ulcers in his legs. Unable to walk unaided, he was carried by trams that shuttled him up and down the corridors of Westminster Palace,[1] and suffered from frequent bouts of fever. It was clear that Henry's reign was drawing slowly to an end.

No one could be sure which direction events might take. The court began to fragment into a kaleidoscope of alliances, broadly forming into two separate factions: on the one hand, the conservatives who espoused the traditional values of the Catholic religion and were embodied in the greatest nobles in the land: the Howards – Thomas, Duke of Norfolk, and his son Henry, Earl of Surrey – paired up against the evangelical cause, espoused by 'new' men who had risen up through the court as a result of Henry's favour, such as Edward Seymour, Earl of Hertford, the rising courtier John Dudley, and the king's secretary William Paget. These bonds were by no means static, and were subject to change as much on the basis of personality as any sincerely held belief.

There was, however, one aim common in the minds of all. For whoever gained access to the dying Henry sought not only to influence his judgement during his reign, but to control his son in the next.

Everything was to play for – at the beginning of the year it seemed that the conservatives had the upper hand, and amidst rumours that Henry might even return to papal obedience they boldly engineered a plot to bring down Katherine Parr, attempting to persuade Henry that she was a heretic. This all fell on deaf ears, for Henry suddenly made a spectacular about-turn, telling an astonished Cranmer that he wished to see the mass abolished within six months. What – or who – had made Henry change his mind?

A likely explanation can be found in Henry's reluctant decision to abandon his hopes of conquest and military glory in France, for the end of the war brought with it the return of two of Henry's favourite courtiers and companions, Edward Seymour, Earl of Hertford, and John Dudley, Viscount Lisle. Edward Seymour's position amongst the nobility was unique. The elder brother of Jane Seymour and Edward's uncle, the king held him in close regard, raising him to an earldom in 1537. He could be proud, tactless and lacking in popularity, often alienating his fellow courtiers, particularly the members of the ancient nobility who regarded him as somewhat of an arriviste. But no one could deny that he was a brilliant soldier renowned for his excellent military leadership.

Unlike Seymour, Dudley could not count on family ties for influence. His father, Edmund Dudley, had been one of Henry VII's deeply unpopular chief ministers, executed for treason upon the accession of Henry VIII. At the time, John Dudley was just six years old. Adopted by Sir Edward Guildford, who persuaded the king to reverse the attainder★ against the Dudley property two years later, Dudley slowly found favour at court and by 1542 had been elevated to the peerage. His military reputation both at land and sea continued to excel, culminating in his appointment as Lord Admiral in March 1546. Edward Seymour wrote admiringly of him to the king: 'I can do no less than to recommend him unto your highness as one that has served you hardely, wisely, diligently, painfully, and obediently as any that I have seen'.[2]

Returning to court from France, Seymour and Dudley immediately took their places as the king's closest advisers, holding the king's ear as they whiled away the hours at cards. Neither probably cared much either way about the direction religion might take – they were perfectly content to follow whatever course Henry chose – were it not for the threat that their great political rivals, the Howards, posed. But both realized that if they were to secure their political survival into Edward's reign, it would be impossible not to take one side or the other.

Fortunately, both men had a common ally in Sir William Paget, the king's secretary, whose reputation for secrecy and political manoeuvre would later earn him the title of 'master of practices'. And it was to him they turned for a solution; naturally Paget already had a plan in mind – to bring about the final downfall of the Howards.

For though Thomas Howard, the Duke of Norfolk, was the most

★ Punitive confiscations by the crown of the property, land and title of a guilty party.

powerful and esteemed nobleman in the land, his son Henry, Earl of
Surrey, was a brash and volatile young man, confident that he could
always fall back upon his exalted family background. Yet Surrey's fool-
hardiness on the battlefield in France had cost him his position as
Lieutenant of the King's Forces, and, more importantly, the king's favour.
Bitter and resentful that his inferiors – Seymour and Dudley included –
should be promoted above him, Surrey grumbled to a friend how 'These
new erected men would by their wiles leave no nobleman on life'.[3] As
the evangelicals grew ever more powerful at court, Surrey's behaviour
merely alienated him even further from his enemies. Fast becoming a
scapegoat, he was unaware of the forces being ranged against him. He
even wrote to Paget addressing him as 'my friend' and later attempted to
win his support by offering him the position of chancellor.[4] Paget had
other ideas in mind. As early as 1545 he had been sending Seymour
letters urging him to befriend others at court, particularly those who had
valuable personal contact with Henry. Soon, with the secretary's help,
Seymour presided at the head of a faction determined to imprint their
dominance upon the court in spite of any who opposed them.

Despite every sign that Henry's favour was turning towards the evangelicals, nothing could be taken for granted and the situation remained
fraught. The cost of espionage escalated, to the concern of the French
ambassador, who found that despite offers of great quantities of gold, no
one would speak for fear of being accused of treason. At court, anxiety
over the future turned to anger and even violence as tempers in the
council flared.[5]

The crucial turning point seems to have come in mid October, when
the conservatives, led by the Howards, lost control of the Privy Chamber
to the evangelicals, who now dominated the household with complete
access to the king. At what cost, the conservatives would soon discover,
though by now the power that had once seemed surely within their
grasp had all but ebbed away. By December 1546, as illness left Henry
dangerously close to death, the council even took to meeting at Edward
Seymour's house.[6]

Henry continued to reaffirm his belief in the evangelical cause. During
the autumn heretics formerly condemned were pardoned and bibles were
printed in England for the first time since 1542. By mid December there
was already talk that 'There will be a change of religion in England, and
the king will take up the gospel of Christ', and one of Henry's final

diplomatic encounters was with an envoy to whom Henry reiterated his commitment to the reformed faith within earshot of four leading councillors.[7]

Whilst the chance was there – and before Henry again changed his mind – Paget, Seymour and the other evangelicals decided to strike first and secure their dominance of the court, finally defeating the conservative faction. They had good reason to be bold, for they had been aided by the defections of the chancellor Thomas Wriothesley and Richard Southwell to their cause. Though both men were Catholics, they now realized which way the wind was blowing, and as was often the case during the twists and turns of the Reformation, religious allegiances became subordinated to the desire for power. They were welcomed into the fold, for between them they had what the evangelicals had been looking for – evidence that would destroy the Earl of Surrey and finally bring down the Howards.

On 2 December Southwell told the council he had information concerning the Earl of Surrey 'that touched his fidelity to the king'. Surrey was arrested and taken for examination at Wriothesley's house, whilst the Howard family home at Kenninghall, Norfolk, was raided by the king's agents in a quest for evidence. What they discovered there, they claimed, was undoubted proof that Southwell was correct, for its walls had been newly decorated with heraldic badges displaying the letters H and R on either side of a broken pedestal, with the royal arms at the top. In an age when visual imagery was a vivid representation of meaning and intent, this, the government claimed, could be taken as nothing less than treason: HR stood for 'Henricus Rex', with the broken pillar a representation of a ruined commonwealth vanquished by the Tudors but to be restored under the Howards. Surrey later denied the charge, claiming that the pillar represented his own noble house, broken by the king's might, with HR standing for 'Hereditas restat'. But no one believed him.[8]

Besides, fresh investigations had discovered that Surrey had taken to quartering his arms in his heraldic shield with those of Edward the Confessor – in effect claiming that the Howards had as equal a claim to the throne as the Tudors themselves. Although told by the herald Garter King-of-Arms that 'it was not his honour to do so', Surrey refused to listen. Surrey's sister recalled how the earl had worn 'a cap of maintenance purple . . . and with a crown . . . underneath the arms was a cipher, which she took to be the King's cipher. H.R.' His close friend George Blagge further admitted that Surrey had told him his father was 'most meet to rule the prince', but in the end it was the testimony of Surrey's sister, that her brother had urged her to 'delight the king' with sexual favours in an attempt to control him, that would put the verdict beyond any reasonable doubt.[9] By 12 December 1546 both Surrey and Norfolk were in the Tower.

Surrey was tried on 13 January 1547 in the Great Hall of the Guildhall. He spoke from nine o'clock in the morning to five o'clock in the afternoon. He remained proud to the last, denying every charge, though a last-minute confession from his father in the Tower sealed his fate. Found guilty, he was led back to the Tower ranting against the 'conjured league' that had destroyed him. He was executed six days later.

Henry had been horrified by Surrey's actions, and was reported to have been 'much perplexed' by the whole affair. His health worsening, he now remained secluded in his bedchamber, surrounded by only a few trusted courtiers. On 24 December 1546 he had spent three hours going through the accusations levelled against Surrey. With a trembling hand he helped to frame the charges, adding (marked in italics): 'If a man compassing with himself to govern *the realm do actually go about to rule the King* and should for that purpose advise his daughter or sister to become his harlot *thinking thereby to bring it to pass and so would rule both father and son*.'[10] Knowing the end of his life was drawing ever nearer, Henry must have realized exactly what was at stake, for though he was not yet in the grave, already the fate of his son was at risk – too young to rule himself, Edward would be an easy target for the unbridled ambitions of politicians and courtiers, and would remain so unless precise guidelines were drawn up on how a regency council should rule during his minority.

Henry decided to act; he would make one final last will and testament outlining his intentions in full. This was exactly what Paget and the evangelicals had been hoping for – the chance to permanently exclude the conservatives from government. For though Henry may have believed that his own supremacy left him fully in control, the reality was far different, for he had become a puppet in the hands of those closest to him, his very thoughts and intentions manipulated with a subtlety that even the most astute struggled to recognize.

In the event of the succession of a minor, the 1536 Succession Act had empowered Henry to name a council of guardians, appointed by his last will as his executors. The list had remained unaltered since Henry last drew up his will upon his departure for France in 1544. But now all this was to change, for Henry told his attendants that he wanted to revise the list – with certain names 'he meant to have in and some he meant to have out'.[11]

Going through the checklist, Sir Anthony Browne, the master of the horse and a renowned conservative, was the first to notice the change: surely Stephen Gardiner, the Bishop of Winchester, had been forgotten? But Henry had not forgotten the bishop – he had left him out deliberately, he told Browne, for he was so stubborn that he thought no man would be able to control him. But Browne did not take the hint and persisted. 'Have you not yet done to molest me in this matter?' Henry retorted, threatening to throw Browne out of his bedchamber. Henry knew exactly what he was doing. The name of Thomas Thirlby, Bishop of Westminster, was also deleted since he had been 'schooled' by Gardiner. When the new list of executors was finally completed – the men who would hold real power under Edward's reign – it read like a roll-call of those either supportive or compliant to Paget's and Seymour's cause.[12]

The new will, written out under Paget's dictation, was ready by 30 December 1546. After laying out the succession, following that set down in 1544, there came the changes: Katherine's position as regent was revoked – a measure of which she remained uninformed; sixteen executors were to act as Edward's councillors, whilst twelve assistants were to provide aid and counsel 'when they or any of them shall be called'. This would allow for a functioning regency council to act in Edward's name until at least October 1555. Henry's intentions were clear: all voices were equal and decisions were to be taken by a majority vote with no one individual acting supreme. With the regency council, Henry sought to create a system that would create a realistic framework of government, seemingly free from manipulation, to act in Edward's name. It was to be a constitution for the new reign.

There was, however, one particular paragraph that has caused more raised eyebrows and has been the subject for more debate amongst historians than any other. Named the 'unfulfilled gifts clause', it read:

> Furthermore, we will that all such grants and gifts as we have made, given, and promised to any, which be not yet perfected ... shall be perfected in every point towards all manner of men for discharge of our conscience, charging our executors and all the rest of our councillors to see the same done, performed, finished and accomplished in every point.[13]

In effect, Henry was giving *carte blanche* for his councillors to reward themselves with whatever grants of land and titles they so wished. The clause seems so remarkable that many historians have doubted whether Henry was even aware of it, suggesting that it was inserted at a later date when he was dying and incapable of knowing its final contents. If this was the case, Henry's will should be considered one of the greatest forgeries ever committed. The evidence certainly seems compelling, for Henry never actually signed the will with his own hand. Instead it was stamped at its beginning and end by a clerk using a 'dry stamp' – a carved impression of Henry's signature – and the impression inked in. This was not unusual, since Henry often had little time for the routine of business, and had regularly delegated the chore of signing documents to officials who held the stamp since September 1545, but it makes the question of when the will was actually stamped difficult to establish. To avoid the risk of its abuse, a list was kept of the times the dry stamp was used and the reason Henry's signature was needed. The entry for the will records that it was stamped and placed in a sealed box on 30 December, yet there is more to the story than this, for the entry comes as eighty-fifth on the list, *after* other entries dated 27 January – the day before Henry's death. Written on an extra piece of parchment, the entry was tacked on to the list at the last moment. This suggests that the will was not stamped on 30 December as the officials would want us to believe, but rather during the final few hours of Henry's life when Henry, slipping in and out of consciousness, would have been oblivious to the conversations taking place in the corridors of power outside his bedchamber. How much could Henry have really grasped what was going on? Very little, one suspects.

Yet the truth of the matter is somewhat more complex, for Henry's tenacity and determination to hold on to what was left of his failing life was extraordinary. His schedule remained as busy as ever: on 17 January he received the French and Imperial ambassadors (though the meeting was kept short 'in consequence of his indisposition') and even fussed around with ordering apple trees for the Privy Gardens. Three days later plans for Edward's creation as Prince of Wales were being organized, yet no efforts were made to bring him back to the capital. Whilst Henry had begun to face the inevitable, death was hardly a thought that he wished to dwell upon, making it extremely difficult for any plans for Edward's future reign to be properly laid. Henry had talked with Paget about creating new members of the nobility to replace the Howards, but these plans were never properly finalized before the onset of Henry's final illness.

When Henry did finally reach that point, the evangelicals, led by Seymour and Paget, seized their moment, for now they could dictate the final contents of Henry's will. According to John Dudley, they certainly manipulated Henry's choice of councillors, for it was when Henry was 'on his death bed' that the lists of executors for the will – those who would qualify for automatic membership of Edward's regency council – were drawn up. Hearing the name of Thomas Seymour, Edward's younger uncle, Dudley recalled how Henry had cried out '"No, no", though his breath was failing him'. Yet Seymour was sworn on to the council just four days before Henry died, after Paget had declared that Henry had remembered 'his good service' and minded 'to have him trained in the knowledge of his Majesty's council'.[14]

But there is no clearer evidence that the will was altered during this stage than the words of Paget himself, who explained later to the council that Henry 'being remembered *in his death bed* that he had promised great things to divers men, he willed in his testament that whatsoever should in any wise appear to his council to have been promised by him, the same should be performed'. If Henry's will was altered – and the mechanics of this remain unclear – this was the moment that the 'unfulfilled gifts' clause was added. Whether Henry himself ordered its inclusion depends on whether one takes Paget and his clique as reliable witnesses. After all, there were no others to corroborate their story.

With a new will drawn up, all that was needed was for the dry stamp to be applied and the will to be registered on the entry list at the eleventh hour, as it was. Henry could go to his grave never knowing the full content of his last will and testament. By 1567, Elizabeth's own private secretary was being challenged by an agent of Mary Queen of Scots to reveal the inside truth behind Henry's will, how, as the king's death approached, 'some, as well known to you as to me, caused William Clerk ... to sign the supposed will with a stamp, for otherwise signed it was never'.[15]

Yet the question of whether the will was forged or not seems to miss the point. Whilst Henry remained secluded, surrounded by one faction bent on destroying the other, evidence could be filtered to give the best gloss, whilst counsel could be directed for the purposes of self-interest. The will cannot therefore be treated as entirely the product of Henry's own making. Nevertheless, whether this really was the beginnings of a conspiracy or not, or whether it was the result of a king determined to retain his authority to the very last, the spectre of a sick and dying king subjected to the ruthless application of pressure reveals how complete the evangelical triumph had been. It was Paget who had had complete access to the king as he drafted rewards and new titles for the nobility, Paget who had acted the driving force in the process, suggesting and criticizing the choice of names, grants and titles to be handed out. The entire court was indebted to him. The Imperial ambassador considered that, as a result of his revelations, Paget had become 'the person in most authority'. 'The whole body of Governors are to some extent under obligations to Paget,' he observed, 'as indeed they appear to recognise by the great consideration in which they hold him.'[16] As for the 'unfulfilled gift' clause, forged or not, it became, in effect, a blank cheque, invoked in nearly thirty patents issued in Edward's first year. In all, Crown lands worth more than £3,200 per annum had been handed out. Through it, Seymour and Paget had bought and rewarded the support they needed to achieve their sole aim – to make Seymour Lord Protector of Edward and of England.

By 27 January 1547 Henry's doctors knew his death was approaching, although for fear of punishment they refused to tell him.[17] Anthony Denny volunteered to break the news. Approaching his deathbed, he informed Henry he was 'to man's judgement not like to live'. He should now 'prepare himself to death, calling himself to remembrance of his former life, and to call upon God in Christ betimes for grace and mercy, as becometh every good Christian man to do'.

'Yet is the mercy of Christ able,' replied Henry, 'to pardon me all my sins, though they were greater than they be?'

He wanted Cranmer to hear his confession. But first he would 'take a little sleep; and then, as I feel myself, I will advise upon the matter'. An hour later he awoke, 'feeling feebleness to increase upon him'. Cranmer was summoned immediately. By the time the archbishop had arrived, Henry had already lost the power of speech. His body was rapidly failing. Barely recognizing the archbishop, he held out his hand, 'but could utter no word unto him, and scarce was able to make any sign'. Cranmer exhorted him to 'put his trust in Christ, and to call upon his mercy'. Realizing that the king could no longer speak, he urged him to 'give some token with his eyes or with his hand, that he trusted in the Lord'. Gripping his hand, Henry wrung it, 'as hard as he could'.[18] By two o'clock in the morning of 28 January 1547, Henry was dead.

Outside the king's bedchamber, Paget and Seymour talked alone. We do not know the exact words that passed between them, but two years later, Paget reminded his friend of their conversation: 'Remember what you promised me in the gallery at Westminster before the breath was out of the body of the king that dead is. Remember what you promised me immediately after, devising with me concerning the place which you now occupy ... And that was to follow mine advice in all your proceedings more than any other man's.'[19] The intrigue that would come to define Edward's reign had begun.

An hour later, Edward Seymour and Sir Anthony Browne were making haste towards Hertfordshire to fetch Edward. Bringing him to Enfield, they broke the news of his father's death to the new king and his sister Elizabeth. Despite Henry's long illness, the news came as a surprise. Tradition dictates that they clung to each other, weeping. The next day, the earl wrote to the council, informing that they would be riding back by eleven o'clock and aimed to be at London and the Tower by three o'clock.

The transfer of power seemed to be going to plan. But in his haste, Seymour had taken the key to the box containing Henry's will. Paget wrote immediately, requesting the key and demanding to know if the box should be opened. Seymour agreed, but believed its contents should be kept secret between them. 'It might be well considered how much thereof were necessary to be published,' he added. 'For divers respects I think it not convenient to satisfy the world.' Part of its contents should be read to the Parliament on the following Wednesday. 'In the meantime we should meet and agree so there may be no controversy hereafter.'[20]

But already everything was slotting neatly into place. Riding back from Enfield, Seymour raised the prospect of his possible appointment as Protector with Anthony Browne, the conservative who had nearly fallen foul of Henry's anger, who agreed it was 'both the surest kind of government, and most fit for that Commonwealth'.[21] By the time the council wrote to Seymour on 30 January 1547, desiring to know his opinion of the traditional royal pardon issued at the beginning of a new reign, his authority seemed a *fait accompli*. The earl nevertheless remained cautious, replying to the council that he was unsure whether he had any power to make any such decisions, yet adding a significant proviso – 'in case we have the authority so to do it, in our opinions the time will serve much better'. His imperious tone, however, revealed his full intentions to become the figurehead for government: 'We do very well like your device for the matter ... we would wish it to be done when the time serveth most proper for the same.'[22]

Life at court continued much as normal, with Henry's death kept secret for the time being – the usual practice to ensure that the transition of power could be achieved as smoothly as possible. The etiquette of court life remained the same – with dishes still being brought to the dinner table to the sound of blaring trumpets.[23]

On the morning of 31 January, three days after Henry had died, a tearful Wriothesley informed the House of Commons of the king's death and his intentions as set out in his will, yet he read only the relevant sections regarding the succession of the Crown.[24] As Seymour had intended, its full contents – including the unfulfilled gifts clause – were not disclosed.

Behind the scenes events were moving fast. The same day a meeting of the executors resolved under oath to honour Henry's will, yet to avoid disorder and confusion they unanimously agreed that Seymour should 'be preferred in name and place before others, to whom as to the state and head of the rest all strangers and others might have access', explaining their decision that as the closest of the king's relations (that 'tenderness and proximity of blood ... being his uncle') and bearing in mind his considerable experience in affairs of state, he was to have 'first and chief place among us, and also the name and title of the Protector'.[25]

Seymour's appointment as a kind of chief councillor was hardly an unnatural solution. As Edward's elder uncle on his mother's side, many would have probably assumed that he would have been the best man for the job. Though Henry remained suspicious of such authority and had sought to create a council of equals, his will had allowed for the executors to do anything they considered 'meet, necessary or convenient' for Edward's benefit if they agreed a majority decision in writing.

But in doing so, Henry's clear instruction, that the sixteen executors, each with equal authority and governing together on behalf of Edward until he reached the age of eighteen, had been shattered. The news probably came as a shock to many, and particularly to Katherine, who had assumed that she would take charge of Edward as his stepmother, not least since she had already begun to sign her letters 'Kateryn the Quene-Regent'.[26]

That afternoon Edward entered the city gates of London, clearly delighted by the welcome of an ecstatic crowd and the endless salute of guns fired from ships on the Thames.[27] Arriving at the Tower, he would remain lodged there until his coronation, his rooms hung with cloth of arras and his cloth of estate. Only a week earlier he had been spending his time writing thank-you letters for his New Year's presents. His favourite present had been from Katherine, a miniature of Henry and herself, 'expressed to the life'. 'It delighteth me much', he wrote to her, 'to gaze upon your likenesses, though absent, whom with greatest pleasure I would see present . . . I give you greater thanks for this New-Year's gift than if you had sent me costly garments or embossed gold or any other magnificent thing'.[28] Now he wrote to console her:

> It hath seemed good to God that my father and your husband, our most illustrious sovereign, should end this life, it is a common grief to both. This, however, consoles us, that he is now in heaven, and that he hath gone out of this miserable world into happy and everlasting blessedness. For whoever here leads a virtuous life, and governs the state aright, as my noble father has done, who ever promoted piety and banished all ignorance, hath a most certain journey into heaven. Although nature prompts us to grieve and shed tears for the departure of him now gone from our eyes, yet Scripture and wisdom prompt us to moderate those feelings.[29]

The new king also wrote to his sister Mary with equal stoicism. 'We ought not to mourn our father's death, since it is his will, who works all things for good,' he remarked, adding: 'So far as lies in me, I will be to you a dearest brother, and overflowing with all kindness.'[30]

Meanwhile, preparations began for Henry's funeral. After the corpse had been seen by the council and the nobles at court, preparations were made for the burial. Commands were sent out to the apothecaries and surgeons to embalm the corpse. As the assembled team took a knife to the body, they found his arteries so clogged and swollen that 'there was hardly half a pint of pure blood in his whole body'.[31] A plumber and carpenter were appointed to encase it in lead; compensating for Henry's massive weight and proportion, the coffin was built around the body as it lay on the bed.

Set upon trestles beneath 'a rich pall of cloth of gold', the coffin was placed in the middle of the Privy Chamber, surrounded by lights. For five days, a continual vigil was held day and night by his chaplains and thirty Gentlemen of the Privy Chamber, during which masses, prayers and obsequies were made. Every wall was dressed in black cloth, and garnished with escutcheons of Henry's arms, descents and marriages.

Back in the chapel, an enormous hearse to hold the coffin had been created, surrounded by banners, escutcheons and standards of St George and Henry's royal ancestors. At its four corners were four banners of saints beaten in fine gold upon damask. On the hearse were eighty candles, each two feet tall, the wax weighing over 1,800 pounds. At its foot, where Henry's body would be laid, was an altar draped in black and covered in precious stones. Once the corpse lay in state, mass would be said continually at its table.

In the meantime, the court busied itself in preparations for the funeral as orders were given for each man and woman to put on their 'mourning weeds'. On Wednesday 2 February, Candlemas Day, between eight and nine o'clock at night, the hearse was lit. Henry's body was removed from the chamber and taken to the chapel. Covered with 'a rich pall of cloth of tissue, crossed with white tissue, and garnished with escutcheons of his arms', the coffin was carried by Gentlemen of the Privy Chamber. Behind followed the nobility placed according to their degrees, torches in hand. When the procession reached the chapel, the coffin was placed within the hearse, a pall of a rich cloth of tissue garnished with escutcheons and a cloth of gold set with precious stones were laid over the coffin. Throughout the night the gentlemen ushers kept watch over the body.[32]

Feelings over Henry's death were mixed, however, the Earl of Oxford even going so far as to mount a play at Southwark that clashed with a dirge that the Bishop of Winchester, Stephen Gardiner, had organized for the king's departed soul. Gardiner wrote furiously to Paget: 'They in game or I in earnest; which [to] me seemeth a marvellous contention, wherein some shall profess in the name of the commonwealth, mirth, and some sorrow, at one time ... what the lewd fellows should mean in the contrary I cannot tell, nor cannot reform it.'[33]

Gardiner was not the only one smarting from his exclusion from the new regime. As a mere assistant to the will, Seymour's younger brother Sir Thomas had not been invited to the meeting of executors that elected his brother Protector. As Edward's younger uncle, he considered this an affront to his status. Shortly after the meeting had ended, Sir Thomas was approached by John Dudley. Dudley was considered a good friend of the Seymour brothers, 'trusted of them both and loved of them'. He informed him of the executors' decision to elect his elder brother Protector, and urged him to demand at the next council session to 'have his voice to be the governor of the king's person' and promising his help and assistance to achieve this, after all 'it was so reasonable a request that he knew no man would deny it him'.

An enthusiastic Sir Thomas thanked Dudley for his advice. He was too proud and foolish to realize Dudley's intent, for he had probably never seen the other side to Dudley's character: a cold and ruthless streak with a Machiavellian sense of purpose to all his political dealings. 'He had,' said Sir Richard Morison, 'such a head that he seldom went about anything but he conceived first three or four purposes beforehand.' According to a later Elizabethan writer, he intended none other than to set brother against brother until he had engineered the fall of both. If this was the case, then Sir Thomas was easy game and ready to fall straight into the trap. At the following packed council meeting he stood up and demanded the governorship of his nephew Edward. Without uttering a word, Seymour rose from his chair and departed, leaving Sir Thomas and the rest of the council astonished.

Later in the day, Dudley, continuing his wiles, paid a visit to Seymour, telling him: 'My Lord, did not I tell you ever that he would withstand all your intents and purposes and he only would envy your state and calling to this room; his heart being so bidge that he will never rest till he do overthrow you again.'[34]

But the next day Sir Thomas, having failed in his attempt to become governor, *was* appointed Privy Councillor. His elder brother had decided upon a compromise. Sir Thomas had, after all, been made a councillor in the last days of Henry's reign, and though the appointment had been annulled upon the king's death, the new Protector needed his brother's support since his own position seemed tenuous. Though the Protectorate had been 'secretly agreed' at the meeting on 31 January, nothing had been set down 'in writing' as the terms of Henry's will dictated. At the first meeting of the executors, Seymour had apparently faced resistance from Wriothesley who 'was sore against him'.[35] Wriothesley was one of the few councillors whose personality and authority were great enough to mount an effective challenge to the Protector's plans; according to the Imperial ambassador he was, with Seymour, Dudley and Paget, among the four who 'will take into their hands the entire direction of affairs . . . each one will strive his best for his own advancement'. And though he had been instrumental in defecting to the evangelical cause and bringing about the downfall of the Earl of Surrey, it was becoming clear that his allegiance and committed support was waning in the light of Seymour's unexpected appointment as Protector.

But if hearts and minds could not be won, they could certainly be bought. Here the 'unfulfilled gifts' clause came into its own, with Wriothesley, like the others, won over with offers of promotion – in Wriothesley's case to Earl of Southampton. On 1 February he declared to Edward in a formal ceremony before the lords that it had been 'agreed with one assent & consent' of them all, that Seymour should be his Protector. 'It was expedient,' he told Edward, 'for him [Seymour] to hold such a position during his youth.' The Lords then answered 'in one voice' that 'there was none so meet ... in all the realm as he' and that they were 'well content'. Seymour thanked them, and asked for their support, as they all cried together: 'God save the noble King Edward!'[36]

Edward removed his cap. 'We heartily thank you, my lords all,' he replied, 'and hereafter in all that you shall have to do with us for any suits or causes you shall be heartily welcome to us.'[37] The entire charade probably seemed perfectly natural to Edward; little did the boy know just quite what deals had been struck and what frictions remained behind his throne. For the moment it was a picture of perfect concord and unity. It would not last long.

3

A SECOND JOSIAH

After Henry's body had lain in state for ten days, his coffin was transferred to Windsor in a procession stretching over four miles. At the front were two hundred and fifty paupers wearing mourning gowns and carrying torches, accompanied by two carts laden with supplies to replenish those that had extinguished. Carried in a gilded chariot pulled by seven horses, a funeral effigy of the late king lay on top of the coffin, dressed in velvet, gold, and precious stones, which according to one observer 'looked exactly like that of the king himself . . . just as if he were alive'.[1] Behind followed guards and officials dressed in black and each according to their degrees. The procession stopped the night at Syon, where one grisly story recalls how 'there the leaden coffin being cleft by the shaking of the carriage, the pavement of the church was wetted with his blood. In the morning came plumbers to solder the coffin, under whose feet . . . was suddenly seen a dog creeping, and licking up the king's blood.'[2] The following day the procession continued its journey to Windsor, greeted along the way by scholars from Eton and the townsfolk of Windsor. There in the chapel at Windsor Castle, the coffin was placed in a hearse thirty-five feet in height, covered with tapers and candles that consumed 4,000 pounds of wax.[3]

On 15 February Henry's burial took place. Stephen Gardiner, in his role as chaplain to the Order of the Garter, preached the funeral sermon as Jane's vault was uncovered and Henry's body was laid to rest beside her, as was his wish. It took sixteen yeomen of the guard using five linen towels to lower the coffin into the vault. Then according to the ritual of custom, the officers broke their staffs, throwing them into the pit, 'not without grievous sighs and tears'. Later, when Edward came to write up his journal he considered this act particularly puzzling, describing how 'the officers broke their staves, hurling them into the grave. But they were restored to them again when they came to the Tower.'[4]

That night the Lords hastened to London on horseback. There were more important ceremonies to prepare for. The next day they gathered in the Tower, where they all received their rewards for their agreeing to Seymour's place as Protector. Seymour himself was elevated to become Duke of Somerset, Dudley and Wriothesley the earls of Warwick and Southampton, and Katherine's brother, William Parr, Marquess of Northampton. There were peerages for Sir Thomas Seymour, Sir Richard Rich, Sir William Willoughby and Sir Edmund Sheffield. At the same time Dudley was granted the staff of Great Chamberlain, whilst Thomas Seymour replaced Dudley in his former office of Lord Admiral. To finish the day, Edward attended his first chapter of the Order of the Garter, 'his George about his neck and his Garter about his leg'.

On Saturday 19 February, the day before the coronation, Edward made his procession from the Tower of London towards Westminster. It was to be the main occasion for Edward to be shown off to his people and for his subjects to catch a glimpse of their new king. Crowds gathered along swept and freshly gravelled streets as Edward left the Tower at around one o'clock, riding on horseback and dressed in a vivid white jerkin of velvet – to make sure that he was easily recognizable amongst the massing throngs – and embroidered with silver and decorated with diamonds, rubies, and pearls fashioned in lovers' knots. His gown was a fine mesh of gold with a cape of sable, whilst the horse he rode upon was draped in crimson satin beaded with pearls.

At the front of the procession the king's messengers walked side by side in pairs, followed by his gentlemen and trumpeters, chaplains, the esquires of the body and the nobility on horseback, each according to their degree. Ambassadors and representatives of nations across Europe were paired with members of the council.

The Imperial ambassador Van der Delft was far from impressed. First kept waiting at the Tower, he then had his oration to Edward in French interrupted by Seymour, now Duke of Somerset, who asked him to address the king in Latin 'which he said he understood better than French'. 'Truth to tell,' he wrote, 'he seemed to me to understand one just as little as the other; although the Archbishop of Canterbury had assured me that the King knew Latin as well as he did himself.' Matters were not helped that he found himself in the procession alongside Cranmer, who, opposing the ambassador's Catholic belief, refused to speak to him during the entire ceremony, acting 'the part of a dumb man all the way'.[5]

After the gentlemen ushers, and the Marquis of Dorset bearing the 'naked' (drawn) sword of state in his role as Constable of England, Edward finally appeared flanked by John Dudley and Somerset, who kept particularly close to his side. Next came the henchmen, the Gentlemen of the Privy Chamber, the pensioners and the guard 'with their halberds in their hands'. Along the route gentlemen with 'tipstaffs' cleared the way in front – one observer recognized them as Somerset's own retainers, a clear sign that the duke was tightening his grip upon power.

The entire scene was depicted in a mural at Cowdray House, the home of Sir Anthony Browne, the master of the horse, who rode behind the king on a horse trapped with gold. Surviving only now as an eighteenth-century drawing, the procession makes its way through the winding narrow streets, stretching out across the entire length of the city. From the highest garret windows four storeys up faces peer out as the king passes beneath. At the corners of the painting, men and women run to catch a glimpse of the new king passing by Cheap Cross; a few even stand on rooftops. Tapestries, competing for space, hang down from parapets erected for the occasion. One chronicler observed that every house along the route 'was richly hanged with coverlets and carpets of tapestry and arras', whilst another account noted that out of every window were hung 'clothes of tapestry, cloth of gold and cloth of tissue ... as richly as might be devised'.

Along the first part of the route, Cheapside was 'richly hanged with cloth of silver and gold', whilst the members of the craftsmen's guilds stood with their individual banners; facing them on the other side of the road were priests and clerks dressed 'with their crosses ... and in their best ornaments'.

The pageants organized by the city officials had been given only a short time to rehearse, and as a consequence turned into a shambles, with speeches not delivered on time and actors only prepared after Edward had already passed by, causing one historian to describe the coronation procession as one of the 'most tawdry' on record. This is unfair, for many were taken from a sequence written by John Lydgate for the coronation of Henry VI as King of France in 1432. The parallel was a conscious one, since Henry had been the last boy king (excluding the unfortunate Edward V – one of the Princes in the Tower) but it also reminded onlookers of a glorious past when the king held the crowns of both England and France.[6] This time, Edward was to be greeted by four children, each child representing Grace, Fortune, Nature and Charity. A huge fountain, topped with 'a crown imperial of gold' and garnished with pearls and precious stones, sprayed jets of wine through pipes into the street, though a few craftily stole the wine in cups and barrels so that its reserves were drained within six hours.

Further along, Edward reached a stage where a scaffold had been erected. Beneath its roof was a heavenly display, with the sun, stars and clouds devised 'very naturally'. As Edward looked on, from one cloud fringed with silk a phoenix descended on to a mount beneath, covered in red and white roses and hawthorn bushes. A lion wearing a crown soon approached, and after 'making a semblance of amity' to the bird (which involved 'moving his head sundry times') a young cub emerged. At that moment, two angels descended from the mock heaven, clutching the imperial crown, which they set upon the cub's head. The lion and the phoenix then disappeared, leaving the young cub crowned and alone.

The imagery may seem bizarre, but visual displays often reflected a world of allegorical meaning closely pondered upon by Tudor contemporaries. The phoenix was Jane's emblem, the lion Henry's, whilst the roses and hawthorn bushes were representations of the Tudor dynasty. Their union, a marriage ordained by God, had produced the cub, Edward. Now he was to be crowned, his imperial crown delivered from heaven, a sign both of divine favour and of royal supremacy.[7]

At Cheap Cross, Edward was presented with £1,000 in gold coins by the aldermen of London. 'Why do they give me this?' Edward, puzzled, reportedly asked, before being relieved of the heavy burden.

Along the route there were more allegorical depictions, among them, Edward the Confessor, Edward's ancestor and namesake, and the paragon of chivalry, St George, on horseback, these being models of piety and leadership expected from a Tudor king. Plays and songs had been prepared, though few were heard by the king, whose procession 'made such speed' that he had passed by before they could begin. Others were drowned out by enthusiastic chants: 'Sing up heart, sing up heart, sing no more down, but joy in King Edward that weareth the crown!' At the conduit in Fleet Street a child representing 'Truth' – epitomizing the cause of reformed religion – did manage to catch the king's ear, urging him to embrace God's truth as his father Henry had done, 'Then shall England, committed to your guard, rejoice in God, which hath given her nation, after an old David, a young king Solomon.'[8] It would not be the last time the same biblical comparison would be drawn of the young king, for already the expectation was clear that Edward must continue the Reformation from where his father had left off. Henry's Reformation had gone only so far. Like Solomon, it was now Edward's duty to rebuild the Temple.

But for the moment one particular display caught the king's eye. On the south side of St Paul's, a tightrope walker descended from a cable, 'aiding himself neither with hand nor foot', to the ground, where he kissed Edward's foot. Ascending back up to the middle of the cable, he 'tumbled and played many pretty toys', much to Edward's amusement.

By the time the procession reached its destination it was nearly six o'clock and Edward had been riding for over four hours. Ambassadors willing to pay their respects were hurried past and asked to take their leave 'with as few words as possible'. That night, warning was given to all noblemen to be at Westminster 'in their best array' by seven the next morning.

Preparations for Edward's coronation had begun in earnest. The ceremony was undoubtedly the most important event in a king's life. Vesting him in the duties of kingship, the ritual was not merely a symbolic one. It gave him power and defined his authority: in short, it created him.[9]

On 4 February, a proclamation had been issued demanding 'all the nobility, and other subjects claiming to do service' at the coronation should make their claims to a court at Whitehall. On 7 February, these were debated among the council. Many of the ancient nobility expected to perform the tasks that had been the preserve of their ancestors: the Earl of Shrewsbury, for example, was to provide the king's right-hand glove and support his hand while he held the sceptre; the Earl of Oxford, as great chamberlain, to serve the king water in order to wash his hands and face before and after the coronation; whilst the Earl of Arundel, the nobleman with the oldest lineage of all the lords, was to act as chief butler at the coronation feast.

The reward for such service was more than honour-bound. Arundel was given all the wine left in the barrels afterwards, in addition to the best cup served to the king; Oxford, the silver basins and towels once Edward had finished with them. The officers at Westminster Abbey received a hundred loaves of bread and eighty-eight gallons of wine. More unusual requests were also granted, such as Nicholas Leghe's to make a 'mess of pottage called degeront', but Robert Puttenham's desire to act as 'marshal of the king's whores' in order to 'drive out all harlots in the king's house and to dismember all malefactors adjacent' was probably sensibly refused.[10]

At nine o'clock on 20 February Edward was taken by barge to Whitehall, where he was received at the privy stairs by the guard and pensioners with their axes in hand. Passing into the chamber of the Court of Augmentations, he donned his Parliament robes, a robe of crimson velvet 'furred with powdered ermines throughout'. The procession then made its way to Westminster Abbey.

The coronation regalia was carried by the most prominent members of the nobility whilst Edward proceeded under a canopy borne by the barons of the Cinque Ports. He was assisted by Shrewsbury to his right and Cuthbert Tunstall, Bishop of Durham, on his left. Behind him, Dudley, Northampton and Thomas Seymour bore his train, followed by the Gentlemen of the Privy Chamber, the nobility in their robes of estate, the pensioners and the guard and the servants at court.

At Westminster Abbey, the choir had been hung with cloths of arras, the floor strewn with rushes. A dais seven stairs tall had been erected, on top of which the throne was set between two pillars, a white chair covered with damask and gold. To compensate for Edward's small stature, two cushions had been placed on the seat, one of cloth of tissue, the other of black velvet embroidered with gold.

The coronation followed the rules set down in the *Liber Regalis*, which had dictated the ceremony of crowning kings since 1375.[11] But there were important changes. The coronation ceremony had been shortened, 'lest their tedious length should weary the king, being yet of tender age'. This cut the length of the entire ceremony, including the coronation banquet, down from twelve hours to around seven.

Cranmer read the first part of the coronation address, the presentation of the king to the three estates. But instead of repeating the traditional formula, 'Will ye sirs at this time, and give your wills and assents to the same consecration, enunction, and coronation?' the archbishop had changed the text to read, 'Will ye *serve* at this time . . .' This alteration enforced a dramatic transformation in the relationship between the king and his people. The question had in effect been turned upside down, marking a significant shift in the theoretical powers of the monarchy; whereas before the presentation underlined that it was the people who had the ultimate power to choose their king, now it had become a reminder of their bounden duty to serve the king regardless.

'Ye, ye, ye, God save King Edward!' the audience replied unwittingly. Cranmer next administered the coronation oath. Since the fourteenth century, kings had sworn an oath that set out the five requests of his people: to confirm liberties and laws that had been granted to the English people by kings before him, then those of the clergy, a promise of peace and concord to clergy, Church and people, to be just and merciful and to observe 'such laws as . . . shall be chosen by your people'.[12] This was drastically altered by Cranmer. References to laws and liberties were removed – in future it would be the Crown that decided what should constitute these. Peace and concord would be promised only to Church and people, significantly excluding the clergy, who found the clause ensuring the protection of their liberties deleted entirely. Reformation of the Church could now be enabled by royal prerogative, the king as lawmaker. To confirm this, the final part of the oath was rewritten to reverse its meaning entirely: now the people, not the king, had to consent to new laws.[13]

Before the anointing took place, Cranmer explained these changes in a remarkable sermon. He addressed the king: the oaths he had given, he told him, were not to 'to be taken in the bishop of Rome's sense'. The clergy had no right to hold kings to account, 'to hit your majesty in the teeth'. The Archbishops of Canterbury had crowned Edward's predecessors, but once God's anointed, they could not reject them. Indeed the coronation ceremony itself had no hold over Edward, who could act as he wished. Nevertheless, God required from kings and rulers 'religion and virtue'. As 'a messenger from my Saviour Jesus Christ', he reminded Edward of his princely duty with a comparison from the Old Testament:

> Your majesty is God's vice-gerent and Christ's vicar within your own dominions, and to see, with your predecessor Josiah, God truly worshipped, and idolatry destroyed, the tyranny of the bishops of Rome banished from your subjects, and images removed. These acts be signs of a second Josiah, who reformed the church of God in his days. You are to reward virtue, to revenge sin, to justify the innocent, to relieve the poor, to procure peace, to repress violence, and to execute justice throughout your realms. For precedents, on those kings who performed not these things, the old law shows how the Lord revenged his quarrel; and on those kings who

fulfilled these things, he poured forth his blessings in abundance. For example, it is written of Josiah in the book of Kings thus: 'Like unto him there was no king before him that turned to the Lord with all his heart, according to the law of Moses, neither after him arose there any like him.' This was to that prince a perpetual fame of dignity, to remain to the end of days.[14]

The image of Edward as a 'second' Josiah was a powerful one, which would be cited frequently during his reign. It was an expression both of Edward's own supremacy and the mission that lay before him. The genesis of Cranmer's argument had already been expressed in a royal proclamation issued on 31 January 1547. This declared that Edward had come to the throne 'fully invested and established in the crown imperial of this realm'. No legal action or further recognition would be required to confirm his authority.[15] A striking coronation medal, produced in gold and silver, also reflected this idea, showing the young king clad in armour girded with the sword of faith. Inscriptions on the obverse in Latin, Greek and Hebrew stressed his supremacy. What this all amounted to was a powerful message: Edward was like no other king that had gone before him. He was the first king to be born with the title of Defender of the Faith, and the first to be crowned with the powers that the royal supremacy brought with it; no king, before or since, was ever given such a unequivocal mandate for absolute rule.

The litany and anointing finished, Edward took his place on the throne. Crowned in turn with St Edward's crown, the imperial crown and his own specially made crown that was both light enough to wear and small enough to fit his head, he was then given the sceptre, St Edward's staff and the orb and spurs, though these were immediately taken off so that they might not 'encumber' the boy.[16] He held the orb in his left hand and, with the Earl of Shrewsbury's help, the sceptre in his right.

Somerset came forward to kneel, pledging his life and limb to the new king. Next it was Cranmer's turn, before the entire nobility came forward, each taking turns to kiss the king on his left cheek. Because 'time would not serve' for them to make their homage individually, they then knelt down together for Somerset to declare it 'in general'.

Events soon moved to the Great Hall at Westminster, repainted, and with its windows glazed for the occasion. Its floors were strewn with rushes, and rich cloths of arras hung around the walls, whilst the stairs leading to the hall were covered with red carpet and over the king's seat 'was a very rich cloth of estate'.

The nobility took their places to serve the king at dinner. At the end of the first course, the herald then proclaimed Edward's style in Latin, French and English, before Edward, Somerset and Cranmer moved to the centre of the hall with the rest of the nobility for a void – a kind of drinks party where everyone stood eating dessert – before removing to Whitehall, where challenges and feasting continued into the evening, culminating in a play against the Pope, complete with pilgrims' staves and caps of crimson and black satin 'for priests in play'.[17]

Over the following two days royal jousts were held, which Edward watched from his gallery. Six challengers, including his uncle, Thomas Seymour, ran six courses against twelve defenders, and 'for their ladies' sake' the defenders ran an extra two. The banquets continued, together with another play 'where was also made a mount, with the story of Orpheus right cunningly composed'.

Everyone seemed impressed, apart from the Imperial ambassador Van der Delft who, despite not having been invited to attend the coronation banquet, complained that the entertainments were unremarkable; he had heard that other ambassadors were not treated satisfactorily and had found it difficult to find a seat in the confusion. What Edward thought of the occasion, his terse diary entry reveals little. Recalling the ceremonies that encircled him, he merely remarked that he sat next to his uncle and Cranmer, 'with the crown on his head'.[18]

Somerset's and Paget's triumph seemed complete. The terms of Henry's will had been overturned and their supporters satisfactorily rewarded. The Imperial ambassador Van der Delft observed how Somerset 'governs everything absolutely', acting only on Paget's advice and counsel. The routine of government business was now being conducted only through them, and those seeking to present petitions to the king were advised to submit them to Somerset 'who hands them to the Secretary as the late King used to do'.[19]

Yet Somerset's own authority remained ill defined. Though he could count on the support of his fellow council members – so long as he did everything according to their permission – there was still no legal justification for the Protectorate, and as foreign ambassadors had already begun to question his ability to act in the king's name, a royal commission under the Great Seal would be needed to affirm his position. And there were other problems: the co-option of his brother on to the council had forced Somerset to create another seat at the board. This made it difficult not to accept others who had a stronger claim to a seat on the council – its membership would eventually need to expand if these men sought advancement and challenged what must have seemed like blatant nepotism.

This aside, cracks in the evangelical faction had already begun to appear. In particular, the Imperial ambassador Van der Delft predicted 'some jealousy or rivalry' to arise between Somerset and Dudley: 'Although they both belong to the same sect they are nevertheless widely different in character: the Lord Admiral [Dudley] being of high courage will not willingly submit to his colleague. He is, moreover, in higher favour both with the people and with the nobles than the Earl of Hertford [now Duke of Somerset], owing to his liberality and splendour.' Somerset, on the other hand, was 'not so accomplished in this respect, and is indeed looked down upon by everybody as a dry, sour, opinionated man'.[20]

For the moment, however, Somerset's attention was drawn else-where – towards the Lord Chancellor, Wriothesley. For though he had agreed to support the Protectorate, Van der Delft considered he had done so out of fear; perhaps believing that Somerset's ambitions could be reined in, the earl later told the ambassador he would resist any further changes that went beyond the provisions set out in Henry's will, claiming that he had prevented Somerset from gaining even further powers. And despite his reward of an earldom, Wriothesley seems to have been determined to resist Somerset's further plans for advancement, being, according to one observer, 'sore against' him.[21]

As chancellor, Wriothesley was also keeper of the Great Seal. This needed to be affixed to every patent for its authentication, giving him, in effect, a veto on each royal patent and commission. This point was not lost upon Somerset: Wriothesley would need to be dismissed if he hoped to further establish his powers as Protector. And he did not wait long to seize the opportunity.

In fact, Wriothesley played straight into his rival's hands. Two days before the coronation he had commissioned four civil lawyers to hear cases in his absence in order to concentrate upon his business in council, importantly without the new king's warrant. A team of common lawyers declared this to be 'to the great hindrance, prejudice and decay of the said common laws', demanding that Wriothesley be removed from his position as chancellor. The council, examining the charge, felt unable to pass judgement. This at least was the case according to the draft of the proceedings. (However, when the final version of the indictment was copied into the Privy Council register, this fact was curiously omitted.)[22]

Wriothesley was charged on 5 March. While under examination the final indictment read, 'he had not only menaced divers of the said learned men ... but also used unfitting words to me, the said Protector, to the prejudice of the King's estate and the hindrance of his Majesty's affairs'.[23] 'What danger might ensue,' the charge read, 'if the great seal of England, whereby the king and realm might be bound, should continue in the hands of so stout and arrogant a person as durst presume at his will to seal without a warrant.' The seal was taken from Wriothesley's hands, and the earl placed under house arrest.

The *coup d'état* that had seen the Earl of Surrey executed, Henry VIII's will forged and Somerset appointed Protector was complete. Wriothesley accepted his conviction dutifully, requesting that 'in respect of his old service he might forgo his office with as little slander and bruit as might be'. Yet this seems to have been, according to an observer, 'for the safety of the rest', and Wriothesley claimed that he had stepped aside so as not to excite 'divisions in the realm'.

The conservatives that had joined Somerset in hope of greater reward and favour were bitterly disappointed by Wriothesley's fall, but before they could act they were outpaced by Somerset, who ordered several to be confined to their houses. There was clearly a recognizable faction that Somerset believed was capable of opposing his plans, probably including the Catholic Stephen Gardiner, Bishop of Winchester, and the Earl of Arundel who were 'known to be opposed to any change in their ancient religion'. Thomas Seymour at least recognized this, calling for Mary and Wriothesley to be thrown into the Tower.[24] Somerset, however, remained cautious, refusing to allow Wriothesley to depart from London for his estate at Titchfield, near Gardiner's own residence, the Imperial ambassador believing it 'quite probable' that Somerset had done this to prevent the two men from arranging to meet.[25]

Meanwhile Somerset began his final assault on Henry's will. On 1 March 1547 the executors and assistants of the will were amalgamated to create a single Privy Council. On 12 March, with only seven members present, it requested a new commission granting the board full authority during Edward's minority. Somerset's powers were also extended, and he was now given full power and authority to decide matters 'both private and public, as well in outward and foreign causes'. He could add or remove councillors at will and convene the council 'as he shall think meet to call unto him from time to time'. He could even act without its approval.[26] In effect, he had become *de facto* king.

Somerset began to behave like one, ordering in regal fashion for two gilt maces to be carried before him, whilst in a letter to Francis I, he addressed the French king Francis I as his brother, an affront that provoked a reply that he should be reminded of who and what he was. He granted himself an annuity of 8,000 marks (£1.6 million) to support his dignity, and that summer his arms were changed to resemble the royal arms his sister Jane had borne.[27] A prayer issued to mark his appointment as Protector gives an insight into his behaviour. For Somerset, it was God's will that had committed an anointed king to his charge. He considered himself his 'minister', 'a shepherd for thy people' and 'sword-bearer for thy justice':

> O my Lord and my God, I am the work of thy hands: thy goodness cannot reject me. I am the price of thy Son's death Jesus Christ . . . I am written with the very blood of Jesus; thy inestimable love will not cancel then my name. For this cause, Lord God, I am bold to speak to thy Majesty. Thou, Lord, by thy providence hast called me to rule; make me therefore able to follow thy calling.[28]

By May 1547, Van der Delft informed Emperor Charles V that Somerset's power was now so great that no mention was made of the king's court for all business was now being transacted in Somerset's house. The records of the minutes of the council show that after the end of May, only a few councillors signed the book every fourth day, suggesting their authority had diminished to mere administrative formulas. After 1 January 1548, the signatures cease to appear. Soon Somerset would be controlling the government entirely by himself.[29]

Somerset also gained complete control of Edward, packing his household with his supporters and followers, including the crucial appointment of his brother-in-law, Sir Michael Stanhope, as a Gentleman of the Privy Chamber. Stanhope, who in August 1547 was made Chief Gentleman of the Privy Chamber, became in effect Edward's governor, controlling his every move and directing who might, and who might not, gain access to the prince.

Somerset had even begun to sign royal warrants on Edward's behalf.

When the French ambassador, Odet de Selve, queried the practice, Paget assured him that Edward had been learning to make a new signature, changing the one he had used before his accession: 'Now he knows how to do it, and in future he will sign all official papers.' De Selve did not believe a word.[30]

MILDER CLIMATES

During the last days of Henry's life, the conservative preacher John Feckenham had preached a sermon at St Paul's Cross, hinting of the troubles to come if a boy king came to the throne: 'What a world shall it be when they shall have the rule, for if they have the swing it will be treason shortly to worship God.' Feckenham's ominous message would have struck a chord with everyone in the audience. For thirty-eight years the country had been dominated by Henry VIII; few could remember a time before. Now no one knew quite what to expect. But Feckenham would be proved right – the world would soon be a very different place.[1]

Henry's death had removed the greatest obstacle to further unimpeded reform of the Church. But when he was urged to press on with the Reformation, Cranmer was already worried about the speed at which events had begun to progress. Under Henry, saints' images had been condemned, but had been allowed to stand, providing they were not the focus of worship. For the religious evangelicals, opposed to any form of religious imagery, this did not go far enough – they wanted them smashed and broken up, so that there would be no distraction from observing the true word of God as set down in scripture. Even before Henry's body had been laid in the grave, the parishioners of the city church of St Martin in London had ripped out their church interior, replacing rood figures with the royal arms, saints' images with biblical texts declaring, 'Thou shalt make no graven images, lest thou worship them.' Examined by the council, they alleged the roof was in ruin, the crucifix and images 'being old were so rotten . . . that they fell to powder'. They received a reprimand for their 'arrogancy and proud hastiness' yet only because they had 'run before they be sent, to go before the rulers, to alter and change things in religion without authority'.[2]

According to Van der Delft, events were certainly 'taking a strange turn': unrestrained since Henry's death, 'the people are beginning to adhere strongly to the sects' with the council ordering evangelical preachers to give daily sermons before Edward at court, where they seemed 'to vie with each other as to who can abuse most strongly the old religion'. On Ash Wednesday Nicholas Ridley had denounced images of saints and others quickly followed him. Broadsheets and plays condemning Lent flourished, provoking protests from Stephen Gardiner to the council. 'Lent remaineth still, my lord, and shall, God willing,' Somerset replied sarcastically, for being 'a great enemy to the pope' and 'so earnestly addict' to the new faith himself he was perfectly content for the reformers to continue their attacks.[3]

The nature of Somerset's own religious affiliation has been the subject of much debate. However, his patronage of Protestant ministers such as William Turner, Thomas Becon and John Hooper suggests that Somerset was something more than a mere moderate in reform: in 1539, he had dined with the firebrand Hugh Latimer and his players had performed plays in London with reformist messages. It was probably his second wife, the Duchess Anne Stanhope, who had guided him along this path. She had been suspected of protecting the radical Anne Askew; whilst under her influence, their six daughters had been brought up in 'good literature and in the knowledge of God's most holy laws'.

In any case, Somerset's own position as Protector was to act as tutor and instructor to Edward, preparing him, and his kingdom, for when he obtained his majority. For William Forrest, who dedicated 'The pleasant poesy of princely practice' to Somerset in 1548, sharp contrasts were to be drawn with the fateful minority of Edward V, brought to an all too sudden end by the usurpation of his uncle Richard III: Somerset was 'not Richard rager of cruelty, to whom the fourth Edward his children betook' but a 'true Theseus. . .'[4] For the reformers, this meant Somerset was 'bound in conscience to set forth God's lively word' and ordained by God himself 'to make so godly a ready way in the hearts of all'. God's temple 'that long hath lyen waste' would now be re-edified and built up once more.[5]

Gardiner quickly recognized that it was with Somerset he needed to fight his corner, reeling off lengthy correspondences against the attacks on images, urging him to inflict no religious changes upon the realm until Edward was old enough to make that decision for himself. Yet as the attacks on images grew more frequent as rumours circulated of religious change, a proclamation was issued on 24 May denouncing 'lewd and light tales told, whispered, and secretly spread abroad by uncertain authors, in markets, fairs, and alehouses' and explicitly denying any such intention. Officially, for the moment little had changed. Edward continued to hear mass in his chapel, hearing four services on Easter Sunday. The French king Francis I's death at the end of March was mourned with a solemn dirge at St Paul's and an obituary was kept in every parish church across London, though this would be the final time that the funeral rites of the old Church would be used at a state ceremony. All this was a 'smokescreen tactic' used to prepare the way for reform.[6]

At the same time, evangelical preachers continued their attacks regardless. Terms of abuse for the sacrament, such as 'Jack in the Box' or 'Round Robin', floated freely, with Somerset doing little to prevent them. Meanwhile, the recantation of the Catholic preacher Dr Smith at St Paul's Cross on 15 May, during which he threw his own books into the flames, came as a devastating blow to the conservative cause. Sensing the direction of things to come, those of deep Catholic conviction decided to leave the country for France or Italy, conveying with them their treasured relics. That same month another preacher chose a more desperate course, leaping from the steeple of St Magnus Church into the Thames, where he drowned.

Their worst fears were soon confirmed. In the summer it was announced that a royal visitation of the entire country would take place, with thirty commissioners appointed to scour the land, armed with a set of injunctions. Issued on 31 July, these were largely based on Thomas Cromwell's orders of 1538, highlighting the benchmarks of Henry's reforms: encouraging scripture reading by the laity and services in the vernacular whilst attacking pilgrimages and image worship. But there were also significant differences. The use of rosary beads was condemned outright, whilst parish processions and the ringing of bells were now abolished. The use of candles was prohibited other than on the altar before the sacrament, thereby quenching the lights around the rood-loft, and decisively ending the purpose of local guilds that existed to maintain them. Any images 'abused', even stained glass, were to be removed and destroyed. However, what constituted 'abuse' was so loosely defined that it could be taken as *carte blanche* for the total suppression of all images. This was deliberately intended, with a delighted Cranmer writing to a friend that he knew the council would leave 'such like matters unto the discretions of the visitors'. In any case, the commissioners could be trusted to do their job well enough, for they had been handpicked by none other than the archbishop himself.

★

With Wriothesley disgraced and the conservatives finally destroyed, Somerset's authority now went unquestioned. If eyebrows were raised, no one felt the need to complain, other than the ambassadors, who found it difficult to discover any gossip, with court business being 'so strictly and narrowly done as to give very little satisfaction'. The council, owing their places to the Protector, all worshipped him. Even Dudley seems to have been happy to leave Somerset to bear the burden of state which he undertook tirelessly and with complete control – 'nothing whatever is done without its passing through his hands'.[7]

But not everybody was so content to allow Somerset's powers to continue unchecked. Since his disappointment at the council chamber, his brother Sir Thomas Seymour had refused to come to terms with his brother's appointment as Protector. 'Why was he made Protector? There is no need of a Protector,' he protested. 'It was not the King's will that dead is that any one man should have both the Government of the King . . . and also the Realm.' Looking through the chronicles, history showed that in the minority of Henry VI the offices of Protector and Governor of the king had been kept separate. Why could he not be Governor instead?[8]

Not satisfied with his new title, lands and income, he resolved that another route to power and influence needed to be found – through marriage. The French ambassador reported that he first considered making suits to Anne of Cleves or Princess Mary, whilst another report suggests he made an attempt for Princess Elizabeth. According to the Imperial ambassador Van der Delft, he approached Somerset, requesting his support for a proposed marriage to Mary. Somerset reproved him sharply, replying that 'neither of them was born to be King, nor marry King's daughters'. It was enough that their sister Jane had been fortunate enough to marry a king; besides, he added, he knew Mary would never consent to marry. Seymour retorted that he only asked for his support, 'he would look after the rest'. Yet soon Seymour had changed his mind, deciding to turn his attention to his former flame, Henry's widowed queen, Katherine Parr.

Katherine had watched Henry's funeral from her gallery dressed in mourning blacks. His death had come as a relief. Now she was free, not only to practise her Protestant faith, but to live as she wished. According to the seventeenth-century Italian historian Gregorio Leti, she had been unhappy in her marriage to the prematurely aged Henry, feeling he had done her a great wrong by marrying her. Perhaps she looked back to a time before, when she had been pursued by Thomas Seymour shortly after the death of her second husband, Lord Latimer. Then Henry's wishes had thwarted her desire. Now, realizing Seymour was keen to rekindle their romance, Katherine must have seen a new beginning opening up before her.[9]

Seymour was fast to take up where he had left off, and according to one account was already making overtures towards her the day after Henry's death. At first Katherine rejected his advances, but she did not hide the evident feelings of desire that she had kept suppressed for so long: 'I would not have you to think,' she wrote to Seymour, 'that this mine honest goodwill towards you to proceed of any sudden motion or passion.' Her mind had been 'fully bent the other time I was at liberty to marry you before any man I know'.[10] It had been God's will that she renounce those feelings to marry Henry, and she was determined that a two-year period of mourning for her dead husband must pass before she could even consider marriage. Seymour was undeterred. He teased her, playing on her sexual frustrations. Scribbling a poem into the back of one of Katherine's religious tomes, he urged her to:

> Blush not fair nymph,
> The master of noble blood
> I fain avouch it,
> And of manner good
> And spotless in life
> Of mind sincere and sound:
> In whom a world of virtues
> Doth abound;
> And sith beside if
> Ye licence give withal
> Set doubts aside
> And to some sporting fall:
> Therefore, suspicion, I do banish thee
> That casts there, hence nymph
> Doth terrify
> And bless
> Thou will be down
> I only suspicionless.[11]

They soon became lovers. At first the affair was kept closely guarded, with moments snatched in between a flurried exchange of letters. Katherine's visits to Edward provided clandestine opportunities to meet at court: 'I think to see the King one day this week,' she wrote to Seymour, 'at which time I would be glad to see you, though I shall scarce dare ask or speak ... When you be at leisure let me hear from you. I dare not desire to see you for fear of suspicion.'[12] But as their desire rose, it was becoming increasingly difficult to conceal their passion.

Katherine moved into her dower house at Chelsea – away from the eyes at court, it was the ideal setting for Seymour to pay secret visits by night. Letters were sent and received, their contents, upon Katherine's urging, were quickly burnt: 'Your letter being finished ... I remembered your commandment to me,' Seymour wrote, 'wherewith I threw it into the fire, be minding to keep your requests and desires.'[13] Yet the survival of both their letters suggest that neither was quite so willing to part with these tokens of love and affection.

Katherine confided her feelings to her friend Lady Paget, who urged marriage. But Katherine was hesitant. She wished 'it had been her fate to have him for a husband' but she was mindful of her position as queen. She had even kept the affair secret from her sister Anne who, when Katherine finally revealed the news, 'did not a little rejoice'.

As a growing number of friends discovered the secret of the affair, it became increasingly difficult to keep it hidden and rumours soon abounded. Meeting Seymour in St James's Park, Princess Elizabeth's servant Katherine Ashley challenged him over his marriage plans. Seymour boasted 'he would prove to have the queen', to which Ashley retorted that she thought this 'was past proof as I had heard he was already married to her'.

Ashley was right, for sometime between mid May and the beginning of June the couple had wed in secret, with one commentator believing the marriage had taken place as early as thirty-four days after Henry's death. If this was true, then Katherine was playing a dangerous game – if she had become pregnant, there would have been no certainty that the child was Seymour's or Henry's. Katherine remained unwilling to commit herself, having doubts to the last. She claimed she was his 'loving wife in her heart' but was determined 'never to marry, and break it when I have done, if I live two years'. Nevertheless, Seymour got his way.

News of their marriage could not stay secret for long. 'I wish the world was as well pleased with our meaning as I am well assured [of] the goodness of God's,' Katherine had lamented, 'but the world is so wicked that it cannot be contented with good things.'[14] Instead she suggested that they find support for their union amongst the most powerful members of the council and court. Seymour tested Princess Mary's reaction. It was not good. Mary considered it 'strange news', writing that if Katherine was keen, there was little she could do. In any case, 'being a maid' she was 'nothing cunning' about 'wooing matters'. Instead, Mary appealed to her dead father's memory: if Katherine was not willing, certainly she would not 'persuade her to forget the loss of him, who is as yet very ripe in mine own remembrance'.[15] Privately Mary was horrified at the prospect, and blamed Katherine for the affair. She possibly even appealed to Elizabeth to discourage the queen, but her half-sister, not wishing to stir up trouble, told her that they lacked any influence at court and should suffer with patience what was impossible to prevent.

Seymour would have to look elsewhere for support and he knew precisely whom to turn to. His confidence rested in the fact that he had managed to remain in regular contact with Edward through John Fowler, a Gentleman of the Privy Chamber, whom Seymour gave a bribe of £10 (£3,000) shortly after the coronation and before long was in his regular pay. Despite being almost continually in the presence of other gentlemen of the chamber, Fowler was soon able to converse with Edward and soon struck up a close friendship with the king, speaking to him alone.

It was not long before Seymour was calling in the favours. At the end of February he had met with Fowler over a drink and asked whether Edward had mentioned him – and in particular whether the king had ever wondered why he had remained unmarried. Would Edward be happy for him to marry? And who should he take as his bride?

Without asking too many questions, Fowler approached Edward a few days later, somewhat unsubtly repeating Seymour's queries. Edward's first reply was to suggest Anne of Cleves, but then, giving the matter more serious attention, answered that he thought Mary to be the best choice, if only 'to change her opinions'. When Seymour heard, he laughed. 'I pray you, Mr Fowler, if you may soon, ask his Grace if he could be contented I should marry the Queen.' He also wanted to know if Edward would write a letter on his behalf in support of the marriage.

It was at this time that Seymour, without Fowler's knowledge, began to visit Edward in private. It was not long before he had persuaded him to write a letter to Katherine, dated 25 June. Despite Edward writing to Katherine at the end of May urging her to 'continue to love my father', now the king seemingly endorsed her relationship with Seymour, since the letter ingeniously made their marriage appear as Edward's personal request to Katherine. Moreover, it gave specific assurance that Edward would safeguard Katherine against any reaction from Somerset, who the couple knew would be furious at their secret union: 'Wherefore ye shall not need to fear any grief to come, or to suspect lack of aid in need; seeing that he, being mine uncle, is so good in nature that he will not be troublesome . . . if any grief shall befall, I shall be a sufficient succour.'[16]

The entire letter was no doubt composed by Seymour, who probably dictated it to the king. At his young age, Edward certainly was easily led. A visitor to the king's court in April recalled how, shortly after his accession, Edward began to make a habit of swearing and blaspheming, invoking 'God's blood'. Asked by his tutor where he had learnt such phrases, Edward replied that one of his classmates had told him that it was expected that 'kings always swore'. Edward was made to stand by while the boy was whipped – 'He had also deserved the same punishment,' he was warned.

When news of his brother's marriage leaked out, Somerset was furious. Edward's blessing made Somerset all the more enraged, and the king was not immune from the brunt of his anger, noting in his journal that 'the Lord Protector was much offended'.[17] But it was his wife Anne, the Duchess of Somerset, who took the greatest offence to the union. Described as 'a woman for many imperfections intolerable, and for pride monstrous, subtle and violent' who held Somerset under her sway 'by persuasions cunningly intermixed with tears', she detested Katherine.

Formerly Katherine's lady-in-waiting, Anne demanded that as wife of the Protector she be given precedence over the queen. Matters came to a head when Katherine paid a visit to the court and insisted that her superior rank be observed, commanding the duchess to carry her train. This Anne refused outright, objecting, 'It was unsuitable for her to submit to perform that service for the wife of her husband's younger brother.' Katherine chose to pass over the affront in silence, but Anne now set herself against the queen with a vengeance, claiming, 'I am she who will teach her.' Katherine was undeterred, writing to Seymour that she had prayed for the duchess's (whom she nicknamed 'hell') 'short dispatch'. Their rivalry would come to exacerbate the tension between the two brothers, driving them further apart. 'Between the train of the Queen and the long gown of the Duchess,' one observer later wrote, 'they raised so much dust as at last to put out the eyes of their husbands.'[18]

Katherine was equally annoyed at Somerset's appointment as Protector as Thomas Seymour. She had expected to be appointed regent, and had briefly fought to claim the title, seeking legal opinion to strengthen her case. Now Somerset refused to deliver the jewels that Henry VIII had bought for her and left her in his will, claiming that they were the property of the state. This not only included her wedding ring and other personal jewels – one in the shape of the initials 'H' and 'K' intertwined – but also a cross of gold left to Katherine by her mother. Katherine marvelled at her treatment: 'What will he do to other that be indifferent to him, I judge not very well,' though she urged Seymour not to cause further trouble on her behalf: 'With all heart not to unquiet yourself with any of his unfriendly parts . . . bear them for the time, as well as ye can.'[19]

But soon the duke's behaviour proved too much even for her. When Somerset began to grant leases on her dower lands without her prior consent, leasing a park to a gentleman who subsequently refused to grant her any rights to her own property, her temper boiled over: 'My lord, your brother,' she wrote to her new husband, 'hath this afternoon made me a little warm. It was fortunate we were so distant, for I suppose else I should have bitten him.'

For the moment Somerset's thoughts lay elsewhere. The diplomatic situation remained tense, with England dangerously isolated. In August 1546 William Paget had prepared a memorandum outlining the problem. France would soon want to revenge the loss of Boulogne, recently captured by Henry. The emperor, under the influence of the papacy to recover its 'usurped power and tyranny over this realm', could not be trusted. These fears were realized upon the death of Francis I, when resumption of war with France became all but inevitable, since the new king Henry II was determined to win back Boulogne. His accession also saw a return to power of the Guise family, who at the same time had recovered their strengths in Scotland where Mary of Guise, the widow of James V and mother of Edward's supposed future bride, Mary Queen of Scots, gained ascendancy over her rivals and looked to ally her country closer to France. It was extremely unlikely that she would agree to the marriage arranged between Edward and her daughter.

It was under these circumstances that Somerset decided once again to invade Scotland. It was a problem upon which he had become fixated. He recalled a dream in which he returned in triumph from a victory against the Scots, receiving the compliments of the king, only to realize he had accomplished nothing.[20] As early as 1544 he was aware of how little Henry VIII's campaigns had achieved. The problem was an obvious one: as soon as the army returned home, Scotland had recovered its strength. The answer, Somerset considered, lay in the total conquest and union of Scotland with England. To achieve this, Somerset believed that garrisons needed to be maintained in Scotland, manned by English troops or foreign mercenaries. Garrisoning had begun in Henry's reign, but they were costly to maintain. It was a price Somerset thought worth paying. Later he told the Imperial ambassador that with them, he would be 'able to win not a battle alone, but a country'. In fact, it was a decision that would prove disastrous.[21]

After a summer of busy preparation, on 30 August 1547 Somerset reached Berwick accompanied by sixteen thousand troops. At the same time, a naval force of eighty vessels and over nine thousand sailors sailed up the coast. An offer of peace was made, conditional upon the acceptance of a treaty of marriage between Edward and Mary. Once this had been rejected, the battle lines were drawn up at Pinkie, near Edinburgh. The Scots clearly had the upper hand, both in terms of numbers of men and the impregnable location they had chosen. But rather than defend their position, they chose to attack – with fatal results. With the English broadsides pounding the advancing Scottish army, it fell into disarray. Its ranks broken, the Scots fled in panic. Where their army had stood was now 'a wood of staves strewed on the ground as rushes in a chamber'. The Scots split in three directions: one, towards the beach at Leith; the second towards the walls of Edinburgh, hoping to escape through its breaches into the city; most fled towards Dalkeith, into a marsh where pursuit proved impossible.

The English sensed a rout. Following on their heels, the chase continued for five miles westward, from Inveresk through Edinburgh Park and on to Leith. Lasting for five hours, between one and six o'clock in the afternoon, it turned into an orgy of killing. Most Scots were hacked down by blows to the head or neck. As they ran, weapons were thrown aside in the hope of gaining speed over the enemy, though this merely played into English hands: the weapons of the dead, lying scattered on the plain, were taken up against those still living by those whose own swords had been shattered through overuse.

A few Scots put up a defiant stand, lashing at the legs of the English horse, slitting open their bellies. Some lay in furrows and feigned death, only to escape later whilst others hid in the river 'with scant his nose above water for breath'. In desperation, men threw their shoes and doublets aside and ran in their shirts. Some, running until they were breathless, died through sheer exhaustion.

When the 'battle' had ended, 'the dead bodies lay as thick as a man may note cattle grazing in a full replenished pasture'. The river ran red with blood. Some thirteen thousand Scots had lost their lives. 'The mortality was so great,' one observer recorded, 'as it was thought the like aforetime had not been seen.' The corpses lay strewn, 'some with their legs off; some but hought [ham-strung] and left lying half dead: others, with the arms cut off; divers, their necks half asunder; many, their heads cloven; of sundry, the brains pasht [smashed] out; some others again, their heads quite off: with a thousand other kinds of killing'.[22]

Edward was overjoyed. He had written to Somerset on 24 August, commending him for 'striving that this kingdom be quiet and replenished with true religion'. Sending a 'little present' of advice, he begged his uncle to 'ever remember these virtues, namely equity and justice; secondly, faith and true religion; lastly, fortitude and bravery'. When he discovered from Somerset's reply that Catholic priests and monks had been amongst the front ranks of those hacked down, he was ecstatic: 'For I hope that they will be conquered and routed, and at last, that all the ringleaders of this tumult and mischief are going out of the world. However, there is no doubt we shall conquer; for we fight for the cause of God, they for that of the pope. God grant you victory!'[23]

As news of the English victory spread, a procession was held in St Paul's where the *Te Deum* was sung in English to give thanks for the victory. Celebrations continued well into the night, with bonfires and banquets on every street.[24] Yet Somerset left to return to London shortly after his victory rather than pursue his advantage up through Scotland. He had become suspicious of his brother. In particular he had grown worried by Sir Thomas Seymour's influence over Edward. The French ambassador recorded how he had heard that Seymour had begun to form a faction against his brother and was determined to become Edward's governor. The feud between the two had taken a new turn before the Scottish expedition when Somerset reprimanded Seymour over his laziness in discharging his official duties as Admiral; Somerset was lenient, choosing not to dismiss his brother, but Seymour did not see it that way. Directly after their confrontation, he rushed straight to the king's apartments at St James's Palace, demanding an audience with him. Edward, however, was at school and did not appear; perhaps he had been briefed to keep out of the way.

Seymour had chosen to remain in London during the campaign, infuriated that Somerset had appointed 'so drunken a soul' as Sir Richard Page as Edward's temporary governor rather than himself. But with his brother absent, there was no better time and opportunity to win the king's favour and his share of power. He began to visit Edward freely, telling him that Somerset's invasion was a waste of money and men. Seymour had also found a new means of winning the boy's favour – through naked bribery. For though Edward had inherited one of the most luxurious courts in Europe from his father, he received – or at least he felt he received – little money to spend from the Privy Purse. 'My uncle of Somerset,' Edward was heard to remark, 'dealeth very hardly with me, and keepeth me so straight that I cannot have any money at my will.'[25] Perhaps this was Somerset's method of punishing Edward for agreeing to Katherine's secret marriage? If it was, then it backfired badly, for instead, Seymour began to give Edward an allowance through the hands of John Fowler. Edward quickly grew accustomed to these regular payments, commanding Fowler to tell the Admiral how grateful he was, adding 'I should like some money now'. Fowler wrote to Seymour:

> The King's Majesty is in good Health, thanks be given to God, and has been heartily recommended to the Queen's Grace and to your good Lordship: And his Grace willed me to write to your Lordship, declaring to me that his mind and love, notwithstanding your absence, is towards your Lordship as much as to any man within England. Also his Grace willed me to write to your Lordship, desiring you, as your Lordship had willed him to do, if he lack any money to send to your Lordship. His Grace desires you, if you conveniently may, to let him have some money; I asked his Grace, what sum I should write to your Lordship for; his Grace would have no sum, but as it pleased your Lordship to send him; for he determines to give it away, but to whom he would not tell me as yet ... The King's Majesty desires your Lordship to send him this money as

shortly as you can; and because your Lordship may credit me the better, his Grace has written in the beginning of my letter himself.[26]

At the top of the letter, Edward's hand read: 'I commend me to you, My Lord, and pray you to credit this Writer.' At the bottom, Fowler had added hurriedly: 'I desire your Lordship to burn my letter.'

After Somerset's return, however, Seymour's opportunities to speak with Edward began to dry up. Now he got straight to the point. As Edward later recalled, he told him he 'was too bashful in mine own matters,' asking him why he did not demand to 'bear rule as well as other kings do'. 'I said, I needed not,' Edward recorded, 'for I was well enough.' Leaving for his estates, Seymour demanded Edward believe no slanders or false reports against him until he returned back to court.

Upon his return, Somerset discovered that his brother was not the only problem he faced. When the commissioners enforcing the new religious injunctions had begun their work in September, their enthusiasm got the better of them. On 5 September, images were pulled down at St Paul's. Across the country a programme of mass iconoclasm had begun, with images in churches smashed and medieval wall paintings white-washed over and replaced with the text of the Ten Commandments. At Shrewsbury they made a bonfire of images in the market place, whilst in Much Wenlock, Shropshire, they burnt the local saint's bones. In Durham the royal commissioner went as far as to smash up images with his own hands, jumping up and down upon them.[27]

Resistance was hopeless. When the conservative bishops Stephen Gardiner and Edmund Bonner protested, they soon found themselves in gaol. Others made the most of their situation; many Catholics fled abroad with their treasured relics, but others quickly had them melted down in anticipation of their destruction and confiscation. In the Grey-friars church near St Paul's, men 'pulled up all the tombs, great stones, all the altars, with the stalls and walls of the choir and altars' to be sold.[28] When the council were informed in October that Christ Church, Canterbury, intended to have their pyx of gold and their silver crucifix coined in order to make repairs to the church, they ordered the relics be kept 'entire, safe and whole'.[29]

In an attempt to avoid wholesale destruction and anarchy, the council suggested that any images not abused might be retained, and that windows containing images of the pope could be defaced or covered over rather than smashed, but it was too late. Throughout the autumn the assault on images continued, and on the night of 16 November the rood-loft in St Paul's, along with the images of Mary and St John, were secretly pulled down, killing two workmen. Soon matters had begun to get out of hand elsewhere as further attacks on the sacrament took place and Catholics and evangelicals clashed openly in the pews. In November John Bisse of Wickham was committed to the Fleet for having 'spoken and done inconveniently against the taking down of images abused in the church' and at Hertford the priest John Forest had been forced to abandon his sermon after being shouted down by John Newport who branded him a 'whoremonger and other misnames'.[30]

The government decided to clamp down. The first Act of the new Parliament that sat that autumn was the *Act against Revilers of the Sacrament and for the Communion in both kinds*, declaring that the sacrament 'hath been of late marvellously abused' and threatened to punish offenders with fine and imprisonment. This was followed by a proclamation issued on 27 December against 'irreverent talkers of the sacrament' warning that it was not for 'Human and corrupt curiosity to search out such mysteries as lieth hid in the infinite and bottomless depth of the wisdom and glory of God'.[31]

Yet all the signs were pointing in a different direction, for Somerset had abandoned mass in own household, and when Parliament opened on 4 November the preacher Nicholas Ridley delivered its opening sermon and the mass in English.[32] In December a new Chantries Act was passed, completing the unfinished work of the Henrician dissolution by abolishing all chantries – endowments that had been set up in men's wills in order for continual masses to be sung for their departed souls – which left 2,500 priests redundant and destroyed all organized forms of lay religious activity. This was deliberate. Whereas the previous Act had justified the dissolution on economic grounds, the preamble to the new Act stated that the entire purpose of the chantries was wrong, being based upon superstition and 'vain opinions of purgatory and masses'. Instead, the Act read, their use should be considered for a new direction, for 'good and godly uses, as in erecting of grammar schools to the education of youth in virtue and godliness, the further augmenting of the Universities, and better provision for the poor and needy'. In reality, this was mere window-dressing, for not a penny of the £610,000 (£187 million in today's money) raised from the confiscation of chantry property would be seen by new schools, the money going instead to finance the ever-depleted coffers of the Scottish war and the expensive garrisons there that Somerset had begun to set up. In fact, the dissolution actually reduced the number of schools; those foundations already in existence were inextricably linked to the chantries, and though most were re-founded as the numerous 'Edward VI' schools still in existence, many were not, and in any case there were extreme delays in the process, prompting the Protestant preacher Thomas Lever to remark that the dissolution had resulted in 'the devilish drowning of youth in ignorance'. Eventually, however, private foundations by citizens would more than make up the deficiency in numbers, with the number of grammar schools increasing from 217 to 272 in the course of the reign.

Somerset was also keen to introduce a new political environment to the reign with the repeal of the 'very strait, sore, extreme and terrible' treason laws of Henry VIII. These had been, at the time, 'very expedient and necessary', but now things were different, with the Act explaining that 'as in tempest or winter one course and garment is convenient, in calm or warm weather a more liberal race or lighter garment both may and ought to be followed and used, so we have seen divers strait and sore laws made in one Parliament, the time so requiring, in a more calm and quiet reign of another prince … repealed and taken away'. The 1534 Treason Act, which had made it treason to speak against the king, was repealed, and the traditional definition of treason – plotting the death of the king or his heirs, waging war against him or serving his enemies – was reintroduced. Two witnesses, rather than one, would be required to prove any offence. The new Act also removed all repressive religious legislation, in particular the 1414 Act for the Burning of Heretics and the Act of Six Articles.

The new Treason Act should be seen in its context; Henry VIII had made similar moves upon his accession in a bid for popularity, and even under the new legislation the accused still faced an uphill struggle, being denied counsel with little opportunity to present his case and no right to confront hostile witnesses.[33] An Act against vagrancy passed in the same Parliament shows that traditional ideas of Tudor justice were still current, for it allowed the unemployed refusing to work to be enslaved for two years, their bodies being branded with a 'V' to show their status as vagrants, the mere property of their owners.

Somerset also looked to the Parliament to enhance his already con-siderable powers. Alarmed by Seymour's behaviour and closeness to Edward, he realized the need to secure his position more fully and intended that a bill ratified in Parliament would legally confirm and extend his authority, giving him special precedence in the Lords, a quasi-regal status that would allow him to sit alone 'upon the middle of the bench or stool standing next on the right hand of our siege royal'. Whereas his earlier patent stated that Somerset would have the protectorship of Edward until he reached the age of eighteen, now his powers would remain in force 'until such time as we shall declare to our said uncle our pleasure ... by writing with our hand and sealed with the Great Seal of England'.[34] It seemed that Somerset's authority, now entirely in the hands of the king, would become unfettered.

Seymour was determined to prevent this, however, for he had plans of his own, declaring that he would 'make the blackest parliament that ever was in England'. Intending to force through a bill making him Edward's governor, Seymour, who readily admitted that he was 'an ill speaker himself', began to lobby furiously for support, urging his friends to support the measure.

Seymour also secured a private audience with the king, in which he requested that Edward give his royal signature to the bill; but Edward was uncertain, asking what it was. Seymour brushed his fears aside, saying it 'was none ill', merely intended for Katherine's wellbeing. Yet Edward remained unsure, sticking rigorously to protocol; if the council had allowed it, he would sign, but he would do nothing without their permission. Seymour persisted, demanding he sign the bill now. Feeling threatened, Edward asked Seymour to 'leave him alone'. Later, he called his tutor Cheke to ask his advice: would it be a good idea to sign the bill now? Cheke gave a firm and resounding no.

Seymour had failed to gain the king's signature, but he did not give up. Throughout November, he initiated a campaign to persuade Edward directly. Soon, he told him, he would be able to rule independently. He certainly did not need a Protector to manage his affairs. On another occasion he confronted him once more, telling him that he should rule independently as king within two years, adding suggestively that Somerset was growing old, 'and I trust will not live long'. Edward gave the matter some thought, before replying: 'It were better for him to die before.'

Edward's reaction to Seymour's challenge is confusing. Did he actually want Somerset dead, or did he just believe that Somerset should be relieved of the burden of power to die naturally with his mind at rest? Edward's words certainly do not seem malicious, and they should probably be taken as an innocent intention of charity and kindness, just as he had sought to do when asked about Seymour's marriage prospects and the lonely Anne of Cleves came first to his mind.

Seymour returned to the subject of Edward's poverty. This would have touched a nerve with Edward, who had been brought up with no expenses spared on his clothes and playthings. Now, Seymour insisted, he was 'a beggarly king'.

Was there truth in this? The household records suggest that Edward, as he later told Seymour, was amply provided for. A surviving account of Stanhope's reveals that Edward's Privy Chamber received £1,448 9s 2d (£443,966) to spend, with £213 8s (£65,400) from Somerset personally. Nevertheless, all this paled in comparison to the Privy Chamber expenses of the final five years of Henry's reign, totalling some £243,423 (£75.1 million).[35]

But Edward did not want the money for himself. More important was the need to reward his teachers, musicians and friends lavishly with money or gifts. The total amount spent on rewards given to various minstrels, players and others close to the king was by far the highest expenditure, at £411 14s 2d (£127,000).[36] Such generosity is not necessarily indicative of Edward's own personality; instead it was a strong element of the cultural world of the court. Gift-giving was a reciprocal exchange, but its purpose went far beyond the actual sums of money and the reward: it was a sign of honour, enhancing one's virtue. The ability to entertain and provide hospitality likewise was wound into this complex code of honour. It was this honour, crucial to Edward's own identity as king, which was at stake. Seymour's own words to him highlight this hidden context, which Edward would have full well understood: he was a 'beggarly king' precisely because he had 'no money to play or to give'.

Edward defended himself from the charge. Mr Stanhope, he told him, would provide for him. Seymour then told Edward he would give him more money, through Fowler's hands. Edward buckled. He made a long list of those he wanted Fowler to reward; prominent among the names were preachers whose sermons Edward had listened to at court. Other names and their occupations reflected Edward's own personal tastes and interests: a bookbinder, musicians, a trumpet player and a tumbler feature.

Before long Seymour had given him £188 in gifts, yet Edward was soon out of pocket again and needed more money. Sending another list of gifts and rewards to Seymour, he attached a torn second-hand leaf of paper on which he scribbled: 'My lord, I recommend me unto you and the Queen, praying you to send me such money as ye think good.' Edward continued to refuse to sign Seymour's bill to make him Governor, yet for every letter of recommendation Edward signed, he was slowly being inculcated into giving Seymour what he wanted: his signature on the bill he had resolutely refused to put his name to before.

Edward had ignored Cheke's advice and, faced with the guilt of taking money without any prospect of paying it back, he had little choice. At some stage, Edward finally agreed to sign the bill, but his agreement remained a verbal one. At a final meeting and under pressure from his uncle, Edward told Seymour to leave the bill with Cheke for him to sign later. Despite Cheke's hostility to Seymour's earlier attempt to persuade the king to sign, Seymour still hoped that Cheke might be bribed into submission. Seymour handed the tutor a leaf of paper on which was written: 'My Lords, I pray you to favour my Lord Admiral mine uncle's suit.' If confirmed by the royal signature, it would have caused uproar. Edward's signature was a clear sign of the royal will, and there would be little choice but to obey his decision. 'A king,' Gardiner had noted once, 'is as much a king at four as he is at forty years of age.' For Seymour's part, he intended Edward's personal support to undermine the Protectorate, destabilizing the council and forcing them to admit him into the position of Governor.

But Edward did not sign, for Cheke could not be persuaded to take Seymour's bill to the king. Seymour stormed off in a rage. Cheke then spoke to Edward; without reprimanding him, he made sure that he realized how serious matters had become. On no account was he to sign anything. Edward got the message, reassuring him that, 'The Lord Admiral shall have no bill signed or written by me.'

Seymour's position was now considerably shaken, yet he remained determined to achieve his ambitions. Deluded by a combination of his own self-confidence and jealousy towards his brother, he began to befriend members of the nobility, hoping for their support. His most powerful ally was Henry Grey, the Marquess of Dorset, who had been won over by the alluring promise that Seymour would arrange for his daughter, Lady Jane Grey, to marry Edward. Together with a loan of £500 (and the promise of an extra £1,500 to come), it was enough to convince Dorset to send Jane off to join Seymour's household.

If Dorset had known the scale of Seymour's intrigues it is doubtful he would have had anything to do with the Admiral, for the only means open to him were to plan for open rebellion, if not active civil war, seeking 'the alteration of the state and order of the realm'.

Seymour first needed a ready supply of men, yet this could only be harnessed through landed power. The support of his fellow members of the nobility, the principal power-brokers in their counties, was crucial, and Seymour soon began to fashion his affinity through his contacts. In early 1548 he advised the Marquess of Northampton 'to go and set up house in the North country' where his lands were, 'thinking it to be much for my commodity'. Later he advised Dorset how to increase his strength in his own 'country', advising him 'to keep a good house'. The local gentry should not be trusted since 'they have somewhat to lose'. Instead, every advantage should be taken of the yeomanry – the next stage down on the social class – since they were 'the men that be the best able to persuade the multitude': 'I would wish you to make much of them, and to go to their houses, now to one and now to another, carrying with you a flagon or two of wine, and a pasty of venison, and to use a familiarity with them, for so shall you cause them to love you, and be assured to have them at your commandment.'[37]

Seymour repeated his advice to the Earl of Rutland. The choice of nobles whom he approached seems to have been dictated by his need to counter the power bases of other members of the council, making a specific attempt to charm those disaffected by Somerset's regime. He approached Wriothesley on their way to dinner during late 1547. 'My Lord of Southampton, you were well handled touching your office,' he told him. 'Why should you not have it again?' Soon he was confident that he had the support of at least five councillors.[38] He advised Dorset to keep to his castle in Warwickshire, 'because it were a county full of men, but chiefly to match with my lord of Warwick [Dudley]'. Rutland testified that Seymour 'thought me to be so friended in my county as I was able enough to match with my lord of Shrewsbury'. Seymour was confident that his plans would succeed, boasting to Dorset that 'he had as great a number of gentlemen that loved him, as any nobleman in England'.[39] He believed more gentlemen would take his side than his brother's. He owned a map of England and, as if strategically planning a battle, would gleefully point out where his lands lay, what counties he could control and where he could rely upon his friends for support.

Seymour also began buying and leasing land on a huge scale, increasing his building works at Sudeley Castle and fortified his 'goodly castle' Holt, Denbighshire. Holt was no ordinary castle: it lay at a key crossing point on the river Dee and was regarded as the gateway into North Wales. A survey conducted in Henry VIII's reign described it as 'being more strongly builded with stone and timber than stately lodging or convenient'. It harked back to a foregone age of lordship, when castles were designed to withstand a siege for months at a time.[40]

The position of Admiral brought the power of the navy behind Seymour's schemes. 'Now I shall have the rule of a good sort of ships and men,' he boasted on hearing news of his appointment: 'I tell you it is a good thing to have the rule of men.' He began a lucrative racketeering deal with the pirates he was meant to be combating; the price of their freedom was to be a share of the spoils, later to be distributed as rewards amongst his servants and friends.[41]

But Seymour needed more than booty: in order to finance troops of men he would need money. He had calculated that for his purposes, he would need ten thousand men for a month. They were to be paid six pence a day, the total cost amounting to around £7,500 (£2.4 million). How could Seymour raise this enormous sum? The answer was simply to have the money made for him. Another of his contacts was Sir William Sharington, a fellow Wiltshire landowner, who conveniently held the position of under-treasurer of the mint at Bristol. Sharington was already an accomplished forger who had sought Seymour's protection against prosecution and owed his seat in the Commons to his patronage; all Seymour needed to do was call in the favour.[42]

This was not the only mischief Seymour had turned his eye to, for despite his marriage to Katherine, it was not long before Seymour began to seduce a greater prize: the fifteen-year-old Princess Elizabeth, who had been placed in Katherine's household. One morning Seymour came into Elizabeth's bedchamber 'in his nightgown, barelegged in his slippers'. Soon he would enter before Elizabeth had dressed or even woken from her bed. If she was awake, he would bid her good morning and ask how she did, and 'strike her upon the back, or on the buttocks familiarly'. If Elizabeth was still in bed, he would pull open the curtains and jump in 'as though he would come at her', leaving a terrified Elizabeth to retreat to the corner of the bed. Elizabeth's mistress, Kat Ashley, reprimanded Seymour over his behaviour: 'It was an unseemly sight to come so barelegged to a maiden's chamber.' 'God's precious soul! I will tell my Lord Protector how I am slandered,' he replied furiously, 'and I will not leave off, for I mean no evil.'[43]

Seymour continued to ignore her warnings, on another occasion attempting to kiss the princess. Ashley bade him to 'go away for shame'. 'I could not make him stop,' Ashley explained, though she finally summoned the courage to tell Katherine, who dismissed the whole affair and promised to be present whenever Seymour decided to visit Elizabeth.

At first Katherine seems to have taken her husband's behaviour to be nothing more than innocent playfulness, and even joined in, tickling Elizabeth in her bed. But matters soon turned serious when Ashley discovered Elizabeth with her gown cut into 'a hundred pieces'. Seymour had done it, Elizabeth explained. What was more, 'the queen held her while my lord did so dress it'. If Katherine was merely playing, the mood began to turn sour. Seymour continued to make his visits unaccompanied. Ashley recalled that 'the Queen was jealous over her and him, in so much that, one time the Queen, suspecting the often access of the Admiral to the Lady Elizabeth's Grace, came suddenly upon them, where they were all alone, he having her in his arms'. She told Ashley that Seymour had spied Elizabeth 'cast her arms about a man's neck'. Elizabeth denied it, weeping. Ashley grew suspicious; the Queen, she believed, 'did but fain this' to make her 'take more heed and be . . . in watch betwixt her and my Lord Admiral'.[44]

For though Elizabeth had first shirked Seymour's advances, she had begun to fall for the man who was considered one of the most attractive at court, and struggled to hide her affection for the Admiral, blushing at any mention of his name. Ashley remembered how 'She hath spoken to me of him many times'.[45]

When Katherine discovered the two of them embracing she was enraged with them both: 'Of this was much displeasure,' Ashley recalled, and as a result Elizabeth was sent off to stay with Sir Anthony Denny early in the summer of 1548. But there was also another reason, for at the age of thirty-six, Katherine had fallen pregnant for the first time. As she prepared for confinement, taking care of Elizabeth and her own large royal household could only have come as a burden. But it is telling that before the princess departed, Katherine gave her a few parting words of advice, warning her of the dangers to her reputation that her conduct had caused. It is perhaps even more telling that Elizabeth, for her part, 'answered little'.

Meanwhile the situation over religion was going from bad to worse. Despite the proclamation of 27 December 1547, attacks against the mass were in full swing, their pace dictated by the evangelicals who continued to preach against it at St Paul's to congregations of 'boys and persons of little reputation'.[46] In the new climate of religious and social change, the repeal of Henry's Act of Six Articles now allowed for unrestricted reading of the Bible, with sixty editions being printed during the reign. In 1549 cheap versions, able to be bought in parts, would become available to the poor. In the new unrestricted atmosphere, books once banned were now printed freely. Between 1547 and 1549, three-quarters of all books published were religious works; half of these were Protestant. Instantly the reformers turned the printing press to their advantage, publishing at least thirty-one tracts against the mass in 1548, two by Somerset's chaplain William Turner. In contrast, Catholic works such as Miles Huggarde's ballad against 'The abuse of the blessed sacrament' were suppressed. Cries of 'Jack in the box' derided the sacrament of the altar and priests were denounced as 'godmakers'.[47]

On 6 February the council issued a proclamation aimed at tackling those who 'rashly . . . and of their own and singular wit' encouraged the people to turn away from the 'old and accustomed rites and ceremonies'. Yet again the contradictions continued to surface, for less than three weeks before an order had been sent out abolishing the use of candles, ashes and palms. This was entirely deliberate, for it was Cranmer's policy that the Reformation be ushered in by the back door.[48]

Yet as the commissioners continued their assault upon abused images, continued resistance left the council nervous. On 21 February they wrote to Cranmer, reporting that although the Injunctions had been obeyed, confusion still reigned. There was only one solution. Witnessing that the only places where tumult had subsided were those where images had been completely removed, they ordered that all images in every church should now be destroyed, whether abused or not. Taking the lead, on 3 March the royal chapels were the first to be stripped, with a total of 995oz of solid gold and 16,217¼oz of gold and parcel gilt being destroyed and melted down, including images of Saint Edmund, Saint Cornelius and a gospel book decorated with 322oz of gilt gold.[49]

In chapels and churches across the country, the fabric of ancient religion was literally torn down. The implementation of a new Order for Communion in March came as a decisive break from the traditions of the medieval Church. Not only were bread and wine to be provided for the laity, but inserted into the Latin mass was a liturgical section in English. This meant that the congregation were no longer mere witnesses to the communion, but had become active participants in the service.

At the same time, the suppression of traditional services, such as the processions that so often formed the highlight of the village calendar, meant that for the ordinary man, the changes transformed their entire visual structure of belief. Candles were no longer to be borne at Candlemas, no ashes or palms were to be carried on Ash Wednesday or Palm Sunday, creeping to the Cross was abolished, as was the baking of holy bread. This was the moment that the Reformation entered into the lives of the ordinary parishioner, and this decisive break can be no more clearly seen than in the churchwardens' accounts at Stanford in the Vale, Berkshire, where it was now, not in Henry's reign, that they dated 'the time of Schism when this realm was divided from the Catholic church' for it was now that 'all godly ceremonies & good uses were taken out of the Church'.[50]

For Robert Parkyn, the parish priest of Adwick le Street, Doncaster, the world must have seemed to be at its end. In amazement he wrote how at Rogationtide (25 April and the Monday, Tuesday and Wednesday before Ascension Day) 'no procession was made about the fields, but cruel tyrants did cast down all crosses standing in open ways dispitefully': 'Yea, & also the pixes hanging over the altars (wherein was remaining Christ's blessed body under the form of bread) was dispitefully cast away as things most abominable ... uttering such words thereby as it did abhor true Christian ears for to hear, but only that Christ mercy is so much, it was marvel that the earth did not open and swallow up such villainous persons, as it did Dathan and Abiron.'[51]

Few stirred. In Hull, the destruction of all saints' images in the parish church of Holy Trinity was met with 'much murmuring' yet no one did anything to prevent their destruction, let alone openly express their disgust.[52] But then on 5 April, in Helston, Cornwall, a large mob attacked the home of William Body, a local chantry commissioner, stabbing him to death. Later, they issued a proclamation in the market place that 'they would have all such laws as was made by the late King Henry VIII and none other until the King's majesty accomplished the age of twenty-four years'. The mob swelled to three thousand, forcing the local quarter sessions to be cancelled.

The rising was put down by the gentry, though it disturbed the council enough to place a ban on any unlicensed preaching, blaming clergymen who were 'of a devilish mind and intent' for inciting the people. Only readings from Cranmer's Homilies, issued at the same time as the Injunctions of July 1547, were permitted.[53]

Despite the execution of the ringleaders, on 17 May a general pardon was issued to all those involved in the Helston rising. Four days later five hundred men laid siege to Sir William Cavendish's house at Northaw in protest against his enclosures for rabbit warrens, which they destroyed with gunpowder, slaughtering a thousand rabbits.[54] Yet this episode highlighted a different problem: the growing concern over the activities of landowners enclosing common lands, turning arable land into either pasture for sheep, cattle and other uses or parkland.

Enclosure was not a new problem, and measures had been taken during Cardinal Wolsey's and Cromwell's period of office to curtail the phenomenon of what Thomas More described as 'sheep . . . eating up men'. Yet increasing demand for wool had resulted in landowners keeping great sheep flocks, such as those of the Norfolk gentleman Sir Richard Southwell, who owned between ten and twenty thousand sheep.[55] This created competition between grazing sheep bred for wool, and cattle for milk and cheese, staples in the diets of the poor. Harvests during the first two years of Edward's reign had been good, yet a lack of milk and cheese had inflated prices, creating the assumption of a dearth of provisions due to the greed of landowners. The contribution of preachers and pamphleteers such as Hugh Latimer and Robert Crowley, denouncing 'men without conscience . . . cormorants, greedy gulls, Yea, men that would eat up men women and children', merely stirred further resentment into the debate, making enclosure a convenient scapegoat for every social ill and turning an economic problem into a moral one.[56]

In fact, the underlying cause of social tension was the determination of landlords to raise rents through a variety of means in order to combat inflation. This had risen by a staggering 77 per cent since the early 1540s, mainly due to Henry VIII's policy of debasing the coinage – reducing its silver content and therefore its overall value on the open market – in order to finance war with Scotland and France. The 1540s had also seen a marked population increase, placing further pressure upon the land to feed new mouths – especially in the counties around London, where the population was expanding at a phenomenal rate, from sixty thousand persons in 1520 to two hundred thousand by 1603.

On 1 June Somerset decided to take action, having received not only 'pitiful complaints' from the king's subjects but also by the comments of 'other wise and discreet men', issuing a proclamation announcing an enquiry into enclosures. The commissioners were ordered to enforce existing legislation against enclosures and to investigate 'the corruption and infection of private lucre grown universally among our subjects'.[57] John Hales, a close friend of Somerset's, was appointed as its head, responsible for the counties of Bedfordshire, Berkshire, Buckinghamshire, Leicestershire, Oxfordshire, Northamptonshire and Warwickshire.

For Hales, the commission offered the opportunity to pursue a quite different, more radical, agenda. In 1548 he publicly announced that its purpose was 'to remove the self-love that is in many men, to take away the inordinate desire for riches ... to expel and quench the insatiable thirst of ungodly greediness wherewith they be diseased, and to plant brotherly love among us'. Hales was not alone in his beliefs. Somerset's celebrated concern for the poor would later earn him the epithet of the 'Good Duke' from the highly partisan preacher John Ponet, and despite historians' cautious assertions to the contrary, it does seem that at times Somerset's belief in impartial justice was strikingly different. 'If he were a devil [he] would have him heard,' he declared.[58] The chronicler Thomas Cooper praised him for his 'affability and clemency' which he considered to be 'so great, that all people of every state and degree, as well poor as rich, may at all convenient times have free access to your grace, and have their reasonable suits, complaints, and petitions benignly heard, and according to equity, justice, and good conscience dispatched'. Not even the most powerful were to be spared. On 19 February he wrote brusquely to Lord Cobham that he had heard 'the instant complaint of a poor woman ... alleging that your Lord did her extreme wrong being known to all the county' ordering that the matter be investigated. And he told John Hales that 'maugre [a curse upon] the Devil, private profit, self-love, money, and such like the Devil's instruments, it [the commission] shall go forward, and set such a stay in the body of the commonwealth, that all the members shall live in a due temperament and harmony, without one having too much, and a great many nothing at all'.[59]

If anything, Somerset knew the game he was playing. He was the first politician to realize the full value of popularity, which he osten-tatiously used to supplement his quasi-regal authority: Paget later reminded him 'how the poor saith to your Grace, "Oh! Sir, there was never man had the hearts of the poor as you have." Oh, the commons pray for you, "Sir," they say, "God save your life."'[60]

Somerset also lent his ear to preachers and writers – such as Hales –

who gave sermons and presented him with their works describing a new vision of society, one of equality and fairness far removed from the Tudor world of authority and obedience. Much ink has been spilled over the nature of this so-called 'commonwealth' party that gathered itself around the duke.[61] While there was no coherent membership of such a group, nor were its ideas particularly novel, it is important that their influence upon the Protector was seen to be recognized. Sir Thomas Smith later condemned 'these hotlings' who 'come to kneel upon your grace's carpets and to devise commonwealths as they like, and are angry that other men be not so hasty to run straight as their brains crow'.[62] And though the 'commonwealth' language they used had been in currency since the 1530s, Somerset's declared wish that 'flesh and blood and country might not weigh with some men than godliness and reason' was something new altogether: for the first time, the messages being sent out by the effective ruler of the kingdom were entirely in tune with the reformers' own.[63]

Inspired by Somerset's lead, Hales set fast to work. Unsurprisingly, his exertions met with considerable resistance from landowners. He wrote to Somerset declaring that efforts had been made to pack the juries and bribes were being offered to men to stand as sheriffs. Reading Hales' own account of his proceedings during the summer, it is easy to understand why. During his meetings, audiences gathered to listen to his own sermon-like tirades against 'the great dropsy and the insatiable desire of riches of some men'. Now, in this time of the new Gospel, they would need to be doers as well as 'talkers of God's word'. Only after he had whipped his audience into a frenzy, comparing the greediness of rich men to the destruction of Sodom, did he take the trouble to warn those present not to take the law into their own hands, and 'go about to take upon you to be executors of the statutes; to cut up men's hedges, and to put down their enclosures'.[64]

Soon news of Hales' radicalism had reached the ears of the nobility. On 12 August Hales had heard that Dudley was 'highly displeased' with him, believing that his exhortations had been blamed for stirring the commons against the nobility and gentlemen and a sparking series of riots that had taken place in Northamptonshire and Suffolk.

There were other reasons for Dudley's discontent. Hales' interventions in the local politics of Dudley's own county must have been viewed by the earl as deep intrusions into his personal and territorial

authority, recently stepped upon by the Protector. When in July
Somerset refused to remove a justice to make way for Dudley's own
nomination, he was furious. 'Thus from one degree to another this
matter has been tossed smally to my poor credit or estimation,' he wrote
to William Cecil. He was sure that he had 'base friends who smile to
see me so used'. Yet he added: 'Despite mockery I shall be as ready to
serve as those who have now won their purpose ... If they work no
more displeasure I will be more willing to forgive.'[65]

Dudley's grumblings were probably the least of Somerset's troubles,
for affairs in Scotland had begun again to take centre stage. Despite
attempts to promote the unification of England and Scotland 'under the
indifferent old name of Britons again', Somerset's costly policy of placing
garrisons across the Lowlands – including a base of two thousand five
hundred men at the fortress at Haddington – was becoming an expensive
failure. Matters had taken a sudden turn for the worst with the invasion
of a sizeable French force at Leith in June 1548. Somerset ignored advice
to repel them and the French soon gained the initiative. First Haddington
was besieged, but the real blow came when, on 7 July, Edward's bride-
to-be, Mary, Queen of Scots, was betrothed to the Dauphin and by the
beginning of August, was spirited away out of the realm and into France.
The entire purpose of the war – first begun by Henry in an attempt to
get the Scots to honour the Treaty of Greenwich – was shattered. The
'rough wooing' was over.

What Edward thought of Mary's escape the records do not reveal,
since Edward had yet to begin to keep a full diary. Yet a backdated entry
gives a sense of his enthusiasm and military pride at how the citizens of
Haddington withheld an onslaught from the French at night 'in their
shirts ... [and] slew a marvellous number, bearing divers hot assaults,
and at length driving them home and kept the town safe'.[66] The glimpses
that we do have of Edward in the first few years of his reign are few,
mainly coming from the pens of ambassadors entertained at court. The
Venetian ambassador, Dominic Bollani, visited Edward at the end of
1547, where he found him in his chamber 'dressed in white silk with a
plume in his beret and a sword buckled to his belt, together with two
other most beautiful children of his own age dressed in black'. He dined
with Edward 'to the accompaniment of music of all kinds' though they
spoke little together, and overall the ambassador seems to have
been somewhat disappointed with the ceremonies of the royal court,
which were somewhat shambolic, the first few officers around Edward

continuing the pretence of order, whilst behind them 'the rest crowd[ed] forward in confusion'.[67]

In February 1548 Edward received the French ambassador 'very graciously' at a mock siege at Greenwich, where they spoke Latin in order that the conversation might flow more easily. The king himself refereed the event, stepping in when the hand-to-hand combat became too intense, before informing both sides that they had performed equally well. In April the ambassador again accompanied him on an inspection of the flagship of the Royal Navy, *The Great Harry*, now rechristened *The Great Edward*, where he noted Edward's keen interest in the ship's modernization. The king, he wrote, seemed in good health, and he could not believe that so many thought him sickly, when the opposite was clearly the case.[68]

Edward continued his studies with John Cheke, which now extended to reading classical authors such as Isocrates, Cicero and Pliny. His abilities continued to astound everyone. William Thomas described him as 'the beautifullest creature that liveth under the sun, the wittiest, the most amiable and the gentlest thing of all the world. Such a spirit of capacity, learning the thing taught him by his schoolmasters, that it is a wonder to hear say' whilst reformers were convinced that their king was living up to their expectations: 'We have a king who is firm, learned, and pious beyond his age,' wrote one in September 1548. 'If there has ever existed a Josiah since the first of that name, this is certainly he ... a more holy disposition has no where existed in our time. He alone seems to sustain the gospel by his incredible piety, most holy manners, prudence altogether that of an old man, with a firmness at this age altogether unheard of. So great a work of God ought not to be unknown to the godly.'[69]

There is some evidence to suggest that this is more than just hyperbole. Edward had begun to take notes of the sermons he attended – 'specially if it touched a king' – and during the year had spent time collecting and translating two sets of scriptural passages into French as a present for Somerset. The first was on the subject of justification by faith, with the second on idolatry, accompanied with an attack on the enemies of God who continued to believe in such papistical superstitions. Edward must have been given considerable advice and encouragement from his French tutor, Jean Belmain, who also happened to be Cheke's nephew by marriage, yet Edward was sensitive to the religious controversies surrounding his court, and fully aware of what was going on. When a furious Somerset told him how Thomas Thirlby, Bishop of Norwich, had deceived him, Edward replied, 'Your expectations he might deceive but not mine.' 'How so?' answered Somerset. 'I expected nothing else,' came the king's confident response, 'but that he, who has been so long a time with the Emperor, should smell of the Interim.'[70]★

★i.e., that he is tainted with Catholicism. The Ausberg Interim of 1548 was a temporary compromise between German Catholics and Protestants approved by the emperor Charles V.

5

THE DOWNFALL OF THE
LORD ADMIRAL

Away from court, Katherine's pregnancy was progressing apace, and in June she felt the child move for the first time. She wrote excitedly to Seymour: 'I gave your little Knave your blessing, who like an honest man stirred apace after and before.' The news left Seymour in good spirits, desiring Katherine to 'keep the little knave so lean and gaunt with your good diet and walking, that he may be so small that he may creep out of a mousehole'. In his paranoia he claimed the baby, without doubt a son, would live to 'revenge such wrongs as neither you or I can'.[1] Deciding that Katherine should be removed from the unhealthy surrounds of London, he spent £1,000 furnishing her rooms at Sudeley Castle, including a nursery decorated in crimson velvet and taffeta. Her household left court on 13 June.

Despite his position as Admiral, Seymour spent most of the summer at Sudeley. Such neglect of his duties sparked further friction between Seymour and Somerset, who curtly replied to a letter from Seymour protesting against his critics: 'We have no time to reply to your long letter . . . We are sorry that just complaints have been made against you, which it is our duty to receive. Avoid extreme judgements. If the complaints are true, redress them.' Seymour's infuriated reply was ominous: 'It is better to be prepared against a suspicious friend.'[2]

Katherine remained resolute in her affection for her husband, confident in the belief that Edward would redress the wrongs done to his uncle when he reached adulthood. 'You shall see the king when he cometh to his full age,' she told a friend, 'he will call his lands again, as fast as they be now given from him.'[3]

The pregnancy was a difficult one, with Katherine suffering from extreme bouts of morning sickness. During her stay at Sudeley, she took the opportunity to reconcile herself with Mary, who wrote on 9 August congratulating her on the 'good success of your Grace's great belly'. Elizabeth wrote to her humbly, asking for forgiveness and thanking her for warning her 'of all evilnesses that you should hear of me'.

Katherine replied warmly and a grateful Elizabeth responded with 'humble thanks, that your Grace wished me with you, till I were weary of that country ... although it were in the worst soil in the world, your presence would make it pleasant'. She hoped that Seymour would inform her 'how his busy child doth', adding 'if I were at his birth, no doubt I would see him [the baby] beaten for the trouble he has put you to'.[4]

On 30 August Katherine was delivered of a healthy girl, named Mary in honour of the princess. Any disappointment Seymour harboured quickly lifted, and he announced the news to his brother with effusive praise of the child's beauty. 'We are right glad to understand by your letters that the Queen your bedfellow hath had a happy hour,' Somerset replied, 'and, escaping all danger hath made you the father of so pretty a daughter. And although (if it had so pleased God) it would have been both to us, and we suppose to you, a more joy and comfort if it had been this the first a son.' But it was 'the escape of danger' that was to be thanked; sons, no doubt, would surely follow.[5]

But Somerset spoke too soon, for Katherine did not feel well. Lying in bed, in her paranoia she told her gentlewoman that she feared she was dying, saying 'I am not well handled, for those that be about me careth not for me, but standeth laughing at my grief; and the more good I will to them, the less good they will to me.' Seymour attempted to alleviate her distress. 'My Lord,' Katherine replied, 'you have given me many shrewd taunts.' Seymour denied this, but Katherine was insistent that he had prevented her from receiving proper medical care. Two days later she was dead, most likely succumbing to puerperal fever. Her hysteria calmed, she dictated her will only hours before her death, bequeathing to Seymour her entire possessions 'wishing them to be a thousand times more in value than they were'.[6] The preacher Miles Coverdale gave the sermon at what has been considered the first Protestant funeral, taking occasion 'to declare unto the people how that they should none there think, say, or spread abroad that the offering was there done, was done anything to benefit the dead, but for the poor only; and also the lights which were carried and stood about the corpse, were for the honour of the person, and for none other intent nor purpose'.[7] Her chaplain Dr Parkhurst wrote the epitaph for her grave:

In this new tomb the royal Katharine lies,
Flower of her sex, renowned, great, and wise;
A wife by every nuptial virtue known,
And faithful partner once of Henry's throne.
To Seymour next her plighted hand she yields –
Seymour, who Neptune's trident justly wields.
From him a beauteous daughter bless'd her arms,
An infant copy of her parent's charms;
When now seven days this infant flower had bloom'd
Heaven in its wrath the mother's soul resumed.[8]

Katherine's death changed everything. Seymour wrote that he was 'so amazed' that he planned 'to have broken up and dissolved my whole house'. He later admitted he had 'small regard either to myself or my doings'. Realizing the opportunity to be had, Kat Ashley urged Elizabeth to write Seymour a letter of condolence, but she refused 'lest she be thought to woo him'. His mother, Margery, Lady Seymour, arrived to take care of the baby, whilst Seymour visited his brother, who attempted a reconciliation, 'making very much' of him.[9]

Without the backing of the queen's household, Seymour lost much of his status at court. 'I fear your lordship's power is much diminished by the Queen's death,' the Earl of Rutland told him. But Seymour was defiant as the old jealousies returned. 'My Lord of Rutland,' Seymour countered, 'how say ye, if I, a year or two hence – or sooner, as I see occasion – shall say unto the council, "The King's Majesty, for whom I pray very much, is now of some discretion, therefore I would that he should have the honour and rule of his own doings, and not as that is now; for that which is now done, the King's highness beareth the charges, and my brother receiveth the honour thereof."' Deliriously, he looked towards the day when his daughter Mary would revenge the wrongs committed to her mother. 'It will be strange to some when my daughter cometh of age, she shall take place above my Lady of Somerset,' he confided, 'for then she shall be taken as a Queen's daughter not as my daughter.'[10]

Yet Katherine's death also opened new opportunities. Again he was free to marry, and marriage brought with it the prospect of a return to power. Later it was reported that he had been overheard to say 'he would wear black for one year, and would then know where to have a wife.'[11] Immediately after Katherine's death, Seymour had returned her lady-in-waiting,

Jane Grey, to her father, but he was soon anxious to have her back. Her father, Dorset, later testified that not long after Seymour was so persistent that 'he would have no nay'. Did he consider Jane a possible replacement for Katherine? Rumours were soon circulating of their forthcoming union, which Seymour took 'merrily'. Yet Seymour seems to have been set upon marrying Jane to Edward, 'if he might once get the king at liberty'. It seems that Jane was singled out as a bargaining token; her improbable marriage to the king the reward for Dorset's support. It was not the last time she would act the pawn.

Instead, Seymour's eye returned to Elizabeth. He had remained in contact with her over a suit for a property in London, using Elizabeth's servant Thomas Parry as a go-between. Parry was under no illusion as to what was happening: 'They used me but for an instrument, to serve their purposes to be brought to pass, and to have entered further, under the pretence for a suit for a house.' Seymour retained a keen interest in the princess, asking 'whether her great buttocks were grown any less or no?' Yet he seemed more interested in Elizabeth's other attributes, asking Parry 'of the state of her grace's house, and how many persons she kept'; 'what houses she had and what lands'; and 'were they good lands or not and did she hold them for life?'[12]

But Seymour had known from the start that while his brother remained in charge of Edward there would be little prospect of any marriage to the princess. He told Ashley that 'I look not to lose my life for a wife. It has been spoken of, but it cannot be.'[13] When Parry brought the matter up, he lamented, 'Oh, it will not be. My brother will never agree unto it.' Turning red, he began to mutter and stammer. Parry struggled to hear him: 'I think he said,' he recalled, 'I am kept back or under, or such like words.'[14]

Seymour was rapidly alienating himself and was beginning to appear unstable. Soon his activities had raised the suspicions of other members of the nobility. 'For God's sake take you heed what you do,' Wriothesley warned him. 'You may say what you will that you mean well and mind all for the king, but in deed you shall show yourself his greatest enemy . . . You may begin a faction and trouble but you cannot end it when you would.'[15]

Riding with Seymour to Parliament in January 1549, Lord Russell brought up the matter of his rumoured advances upon the princess.

'My Lord Admiral, there are certain rumours bruited of you that I am very sorry to hear.'

Seymour demanded to know what they were.

'I am informed you make means to marry either with my Lady Mary or my Lady Elizabeth. And touching that, My Lord, if ye go about any such thing, ye seek the means to undo yourself, and all those that shall come of you.'

Seymour denied everything. 'I am glad to hear you say so – do not attempt the matter,' Russell continued,

> You know, My Lord, that although the king's majesty's father was a prince of much wisdom and knowledge yet was he very suspicious and much given to suspect. His grandfather also King Henry VII was a very noble and wise prince, yet was he also very suspicious. Wherefore it may be possible, yea and it is not unlikely but that the king's majesty following therein the nature of his father and grandfather may be also suspicious. Which if it shall prove, this may follow, that in case you being of alliance to his highness, shall also marry with one of the heirs of the crown by succession, his highness may perhaps take occasion thereof to have you hereafter in great suspect, and as often as he shall see you to think that you gape and wish for his death. Which thought, if it be rooted in his head, much displeasure may ensue unto you thereupon.[16]

Seymour was also reprimanded by Dudley over his behaviour, demanding he be content in his position as Admiral: 'Neither the king nor I will be governed by you,' he challenged, 'nor would we be governed by your brother, were it not that his virtues and loyalty towards the King and the kingdom make him the man fittest to administer the affairs of the country during the King's minority.'[17]

Typically, Seymour refused to listen. Hearing that the Commons sought to pass a bill ordering that Edward 'shall be better ordered . . . that no man may see him', he planned to stand against it in the Lords. Warned he could be gaoled by Somerset for such an affront, Seymour would heed no advice, saying, 'If the council send for me, I will go – he will not be so hasty as to send me to prison.' Asked how he would escape, he gave no answer.[18] When Dudley discovered his plans, he told him: 'If my Lord Protector knew this he would see you fast in the Tower or else. If I were as he, I would do it.' Whosoever dared to lay a hand upon him, Seymour retorted, 'I shall thrust my dagger in him.'[19]

In desperation, Seymour decided to pin his hopes on the young king. Once, when he had discussed Edward's abilities with the Earl of Rutland, Seymour remarked how he 'would be a man three years before any child living ... within two or three years he would desire more liberty, and the honour of his own things'. 'Of his years,' he told the Marquess of Dorset, 'he is wise and learned.'[20]

He hoped to make Edward realize his point of view. Visiting him at Hampton Court, he walked with Edward in the garden. 'Since I saw you last,' Seymour spoke, 'you are grown to be a goodly gentleman. I trust that within three or four years, you shall be ruler of your own things.'

'Nay,' came the reply.

Seymour did not give up that easily. Ostentatiously counting out each year of Edward's age, he feigned surprise. 'Within these three or four years, your Grace shall be sixteen years old. I trust by that time Your Grace will help your men yourself, with such things as fall in your Grace's gift.'[21]

Yet Edward refused to answer and the conversation soon turned to other matters. It was clear that Seymour would have to find another way to make his nephew see his point of view.

Seymour was certainly up to something. On 24 November he ordered his steward to make preparations at Bewdley where he planned to keep 'as great a house and of large expenses as he did in the Queen's lifetime'.[22] Preparations at Holt Castle had continued in earnest, with its large hall stocked with beer, beef and wheat, whilst Sir William Sharington's coined £7,500 was moved into its treasury. Everything was now in place. But for what? It seems likely that Seymour planned to kidnap Edward, taking him to Holt where he might hold out for civil war. He had been surprised at the lack of security around the king, saying 'a man might steal away the king now for there came more with me than is in all the house besides' and as early as Easter 1548, had told John Fowler that if he could get Edward into his custody 'he thought that a man might bring him through the Gallery to his chamber, and so to his house'. Somehow he managed to obtain a 'double key' for the privy gate into the garden, which he kept in a casket at his house.[23] Plans were meticulously researched, with Seymour travelling frequently to and from the court during twilight hours.

All this activity had left Somerset increasingly suspicious, and informed by Dudley, Russell and Wriothesley of his brother's remarks, he wished to see him immediately. Excusing himself in a hastily written letter, Seymour demanded instead to meet in open council, signing off with the bitter parting shot: 'I wish your grace as well as I would to myself, although ye should do me wrong.'[24]

The time had come for Seymour to act. On 16 January 1549, he broke into the Privy Garden accompanied by two servants. Pistol in hand, he made his way uninterrupted until he reached Edward's bedchamber. But fumbling with the key for the door, he came against an unforeseen obstacle: opening the outer door, he was attacked by Edward's dog. Surprise overcame him and in desperation he shot the creature. Edward's bodyguard awoke, their cries of 'Help! Murder!' raising the alarm as they rushed to Edward's defence.

There they found Seymour, who proclaimed his innocence, for he was only making sure the king was securely guarded. Edward was safe in his bed, no doubt terrified. On the floor lay 'the lifeless corpse of the dog'. It had been, as one guard remarked, 'the most faithful guardian of the King's Majesty'.[25]

'Unless the King's Majesty had accidentally left his dog outside and bolted the inner door of his chamber – which is done very seldom,' John Fowler mused, 'it would certainly have been all over with him.' But was it really an accident? If Edward knew something, he did not let on.

What had Seymour been planning to do with Edward? News of Seymour's coup spread across Europe, with rumours circulating that he had 'attempted, by an unheard of treachery and cruelty, to destroy with his own impious hands, in the deep silence of the night, our innocent king'. But Seymour would have gained nothing from killing Edward, knowing that his own position was dependent upon his nephew: 'Am I not made by the King? Have not I all that I have by the King?' he had told a friend.

Seymour was arrested the next day. The council began to gather their evidence soon after, and the following day his house was searched. 'He has been a great rascal,' Paget confided to Van der Delft. Seymour stood defiant, determined to protest his innocence. 'I am sure I can have no hurt,' he told his guard before his examination, 'if they do me right. They cannot kill me, except they do me wrong. And if they do, I shall die but once. And if they take my life from me, I have a master that will at once revenge it.' But as time drew on and still he heard no news, his confidence waned. He despaired: 'I had thought before I came to this place that my Lord's Grace, with all the rest of the council, had been my friends, and that I had had as many friends, as any man within the realm, but now I think they have forgotten me.'[26] When he was finally examined on 23 February 1549, he refused to make any answer unless his accusers were brought before him.

At some stage, Edward himself gave evidence against Seymour. His testimony sealed Seymour's fate. For Somerset, the king's words must have struck straight through him. Edward was on record as having wished him dead: 'It were better for him to die before.' No longer could Somerset claim that he was Edward's trusted guardian and beloved uncle.

As the evidence unfolded, Seymour's affair with Elizabeth became open knowledge. She was interviewed herself, as were Ashley, Elizabeth's maid and the go-between, Thomas Parry. All three remained tight-lipped, their confessions so similar that their interrogator Robert Tyrwhitt grew suspicious. 'They all sing one song,' he wrote to Somerset, 'and so I think they would not do, unless they had set the note before. For surely they would confess; or else they could not so well agree . . . I do believe that there hath been some secret promise . . . never to confess to death; and if it be so, it will never be gotten of her.'[27]

Elizabeth sought to limit the damage. She wrote to Somerset on 28 January 1549 protesting her innocence. 'There goeth rumours abroad, which be greatly both against my Honour, and Honesty . . . that I am in the Tower; and with child by my Lord Admiral. My lord these are shameful slanders, for the which . . . I shall most heartily desire your Lordship that I may come to the court after your first determination; that I may show myself there as I am,' and urged him to issue a proclamation repudiating such slanders.[28]

But as the questioning intensified, the united front began to crumble. Thomas Parry confessed in the Tower, a shocked Elizabeth condemning him as a 'false wretch, and said he had promised he would never confess it to death'. Ashley lost her job over the affair, being replaced as Elizabeth's Mistress by Lady Tyrwhitt. Elizabeth protested to the council: Ashley 'was *her* mistress . . . she had not demeaned herself so that the council should now need to put any more mistresses upon her'. Told their decision would stand, she 'wept all that night, and lowred all the next day' in vain.[29]

With the evidences and testimonies gathered, Seymour's guilt was a formality. On 24 February 1549, the council reported their findings to the king. In all, thirty-three charges were laid against Seymour. Somerset declared 'how sorrowful a case this was unto him', but he did 'rather regard my bounden duty to the King's Majesty and the Crown of England than his own son or brother, and did weigh more his allegiance than his blood'. He would 'not resist nor would not be against the Lord's request, but as his Majesty would he would most obediently be content'; if he had done the same, 'he could not think himself worthy of life ... and therefore he could not refuse justice'.[30]

Those gathered waited for Edward to speak. They knew what he was going to say, for his words had already been written. But appearances needed to be kept up. Though the charges they brought against Seymour showed all too clearly otherwise, they needed to believe that Edward bore the weight of his majesty himself. Formality and ceremony disguised the instability within the realm, carpeting over the underlying cracks in the implausible structure of Edward's authority. 'We do perceive,' Edward spoke, 'that there is great things objected and laid to my Lord Admiral mine uncle – and they tend to treason – and we perceive that you require but justice to be done. We think it reasonable, and we will well that you proceed according to your request.'[31]

'With these words, coming so suddenly from his grace's mouth of his own motion,' the council register declared, the 'lords and the rest of the Council were marvellously rejoiced, and gave his highness most hearty praise and thanks.' The charade could continue.

On 25 February, a bill of attainder was introduced into Parliament, passing unopposed in the Lords. Out of pity, Somerset was allowed to take his leave. But by the time the bill reached the Commons, it was 'very much debated and argued' and lawyers were brought in to defend the charge that Seymour's doings had compassed high treason. On 5 March the Commons, 'being marvellous full', finally passed the bill, with only twelve dissensions. Seymour was declared guilty of high treason, to be sentenced to death. Somerset signed his death warrant, his signature so shaky that it is almost illegible. Edward gave only sparse judgement: 'I will and command you proceed as you request,' he told the Lords, 'without further molestation of myself, or of the Lord Protector. I pray you, my Lords, do so.'[32]

On 19 March 1549, Thomas Seymour was executed upon Tower Hill. He continued his wiles until the last. While imprisoned in the Tower, he had fashioned a pen out of a piece of metal he had pulled off his jacket, and making his ink 'so craftily and with such workmanship as the like hath not seen' he wrote to Elizabeth and Mary, encouraging them to conspire against Edward. Sewing the letters into the soles of his velvet shoes, he ordered his servants to retrieve them after his death, pleading with the council for his execution to be delayed, so that they might be present at the scaffold. But the letters were discovered and his plans thwarted.[33]

No crowds were there to witness his end. He requested that his daughter Mary be brought to him. It is uncertain whether he did get the chance to see his child, who survived for only another two years. His final words were reportedly: 'I have been brought here to suffer death, for as I was lawfully born into this world so I must lawfully leave it because there is some work to be accomplished which cannot be fulfilled unless I am put out of the way.'[34] A poem, written by Seymour in the Tower, provides an elegant testimony of the state of his mind during the final days of his life:

> Forgetting God to love a King
> Hath been my rod, or else nothing
> In this frail life, being a blast
> Of care and strife till it be past;
> Yet God did call me in my pride
> Lest I should fall and from him slide
> For whom he loves he must correct
> That they may be of his elect.
> Then death hast thee, thou shalt me gain
> Immortally with Him to reign.
> Lord! send the king in years as Noye
> In governing this realm in joy
> And after this frail life such grace
> That in thy bliss he may find place.[35]

It is not known what Edward felt about his uncle's death. When he came to write his diary a year later, he recalled these events only briefly, noting that 'the Lord Sudeley, Admiral of England, was condemned to death, and died the March ensuing'.[36] Elizabeth, however, never forgot the injustice of the Admiral's death. She would later recall how she had heard Somerset say that 'if his brother had been suffered to speak with him, he had never suffered; but the persuasions were made to him so great, that he was brought in the belief that he could not live safely if the Admiral lived, and that made him give his consent to his death'. For now, hearing of his execution, she merely remarked: 'This day died a man of much wit, and very little judgement.'[37]

In the streets, Somerset was openly proclaimed as 'a blood-sucker and a ravenous wolf' and it was predicted 'the fall of the one brother, would be the overthrow of the other'. To combat such discontent, the court preacher Hugh Latimer was wheeled out to smear Seymour's name. 'God had left him to himself, he had clean forsaken him,' he exhorted the crowd. 'Charity, they say, worketh but godly, and not after this sort.' When Katherine had ordered prayers twice daily in her household, he said, Seymour got out of the way 'like a mole digging in the earth'.

> And as touching the kind of his death, whether he be saved or no, I refer that to God only. What God can do, I cannot tell. I will not deny, but that he may in the twinkling of an eye save a man, and turn his heart ... And when a man hath two strokes with an axe, who can tell but that between two strokes he doth repent? It is very hard to judge ... I think of his death, that he died very dangerously, irksomely, horribly ... He was a man the farthest from the fear of God that ever I knew or heard of in England.[38]

Later, Seymour's fall would become a familiar lesson to the ambitious reaching beyond their means: as Sir Nicholas Throckmorton elegized, 'His climbing high, distained by his peers, was thought the cause he lived not out his years.'[39]

In the face of the major security threat that Seymour's intrusions had posed, work soon got under way to make Edward's Privy Chamber more secure. At Whitehall, eight new bolts were placed on its doors and new locks were fitted. And a tighter watch over Edward was ordered at St James's, with 156 mats laid in the Privy Chamber, upon which pallets for resting guards would be laid.

But the damage to Somerset's reputation was irreparable. As one commentator recorded, it was commonly thought that 'the blood of his brother the Admiral cried against him before God'. Later in the year a 'godly and honourable' lady approached him, exclaiming: 'Where is thy brother? Lo! His blood crieth against thee unto God from the ground.' Whatever criticism he faced, it was clear to all that after his brother's death, Somerset was never quite the same person, 'no longer like himself'.[40]

If anything, Somerset's authority had been seriously called into question. Not only had he failed in his duty to protect the king as the governor of his person, but he had heard for himself the king's testimony, suggesting that Edward thought he might be better off dead. His grip upon power had begun to loosen, and the crisis had forced him to bring Wriothesley back on board for a meeting of the entire council and executors on 17 January.

Somerset's words to Elizabeth, that 'the persuasions were made to him so great, that he was brought in the belief that he could not live safely if the Admiral lived', suggest the malign influence of others behind the scene, forcing his hand. Had he been briefed against his own brother? If this was the case, there can only have been one culprit. A Catholic and hardly impartial observer believed that the hostility between brothers had been accomplished 'by the contrivance of Dudley, who upheld and counselled Somerset in all things', whilst the French ambassador had perceived that it was the earl who had first urged Somerset to arrest his brother, before demanding his death.[41]

More revealing is Dudley's careful plotting that an anonymous writer, possibly Somerset's friend John Hales, recalled. Ever since his trick of persuading Thomas Seymour to challenge his brother for the gov-ernorship of Edward, he had sought 'with all diligence to understand their humours; and so by little and a little to compass them both'. Taking Somerset's side in their quarrel, he was a constant presence at Somerset's house 'for as long as Sir Thomas Seymour lived ... always at hand' until after Seymour's death, when he moved into his own residence in Holborn.[42]

The gloss of Somerset's reputation as the 'goodly Duke' had also begun to peel. Expressions of his belief in fairness and the equality of all were undermined by his own lavish lifestyle and accumulation of wealth. Nowhere was this more clear than in the construction of his new palace, Somerset House. Shortly after work had begun in late 1547, the church of St Mary le Strand and a six-acre area of densely populated surrounding tenements were razed to make way for its grounds, plundering religious houses and St Paul's cloister for stone. Work was still continuing in 1549 when the priory church and bell tower of St John were blown up with gunpowder for quarry. But it was the destruction of the charnel house of the cathedral, scattering the bones of long-dead eminent citizens, that shocked and angered even the Protector's supporters. 'Many well disposed minds conceived a hard opinion,' one observer noted, adding: 'These actions were in a high degree impious, so they did draw with them both open dislike from men and much secret revenge from God.'[43] As the building works drew out, growing ever more expensive, even the reform-ers became disheartened with the duke's waning belief; he had become 'cold in hearing God's word', preferring to supervise his masons on a Sunday than listen to sermons. In fact, despite Somerset's total annual income amounting to a staggering £12,734 (£3.2 million), the building works and his lavish lifestyle had quickly consumed this, and his steward later admitted he had frequently urged Somerset to curb his building projects which were resulting in mounting debts.

But his personal problems were far outweighed by the escalating crises that were beginning to face the nation. The now futile war against Scotland was proving increasingly expensive. Somerset would eventually spend £580,393 (£146.1 million) on the campaign, £351,521 (£88.5 million) on troops alone. Since England was unable to recruit the numbers of men needed for garrisoning as well as regular service, he hired a total of 7,434 mercenaries from all nations – Italians, Germans, Spaniards, Albanians, Hungarians and Irishmen. Compared to Henry's vast military expenditure in the last years of his life, Somerset had spent nearly double in half the time.

The rush of religious change had continued, culminating in the introduction of the Book of Common Prayer in Parliament during November and December 1548. The book rendered the Latin mass into English, though its message was essentially one of compromise: 'Indeed it is none other but the old,' Cranmer admitted, 'the self-same words in English which were in Latin, saving a few things taken out.'[44] In fact, the book was remarkably conservative in its content and form, which had been taken from the liturgy of the Catholic reformer, Cardinal Quinones. Few reformers were satisfied, but many realized that it was a concession to the 'infirmities of the age' and expected the book to be a temporary measure. Yet Cranmer's omissions were still significant, for they removed the instructions for ceremonies that were to accompany prayer, though few were actually forbidden. But it was the abolition of the elevation of the host and the Catholic doctrine of the sacrifice of the mass, and the outright dismantling of the traditional cycle of feast and fast days, that brought such a decisive break with the world of medieval Catholicism. And as Cranmer argued during the debate in Parliament, he was prepared to go further, for he no longer believed in transubstantiation either.[45]

As the bishops picked over the academic fine points of the service, confusion reigned across the country. In September 1548 the situation was so out of hand that the council suspended all licences to preach, and by the beginning of the year it was clear that discontent was growing. In Jersey, priests refused to accept the new English service, boasting that before long 'this world will change and their images and old superstitions shall be had in great reverence'.[46]

Soon William Paget was asking Somerset to 'Look backward, whether at your first setting forward, you took not a wrong way.' In Henry VIII's time, 'all things were too straight, and now they are too loose; then it was dangerous to do or speak though the meaning were not evil', but now the opposite was the case, for 'every man hath liberty to do and speak at liberty without danger'. 'The governor not feared; the noblemen contempted; the gentlemen despised,' he warned. 'What is like to follow your grace knoweth better than I, if it be not shortly amended.'[47]

He wrote again on 2 January 1549, this time with his New Year's gift for Somerset – a written 'schedule': 'Wherein as in a glass if your grace will daily look, and by it ready you shall so well apparel your self as each man shall delight to behold you.' It read:

> Deliberate maturely in all things. Execute quickly the deliberations. Do justice without respect. Make assured and staid wise men ministers under you. Maintain the ministers in their offices. Punish the disobedient according to their deserts. In the King's causes give commission in the king's name. Reward the king's worthy servants liberally and quickly. Give your own to your own, and the king's to the king's frankly. Dispatch suitors shortly. Be affable to the good, and stern to the evil. Follow advice in counsel. Take fee or reward of the king only. Keep your ministers about you uncorrupt. Thus God will prosper you, the king favour you, and all men love you.[48]

But Paget found his pleas fell upon deaf ears. Not to be deterred, he wrote again in February urging Somerset to take stock of the desperate situation facing him. France was on the verge of declaring war in order to aid the Scots; meanwhile the emperor remained hostile to the country's religious innovations and the treasury was desperately short of funds. He pleaded for Somerset 'to weigh and ponder my writing again and again and make me not to be a Cassandra, that is to say, one who told the truth of dangers before and was not believed ... And now, sir, lift up, lift up the eyes of your heart and look in what terms and in what compasses you stand.' Without an ally, the realm could not stand alone. The emperor needed to be brought on side, 'to seem to yield with him, to dally with him'. Religious innovations should be stayed, for the changes outlined in the Prayer Book were far too drastic. Meanwhile the nobility and gentry, he argued, should be sent from court into the troublesome counties of Suffolk, Norfolk, Kent, Sussex and Wiltshire to ensure order. The law should be enforced with vigour. 'For so shall you bring in again obedience which now is clean gone ... the noblemen shall be regarded and every other man in his place abroad in the world reputed as he ought to be. Whereby quiet shall ensue among ourselves ... We shall no more say "thou papist" and "thou heretic".'[49]

Paget was not the only one forecasting doom. In a series of lip-smacking sermons preached before Edward at court during Lent, the preacher Hugh Latimer – as well as delivering a thinly veiled assault upon Henry VIII's predilection for wealth and wives – took it upon him to denounce the covetousness and greed of 'you landlords, you rent-raisers, I may say you step-lords, you unnatural lords, you have for your possessions yearly too much'.[50] Latimer was a powerful speaker, whose sermons drew in the crowds. His commanding performances were immortalized in a woodcut printed in John Foxe's *Acts and Monuments*, first published in 1563, where the preacher can be seen standing in a pulpit surrounded by a sea of faces. From his Privy Chamber window, Edward seems to be listening intently, writing down the words of his sermon. Indeed, Bishop Gardiner confirmed that he had been shown Edward's writings where he had written down extracts from sermons 'specially if it touched a king' and a notebook of Edward's, into which he jotted 'the preacher's name, the time, and the place, and all other circumstances', was recorded as being in the library of James I, but has since disappeared. Perhaps into this he had noted Latimer's effusive praise of his abilities, his criticisms of the nobility and the clergy, though he probably chose to overlook the uncomfortable and telling comment, 'Woe to thee, O Land, where the King is a child.'[51]

6

COMMOTION TIME

As spring neared and the authorities prepared for the introduction of the new Prayer Book on Whit Sunday, 9 June, increasing disorder across the country was matched by a general sense of confusion over the government's position on enclosures. Whilst William Paget pleaded with Somerset to end Parliament, 'whereof you have great need, and so much as I never saw in my time', the Lord Chancellor Richard Rich warned justices that law and order was breaking down and there was now a real risk of rebellion. His admonitions were matched by those of the court preacher Hugh Latimer, who complained to Edward and the court that he had never seen so little discipline across the country: 'Men will be masters – they will be masters and no disciples. Alas, where is this discipline now in England? The people regard no discipline; they be without all order.'[1]

Yet in the face of this growing threat, John Hales attempted to introduce three new bills into Parliament, enforcing his programme of social legislation upon landowners, though these were met with such a vigorous reaction that they were instantly thrown out, as Hales later wrote, 'like a lamb being fed to the wolf'. Yet Hales did manage to push through a new tax, the Act for the Relief – effectively a poll tax upon the number of sheep a person owned. For the nobility, many of whom owned flocks numbering in their thousands, the move was deeply unpopular.

What happened next, however, left them stunned. Landowners found guilty of enclosing during the previous summer's commissions were granted pardon, yet barely a few weeks later Somerset was convinced that they had returned to their 'old vomit' and issued a new proclamation ordering repeat offenders to be punished. Even the tone of the proclamation was remarkably hostile to the landowning classes, condemning them for their greed and covetousness, and seemed even to side with the poor and the ordinary man.[2]

At least that was what men thought as news of the proclamation travelled across the country. By 8 May riots had broken out in Frome, Somerset, with protesters ripping down enclosure hedges, claiming that it 'was meet and lawful for them to do' for they had heard of a proclamation that had been sent into the county allowing them to carry out their destruction. The direct link between Somerset's own legislation and commissions against enclosure and popular disorder was clear. Secret meetings continued, as fences were plucked down with 'lewd and unfitting talk' being spoken amongst artificers: 'Why should one man have all and another nothing?'[3]

Soon other sporadic disturbances had started to break out – on 19 May enclosures were pulled down in Bristol and an armed clash took place in a nearby marsh. The castle was promptly armed with guns and gates were rebuilt, with nightly watches.[4] The following day a decisive moment came when Sir William Herbert's park at Wilton, Wiltshire, was destroyed and his enclosures pulled down, the protesters insisting that they would obey the king but 'will not have their commons and their grounds to be enclosed and so taken from them'. Herbert was enraged, and ordered two hundred men to attack who 'slaughtered them like wolves among sheep'. News of his actions soon spread, and in Hampshire there were reports of preparations for a rising, to kill 'the villain' Herbert.[5]

In an attempt to calm the situation, Somerset issued a proclamation on 23 May condemning those who had destroyed hedges 'at their will and pleasure', only to allow another proclamation to be issued a few weeks later promising pardon to all, as long as they were sorry for their acts 'of folly and of mistaking'.[6] In the confusion, the rioting continued. In Kent, Surrey, and Sussex a spate of risings were organized by 'a captain they called Common-wealth'. The local gentry knew instantly at whom to point the finger, for the ringleader had also named himself after the preacher Hugh Latimer and went around with Somerset's name 'in his mouth'. The rebels' actions were certainly threatening, but the risings were remarkably composed – despite the damage caused to enclosures – one chronicler remembering how the rebels 'paid for their food in every place'.[7] But as news of the risings encouraged others to take direct action themselves, soon the nobility found their parks destroyed and their deer slaughtered, and by 18 June Dudley was complaining how his park – 'the fairest pasture which would have borne much hay' – had been ploughed up and planted with oats.[8] Meanwhile Somerset's behaviour grew increasingly erratic. Declaring in open council that 'the peasants' demands were

fair and just'; he had 'grown in great cholerick fashions' lashing out at
his fellow councillors who thought to criticize him 'so sharply sometimes'
that few dared to speak out against him. One gentleman at court had
received such a savaging from the duke that he had come to Paget's
chamber weeping 'almost out of his wits, and out of heart'.[9]

But it was in Cornwall, far from the reach of central authority, that
the spark of rebellion finally ignited. The region lacked a ruling magnate
of authority and local justices struggled to contain violence, as William
Body's lynching and the subsequent near uprising that ensued the previous year had proved. The recent tax upon sheep and woollen cloth had
been received with deep dismay, and rumours had already begun to
spread that 'they should be made to pay, first for their sheep, then for
their pigs and geese also'. The region was also notably conservative in
religion, and despite the council sending a preacher to aid its conversion to
the new faith, this only added to the growing uncertainty and division.[10]

The new service of the Book of Common Prayer was first performed
on Whit Sunday in the parish church of Sampford Courtenay, on the
northern edge of Dartmoor, sixteen miles west of Exeter. It took place
with little resistance. However, by the next day the mood had changed.
Possibly the villagers had heard news of a rising that had begun in
Cornwall, the precise details of which remain unspecified.[11] Encouraged
by these events, the local priest was ordered to 'keep the old and ancient
religion as their forefathers before them had done and as King Henry the
eight by his last will and testament had taken order that no alteration of
religion should be made until King Edward his son were come to his full
age'. As Edward was a child, they insisted, he 'could do nothing'; they
therefore would do likewise. Donning his Catholic vestments, the priest
delivered the familiar mass. It was a small victory for the villagers of
Sampford, but their defiance was the flashpoint in the south-west for
what would later become known as the Prayer Book rebellion.

The situation soon began to turn ugly when a local gentleman who
attempted to resolve the situation was seized and hacked into pieces, his
remains being hastily buried in the churchyard. (However, care was taken
to bury the body along the line of north and south, marking the dead
out as a heretic and outcast from the village.) Further antagonism from a
local gentleman and Protestant stalwart, Sir Peter Carew, proved equally
disastrous when, against the will of the local justices, he attempted a
direct confrontation with those he considered rebels, and one of his
servants decided to torch a nearby barn. It was now clear that there would

be no backing down on either side as 'the common people ... noised and spread it abroad that the gentlemen were altogether bent to overrun, spoil and destroy them'.[12] As Carew and the local magistrates fell into further disagreement, the rebels barricaded nearby villages, blocked highways with felled trees and set ambushes trapping unsuspecting gentlemen who were promptly imprisoned.

When news of the growing rebellion first reached the court, Edward was reported to be 'very much grieved and in great perplexity'. Somerset, hopelessly out of touch, remained calm. Writing to Lord Russell – who had been dispatched to restore order – he ordered him to contain the rebellion at Sampford Courtenay, clearly unaware of the rebels' joint advance to Exeter. Already his resources were overstrained both in Scotland and with the enclosure riots elsewhere. No military support was forthcoming, and Russell would have to make do with the small force provided.[13] Meanwhile, he was struggling to raise soldiers in Wiltshire and Somerset and began to talk of retreat. A rebel force focused on marching to London could simply have outmanoeuvred him, slipping past through Dorset, yet they failed to seize their moment.

Fortunately for Somerset, London was not on the rebels' agenda. Two thousand rebels now marched in procession towards Exeter, led by priests, robed and chanting, the pyx carried beneath its canopy, surrounded by incense and tapers. At the centre of this litany was the banner of the Five Wounds of Christ. It was the same emblem that had headed the Pilgrimage of Grace of 1536. The visual image of the five wounds on the banner reflected and embodied the hopes of the rebels. A bleeding heart surrounded by two pierced hands and feet represented Christ's final sacrifice – a vision of deliverance that now not only gave the rebels hope in their cause, but demonstrated equally their determination that, like the pilgrims before them, they would not turn from their own sacrifice.

Their demands were just as uncompromising, prefaced with the peremptory and uncompromising formula 'We will have'. Whilst for those who refused to obey them, 'We will have them die like heretics against the holy Catholic faith'. The articles prompted a furious reply from Cranmer, incensed by their impertinence and indignation. 'O ignorant men of Devonshire and Cornwall,' he declared. 'Standeth it with any reason to turn upside down the good order of the whole world, that is everywhere and ever hath been, that is to say the commoners to be governed by the nobles, and the servants by their masters? Will you now have the subjects to govern their King, the villains to rule the gentlemen, and the servants their masters? If men would suffer this, God will not ...'[14]

It is easy to see why Cranmer was so incensed by the western rebels. Ordering that all the new Prayer Books be gathered up and burned in bonfires, they demanded no less than the complete re-introduction of the Act of Six Articles of 1539 and the suppression of the English Bible. Instead, they ordered that the Latin mass be restored, 'as was before, and celebrated by the Priest without any man or woman communicating with him' and the hanging of the sacrament over the High Altar 'to be worshipped as it was wont to be'. Communion of the laity should take place only at Easter and then only in one kind; baptism only on weekdays; prayers for the dead should be re-introduced, as should 'holy bread and holy water made every Sunday, palms and ashes at the times accustomed, images to be set up again in every church, and all other ancient old Ceremonies used heretofore, by our mother the holy Church'. Memorably, they refused to receive the new Prayer Book service 'because it is but like a Christmas game' instead insisting that 'we will have our old service of Matins, mass, evensong and procession in Latin not in English' before adding bluntly that 'we the Cornish men (whereof certain of us understand no English) utterly refuse this new English'.[15]

As the rebels encircled Exeter, the city gates were bolted shut ready for the siege to begin. The suburbs outside the walls were taken immediately. Once the highways leading into the city were barred with felled trees and bridges broken up, watches were kept on them, so that no man could pass 'without sufferance'. Since the markets had been abandoned, food supplies now ceased, whilst conduits supplying water into the city were smashed and the lead from the pipes turned into shot. The rebels set fire to the city gates, which were soon being pounded by their guns. Some bragged that the townsmen, trapped, had become merely birds in their coop.

To little avail, Somerset had attempted to placate the western rebels by issuing a proclamation on 2 July offering to regulate the prices of their cattle and food, hit by the impact of high levels of inflation. He wrote to the rebels on 8 July with the threat of vengeance, in a last attempt to persuade them to lay down their weapons, but three days later, when this had failed, he issued a proclamation with the intention of setting both 'a terror and division amongst the rebels'. Condemning them as traitors, it threatened them with forfeiture of their property which was then to be granted out on a first-come, first-served basis. The following day, however, a second proclamation was issued, contradicting the first entirely by declaring that those seeking repentance would be pardoned and made exempt from any 'actions, suit, violence or compulsion' sought by those who had suffered injury or loss at their hands. Immediately Russell complained that the situation was unworkable and would do more harm than good. Somerset simply failed to understand that for those who had turned against their king in desperation, confiscation of their property would be of little concern. And, by pardoning those already denounced as traitors, mixed messages were being sent both to the rebels and to those that had already suffered at their hands, about whose side the government was really on.[16]

Yet Somerset's attentions were also being diverted elsewhere, for risings had sprung up in Essex, Suffolk, Sussex, Hertfordshire, Oxfordshire and Buckinghamshire. On 1 July Somerset had summoned a list of gentry and nobility from the Home Counties to meet at Windsor Castle, probably to send an army to march westwards to tackle the Devon and Cornish rebels. In hindsight it is easy to see how this was a spectacular mistake. No sooner had the gentry left their estates than popular uprisings swept through precisely these areas – deserted by the very men who also provided the local authority and order that was so desperately needed. This 'rebellion of the Commonwealth' set up camps – the rebels soon became known as 'the camp men' – from which they issued their own sets of petitions to Somerset, some even embellished with 'sundry texts of scripture'. But what is remarkable is Somerset's leniency towards the protesters, witnessed in a set of his letters to various rebel camps. In these, Somerset not only granted the rebels pardon, but with a striking tone of deference, basically admitted that their grievances were valid, 'for the most part founded upon great and just causes', and telling them that he intended to recall Parliament to address their concerns.[17]

In unbridled desperation Paget sent Somerset one final warning, stating how he could see 'that coming which I have now feared of good time, the destruction of that goodly young child, my sovereign Lord, the subversion of the noble realm of England, and the ruin of your Grace':

> Remember what you promised me in the gallery at Westminster, before the breath was out of the body of the King that dead is: remember what you promised immediately after, devising with me concerning the place which you now occupy . . . And that was, to follow mine advice in all your

proceedings, more than any other mans. Which promise I wish your Grace had kept; for then I am sure things had not gone altogether as they go now. If your Grace remember, I wrote you a letter upon either Christmas day or Christmas eve at night: which letter I would to God you had pleased to have considered and followed, and to have kept me as men of war use to keep their spies, till they see the effects of their advertisements, and thereupon to have used me accordingly. I was a Cassandra, I told your Grace the truth, and was not believed: well, now your Grace seeth it. What seeth your Grace over the King's subjects out of all discipline, out of obedience, caring neither for Protector nor King, and much less for any other mean officer. And what is the cause? Your own lenity, your softness, your opinion to be good to the poor . . .

Now the common people had 'become a king; a king appointing conditions and laws to the governors, saying, "Grant this and that, and we will go home". Alas! Alas! that ever this day should be seen in this time'. Somerset had attempted too much too soon. No man, he believed, had 'put no more so many irons in the fire at once, as you have had within this twelve month. War with Scotland, with France . . . commissions out for this matter, new laws for this; proclamation for another.' Again Paget reminded him of another of their conversations, this time when Edward had arrived at the Tower as king. There he had warned Somerset of the perils of 'Liberty, liberty . . . your Grace would have too much gentleness'. All this might have been avoided, Paget complained, 'if your Grace would have followed my advice. In giving whereof, as I have been somewhat frank with your Grace apart, and seen little fruit come of it.'[18]

Still his advice fell on deaf ears. Almost perversely, Somerset issued another enclosure commission on 8 July giving the commissioners new powers not just to inquire into enclosures, but to pull them down themselves. How many actually began their work is uncertain, but it seems that they were met with bewilderment, their work beginning sporadically, delayed by 'the folly of the people seeking their own redress unlawfully', in Essex, the Midlands, Dorset, Warwickshire and Kent, where in order to suppress risings, the commissioners even paid for the cost of the demonstrators' journey home.[19]

Over the next few days further proclamations were issued, each one seemingly contradicting the next – on the one hand pardoning the rebels, on the other threatening them with even more severe punishment. And all the while the risings were spreading further afield, into Essex, Suffolk, Cambridge and East Anglia.[20]

Writing to Russell on 10 July, Somerset, confident that this mixed strategy of conciliation would work, assured him:

> You shall understand that now, thanks be unto god, they be appeased and thoroughly quieted in all places, saving only in Buckinghamshire, there a few light persons newly assembled, whom we trust to have appeased within two or three days. And thus one thing we assure your Lordship, that in all places they have not only confessed their faults with very lowly submission, but also for religion declared themselves in Suffolk, Essex, Kent, Hampshire, Surrey and many other places so well persuaded as, hearing of your rebels, they desire to die against them in that matter.[21]

The next day he wrote to the Marquess of Dorset and the Earl of Huntingdon in a similar manner, ordering that no action be taken and urging them and their gentlemen to remain 'a sunder at your several dwellings' in case 'the people should by bruits conceive ye would overrun them before they commit evil'.[22]

The nobility found their patience being tested to the limit. Though the Earl of Arundel was able to pacify his tenants from stirring by inviting them to a banquet at his castle to listen to their complaints, Lord Grey of Wilton ruthlessly disposed of rioters in Oxfordshire, killing two hundred of them, much to the satisfaction of those who believed his actions were 'better than ten thousand Proclamations and pardons for the quieting of the people'. The use of members of the government to restore order in their home counties was a clear success, particularly in the north, where the swift actions of the earls of Shrewsbury and Huntingdon prevented any major rebellion breaking out. Within days Somerset could assure an anxious Paget that 'there is no likelihood of any great matter to ensue thereof'. Nevertheless, the situation remained on edge, best described in the words of the Earl of Arundel, as in 'a quavering quiet'. All this was soon about to change.[23]

When fresh troubles sparked in the market town of Wymondham, near Norwich, it marked the beginning of a series of very different risings that would spread throughout Norfolk, Suffolk and Cambridge. The best documented and well known of these centred around Norwich itself, becoming known as Kett's rebellion, after its leader Robert Kett.

A grandfather aged fifty-seven, Kett was hardly a revolutionary filled with youthful vigour. A tanner and farmer by occupation, he was of a

relatively wealthy background.[24] Why he chose to lead one of the largest
Tudor rebellions remains unclear to this day. Social conditions in
Norwich, where he marched initially, created a groundswell of support
for Kett. With a population of around thirteen thousand, Norwich was
the second largest city after London, but the majority of its citizens also
lived in extreme poverty, with 6 per cent of the population owning 60
per cent of land and goods. Recent years had seen the decline of the
staple textile industry, leading to mass unemployment. And with the
county's leading gentry absent – having been recalled to Windsor to
muster against the western rebels – this made the city a dangerous hotbed
for disorder and sedition. Soon there were reports that Kett's forces had
swelled to nearly sixteen thousand men.

Camping on nearby Mousehold Heath, Kett ensured that a semblance
of order was kept amongst his supporters. Declaring themselves 'the
king's friends and deputies' they issued warrants in Latin. Governors
were appointed to represent twenty-four of the county's thirty-two
hundreds, whilst Kett ordered justice to be dispensed beneath a great
oak, which became known as the Tree of Reformation. Complaints were
heard and speeches addressed to the assembled crowds, urging them 'to
restrain the needy and hungry common people from this importune
liberty of rifling and robbing'. Gentlemen who were considered to
have committed injustices were tried, and sentences issued to offenders,
including imprisonment and forfeiture of property. The guilty often
escaped lightly, although for many gentlemen held to account by their
social inferiors the humiliation must have been punishment enough.[25]

Whereas it was easy to condemn the western rebels for their ignorance,
Kett's rebels were fully supportive of the regime and its new Prayer Book,
using its service rather than burning it in disgust. The twenty-nine articles
sent down from Kett's camp reflect this loyalty to the regime – they
certainly would have been horrified to find themselves branded as rebels.
No more clearly is this demonstrated than in the tone of the language in
which the articles were couched, with their customary humble request
of 'We pray that' prefacing each article contrasting sharply with the
insolent challenge 'We will have' of the demands of the western rebels.[26]

By now Kett's camp had made contact with separate camps in Suffolk –
a series of planned demonstrations the timing of which suggests advance
co-ordination. In particular, camps had been set up around the administrative centres of local government – Bury in the west, and Melton in
the east, where more than a thousand rebels had gathered, consuming

320 sheep and 4,000 rabbits. Only fragments of information about these camps have survived, since local magnates Sir Anthony Wingfield and Thomas, Lord Wentworth, were able to quell them with pardons and promises, as one Suffolk rebel would later recall bitterly: 'Then we were promised enough and more than enough. But the more was an hawlter.'[27]

Back in the capital, however, Somerset seemed oblivious to the growing crisis. 'The king, the Lord Protector, and all the Court are merry,' wrote one courtier.[28] Somerset admitted privately to Russell that events in Norwich 'were not in so good order and quiet as we would wish' though he was still willing to make excuses for the rebels and treat them with consideration, since he believed 'their articles be not such as your matters, raves and spoiling of Towns ... they stand for private reformation and yet must they tarry a parliament time'. Yet Edward was not completely unaware of the danger, as two thousand horsemen and four thousand soldiers were drafted in to act as his personal bodyguard.[29] When this raised the alarm among Londoners that the king himself had been deposed, Edward rode through London in procession on 23 July – removing his cap each time he passed by men in the crowds – the reason for which he later recalled was, 'because there was a rumour I was dead'. His other diary entries reveal his admiration for the feats of Lord Grey of Wilton, who 'did so abash the rebels that more than half of them ran their ways, and others that tarried were some slain, some taken, and some hanged'. And it is surely not a coincidence that during the commotions themselves, on 28 July, Edward penned one of his first Latin *Orationes* – a short essay in argument and composition – on the horrors of war ('Dulce bellum inexpertis') arguing that 'bravery is shown by rebels but all the same sedition and that movement and that motion of subjects against the leader is not honourable'.[30]

For the reformers, eager to make sure that their cause was not tainted with rebellion, the actions and the language of Kett's men was highly disturbing. Edward's tutor John Cheke penned *The Hurt of Sedition*, a polemical diatribe against rebellion, which specifically engaged with those rebels who shrouded their complaints with the evangelical and Commonwealth cause: 'And yet ye pretend that for God's cause and partly for the commonwealth's sake, ye do arise, when as yourselves cannot deny, but ye that seek in word God's cause, do break indeed God's commandments, and that ye seek the commonwealth have destroyed the commonwealth'.[31] No one had more to lose than Archbishop Thomas Cranmer, who was hardly going to allow his project of religious reform to be derailed now. Making a personal appearance at the pulpit at St Paul's on 21 July, he delivered a blistering sermon against those rebels who dared to claim allegiance to the Protestant faith:

> It is reported that there be many among these unlawful assemblies that pretend knowledge of the gospel, and will needs be called gospellers; as though the gospel were the cause of disobedience, sedition, and carnal liberality, and the destruction of policies, kingdoms, and commonweals, where it is received. But if they will be true gospellers, let them be obedient, meek, patient in adversity and long suffering, and in no wise rebel against the laws and magistrates.[32]

His address was received with wide acclaim, so that by the evening his chaplain John Joseph was forced to repeat the sermon 'because all heard him not before'. Meanwhile the conservative Bishop of London, Edmund Bonner – whose inaction over introducing the new Prayer Book and preventing masses being said in the capital had already earned him a sharp rebuke – was ordered to personally denounce the western rebels, warning them that they would be 'swallowed down alive into Hell'. The threat of rebellion was far too great not to be taken seriously – there were certainly figures looking to raise dissidents among the more volatile types, in particular servants and apprentices.[33] As the City leaders worked hard to extinguish any trouble before it began, night watches were extended into the day, as guns and weapons were seen being moved from the Tower and placed on the city walls. The City gates were strengthened, and a drawbridge was constructed over London Bridge.[34] Martial law was declared on 18 July, with any mention of rebellion strictly forbidden. The penalties were severe, with public hangings of those suspected of any slight disobedience organized as a macabre warning to all. Before his summary execution, a bailiff from Romford explained from the ladder of the gallows that his only crime had been to mention that 'many men be up in Essex, but, thanks be to God, all is in good quiet about us'.[35]

Still Somerset seemed oblivious to the growing threat around him. With blind optimism, he informed Russell how the rest of the country was on 'good terms of obedience, saving some of the light sort remaining tickle, but no great number'. The Marquess of Northampton had been dispatched to deal with the rebels at Norwich, though Somerset was confident 'there shall be no great matter, for presently are there come hither half a dozen chosen of their company who seek the King's Majesty's mercy and redress of things'.[36] The same day he wrote in person to Kett and the Norfolk rebels. He believed they were 'good people' but had been led astray by 'idle persons and needy and seditious men . . . they with some naughty papist priests that seek to bring in the old abuses and bloody laws'.

Somerset decided there should be one last chance for Kett and his rebels to surrender. When this was refused, however, the rebels' assault led by naked and 'bear arssyde' boys took the city by surprise, leaving Norwich in rebel hands and the royal herald fleeing for his life back to the court. Elsewhere the news was no better: in Yorkshire three thousand men had gathered, demanding that 'there should no king reign in England: the noble men, and Gentlemen to be destroyed: And the Realm to be ruled by four governors to be elected and appointed by the Commons'.[37] Back in the west, despite Somerset's promises to send further troops, Lord Russell was growing increasingly nervous; his men had begun to defect to the rebel cause, leaving him 'in more fear than he was feared'. As his retinue dwindled, he sent letters requesting reinforcements. No prospect of help was forthcoming, and he was left to fall back on his own devices, raising money from loans made by merchants at Bristol. Complaining to Somerset of 'the smallness of [his] own power', Somerset's vacillating reply was hardly encouraging, merely urging economy: his men should not shoot too many arrows, since the rebels would simply gather them up to be used against royal forces.[38]

In Exeter, with little hope of a reprieve to come, the citizens matched the rebel onslaught with equal resilience. Yet others inside the city rallied to the rebel cause: as the siege drew on, rations became scarce and with the danger of famine looming, the commons grew 'very impatient to endure the continual barking of their hungry bellies'. Soon bakers were forced to make bread from bran, whilst the poor, being considered more susceptible to rebellion, were granted a weekly dole, and what few foodstuffs there were, granted to them free or at a reduced rate. The meat from cattle caught near the city walls was distributed to them, and even the prisoners were provided for, albeit with a diet of horseflesh.

By the end of July, his patience dwindling, Somerset's tone towards the western rebels had changed. 'Sharp justice must be executed upon those sundry traitors which will learn nothing but by the sword,' he wrote to Russell, dictating that those speaking traitorous words against the king should hang to set an example for all: 'That will be the only and the best stay of all those talks.' Having received Somerset's orders, Russell finally made his advance on 28 July. In a pitched battle at the nearby village of Clyst the rebels put on a brave display of resistance – Lord Grey later remarked that in all his military career he had never seen men fight with greater 'valour and stoutness' – leaving over a thousand dead. On the king's side, there were forty fatalities with over a thousand injured, though one chronicler reported that many more were killed 'but no one was allowed to talk about them'. When Russell's army finally arrived at Exeter on 6 August, the city's final liberation was something of an anticlimax, for the rebels had already fled. In an effort to seem useful, the soldiers did help gather food and cattle from the surrounding countryside for the starving citizens, some of whom subsequently died from overeating. The next day Russell dutifully dispatched his report of the fighting and his victory to the council and Edward, who was evidently impressed, taking care to write in his diary a few months later every detail of the hard-fought campaign. Russell remained in the city for ten days, punishing the surviving rebels and rewarding his supporters with grants of forfeited lands. The ringleaders were dealt with severely, with one vicar named Robert Welsh hanged in chains from the top of his church tower in his mass vestments, 'having a holy water bucket, a sprinkle, a sacring bell, a pair of beads and such other like popish trash hanged about him', his body left dangling until it was cut down in Mary's reign.[39]

Despite having recaptured Exeter, Russell was reluctant to venture into the lawless west until his forces had regrouped. Discovering that the rebels had retreated back to Sampford Courtenay, Russell ordered Lord Grey and Sir William Herbert to launch an attack. In the end, the rebels were overcome by the sheer numbers of the royal troops. The western rebellion had ended where it had all began. Those rebels still standing fled, disappearing into the West Country lanes, yet they were soon tracked down across the county by a ruthless Sir Anthony Kingston, who as provost marshal ordered the summary execution of all those suspected of participation in the rebellion. Others escaped into Somerset, though their freedom was short lived, with one hundred and four prisoners captured at Kingsweston being conveyed to Wells, where payments to Sir John Thynne, Sheriff of Somerset, hint at their fate: two shillings to a poor man for serving as executioner, twelve pence for wood to burn the entrails of the guilty.[40]

In Norfolk, however, the situation was going from bad to worse. The Marquess of Northampton arrived at Norwich on 31 July with a force of 1,500 men, having succeeded in mopping up various rebel camps around Suffolk. He had been given specific orders not to offer battle, but instead to station his troops outside the city, blockading the supply lines to the camp. Northampton had different ideas. Thirsty for glory, he marched into the city where, amongst its narrow winding lanes and backstreets and with its walls long dilapidated and in need of repair, his troops were a sitting target for a rebel attack. When this came, military superiority could not match the sheer determination of the rebels, who, streaming down from Mousehold Heath, fought with 'hellish fury'. When the young and headstrong Lord Sheffield, anxious to prove his valour and nobility, fell from his horse during a surprise ambush, he was held prisoner before being beaten to death with a club. When news of Sheffield's death reached the marketplace, Northampton fled, prompting scenes of general panic. Men fled in terror, throwing off their gowns in hope of faster escape. Wives and children were left behind, even 'some that were with child, some that were sick and diseased', their sound of weeping filling the air. In the confusion, buildings were set alight. For the moment, as the rebels ran loose through the city looting and ransacking shops and houses, it seemed as if the world was at its end.

Kett may have won the day, but the victory over Northampton was entirely futile. Though Kett had gained the tactical advantage, he could no longer claim to be acting as the king's representative. The only hope now lay in open defiance.

Back in London, the news of Northampton's defeat stunned everyone. London prepared for the worst, with ditches being converted into moats whilst the authorities kept on the lookout for troublemakers. Unsurprisingly, the city authorities focused their attention on known preachers who had a record of encouraging sedition. Certainly there were those who sought to enflame the situation. A saddler was committed to Newgate prison 'for that he enticed men's servants and apprentices ... to go with him to the rebels at Norwich', whilst Anthony Roberts of Tonbridge, Kent, was arrested as a suspected rebel, and soldiers were expelled from the city, with two arrested for uttering 'slanderous and seditious words'. The watch at Tower Hill was attacked by an apprentice carpenter, and on another occasion had arrows fired at it.[41]

Somerset had no alternative plan of action. For a week the council met continuously, uncertain how to proceed. Initially it was decided that Somerset would ride against the rebels; the Earl of Shrewsbury was ordered to muster on 3 August, whilst a letter issued on 6 August informed that 'a main force ... in the order of our said uncle' would 'weed and try out our good subjects from the evil, to minister, aid, and comfort to the one, and contrarywise to extend the rigour and extremity of our sword to the other'. German mercenaries were eventually persuaded to fight with the promise of a month's pay for one day's fighting. On 7 August, however, it was decided that Dudley would be Lieutenant General, though he urged that, to save face, Northampton should remain as commander-in-chief.

Why Somerset decided not to command an army against the Norfolk rebels has been long debated by historians, with some suggesting that the duke could not in conscience bear to confront men with whose aims he held such sympathy. This seems unlikely, for with his patience running short, he now considered the rising as 'a plague and a fury amongst the worst sort of men'.[42] Whatever Somerset's reasons, it was probably a wise decision, for on 8 August the French king Henry II declared war on England and began to lay siege to the English-controlled territory of Boulogne. Hearing of the French declaration, Dudley reflected that at least war was preferable to 'coloured friendship' and urged for men to put their faith in the Lord.

Dudley's own behaviour during the risings is mysterious. On 12 July he had written to Somerset, complaining of illness. He hoped to return to court soon 'for the staying of the fury of this people', but uprisings had taken place near his own residence. Still Dudley seemed reluctant to give his full assistance to crushing the revolts. He had sent orders to defend his castle, 'which is but a very slender house of strength', and was unsure that it would not fall to rebel hands: if the entire county was to rise, he wrote, 'I shall be [able] to do no service'. According to a servant of the Earl of Rutland, Dudley then came 'very lustily on to the court'. He remained in London until 31 July, the day before Northampton's defeat, when he departed on an undisclosed mission with five hundred men, the Imperial ambassador reporting that his destination was Wales. Whatever Dudley was planning, certainly according to one chronicler, 'most men in those days thought that the displeasure of the Earl of Warwick [Dudley] conceived against the Lord Protector in the time of rebellion was a great cause of the trouble at this time'.[43]

On 12 August Dudley led a force numbering over five thousand out of the capital, joining forces with Northampton at Cambridge. Meanwhile the rebels had taken over the cathedral, camping there during the nightly rainfalls. The mayor's deputy procured preachers 'to go up among them & preach God's word' yet to little avail, 'for so impudent were they & out of order'. With spies watching out from the steeples and towers of the city, the sight of Dudley's approaching army was spotted a mile off, causing so much panic that Kett himself climbed up to view the troops marching over the horizon.

Dudley offered the rebels a choice: they might quietly open its gates or 'else to look for war at his hands'. A pardon was offered to all except Kett, and all seemed to be going well until the herald came to announce the pardon on Mousehold Heath, when a young boy pulled down his breeches 'and did a filthy act', incensing Dudley's men who shot him dead. Uproar ensued, though amidst the confusion, Kett's next move was a startling one. He decided to meet with Dudley. As he rode down the hill with the herald, however, he was prevented from doing so by his own men, who taunted him into remaining.

Dudley was now in no mood for compromise. Demanding that the city gates be broken down immediately, his army opened fire on the main gate, smashing down the portcullis. Fighting broke out in the streets and continued throughout the afternoon. Dudley made at once for the marketplace where, in a calculated gesture of strength, forty-nine rebels were rounded up and promptly hanged. Such was the congestion that the ladders up to the gallows broke and had to be repaired at a cost of three pence. Hearing of this, the citizens and the servants came out of hiding, crying for pardon, which was duly granted.

Dudley's troops now held the city, but the rebels' retreat would only be a temporary lull. Playing on their intimate knowledge of the city, they decided to assemble into three separate companies, patrolling the streets in hope of cutting off their enemies. When, in a series of ambushes, the rebels managed to seize two cartloads of munitions and cannon, it seemed that their tactics had worked. However, with Dudley occupying the city and their supply lines cut off, the only option for Kett was to continue his attack. Despite a ferocious onslaught by the rebels that night – leaving a large part of the city in flames – Dudley stood his ground, his men repulsing their attackers in spite of heavy losses.

When certain citizens urged his withdrawal, Dudley refused outright, and in a calculated gesture of military honour, ordered his men to kiss their swords, binding them under oath that none would depart until they had 'vanquished the enemies or lost their lives'. Such bravery disguised the fact that reinforcements were soon at hand, for the following day, 26 August, a thousand Swiss mercenaries arrived from London. As Dudley's men jubilantly fired volleys of shot, the rebels sank into despair. Kett became increasingly withdrawn. When a snake leapt from the branches of a rotten tree on to his wife's bosom, no one doubted it was an omen of worse to come. In desperation, one prophecy offered him comfort and hope:

> The country gruffs, Hob, Dick and Hick
> With clubs and clouted shoon
> Shall fill up Dussindale with blood
> Of slaughtered bodies soon.[44]

Kett urged his followers to leave Mousehold Heath and journey to the wider plain of Dussindale. As dusk fell the rebels burned their huts and fortifications. Men in Dudley's army watched the rising smoke in amazement, as the rebels slipped away into the night, carts laden with goods and armaments, making their way on to the open plain.

Dudley knew that his opportunity had come. Before the rebels entrenched themselves they remained vulnerable: he would attack tomorrow. Meanwhile, the rebels worked throughout the night, fortifying their position with trenches. They had taken their gentlemen captors with them; chained together in a form of human shield, they were to be the first line of defence.

The next morning, Dudley's troops marched out of the city gates towards Dussindale. When the offer of a final pardon was refused by Kett and his rebels, Dudley ordered his troops forward with a rallying speech; they should take the rebels not for men, but 'brute beasts imbued with all cruelty': 'Neither let them suppose that they were come out to fight, but to take punishment.'

As the Royal Standard advanced, a rebel gunner fired the first shot. The cannonball cut through his thigh into the horse's flank, killing both. The army returned fire. As they charged, the gentlemen tied in the human chain managed to break free, though a few were accidentally killed by the Swiss who 'knew not what they were'. The front rank, including Kett, scattered and fled.

Deserted by their leaders, those remaining vowed to fight to the last man. Gathering up weapons from the ground they barricaded themselves behind carts and carriages. Dudley was so moved by their courage that he sent a herald to offer pardon. Only once the earl had confirmed the promise in person did the rebels believe it was genuine. 'God save King Edward, God save King Edward,' they cried, laying their weapons aside.

One soldier recalled how some 'blinded with desperation' were presented to Dudley, and 'utterly refusing the king's pardon chose only to try the quarrel with the extremity of the sword'. The battle was over by four o'clock. Back inside the city, two barrels of beer were opened at the market cross in celebration.[45]

It had been less a rout than a massacre. Cut down by Dudley's horsemen, at least two thousand had been killed, though estimates ranged as high as three thousand five hundred. On the king's side, the losses were put at forty. Among the casualties was Sir Andrew Flammock, hit in the chest with a club, the blow of such ferocity that despite wearing a suit of mail 'it made him void blood both ways'. Hastily making his will, he died of internal injuries shortly afterwards.[46]

Fleeing from the battlefield, Kett rode towards Swannington, eight miles north-west of Norwich. His horse tired and he was forced to hide in a nearby barn. Spotted by two farm labourers, he was brought to a farmhouse where exhaustion and hunger overcame him. He was left under the supervision of an eight-year-old child, but he 'had not the spirit to depart'. The next day an armed guard was sent to return him to Norwich.

The executions began the following morning. Nine rebels were hanged, drawn and quartered at the Oak of Reformation, their heads 'fixed on the tops of the towers of the city, the rest of the body bestowed upon several places, and set up to the terror of others', and by the end of the day three hundred had been hanged. The local gentlemen looked for further reprisals but their vengeance was tempered by Dudley, who urged for justice and mercy. On 29 August a large crowd heard a service at St Peter's church, overlooking the marketplace, where Dudley himself spoke, giving thanks to God. In celebration of his victory every household set up the sign of the ragged staff – Dudley's coat of arms – outside their doors. It was a proud moment for the earl, who later hung a map of his expedition to Norwich in his London home beside the charts of his other campaigns in Scotland.[47]

On 7 September Kett was brought to London together with his brother William. Taken to Newgate, the crowds gathered to see him ride bareback through the city. Placed on trial, the verdict was never in doubt. Kett and his brother were to be taken from the Tower to Tyburn 'and on that gallows hanged, and while yet alive, that they be cast on the ground, and the entrails of each one of them be taken out and burnt before them, while yet alive, and their heads cut off, and their bodies divided into four parts; And that the heads and quarters of each of them be placed where our Lord King shall appoint'.[48]

Shortly after the trial, however, it was decided that the brothers should be sent to Norfolk to die. There their fate would be a message to all who might be tempted to follow their course – especially former followers who surviving the initial reprisals had now returned to their homes and ordinary lives. On 7 December they were executed; William was hanged from the west tower of the Abbey at Wymondham whilst Robert was taken to Norwich where he was dragged behind a cart from the Guildhall to the castle. There he was hanged in chains from the castle wall, his body left hanging until the flesh fell away from the rotten corpse. Five hundred years later, in 1949, a brass inscription was affixed to the outer wall of Norwich Castle commemorating the dramatic days of that summer. Erected by the citizens of Norwich, it reads: 'In reparation and honour to a notable and courageous leader in the long struggle of the common people of England to escape from a servile life into the freedom of just conditions.'

What were Kett's motives? He had lived a comfortable life, and as he approached what then would have been his twilight years, he could have looked forward to a quiet retirement. Instead, he chose to join, and then lead, rebellious dissidents, ending his life in torturous agony. But there is perhaps more to the story. In particular, Kett's bizarre decision to meet with Dudley needs further explanation, especially given his earlier refusal to negotiate with either the city authorities at Norwich or the Marquess of Northampton. Kett's behaviour hides an illuminating secret, for Kett was in fact Dudley's tenant, having purchased land from him in 1543. As he rode down the hill to meet Dudley, did he know full well what the earl was going to say, or ask him to do?

To suggest that Kett had been Dudley's agent, urged to encourage rebellion against Somerset, is probably fanciful, though significant questions must remain over the behaviour of another figure – Sir Richard Southwell, Dudley's friend and steward of the former Howard lands in Norfolk. After the rebellion had ended, Southwell was accused by a local gentleman Sir Edmund Knyvett 'to have been one of the authors of this rebellion'. Here the intrigue deepens, for Southwell employed none other than Robert Kett's brother as his deputy-bailiff. Southwell himself was treasurer for the king's forces, though his efforts seem to have been somewhat misdirected. Among the exchequer receipts detailing the charges of the costs of the rebellion, is the following entry:

of such money as Robert Kett principal leader of the said Rebels had from Sir Richard Southwell then having charge of the King's treasure sent down by him for the suppressing of the said rebels and tried out by the said earl upon the examination of diverse the said rebels to be conveyed in particular sums amongst diverse persons which was by the said earl gathered together and delivered over to this accomptant ... £497 15s.[49]

In effect, Southwell had been secretly funding the rebel cause from the king's own coffers. But there was more to indict the guilty party. Southwell later broke into William Cecil's chamber at Savoy, stealing Knyvett's deposition against him. One account also recorded that while Kett resided in the Tower, none of the council came to visit him 'but only Southwell'. The following January, Southwell found himself in the Tower and fined £500 for writing 'bills of sedition in his own hand'. Could these have possibly implicated Dudley – with his link back to Kett – and other members of the council in the organizing of the rebellions? Intriguingly, when Southwell drew up his will in 1564, he left the considerable sum of £40 to his servant Richard Kett.[50] Kett's son, perhaps? The case remains open.

There were others who had an interest in benefiting from the commotions, not least Edward's sister, Princess Mary. A staunch Catholic, she had become an increasingly vocal critic of his government and their religious policies. But it was not the princess that concerned the council most. Instead it was the actions – and religious affiliations – of her household. Mary's open opposition to the Reformation made her the obvious figurehead for conservatives. Her affinity began to be shaped along religious lines, and her own court became a magnet for Catholics to hear mass according to the traditional rites secretly and without fear of prosecution. During 1547 Mary was hearing as many as four masses a week and when she visited Norfolk in December 1548 'she was much welcomed ... wherever she had power she caused the mass to be celebrated, and the services of the church performed in the ancient matter'.

Mary's position was a simple one. To her, the mass and other traditional rites represented the only true religion. Edward was still a minor, whose authority was insufficient to force through religious change. She believed that the king was being misled by his council, and had every confidence that he might reverse their decisions. According to her mistress and Edward's former playmate Jane Dormer, the king had told her that she might continue to practise her faith privately, adding, 'Have patience till

I have more years, then I will remedy all'.[51] Perhaps with this in mind, Mary wrote bitterly to the council upon the passing of the Act of Uniformity in January 1549, arguing that religion be left untouched until her brother obtain his majority.[52]

Mary would not have normally have posed any serious threat to the council, had it not been for the wholehearted support of her cousin, Emperor Charles V, who was equally determined that his Tudor cousin be allowed to retain her right to hear the Catholic mass. In early May 1549 he ordered Van der Delft to demand 'a written assurance, in definite, suitable and permanent form, that notwithstanding all new laws and ordinances made upon religion, she may live in the observance of our ancient religion'.[53] At the end of May the ambassador secured a meeting with Somerset. The Protector refused to accept and hoped, for the sake of the kingdom, that Mary might eventually conform. For now he would not personally enquire into her conduct or the worship of her household. According to Van der Delft, Somerset ended the meeting declaring that 'she shall do as she thinks best till the King comes of age, and meanwhile she shall find me her good servant, as I have always been'. For Mary, this was the definite promise that she had been looking for − a pledge that she could continue to enjoy her religious freedoms. For Somerset and the council, it was a mistake that would come back to haunt them.[54]

On Whit Sunday, in defiance of the introduction of the Prayer Book, Mary celebrated mass in her chapel at Kenninghall with particular pomp. On 16 June the council delivered a restrained letter ordering her to desist and to use the new Prayer Book instead. Mary wrote back on 22 June. 'I have offended no law,' she replied, 'unless it be a late law of your own making, for the altering of matters in religion, which, in my conscience, is not worthy to have the name of a law.'[55] The matter was becoming serious. Mary's resistance was becoming a thorn in the council's side, but her position made it too sensitive to tackle the problem directly. Instead the council summoned her senior household staff to appear before them. This prompted another glaring response from the princess, but with rebellion in full flare, Somerset decided to back down. Indicating his own wish to tolerate Mary's private worship (if only she would 'do as she pleases quietly and without scandal') he issued a dispensation for mass to be said in her private chamber 'in the presence of yourself and not more than twenty ladies and gentlemen appointed by you'.[56]

In the meantime, as commotion raged across the country, the council discovered some startling information. A direct link had been found between Mary's household servants, if not the princess herself, and the ongoing rebellions in the west. It warned Mary on 18 July that 'certain of your servants are reported to be chief in these commotions'. One of her chaplains had been active amongst the rebels at Sampford Courtenay and her servant Thomas Poley 'a captain of the worst assembled in Suffolk'. Her household servant named Lionell was 'of like credit with the rebels in Suffolk'.[57]

Mary wrote back rejecting all such charges. The commotions, she wrote, 'no less offend me, than they do you and the rest of the council'. Concerning her chaplain being at Sampford Courtenay, 'I do not a little marvel; for, to my knowledge, I have not one chaplain in those parts'. Thomas Poley had remained at her house all the while 'and was never doer amongst the commons, nor came in their company'. She did have, however, another servant living in Suffolk of the same name; 'Whether the commons have taken him or no, I know not, for he resorteth seldom to my house.'[58]

Mary was probably telling the truth, for she herself was not entirely immune from the rebels' violence, as they even partly destroyed the enclosures of her park at Kenninghall, though they stopped short of any further action, declaring 'she was kept too poor for one of her rank'.[59] Nevertheless, suspicion of her complicity lingered. Sir Thomas Smith, writing to William Cecil, cloaked his accusations in Latin and the masculine gender when he spoke of 'Marius and the Marians, the fear of which torments me to the point of destruction'.[60] If Mary was not directly involved in the risings herself, there were certainly religious conservatives ready to do her bidding.[61] Perhaps most tellingly, Sir Richard Southwell – whose complicity with the rebels seems beyond doubt – was also keeper of Mary's estate at Kenninghall.

Paget also worried that rebellions might be linked to more sinister dealings. 'I trust for our benefit,' he wrote to Sir William Petre, 'if we may appease our things at home, and lean not too much to such new fantasies as set forth innovations which be dangerous ... To alter the state of a realm,' he insisted, 'would ask ten years' deliberation.'[62]

For the moment, the greatest threat to the nation since the Peasants' Revolt in 1381 had finally been brought under control, but not without a price. Thousands of rebel lives had been lost – perhaps even the largest number of the entire Tudor period. Crushing their resistance had not come cheaply either, with the cost of organizing troops amounting to a total of £28,122 7s 7d [£7,081,746]. In many ways, Somerset had been fortunate – had either Kett or the western rebels decided to march on London it might have been a very different story. Yet for the nobility and gentry of the realm, it was Somerset's behaviour during the Commotion time that had proved most alarming. Not only had his proclamations, with their promises of reformation of enclosures, encouraged men to take the law into their own hands, but Somerset had also given written assurances to the rebels that their concerns would be redressed at the following Parliament. Sir Anthony Aucher complained to William Cecil that the local gentlemen were shocked at Somerset's lenient treatment of the rebels. The 'commonwealth' Latimer had been pardoned and others arrested and sent up to London had come away unpunished. His fellow gentlemen were growing jealous and resentful of Somerset's close friendship with them. 'To be plain,' added Aucher, 'I think my lord's grace rather to will the decay of the gentlemen than otherwise.'[63] He warned of worse to come, for there was talk amongst 'these commonwealths' that 'if they have no reformation before St Clement's Day [23 November] they will seek another way'. Somerset may have avoided disaster at the hands of Kett and the western rebels, but having lost the support and confidence of the nobility and those he depended upon to ensure law and order, he now faced an even greater challenge of retaining his weakened position as Protector.

7

COUP D'ETAT

Be pleasant and a flatterer as some other is
What need I tell truth and myself cast away.
The wicked I see to gain most riches
The weathercock scapeth best every wind.
Sir Thomas Smith, poem written in the Tower, Winter 1549[1]

'Matters in this realm are restless for change,' the Imperial ambassador Van der Delft wrote on 15 September. The council was split, whilst Dudley and Somerset had fallen into open dispute. Paget had lamented the condition of the realm with tears in his eyes. He had written to Somerset at the end of August, urging him to end the war with Scotland: 'How we are exhausted and worn to the bones with these eight years wars both of men, money and all other things … your grace and my lords know better than I.' 'Civil spoil and ruin' now threatened.[2]

But Somerset did not listen, writing to a friend that 'the realm was never in more quiet'.[3] Soon Paget was begging Van der Delft to reason on his behalf. In August the secretary had blamed Somerset's ineptitude on the duchess, but now Somerset's paranoia had become intolerable and he could not see two councillors speaking together without becoming jealous. Relations had broken down between them and Paget now reckoned some other means of maintaining the kingdom would have to be looked for.

The polity was also rapidly deteriorating. 'No improvement is observed in the keeping of order or the administration of justice,' Van der Delft observed. 'The people are all in confusion, and with one common voice lament the present state of things.' He was not alone in his thoughts. When he visited Dudley, the earl displayed his open discontent with the Protector: 'Now was the time,' he added, for the emperor 'to come forward as the King's father.'[4]

Dudley's patience finally broke when his request for certain offices to be granted to the family of his late neighbour Sir Andrew Flammock, in consideration of his service against the rebels, was turned down by the Protector. Instead, they went to Thomas Fisher, Dudley's 'mortal enemy'. Dudley returned to court accompanied by his captains and demanded to speak with Somerset. The interview was stormy – Dudley demanded money for his captain's wages, only for Somerset to reply that there was none to be had. According to a later account, Dudley persuaded his following that Somerset was 'a coward, a nigard, covetous and ambitious'. They would have no reward, he told them, unless they would 'play the knave as Fisher did': 'You saw the altercation I had with the Protector, and all in order that you should be well rewarded. I hope, therefore, you will hold your men ready if I should want them.' They agreed; they were entirely at his service.[5]

With the support of his troops secured, Dudley decided that now was his chance to bring Somerset down. At Greenwich, where he was able to secretly consult with his friends, the plans were laid for the Protector's demise. Meanwhile Somerset, unaware of the growing threat to his position, had gone hunting into Hampshire with his wife.

The exact sequence of events is unclear, but the official version of those lords of the council who gathered around Dudley and against Somerset which was later recorded in the minutes of the Privy Council admitted they had consulted together about 'how to bring things into frame again'. They resolved to travel to Hampton Court to confront Somerset in person, yet only, they would later insist, for 'friendly communication ... about the reformation of State'.[6]

To the last Somerset remained completely unaware. On Tuesday 1 October he returned to Hampton Court, where council business continued to be conducted as normal. On 3 October he even signed warrants for the payment of military wages – amounting to £16,000 (£4 million) – after William Paulet persuaded him that 'there was many poor men did daily cry out to him for money'.[7] In fact, he had paid for his own coup.

On Friday 4 October there was talk that Dudley and the Earl of Arundel had turned against him. When Dudley refused to attend court, Somerset panicked and the following day issued a proclamation desperately commanding men to come immediately to Hampton Court armed to defend the king 'against whom certain hath attempted a most dangerous conspiracy'. But Somerset still had no idea what was being planned. Over the next few days he sent a flurry of letters – including to Lord Russell and Sir William Herbert, whose army had yet to return from subduing the rebellion in the west – requesting armed support: 'We be given to understand by insinuation of rumours that a certain conspiracy is in achieving against us.'[8]

As they were about to set off for Hampton Court to confront Somerset, the lords received news of the proclamation. Their plans would have to change. In their own explanation of events, the 'novelty' of Somerset's actions had taken them by surprise. Mustering their forces immediately, they began to prepare to take their stand. Riding through the city armed, their retinues followed behind 'attending upon them in new liveries, to the great wondering of many'.[9]

At four o'clock in the morning a messenger from London arrived at the gates of Hampton Court with news that the capital was filled with horsemen – perhaps at least two thousand – which 'seemed then to be such as would have no repulse'. It would soon become clear that the troops were massing around Dudley's residence at Ely Place in Holborn.

Weapons and five hundred harnesses were mustered immediately, whilst cobblestones were dug up to be used as projectiles and beams were ramped up against the back gates. Edward was transferred from the protection of his guard into Somerset's own lodging, a move that caused such confusion amongst his servants that Edward had to be brought out to prove that he was safe. Another proclamation, more urgent in tone, was issued, denouncing the lords and their 'false surmises'. The next day the frantic letter-writing continued. Throughout the day Edward noted that 'people came abundantly to the house'. Soon, four thousand peasants had assembled at the palace gates. Divided into squadrons and assigned quarters, captains were appointed to choose the most able men, though due to severe lack of food and fresh water, those without sufficient arms were sent home. Somerset then addressed the assembled crowd, claiming that Dudley and the lords were 'minded to make the Lady Mary regent and pull down me from the Protectorship'. He recalled a story that they knew all too well – that of Richard III and the murder of Edward V; and comparing the lords' actions, he warned how they sought to harm Edward, who he claimed was 'the apple of my eye; whose health is my comfort . . . and whose death is my fault and ruin'. He had been chosen by God to protect the king, and would do so to the last, pledging, 'I myself will be one of the first that will die in the gate, if they come in by any forcible manner into the court'.[10]

Meanwhile handbills in support of Somerset's cause, inscribed on the back 'Read it and give it forth!', were scattered on the streets of London.

One, written by an unidentified 'Henry A' encouraged men to 'Remember yourselves with loyal obedience, and be not carried away with the painted eloquence of a sort of crafty traitors, which draw at one mark and shoot at another'. The lords were denounced in the harshest terms. They were 'come up but late from the dunghill; a sort of them more meet to keep swine than to occupy the offices which they do occupy', for though they had described themselves as the council, 'yet they lack the head: then may ye call it a monstrous Council, for truly every body is nothing without the head. But the Lord shall destroy such a body at his pleasure!'[11] Another appealed to the Commons in other counties, setting Somerset's godly reputation against the avarice of the other nobles and gentry: 'Good people, in the name of God and King Edward let us rise with all our power to defend him and the Lord Protector ... for whom let us fight, for he loveth all just and true gentlemen which do no extortion, and also the poor commonalty of England.'[12]

Meanwhile on Sunday, 6 October, the lords met at Dudley's house in Holborn. Considering their position, they realized matters had now reached crisis point. Rebellion, despite 'the great slaughter and effusion of blood', had left the king's subjects in such disobedience that 'if speedy remedy be not provided both his Majesty's most royal person and the whole state might be brought into peril'. The blame lay firmly with Somerset and his 'ill government'. Despite repeated warnings both in council and in private, he had 'not only refused to give ear to their advises, but also minding to follow his own fantasies (wherefrom all the said disorders and mischiefs had before grown and arisen)' had carried on regardless.[13]

The lords in London sent out letters to the other nobility across the country ordering them to ignore Somerset's proclamation and repair to London armed. One reply survives – that of the conservative Henry Parker, Lord Morley – who pledged his uttermost support 'with that poor power I have ... to live or die'.[14]

Morley's involvement raises important questions that need answering. For Morley was also a prominent supporter of Princess Mary – was he part of a far greater conspiracy that had planned far in advance to engineer Somerset's fall in order to give Mary control of the kingdom? Somerset's speech to his followers at Hampton Court had accused the lords of being 'minded to make the lady Mary regent', yet the lords denied this in a letter to Mary on 9 October 1549. 'Among many his untrue and idle sayings,' they said, he 'declared that ... we would have removed him from office, and that we minded to have your Grace to be Regent of the realm ... which as God knoweth, we never intended ... neither any of us at any time, by word or writing, hath opened any such matter to your Grace, as your honour knoweth.'[15]

This was a convenient fiction to cover both their backs, for earlier in August 1549, Mary had received 'trustworthy information' that Dudley and Wriothesley, together with the Earl of Arundel and the treasurer, William Paulet, were 'working against the Protector and his new Council and sending to sound her to see if she would lend her favour to an attack on the Protector'. Mary asked her cousin the Emperor Charles V for his advice, though her plea seems more like a call for support. Charles' reply on 17 September 1549 killed the plans dead. 'As for certain Councillors' machinations against the Protector,' he wrote, 'it does not for the present seem opportune that such an important change take place in England ... it would be exceedingly hazardous for the Lady Mary to take any share in such proceedings.'[16]

This all suggests a plot to overthrow Somerset being hatched much earlier than the official record of the lords' actions would lead us to believe. The intrigues had begun perhaps as far back as early June, and in late May, shortly after Sir William Herbert's park had been destroyed, it was reported that Dudley had 'come very lustily on to the court'.[17] On 2 June Wriothesley had refused to serve on an embassy to France on account of his ill health, something which clearly rattled Somerset, since the earl wrote again three days later, professing that he 'shall never have cause to repent any your goodness towards me for I pray God that I live no longer than I shall show myself an honest man towards you'. By July 1549 Wriothesley's principal residence at Titchfield in Hampshire may possibly have become an alternative focus of power to Somerset's court; one woman even travelled from London to have her grievances addressed.[18]

But as the coup against the Protector now gathered pace, the lords needed the crucial support of the capital if they were to stand any chance of succeeding in standing up to Somerset and his growing bands of supporters. Though Somerset had become deeply unpopular among Londoners through his lavish building programme at Somerset House – 'There is not a man in town who does not curse the Protector,' the Spanish ambassador remarked – there was no guarantee that this would translate into unequivocal military backing. The Lord Mayor and his aldermen were summoned to Dudley's house. There the lords denounced Somerset's 'pride, covetousness, and ambition' which 'ceaseth not daily' with the meeting ending with both sides agreeing to arrange an assembly of aldermen to consider requests for military assistance. Meanwhile they assented to strengthen the watches, both night and day, around the city walls.[19]

Amidst the confusion, support for the lords was steadily growing. On 7 October, they made the point of meeting openly in a public house in the centre of the city, conferring at length both before and after dinner. The Earl of Shrewsbury and Lord Rich arrived in London that day, followed by the Earl of Derby the next morning. 'Now the entire nobility is here in arms,' Van der Delft remarked. Seventeen of the twenty-five councillors had now taken Dudley's side. Two councillors visited Van der Delft, taking time to explain the situation. They now 'hoped to regain the esteem and reputation they had lost in so short a time through the bad government of the Duke, who had had no care but to build houses for himself and deliver the realm to the enemy'. Every means had been tried to reason with him, they said, but in vain. 'Things shall be righted now or never.'[20]

But the city still held back its support. At the meeting held in the Guildhall on the afternoon of 7 October, letters from both Somerset and the lords were read out and their contents 'ripely and deliberately debated and pondered'. The aldermen unanimously agreed to side with the lords to defend both Edward and the city, but significantly only agreed to assist the lords in defence of the city against attack and declined to provide an armed force to march upon Somerset.

The next day the city authorities reconvened at the church of St Thomas à Becket. This time the lords had turned up in person. The Master of the Mint, John York, spoke of 'the great abuses of the said Lord Protector, desiring all the citizens to be aiding and assisting with the lords for the preservation of the king's majesty's person, which they greatly feared'. In response, the aldermen promised their support 'to the uttermost of their lives and goods', but still gave no assurance of armed force. Robert Brook, recorder of the city, requested they send five hundred men since Somerset 'had abused both the king's majesty and the whole realm'. But one alderman disagreed, citing a story in Fabyan's chronicle of a similar dilemma that occurred during the reign of Henry III. Then the city fathers had taken the side of the nobility against the king, for which Henry III never forgave them, and their liberties had been taken away amidst widespread persecution. His speech was enough for the citizens to stay their support, demanding that they needed more time. The discussions continued over the next few days, with an eventual agreement to provide five hundred men and one hundred horse to march in an armed force against Somerset.[21]

In the meantime, Somerset had been making his own preparations, organizing his troops to advance upon London on the afternoon of 7 October. The duchess was sent away weeping, 'very badly handled in words' by all those present 'who put all this trouble down to her'. It became impossible to feed the growing number of peasants that had turned out on the Protector's behalf, and still more were sent home. Mounting his horse and about to depart for London, Paget recognized a friend of Van der Delft: 'When you return to London tell the Emperor's ambassador in what condition you saw me, and that he was a great prophet,' he said, tears welling in his eyes.[22]

Orders were sent out to Sir Edward Wolf to take the Tower of London, yet upon his arrival he found the lords had already secured its gates. Returning on the way to Hampton Court at full speed, he met Somerset, Edward and his party en route to the capital. Another solution would now have to be found. Somerset gave the order to turn back, towards the stronghold of Windsor Castle.

The confusion and alarm were startling to Edward, who recorded later in his journal: 'That night, with all the people, at nine or ten o'clock at night, I went to Windsor, and there was watch and ward kept every night.' He had listened to Somerset's speech and apparently believed every word. Making his way on horseback, observers reported him armed, carrying a little drawn sword, saying, 'My vassals will you help me against those who want to kill me!'[23]

Arriving at Windsor without warning, there was little provision to sustain the royal household and its entourage. The lords, learning that the king had been taken to Windsor without food were 'most sorrowful for the same' and sent provisions 'with a most inestimable care'.

Amongst Somerset's camp there was both confusion and division. Sir William Petre was sent to London to gauge the lords' opinions, but he did not return. Rumours abounded – that Somerset had sent a ship 'to the French King laden with gold and silver in barrels like Gunpowder ... which ship was taken'. A memo was drawn up urging that letters be written to the lords, 'willing as many as were honourable to repair to him against his enemies, or else they sought his blood as well as his uncle's'. Significantly, it also commanded: 'send a letter to my lord of Warwick [Dudley] only from the king.'[24]

Letters shuttled between the lords at London and Windsor, each stating their determined position. 'We mean nothing else but the surety of his Majesties person,' the lords in London wrote to the few remaining council members at Windsor. 'If the Duke of Somerset would at any time have heard our advices, if he would have heard reason, and acknowledged himself a subject, our meanings was to have quietly communed with him for redress of all things without any disturbance of the realm ...' They urged for reconciliation, but it seemed both sides were gearing up for civil war. The same day Somerset wrote to the lords: 'If you will take no other way but violence ... our allegiance doth bind us, to the extremity of death, and put all into God's hands, who giveth the victory as it pleaseth him.'[25]

Men continued to arrive from the surrounding countryside, in support of the Protector. One gentleman from Kent brought with him 352 men, encouraging them that they would meet the king in person: 'I was sure that my Lord Protector ... could be no traitor ... If the Lords of London should have the upper hand that then if they should put the Lord Protector to death ... the king would revenge his uncle's death at his full age.'[26] Yet Somerset knew it was vital to secure the support of Lord Russell and Sir William Herbert and the royal troops under their command if he was to have any chance of victory. Ironically, he had written to them on 25 September ordering their return to London on 8 October 'for matters of importance'. Now letters, signed both by the Protector and the king, were sent urging them 'to come forth to the court with all diligence'.[27]

One, unnoticed until now, reveals Somerset's desperation to the full. 'If ever noble men were desired,' he wrote on 9 October, 'if ever there was cause why ye shall repair to the King's majesty and be most welcome and looked for, now is the time my Lords ... Such a time as never was before, and as we wish and with inward tears of our heart most humbly pray to god, never may come again ... There is no time now for you to go back, nor place to shrink.' Comparing the situation with the rebellions of the summer, he believed they were in no less danger – 'that was on the inferior members, this is in the head & chief rulers of the commonwealth'. He condemned the lords' 'almost disloyalty' to their king, 'whose presence in such a time should be his most stay and comfort whose innocency and tender age would more any infidel or

Jew to take compassion as you see they do not'. With their help, he predicted, 'it should not be two days before these tumults should have an end'.[28]

Somerset's pleadings were in vain, for that same day he received a letter from Russell and Herbert, urging him to step aside 'rather than any blood be shed; which if be once attempted, and the case brought to that misery that the hands of the nobility be once polluted each with other's blood, the quarrel once begun will never have end'. In a private quarrel such as this, they wrote, they would pledge their support to the lords. With 'great lamentation and sorrow' they had heard of 'the civil dissension which has happened between your Grace and the nobility ... A greater plague could not be sent unto this realm from God; being the next way to make us, of conquerors, slaves, and to induce upon us an universal calamity and thraldom.' Somerset's tactic of appealing to the commons against new-born men who he claimed had risen 'from the dunghill' had backfired spectacularly, for Herbert and Russell, newly risen themselves, had discovered his proclamations themselves by which 'we, and these other gentlemen we have served ... do incur by these means much infamy, slander and discredit'.[29]

Resistance was pointless; all Somerset could fight for now was his life. He offered his submission to Edward in front of his council at Windsor. In no way had he meant to cause 'any damage or hurt, but to defend only, if any violence should be attempted against your highness' and was willing to negotiate with two independent commissioners present.[30] The articles were sent to the lords, together with a letter addressed solely to Dudley, once his close friend, now rival:

> My Lord, I cannot persuade myself that there is any ill conceived in your heart as of yourself against me; for that the same seemeth impossible that where there hath been from your youth and mine so great a friendship and amity betwixt us, as never for my part to no man was greater, now so suddenly there should be hatred; and that without just cause, whatsoever rumours and bruits, or persuasion of others have moved you to conceive; in the sight and judgement of almighty God, I protest and affirm this unto you, I never meant worse to you than to myself; wherefore my lord, for God's sake, for friendship, for the love that hath ever been betwixt us or that hereafter may be, persuade yourself with truth, and let this time declare to me and the world your just honour and perseverance in friendship ...[31]

In one last throw of the dice, Somerset turned to his nephew to save him. The same day Edward wrote a letter, probably under dictation from Cranmer, to the lords:

> As far as our age can understand ... we do lament our present estate being in such an imminent danger; and unless God do put it into the hearts of you there to be as careful to bring these uproars unto a quiet ... we shall have cause to think you forget your duties towards us, and the great benefits which the King our lord, and father, of most noble memory, hath employed on every one of you. For, howsoever you charge our said uncle with wilfulness in your letter ... we trust that both you and he may continue ... without superstition, by a friendly determination and agreement among yourselves ... Each man hath his faults; he his and you yours; and if we shall hereafter as rigorously weigh yours, as we hear that you intend with cruelty to purge his, which of you all shall be able to stand before us?[32]

Paget, Cranmer and Sir Thomas Smith further wrote to the lords that day, begging them to spare Somerset's life: 'Life is sweet, my Lords, and they say you seek his blood and his death ... we beseech you again and again, if you have conceived any such determination, to put it out of your heads, and incline your hearts to kindness and humanity, remembering that he hath never been cruel to any of you; and why should you be cruelly minded to him?'[33]

Paget's own role in the coup remains mysterious, for it seems that his hand had a part to play in the downfall of his former friend and patron. When news of the lords' conspiracy broke, Somerset believed Paget was 'as evil as the best of them' and assumed he would be defecting to their side. The Duchess of Somerset also wrote, pleading for his loyalty in this 'miserable unnatural time'.[34] But Paget had different ideas, dispatching his servant with a secret message to the lords. He would be able to secure the arrest of Somerset and his household, he told them. They replied, thanking him for his 'wise and stout doings', to which a grateful Paget wrote back acknowledging the 'favour you have showed me', adding, 'I have always borne you my good will: so being the same increased by this I shall continue it during my life'.[35]

Paget knew that it was time to jump ship, a fact made all too clear when, on 8 October, the lords issued their own proclamation, sealed with the Great Seal yet without royal authority, 'containing the truth of the Duke of Somerset's evil government'. It proved to be a turning point:

'After which time,' Edward later wrote in his journal, 'few came to Windsor but only mine own men of the guard, whom the Lords willed, fearing the rage of the people so lately quieted.'[36]

Yet events were beginning to take a more desperate turn. The lords heard on 9 October that Somerset had openly declared that 'if the lords intended his death, that the king's majesty should die before him'. It was at this moment that his fate was decided, for the lords now considered him unworthy to remain as Protector. Resolving that Somerset must now be deposed from his position, a carefully orchestrated plan was prepared to bring him down. The key figure in the design was Sir Philip Hoby who, despite being a former 'creature' of Somerset's, had secretly defected to the lords after delivering the duke's previous letter to them. Acting as the lords' secret agent, Hoby agreed to return to Windsor with a message of support and comfort. But he also carried with him another packet of correspondence, addressed separately to Edward, Cranmer, Sir Thomas Smith, Paget and the entire household at Windsor, blaming Somerset for the realm's failure and urging them to withdraw their support. The idea – if everything went to plan – was to create a false sense of security in the duke's mind while giving those closest to him the opportunity to desert.

Yet before events could be put into motion, the lords hesitated, for they had yet to hear back from Russell and Herbert to whom they had sent letters urging their – and their troops' – support.

Hoby promptly set out towards Windsor with the lords' reply. Halfway along the route, however, Hoby suddenly turned back, claiming to have lost the lords' letter. Telling his servant he would return to London to obtain new copies, he urged him to continue on to Windsor, to tell Somerset and the court that 'all was well'.

Of course there had been no 'lost' letter. Instead, the entire charade was devised by the lords, in order to play for time while they waited for Russell and Herbert's response. That arrived later in the day. It was the news the lords had been hoping for, for they declared their unequivocal loyalty to the lords' cause. Somerset had gone too far and needed to be removed. With the support of Russell and Herbert, and with their troops ready to fight against the protector, they knew now that for Somerset the game was nearly up.

Hoby finally arrived at Windsor with the letters mid morning on 10 October. The first, addressed to Somerset, he read aloud to the court:

Of their faiths and honours they do not intend, nor will hurt, in any case, the person of my Lord the Duke, nor none of you all, nor take away any of his lands or goods, whom they do esteem and tender as well as any of you, as they ought, and as one whom they are not ignorant, no more than you, that is the King's uncle.

They do intend to preserve his honour as much as any of you would; nor meaneth not, nor purposeth not, no manner to hurt him, but only to give order for the Protectorship, which hath not been so well ordered as they think it should have been; and to see that the King be better answered of his things, and the realm better governed for the King's Majesty. And for you, my Lords and Masters of the Council, they will have you to keep your rooms and places as you did before, and they will counsel with you for the better government of things.[37]

'My Lord,' Hoby said, turning to Somerset, with the Judas words: 'Be you not afraid. I will lose this, my neck, if you have any hurt.' Those present wept for joy, praying both to God and for the lords. Paget fell to his knees weeping. Clasping Somerset, he said: 'Oh my lord, oh my lord, ye see now what my lords be.'[38]

But of course that was not the only letter Hoby had come to deliver. Without Somerset's knowledge, Edward personally received a private letter from the lords, which he remembered declared Somerset's 'faults, ambition, vainglory, entering into rash wars in mine youth, negligent looking on Newhaven, enriching of himself of my treasure, following his own opinion, and doing all by his own authority, etc.' Another letter, to Paget, Cranmer and Smith, was couched in harsher terms. Commanding them to have 'continual earnest watch' over Edward, it menaced that 'you will answer for the contrary at uttermost perils'.[39]

Meanwhile, arriving at Windsor in advance, Hoby's servant had handed printed copies of the lords' proclamation denouncing the Protector to the commander of the royal bodyguard, who distributed the charges to 'all the good fellows of credit' whilst they were in 'the houses of office [the lavatories] in the morning'.[40] Within an hour those who had promised to fight with Somerset to the death were seeking his own, but they were ordered to remain silent and wait until they were given the signal to depart. This came as Hoby was delivering his oration, for with one blast of a trumpet the guard laid down their weapons and speedily departed from the palace gates. The gates shut, only the officers of the royal household remained. The deception complete,

Somerset was, at a stroke, isolated and helpless – his authority had vanished.

Once Somerset's men had departed, three of the best chambers were made ready for the lords' arrival. The next morning, 11 October, Sir Anthony Wingfield, captain of the guard, arrived at Windsor with five hundred men. To his surprise, Somerset was removed from his lodging next to the king's bedchamber and placed in Beauchamp Tower under arrest, surrounded by 'a strong and good watch'.

When the guards entered Edward's chamber, the king's reaction was first one of terror. According to the list of charges later brought against him, Somerset had persuaded his nephew and the 'young lords' attending him that the lords 'minded to destroy the king'. Telling Edward 'never to forget it, but to revenge it' he urged Edward's friends to remind him constantly. Now Edward believed they had come to kill him. But it was not long before he had been convinced otherwise.[41] He was found to be suffering from 'a great rheum', caught on the night-ride to Windsor. 'Methinks I am in prison,' he told Wingfield, 'here be no galleries nor no gardens to walk in.' Paget, however, found him to be 'in good health and merry', at breakfast welcoming his new guard 'with a merry countenance and a loud voice', asking 'how your Lordships did, when he should see you, and that you should be welcome whensoever you come' and allowing each gentlemen to kiss his hand, 'much to their comfort'.[42] The ordeal was over – their king was safe.

At around five o'clock in the afternoon of 14 October Somerset entered London surrounded by an armed guard of three hundred horse. Scant respect was paid to him, despite his repeated protestations to the crowds that 'he was no traitor, but as faithful a servant of the King as any man'.[43] On 13 October the office of Protector had been revoked by letters patent. The next day he was placed in the Tower together with members of his household, including his private secretary, Sir Thomas Smith. 'The man that ruled all by his wilfulness is restrained,' Dudley wrote to Lord Clinton abroad at Calais. 'Now things are like to pass otherwise than of long time it hath done, more for the king's honour and the wealth and safety of his realms and subjects.' Others were less sure. 'The duke is now stayed & his troublous head,' Paulet wrote to Lord Cobham, 'whereby great questions shall follow by God's help.'[44]

Somerset was charged on twenty counts of treason. The catalogue of offences included discharging murderers and those charged with treason from prison, tampering with the coinage, commanding 'multiplication and alchemy to be practised', and neglecting the defences in Boulogne and Scotland.

There was the ring of the personal. He had 'rebuked, checked, and taunted' other councillors privately and in public, pointedly refusing their advice. If anyone had disagreed with him, he had threated them with expulsion from the council. His proclamation concerning enclosures had been issued 'against the will of the whole council' whilst the enclosure commission was blamed for causing the rebellions of the summer, which Somerset had done nothing to counter. He had even shown sympathy and support for the rebels, blaming the gentry for their covetousness.[45]

Meanwhile Edward travelled to Hampton Court, where he thanked 'all the company for having rid him of such fear and peril'. Entering London on 17 October, Edward, richly apparelled in a coat 'of cloth of tissue', rode in a procession of over a thousand horse. It was a day of thankful celebration. The streets were freshly gravelled and cloths of gold and arras hung from every house lining the route. People crowded to see that their king was safe; amid scenes of jubilation and the 'melodies of instruments and singing men' played much to Edward's enjoyment.[46] The country had been pulled back from the brink of civil war. For the moment, nobody seemed to care what might follow. For Edward, it had been the most important test of his fragile kingship, one which he had only narrowly survived. As he rode into Westminster, Van der Delft caught a glimpse of his face: 'He certainly looked as if he had had a surprise.'

With Somerset placed in the Tower, a vacuum of power was created at court. But whereas Dudley might have been considered the obvious choice to replace him as Edward's guardian and leader amongst the council, it was in fact Wriothesley who now took centre stage, lodging himself next to Edward and promising his supporters handsome rewards: Sir Thomas Arundel was 'promised to be next to the King' as Comptroller and none other than Sir Richard Southwell 'for his whisking and double diligence' was admitted to the council. 'Every man repaireth to Wriothesley, honoureth Wriothesley, sueth unto Wriothesley,' the preacher John Ponet later remarked, with no decision being taken without his advice.[47]

The earl seems to have become the self-appointed head of a 'Catholic' party, seeking the restoration of the old religion. The Imperial ambassador wrote confidently how 'all the foremost Councillors are Catholics' with even Dudley 'taking up the old observances day by day' and 'intends to range himself on their side, for he has forbidden his household to eat meat on Fridays under severe penalties'.

Officially, however, with the dissolution of the Protectorate, control of Edward and the kingdom now reverted back to the executors of Henry's will. On 15 October these met to appoint a new Privy Chamber for the king. Security around Edward was to be dramatically increased. This entourage was significant, since it assured almost constant contact with the king, with Edward noting in his diary that 'three of the outer Privy Chamber gentlemen should always be here, and two lie in the pallet and fill the room of one of the four knights; that the esquires should be diligent in their office, and five grooms should always be present, of which one to watch in the bedchamber'.[48] The four Chief Gentlemen chosen included Andrew Dudley, Dudley's brother, the evangelicals Sir Thomas Wroth and Sir Edward Rogers, Sir Thomas Darcy and the Marquess of Northampton. It is significant that all were Dudley's political allies. Later it would be alleged that it was through Thomas Cranmer's support that Dudley 'procured . . . great friends about the king'.

But Edward's own feelings should not be discounted too readily. Edward noted in his journal that the appointments were made 'by my consent' and their evangelical outlook parallels the king's own religious development. No more clearly is this felt than in a treatise against papal supremacy that Edward had finished on the last day of August 1549, having spent since December 1548 working on the manuscript. Arranging it in four parts, Edward considered the arguments for and against papal supremacy. The Pope, he concluded, was 'the true son of the devil, a bad man, an Antichrist and abominable tyrant'.

Edward's work was based in part on John Ponet's English translation of a work by the Italian refugee Bernardino Ochino, which had been dedicated to Edward in early 1549. However, Edward did not slavishly copy Ochino; instead he reused his ideas and historical detail to tailor his own argument. But it is clear that the treatise was an original composition. A contemporary note attached confirms that it was the king's own work, even if based on conversation and available books, and Edward's draft manuscript is corrected throughout in another hand, probably by his French tutor Jean Belmain.

'In my father's days,' Edward wrote, 'when [the Pope's] name was struck out of books, he stopped the mouths of Christians with his six articles, like six fists' – forgetting that it was Henry himself who had passed the Act of Six Articles. Edward identified himself with 'the poor lambs of God' writing: 'If they do not do the Pope's bidding, that is to offer to idols and devils, he burns us, and makes us bear a faggot.' Deciding that the remark was far too personal for a king to make, Belmain altered the phrase to 'he burns them, or forces them to make honourable amends'.[49]

Importantly, Edward had dedicated his treatise to Somerset, praising him for his 'great affection towards the divine word and sincere religion'. Edward had already sanctioned the execution of one of his uncles that year – he was unwilling to let another suffer the same fate. One story provides a valuable insight into the dynamics of power during these unstable times. When the Duchess of Somerset was granted an audience with the king, she had begun to plead for her husband's life when Edward asked where he was.

'A prisoner, in the Tower,' came the astonished reply, 'and if Your Grace doth not pardon him, the Council will kill him.'

'Jesu! They told me the Duke was ill – why have they taken him prisoner?' Edward replied, turning to Cranmer: 'Godfather, what hath become of my uncle the Duke?'

Cranmer prevaricated: 'We feared that he might kill you,' he explained gently. 'If my lord had not been imprisoned, great harm had been done.'

'The Duke never did me any harm,' Edward replied, adding: 'He went to the Tower of his own will, it is a sign that he be not guilty.' Cranmer made a further attempt to persuade the king of the lords' reasons, but Edward was insistent – he wanted to see his uncle. Dudley stood in silence near by, musing on the king's words. Securing Somerset's safety might be the best chance of obtaining influence with Edward, influence that would translate into power. Later, at a meeting of the council he rose to address the board: 'We must return good for evil. And as it is the King's will that the Duke should be pardoned, and it is the first matter he hath asked of us, we ought to accede to His Grace's wish.'[50]

This story may hold a kernel of truth. It was noted that the Duchess of Somerset began to take turns in regularly hosting banquets with Dudley's wife, becoming a constant visitor at Dudley's house; and it seems that through his wife, Dudley was also attempting to rehabilitate the Protector's colleagues. Was it also through the duchess's efforts that Dudley realized the only chance of his political survival was ultimately through the young king and his desire to save his uncle?

It is more likely that Dudley became increasingly close to Edward through the appointments of his associates, the Gentlemen of the Privy Chamber, who no doubt kept the earl closely informed of the king's wishes and expectations. And the most important of these was Edward's desire that the Reformation continue as planned.

With Edward's support behind him, Dudley's star was again soon rising, and on 20 October he was appointed Admiral. Significantly, the appointment coincided with the recovery of the evangelical faith, for the same day a royal letter sent to Zurich enthusiastically noted 'the mutual agreement between us concerning the Christian religion and true godliness'. One reformer wrote confidently to another that 'in these difficult and perilous times' the Catholic faith had been cast down, with even more severe penalties being placed on those who neglected the new religious observances: 'There is nothing therefore for the godly to fear, and nothing for the papists to hope for, from the idolatrous mass.'[51]

By the end of October the new posturing was made official in a proclamation which outlined that the progress of the Reformation was not exclusive to Somerset's regime; the government would 'further do in all things, as time and opportunity may serve, whatsoever may lend to the glory of God and the advancement of his holy word', a sentiment echoed by Dudley to the Imperial ambassador. As Parliament opened on 4 November, the evangelicals could gloat that their cause presently stood in a better state than before Somerset's fall.[52]

Yet despite this restatement of the evangelical cause, Wriothesley reassured the Imperial ambassador that the conservative cause still held firm and that Mary would be allowed her mass, saying 'those who have molested her will do so no more, and even though they were to begin afresh she has many good servants, of whom I hold myself to be one'. Wriothesley himself continued to hold great authority, being lodged at court where 'a great number of lords' paid him lip service daily.[53] Little did the earl realize this was all about to change.

With power swinging back to the reformers, the conservatives began to grow restless. In early November, Sir Thomas Arundel, one of Wriotheseley's main supporters and described as being of the 'old faith', renewed contact with Mary, offering to be taken into her service. Mary refused; given that Arundel had been 'a prime instrument in uniting the lords against the Protector' she now wanted nothing to do with any scheme to make her regent. Yet Arundel's posturing was enough to spur Dudley into action. Sensing a conservative challenge, he managed to bar Arundel's appointment to the council. Instead, Thomas Goodrich, the

Protestant Bishop of Ely, and Henry Grey, Marquess of Dorset, were brought on to the council to counterbalance the conservatives' dominance. This would be the tipping point at which the evangelicals would recover their authority, for from now on they held the majority on the council. Sworn on to the board on 29 November, one evangelical believed their appointment placed 'all honest hearts in good comfort for the good hope that they have of the perseverance of God's word'.[54]

Meanwhile Parliament had lain in such a state of paralysis that it was nicknamed 'the still Parliament'. Important legislation, however, heralded an end to the leniency of Somerset's regime. A bill for 'the punishment of unlawful assemblies and risings of the King's subjects' was introduced into Parliament on 9 November declaring it treason for twelve or more persons to assemble with the intention of killing or taking any of the Privy Council, with authority granted to any of the king's officers to use whatever force at their disposal to disperse suspicious crowds. And perhaps with Kett's rebellion in mind, an act against 'fond and fantastical prophecy' was passed on 26 December forbidding the setting forth of prophecy in writing, printing, singing or speaking under the punishment of a year's imprisonment for the first offence, with life imprisonment and the forfeiture of all goods for the second. The milder climates that Somerset had hoped for had grown very much colder.[55]

But during the winter Wriothesley's health deteriorated. Van der Delft began to realize that any hope of a Catholic restoration was looking as fragile as the earl's health, and stood the prospect of being buried with him. 'If he were to fail us now,' he wrote at the end of November, 'I should fear matters might never be righted.' Wriothesley, he remarked, was still in 'good hope' of success and had the backing of a good part of the council. These, however, would 'go astray and follow the rest' without him, 'for there is not a man among them of sound enough judgement to conduct opposition'.[56]

Dudley too fell sick, confined to his chamber 'with a rheum in the head'.[57] However, arrangements were made for council meetings to take place at his house. His growing authority came from Edward's tacit support; how influential this was is not easy to ascertain, but it is likely that Dudley's careful placing of his 'great friends about the king' had had the desired effect. He soon began to earn new friends on the council. Having gained Paget's support during the October coup, the two had been described as 'great friends' and virtually inseparable. Paget brought the Lord Chancellor, Richard Rich, on side; others soon followed.[58]

With the appointment of the Bishop of Ely and Henry Grey, Marquess of Dorset, to the council having strengthened Dudley's hand against the conservatives, he now decided to consolidate this position by rewarding his closest supporters with offices, lucrative rewards and a series of elevations to the peerage. As Dudley's position grew stronger day by day, so the Reformation seemed to be back on track. 'Although our vessel is dangerously tossed about on all sides,' one reformer wrote, 'yet God in his providence holds the helm, and raises up more favourers of his word in his Majesty's council, who with activity and courage defend the cause of Christ.'[59] On Christmas Day the evangelical triumph was nailed with a new letter sent out to all bishops, ordering them to burn all Catholic books and primers whilst proclaiming that the Reformation would continue full steam ahead. Soon bonfires burned in every marketplace and churchyard across the country.

That same Christmas Day Somerset was also allowed to see his wife, the duchess, 'to his no little comfort'. In the afternoon he listened to John Hooper preach a sermon on a psalm of David, no doubt arranged by the new regime since he spoke on 'governors that misordered their vocations, persuading that God punished rulers for their sins, exhorting such to take it patiently and in any wise not to go about to seek revengement, saying that if any did procure or labour to revenge that then God would punish those with double plagues'.[60] Rumours were soon in the air that Somerset would be released on New Year's Day, as the king's gift to him.

Wriotheseley knew he had to act fast if he was to maintain any influence at court, for the return of his enemy would surely spell the end of his political career. Throughout early December he had been entrusted to examine Somerset in the Tower, together with the Earl of Arundel and William Paulet, visiting him daily and questioning him on each point of the list of articles drawn up against him. Somerset gave no answer except that Dudley had been party to his every move. For Wriothesley, it was the perfect opportunity to bring down both his rivals. 'I thought ever we should find them traitors both, and both are worthy to die by my advice,' he remarked one day as they left the Tower. Arundel agreed. The day Somerset was condemned, it was decided, Dudley should be sent to the Tower 'and have as he had deserved'. Paulet remained silent.

That evening Paulet paid a visit to Dudley in secret, revealing to him the entire conversation in the Tower. Warning Dudley how to handle Somerset's punishment, 'for he should suffer himself for the same', at that moment Dudley realized his own fate lay in preserving Somerset's life.

The next council meeting was again arranged to be held at Dudley's house in Holborn, supposedly on account of the earl's recurrent illness. As Dudley lay on his bed feigning sickness, Wriothesley spoke, outlining the charges against Somerset and demanding his execution: he was worthy to die, he remarked, 'and for how many treasons'. Recognizing that Wriotheseley was about to launch an attack on his own involvement in Somerset's dealings, Dudley jumped up 'with a warlike visage' and laying his hand on his sword, said: 'My lord, you seek his blood and he that seeketh his blood would have mine also.'[61]

Wriothesley was arrested and commanded to keep to his house. His supporters were soon rounded up: Sir Richard Southwell was arrested and fined £500 (£125,900) for writing 'certain bills of sedition with his own hand' whilst Sir Thomas Arundel and Sir Edward Rogers, one of Edward's four principal gentlemen, were ordered to remain in their houses 'without further liberty'.

Dudley realized that the conservatives could no longer be trusted. The cull came quickly, with the Earl of Arundel ordered to hand over his staff of office for, according to Edward, 'certain crimes of suspicion against him, as plucking down of bolts and locks at Westminster, giving of my stuff away etc.'. Discovered removing the bolts from the doors to Edward's Privy Chamber by Sir Andrew Dudley, he had replied he 'would not tarry at other men's pleasure to come to the king's chamber'. He was removed from his position as Lord Chamberlain on 21 February and fined £12,000 (£2.7 million).[62]

Wriothesley's health worsened soon after. According to his physician, the diagnosis was tuberculosis. Exiled from court, he must have seen death as a welcome relief; he told Van der Delft he desired 'to be under the earth rather than upon it'.[63] When he was finally granted permission to return to his home at Titchfield on 28 June, he was too ill to travel. He died on 30 July 1550 at his London home, Lincoln House, amidst rumours of suicide. Yet by his death he had come to recognize the inevitable, requesting in his will that the Protestant cleric John Hooper preach his funeral sermon. And amongst his other bequests, he left a gold cup to his 'friend' Dudley.

Few mourned his loss. Two years later, Sir Richard Morison probably spoke for many when he recalled how he had been 'afraid of a tempest all the while Wriothesley was able to raise any. I knew he was an earnest follower of whatsoever he took in hand, and did very seldom miss where either wit or travail were able to bring his purposes to pass. Most true it is, I never was able persuade myself that Wriothesley could be great, but the King's Majesty must be in greatest danger.'[64]

Dudley had destroyed his rivals in a brilliant game of political manoeuvre, but this had come at a price, and political debts would need to be paid. On 19 January Paulet was elevated as Earl of Wiltshire, Russell became Earl of Bedford, whilst Northampton was granted the honorific but no less prestigious title of Lord Great Chamberlain. The rewards served to strengthen Dudley's own position, particularly in the household, where Sir Anthony Wingfield was made Comptroller and Lord Wentworth Chamberlain. The honours list was completed with the elevation of Lord Ferrers to Viscount Hereford.[65] Hearing of the promotions from his cell in the Tower, Sir Thomas Smith, Somerset's private secretary, was less than convinced:

> This day made new Duke, Marquis or Baron
> Yet may the axe stand next the door
> Every thing is not ended as it is begun
> God will have the stroke, either after or before.[66]

8

UNCERTAIN TIMES

At court, tournaments and celebrations attempted to mask the jockey-ing for power.[1] One notable absentee from the celebrations was Edward's sister, Mary. She had been particularly despondent at Dudley's ascendancy, telling Van der Delft that she thought him 'the most unstable man in England' whose conspiracy against Somerset was driven by 'envy and ambition as its only motives'. 'You will see that no good will come of this move, but that it is a punishment from Heaven, and may be only the beginning of our misfortunes,' she told him, adding that she now wished to leave the country. The council were pushing her to attend at court to celebrate the Christmas festivities, but she had declined. 'They wished me to be at court so that I could not get the mass celebrated,' she told the ambassador, 'and that the king might take me with him to hear their sermons and masses. I would not find myself in such a place for anything in the world.' Deciding to pay her brother a visit at a more convenient time when she would be able to stay at her own London residence rather than lodge at court, she resolved that she would remain only for four or five days, 'and avoid entering into argument with the King my brother, who, as I hear, is beginning to debate the question of religion and oppose ours, as he is being taught to do'.[2]

Mary was not the only one with reservations about the direction of things to come. 'Notwithstanding all this great pastime and mirth, the Council is in that unquiteness and trouble among themselves that no man can have no time to speak with them,' a servant wrote to the Earl of Rutland. Van der Delft reported that the Earl of Derby had declared that the sacrament 'should be publicly revered and worshipped', and in a dispute with the Marquess of Northampton told him he would lay down his life for it.[3] It was one example of religious division amongst many. 'People do not make inquiry of a man's good name,' Van der Delft observed on the mood of the court, 'but merely ask whether he belongs to the new faith or the old religion, and he gets treated according to his faith.' The conservatives – in Van der Delft's words 'the partisans of righteousness' – were 'still numerous', and intended to cause further instability. There may have even been an attempt by the conservatives to counter Dudley's new supremacy, for the Clerk of the Privy Council, William Honnings, was arrested on 30 January, accused of assisting the conservative faction by stealing the copy of the judges' opinions on Bishop Gardiner's offences, and later committed to Marshalsea prison.[4]

In their nervousness, for the first week of February the council met at Dudley's house at Ely Place. Having heard reports of a new commotion in the country, they resolved 'to break up the parliament this day and to send the gentlemen home ... with such powers ... to stay the malice of such ill disposed people, as otherwise would lightly be stirred and induced to rise again'.[5]

New insurrections certainly threatened. In Braintree, Essex, plans to burn down the residence of the Lord Chancellor Richard Rich and assassinate a local gentleman before marching on London were foiled.[6] Elsewhere, a weaver in Norwich called for the removal of Dudley's insignia from the city gates, boasting that Kett's body would 'be plucked down from the top of the castle'.[7] 'Slanderous bills' against the council were discovered at the end of March. 'Fine witted young men' were soon arrested and examined, whilst George Ferrers, a client of Somerset's, was detained under suspicion at Dudley's house in Greenwich.[8]

In the meantime, others worked hard for Somerset's release, including William Cecil, who wrote to the Duchess of Suffolk, requesting her own intercession on Somerset's behalf.[9] On 14 January Somerset was formally deposed as Lord Protector. In hope of his early release, two thousand people had waited outside the Tower that day. However, upon his admission to the thirty-three charges laid against him on 27 January 1550, there was probably a mutual understanding that his release would follow shortly.[10] On 6 February Somerset was summoned to the council to receive the king's pardon, and was appointed to remain under house arrest at Syon under a recognizance of £10,000 'until the king's pleasure be further known'.[11]

With the abolition of the Protectorship and Wriothesley's demise, Dudley stepped up to take Somerset's place. But there was no precedent for someone who was not a member of the wider royal family to inherit such a position; Somerset, after all, had been Edward's maternal uncle. Instead, Dudley found a solution in the procedural authority of the Tudor court, in particular that of the Privy Chamber. On 2 February he was granted the office of Lord Great Master of the chamber, a post vacated by the elevation of William Paulet to the peerage. This gave the earl the power to control the operation of Edward's royal apartments, effectively giving him complete access to the king. With this office also came the previously nominal role as Lord President of the Council, a position that was more or less dormant under Somerset's rule. Dudley soon realized that the arrangement would give him the recognized authority he required. Through the Privy Chamber, he would become the head of the king's government in council, acting as its 'lieutenant', organizing meetings and sitting at the upper end of the council table.[12]

As President of the Council, Dudley also held the power to appoint or disbar councillors at will. He immediately took the opportunity to purge his rivals from court. His first official act was to banish the leaders of the conservative opposition from their seats on the council, whilst over the next eighteen months he secured the appointment of ten of his supporters to the board. His dominance was now unrivalled, with Van der Delft considering that he 'is absolute master here, and the Lords of the Council are under his orders', and visiting him daily at his house to 'learn his pleasure'.[13]

At the same time, the lessons of the past had made it clear that a more consensual system of politics needed to be adopted. Somerset had been overthrown for abusing his position and ignoring the advice of his fellow councillors. Having learnt from Somerset's mistakes, William Paget now sought to ensure that this could never happen again. On 23 March he delivered his 'Advice to the King's Council' to the council board, a blueprint for reform that aimed to restore harmony and structure to the machinery of government. He advocated that the council should meet on regular and set occasions: three times a week from eight o'clock until lunchtime, then from two o'clock until four, 'and oftener if the King's affairs so require'.

Most importantly a sense of unity needed to be restored. The events of October and the ensuing winter had revealed to the world the bitter divisions between councillors. Paget now looked to heal wounds and restore confidence in the government. The councillors were to 'love one another as brethren or dear friends', with each able to speak his opinion 'frankly ... without reproof, check or displeasure for the same of any person'. By this means they would gradually recover their authority, 'whereby will come to pass that others shall honour them and have them in great estimation'.[14]

Soon stability began gradually to return to the political arena. As for Wriothesley and Arundel, 'I think they be almost forgotten,' one courtier wrote, 'for I can hear nobody in a manner to speak of them.'[15] By April, Somerset's star was again rising, albeit with Dudley's assistance. On 12 April 1550 he visited Edward at Greenwich, later dining with Dudley. Rumours soon began to circulate of a miraculous political comeback. 'Some say he will be President of the Council,' Van der Delft informed the emperor, 'others that he will be Governor of the King's person; however that may be, there is apparently a great likelihood of his return to high authority.' 'Doubtless the Protector governed us ill,' the English diplomat John Mason had told him, 'but you will see that he will come back into authority as before, and this will happen because there is no one else to take his place.'[16]

Mason was right: as the only adult duke, Somerset was effectively the most important member and leader of the peerage; there was little choice but to restore him to his place in government. By 26 April one courtier reported that the duke had returned to court where 'all men seeketh upon him', and his restoration was finally complete with his recall to the council on 7 May 1550 and re-admittance to the Privy Chamber four days later.[17]

For all his misfortunes, at first Somerset seemed repentant enough. The day before his return to the council he contributed a preface to the Protestant preacher Miles Coverdale's translation of Otto Werdmueller's *The Spiritual and Precious Pearl*. During his 'scourge' in prison, Somerset had read the work and had found 'great comfort and an inward and godly working power much relieving the grief of our mind'. And commenting upon his own fate, added 'Such is the uncertainty of the world and all human things, that no man standeth so sure', humbly recalling a passage from the first book of Kings: 'The lord bringeth death, and restoreth again unto life, bringeth into the grave and raiseth up again, putteth down and exalteth also.'[18]

However, Dudley was not taking any chances, and security around the king remained tight. On 20 April Edward wrote in his journal how it had been decided to increase the security ring around him, with five gentlemen being placed constantly in attendance, and a personal bodyguard to watch over him at all times, both day and night.[19] Licences were issued for members of the council and Gentlemen of the Privy Chamber to keep a total of 2,340 retainers, whilst the Yeomen of the Guard were increased from one hundred to four hundred and the

Company of Gentlemen Pensioners, first founded in 1539 and whose members were increasingly aged, were replaced by a new force of sixty 'men of arms' demobilized from Boulogne.[20] Edward's court must have been transformed into something more akin to the barracks of a militia.

A glimpse of the intense level of security that surrounded Edward can be captured from the ordinances of the Gentleman Usher of the Privy Chamber, set down by Sir Richard Blount. Edward's chambers were to be made 'as sweet as they may be', with fires in every chamber used by the king. Each morning, the pallets that the guard had slept upon had to be removed, window-sills furnished with cushions, and the remains of torches extinguished and taken away. When the king was awake and dressed, the usher was to ask 'his pleasure what time he will go to breakfast' before warning the relevant officers in the kitchen, and when Edward needed to 'go service to the closet' – in other words use the toilet – the cushions he would sit on would need to be tested 'in convenient time'. If Edward wanted to play 'in parks, orchards, gardens and galleries' the usher must investigate the area fully; this was of particular importance if Edward was to 'remove to any strange house', for which there were specific guidelines to check the roofs and floors, making sure that 'all other his Privy Chambers have no backdoors into gardens or courts ... cause them to be stopped if he thinks good ... see there be none lodged under the King's Chambers, and especially the bed chamber.'[21]

Edward's education was also carefully screened, with his texts and reading books carefully selected by his teachers and the council. The reformer John Hooper noted that when a German Lutheran attempted to present Edward with a book 'against the Anabaptists and sac-ramentaries' he was forbidden, since it did not please his tutors and was presumably never given to the king. When the Swiss reformer Martin Bullinger dedicated his masterpiece *De Regno Christi* to Edward, it was presented to him splendidly bound, in a carefully stage-managed ceremony through the intercession of the Marquess of Northampton, who laid it before Edward. Hooper, who had a part in organizing the event, explained to Bullinger that 'I should have presented it myself, had it not been forbidden by our laws for any one to lay before the King either a letter or anything else brought from foreign parts, without previously making it known to the council; and this law no one may violate, until the King shall have arrived at the steadiness of mature age.'[22] When the yeoman of the guard Philip Gerrard overstepped the mark and attempted to present to Edward his own exhortation, explaining how 'the cruelty of the rich sort is wonderful great & daily encreaseth' and blaming the rebellions of the previous summer on 'the great cruelty, exhortation, and a greedy desire to have all of certain gentlemen', he was prevented from handing the manuscript to the king by another attendant John Gates, a loyal friend of Dudley's who had been appointed to the Privy Chamber in January 1550 and now crucially held the dry stamp of Edward's signature.[23] At around the same time, another anecdote from a foreign observer recalled how Edward, 'according to his time of life', 'suffered very free expressions to escape him' when reflecting upon events. On one occasion, Dudley was present in the room where Edward was reading 'some English histories' (probably Edward Hall's *Chronicle*).[24] He 'happened to fall upon a page that contained a narration of the capital punishment inflicted upon [Dudley's] father ... but as the narration did not express the name of Dudley's father, the king, being at a loss, asked him who it could be.' Dudley promptly seized the book from Edward saying, 'Why do you burthen your youthful and tender mind with knowing the romantic tales of the vulgar?' and ushered him out to archery practice.

In reality, Edward's studies had undergone a significant change since Somerset's fall. As soon as Dudley took charge of the Privy Chamber, the Venetian ambassador recalled how the earl had Edward 'taught to ride and handle his weapons, and to go through other similar exercises, so that his Majesty soon commenced arming and tilting, managing horses, and delighting in every sort of exercise, drawing the bow, playing rackets, hunting ... indefatigably'. 'Though he never neglected his studies,' the ambassador added. According to Foxe, this was not always the case, for Edward often arrived late for his lessons having been absorbed in play.[25]

There were also changes made to Edward's tutors. Cox retired from his position as almoner in February, and was replaced by Sir Anthony Cooke, who was granted an annuity of £100 for providing 'training in good letters and manners' to the king.[26] Cheke's tuition provided continuity in the king's education, which by now had progressed on to learning the *Ethics* and *Dialectic* of Aristotle and translating Cicero's *Philosophia* into Greek, before moving on to Aristotle's *Rhetoric*. According to Cheke, Edward could now understand Latin 'with accuracy, speaks with propriety, writes with facility'. Cheke had carefully planned the form that Edward's learning would take, fully grounded in the basis of history. 'My endeavour,' he told his friend Roger Ascham, 'is to give him no precept unaccompanied by some remarkable example.'[27]

Cheke was also determined that Edward should begin to keep a diary, advising him that 'a dark and imperfect reflection upon affairs floating in the memory, was like words dispersed and insignificant; whereas a view of them in a book, was like the same words digested and disposed in good order, and so made significant'. At first Edward began with a brief summary of his life, recording significant events in the third person. Eventually, however, its entries became fuller and more personal, to the point whereby Edward began to make daily entries and the document becomes the single most valuable source for the history of the reign.[28]

But it was in religious affairs that Edward had begun to demonstrate a serious interest. 'In the court there is no bishop, and no man of learning,' the Imperial ambassador reported, 'so ready to argue in support of the new doctrine as the king, according to what his masters tell him, and he learns from his preachers.' Copying out their sermons with his own hand ('a source of pride to his courtiers'), he had even begun to choose his own preachers.[29] That Easter, Edward listened intently to the Lenten sermons at court, urging him personally to press on with the Reformation, despite stirrings from the conservatives that 'as long as the King is in his tender age, his council should do nothing in matters of religion'. The Bible itself, one preacher recalled, 'teacheth how a king in his young age, with his wise and godly council, should abolish idolatry and set forth the true and godly religion of the living God. Thus declareth the notable and godly fact of Josiah.' As Edward sat and listened, he was probably noting down every word. As the sermons continued, however, their message became increasingly uncomfortable to the ears of the council, and when Edward's chaplain preached against the heavy grants of land that had been made in his reign, comparing the nobility to a sponge, 'to suck continually until it be full ... take those greedy sponges and to wrest out all the moisture again', he was arrested immediately and thrown into the Fleet prison.[30]

Not all believed that such blatant posturings of Edward's godliness was genuine, with the Imperial ambassador insisting that the council was merely putting words into the boy's mouth: 'Whence it may be feared that the King's natural goodness will be perverted, and that unless some singular grace of Heaven be dispensed to him he will never learn to aspire to things which he has never learnt to know.' The evidence suggests to the contrary; even Bishop Gardiner, when shown Edward's notes upon sermons, 'showing me how the King's highness used to note every notable sentence, and specially if it touched a king', was convinced of his abilities. Edward's other writings, as discussed below, further suggest that he was fully in control of his developing religious opinions.[31] From April 1550, Edward ordered that regular preaching be extended to weekly sermons, possibly having been influenced by John Hooper's sermon that Easter which urged that 'seeing there is in the year 8,730 hours, it shall not be much for your highness, nor for all your household, to bestow of them 52 in the year to hear'.[32] 'Believe me,' one reformer wrote in March, 'you have never seen in the world for these thousand years so much erudition united with piety and sweetness of disposition. Should he live and grow up with these virtues, he will be a terror to all the sovereigns of the earth. He receives with his own hand a copy of every sermon that he hears, and most diligently requires an account of them after dinner from those who study with him.'[33] And the iconic woodcut in John Foxe's *Acts and Monuments* of Edward listening from his chamber window to Latimer preaching from the pulpit in the Privy Chamber garden in 1549, together with the record of the king's own frequent payments to preachers, suggests that Edward was more than a keen participant in the ideas of reformed religion; he was becoming an integral character in the shaping of the religious atmosphere at court, and therefore the nation at large.

For the reformers, Edward's abilities were never in doubt. Martin Bucer, now resident in Cambridge, thought Edward 'learned to a miracle', being well acquainted with Latin, having 'a fair knowledge' of Greek and also able to speak Italian and French. Edward's studies included Cicero and Aristotle, 'but no study delights him more than that of the Holy Scriptures, of which he daily reads about ten chapters with the greatest attention'. Bucer was probably being fed his information from Martin Micronius, a minister from the newly erected Stranger Church in London, set up for exiled European Protestants, who had Cranmer's full support, the latter writing to him on 20 May that, 'Our King is a youth of such godliness as to be a wonder to the whole world. He orders all things for the advancement of God's glory. He has on every Lord's day a sermon such as he used to have during Lent. I wish the bishops and nobility were inflamed with the like zeal.'[34]

How much of this was true? Admiration for the king's abilities was inextricably bound up with the reformer's own vision of Edward as a sort of new Josiah or Constantine 'exerting all his power for the restoration of Christ's kingdom'. The image of a godly king 'truly holy ... inflamed with so much zeal' was to be held up as evidence of divine favour towards the Reformation that Edward literally embodied: 'wherefore we must entreat God with most fervent prayers very long to preserve him to the kingdom and to the church.' If Edward was held up as the model of godliness, he was also a beacon of light in a world of perceived darkness, 'carnal liberty and spiritual bondage' – a model and example to all. Even in the classroom, a schoolmaster found that by exhorting 'the godly example of so virtuous a Prince,' he was able to 'wrought more in the heads of his unwilling scholars, for their furtherance unto good literature, than all his travail among them in one year past'.[35]

Yet beneath the image of Edward as the godly reformer lay a tension that was to characterize Edward's kingship. Whilst the reformers looked forward to their young Josiah becoming 'the wonder and terror of the world', the aristocracy and the old world at court still expected him to act the Renaissance king and bear majesty with matching splendour and physical courage. There was, of course, no reason why he might not continue to act out both roles. It is telling that the Privy Garden in which Edward listened to sermons on Sundays could be transformed into an arena both for bear-baiting and wrestling matches. The reformers attempted to keep their cherished project on the straight and narrow – Latimer had urged Edward in 1549 not to follow the example of his father in taking too many wives (which, he explained, 'causes much whoredom and divorcing') and owning too many horses, whilst a new preacher to the scene, the young and energetic Thomas Lever, implored him to avoid the company of young noblemen such as Barnaby Fitzpatrick and Henry Suffolk, whose scribbles and attempts at practising their signatures can still be found today in the margins of Edward's schoolwork. Yet Edward did not listen, and remained a normal adolescent who enjoyed riding, hunting and watching sports. Like his father, Edward seems to have been an inveterate gambler, losing a tilting wager of ten yards of black velvet to his Privy Chamber gentleman Sir Thomas Wroth and racketing up the princely sum of £143 17d as 'money lost in play' – either at shooting, tennis, cards or chess.[36]

In fact, as will be shown later, Edward retained much of the values of material splendour and physical prowess that had surrounded his father's court, which were indeed a crucial part of Edward's personality and royal identity. Like Henry, Edward wore nothing but the finest clothes, including 'a square cape of crimson velvet and crimson satin all over embroidered with ... damask gold and silver having a rich border ... pearl faced with crimson satin all over' with twenty-one diamonds set in buttons of gold on the sleeves, and twenty-four prized skins including one of sable elaborately decorated 'with a head of gold contained in it a clock with a collar of gold enamelled black set with four diamonds and four rubies and with two pearls hanging at the ears and two rubies in the eyes' with its 'feet of gold the claws thereof being sapphires'.[37]

It seems that, for the moment at least, Edward began to enjoy the newfound freedoms that Dudley had allowed him, and the summer was spent in pastime and entertainment. After a peace treaty with France had been concluded in March, it was agreed that six hostages should be exchanged as guarantors of the peace. The young lords who had grown up at Edward's court departed to France, whilst in their place Edward received some older playmates, including the impressive Francois de Vendome, Vidame of Chartres, whose influence upon Edward was quickly noticed by the Imperial ambassador: 'He takes him away from his books and his master's lessons, saying to him: "What need has your Majesty of so many books?" And he leads him away to play.'[38]

Certainly Edward's diary entries for the summer suggest that the French ambassadors' visit in May captivated his imagination. Excitedly, Edward wrote how he had watched 'a pastime of ten against ten at the ring', baiting of 'bears and bulls' the next evening, followed by two days of hunting. On 29 May Somerset hosted a banquet in their honour; afterwards they 'went into the Thames and saw both the bear hunted in the river and also wildfire cast out of boats, and many pretty conceits' including tilting between French, English, Italian and Spanish gentlemen that lasted three hours.[39] Two days later Edward was invited to dine at Deptford, where before the meal, Edward watched 'certain men stand upon the end of a boat without hold of anything and ran one at another until one was cast into the water'. Then after supper, Edward vividly described in great detail how he watched a mock siege upon the Thames in which 'clods, squibs, canes of fire, darts ... and bombards assaulted the castle' beating down its walls and sinking a ship 'out of which all the men in it, being more than twenty, leaped out and swam in the Thames'. Writing to the emperor, the ambassador Scheyfve had observed Edward 'very much pleased and amused' by the entire spectacle, adding: 'They say he has a natural liking and taste for all sorts of warlike sports.'[40]

In accordance with the reformers' best expectations, Edward did take up his position as Defender of the Faith. Given Edward's growing interest in the tilt and the hunt, it is perhaps entirely appropriate that Edward's first involvement in religious matters was in that paragon of chivalric expression, the Order of the Garter. The problem of the Order, aside from its similarity to the many thousands of guilds that the government had ordered to be destroyed two years before, was its association with the chivalric ethos of St George. Under Edward's direction, this was about to change. On St George's Day, celebrated by the Order with service and feast, Edward came down into the presence chamber after listening to the sermon preached at court, demanding to know why the Order worshipped a saint. William Paulet volunteered a somewhat unsatisfactory answer, attempting to impress the king with tales of St George's feats in slaying the dragon, but his best efforts only left Edward in fits of laughter.[41]

Behind Edward's ridiculing of the saint lay a serious concern. As an international association, it was necessary that the Order send out the right message about the nature of England's Reformation and the royal supremacy. By the end of the year, Edward had personally resolved to revise its statutes, eradicating all mention of the former royal saint. Edward's successive drafts reveal the strength of his evangelical beliefs. At first he wished to rename the Order for the 'defence of the truth wholly contained in scripture' with the badge for its members to wear being a picture of himself in full representation of his position as supreme head: 'a king graven, holding in one hand a sword and in the other a book, and upon the sword shall be written *Justitia* [justice] and upon the book VERBUM DEI [the word of God]', though after considering alternative designs that included a shield with a red cross upon a white background with the words 'Scutum fidei [shield of faith]' upon the reverse, the final result was an anonymous armed knight on horseback, no doubt much to Edward's frustration. Believing that the 'serpent Satan' had stuffed the statutes 'with doubtfulness and contraries, perverted with super-stitiousness and idolatry, and finally almost destroyed it with bringing in of popery and naughtiness', Edward's early plans seem to have been to turn the Order into an international league against idolatry, the oath for all members to swear reading: 'Will you refuse the bishops of Rome's authority, and fight in your country's cause against him and his erroneous and pestilent heresies?'

More tantalizing are Edward's brief reflections upon the communion, which he considered was 'wholly contained in God's word'. On several occasions, Edward began to consider its very nature, changing its name to 'the supper of our Lord' and striking out the title given by the 1549 Prayer Book, 'the holy communion commonly called the mass'. Edward clearly held hang-ups against any relics of a Catholic past, but was he already turning his back upon the 1549 Prayer Book? Another statement that communion was 'the faithful remembrance of Christ's death, which was once offered up for all, and dwelleth not in man's temples' suggests just that; Edward's beliefs were forming into a coherent whole, anticipating future religious reform.[42]

We should perhaps not read too much into Edward's first formative foray into the complexities of Reformation theology. On the question of the real or spiritual presence in the bread and wine, his defaced jottings reveal Edward was less sure about what he exactly believed. For him, the Lord's Supper was 'the faithful remembrance of Christ's death', yet he drew back from adding the phrase 'and his body and his blood spiritually by some mystery', probably in fear of being mistaken of favouring the real presence.

The first test of Edward's own convictions came in early summer with the case of the heretic Joan Bocher, the wife of a London butcher who had long troubled Cranmer with her Anabaptist views.[43] Despite her imprisonment and formal excommunication, Joan refused to recant her beliefs. Edward recalled how she had been arrested a year earlier, 'but kept in hope of conversion'. On 30 April one last attempt was made to make her see reason, but she refused. 'It was not so long ago that you burned Anne Ayscough for a piece of bread,' she told Cranmer, 'yet came yourself to believe the doctrine for which you burned her.'[44] After much procrastination, a final decision was taken to send her to the flames. This Edward refused to countenance, and despite his tutor Cheke's persuasions, 'all the council could not move him to put his hand' to the warrant. Eventually Cranmer was called in, 'yet neither could he, with much labour, induce the king so to do'. 'What, my lord?' Edward reasoned, 'will ye have me send her quick to the devil in her error?' Cranmer later confessed that 'he had never so much to do in all his life, as to cause the king to put to his hand'. The matter was resolved only when the archbishop agreed to Edward's demands that 'he would lay all the charge thereof upon Cranmer before God'. On 2 May 1550 Joan burned at the stake. For Edward, it was perhaps little consolation to learn that she 'reviled' the preacher John Scory at the pyre with 'raging and railing'.[45]

Joan's burning was to go down as a landmark in Edward's reign, for despite Somerset's legislation to ban the burning of heretics, it was a clear sign that the period of 'warmer weather' had drawn to a close. Indeed, Joan's case should be viewed in the context of growing instability and real fears that a repeat of the commotions of the previous year was about to take place. In April Edward noted in his diary that 'certain were taken that went about to have an insurrection in Kent upon May Day following, and the priest who was the chief worker ran away into Essex . . .' leading to the execution of two men at Ashford and one at Canterbury.[46] In Hampshire 'certain sorcerers' were arrested for attempts 'to consume certain of the chiefest rulers' whilst perhaps more worryingly, a former rebel, Captain Red Cap, had been released from prison in Middlesex to a warm reception by the commons who 'feasted him'.[47] In Norfolk, men looked back to the previous summer upon Mousehold Heath with fondness. 'It was a merry world when we were yonder eating of mutton,' the fisherman John Oldman recalled, while one John White was over-heard remarking that he hoped to have 'as hot a summer as ever was, and as evil and busy a one as the last summer was'. The conditions were certainly ripe for the spread of sedition, for in London the annual rate of inflation was 21 per cent; as the price of flour doubled, the size of a half-penny loaf of bread, the staple diet for many of the poor, shrank drastically, leaving those embittered to fondly reminisce on their champion Robert Kett, who had 'trusted to see a new day for such men as I was'.[48]

By June, the Imperial ambassador had heard news that ten thousand peasants had gathered near Sittingbourne. While this figure was no doubt wildly exaggerated, there were other reports that 'a conspiracy amongst the commons' was planned for Whit Monday, leading to a search through-out the county for 'vagabonds, gypsies, conspirators, prophesiers, all players and such like'.[49] It was only a matter of time, the ambassador warned, until the peasants' granaries were filled, 'they will then rise, as the promises that were made to them have been empty and fruitless . . . that the gentry seize their lands, or at any rate the lands that used to provide them with means of livelihood; that they have doubled the price of land and made them pay rent for last year, when the soil was not cultivated, so that many are dying of want'.[50]

The response of the council was prompt. Sir William Herbert was dispatched to Wales to subdue the 'inconstant disposition of the com-mons' and Russell to Exeter. Letters were dispatched to Justices ordering them to remain on high alert, and a reward of £20 was to be offered to informers with reports of those attempting to raise rebellion. A proclamation in May ordering vagabonds out of London and to 'get themselves home again ... into their native counties' was followed in June by an order to all officers to depart to their commands under severe penalty. Edward noted on 20 June that the mayor had 'caused the watches to be increased every night because of the great frays' and an alderman had been appointed 'to see good rule kept every night', and by July all discharged soldiers were ordered to leave London upon pain of imprisonment. Edward himself was not immune from the concern, recording in his diary how there had been 'a privy search made through all Sussex for all vagabonds, gypsies, conspirators, prophets, ill players, and such-like' and how there had been discovered 'certain in Essex about Romford [who] went about a conspiracy, which were taken and the matter stayed'.[51] The following day he was moved out of the capital to Greenwich for his own safety.

The same month Somerset was commissioned to maintain order in Oxfordshire, Sussex, Hampshire and Wiltshire, departing to Reading on 6 August, whilst Dudley's planned journey into the north to take up his command along the Scottish border was called off because of 'urgent considerations'. Relations between the two had been cordial since the duke's release, with the Imperial ambassador observing that they were again 'in close communication, visiting each other everyday'.[52] Soon it was reported that Somerset was being treated with 'great respect' by men at court; no one could doubt, as the Imperial ambassador remarked, that Somerset had been fully 'reinstated in honour and pre-eminence'.

By the summer, relations between Somerset and Dudley had repaired to the extent that a marriage had been arranged between Dudley's son Lord Lisle and Somerset's daughter Anne, to be celebrated at Somerset's residence at Sheen on 3 June. Plans had been discussed since January, probably by the two mothers. Edward himself attended the ceremony, giving the bride a ring worth £40 as a wedding present. After dinner and dancing, from 'chambers made of boughs' he watched two teams of six gentlemen running the length of a field twice over. Afterwards there were masques organized by the Frenchman Vidame where he 'entertained the ladies bravely'.[53]

What was remarkable was that Dudley had decided to miss his own son's wedding, travelling instead to Hatfield at least three days before the marriage. Others suspected foul play, with one account relating that Dudley had avoided the wedding since he 'suspected he should have been betrayed there'.[54] The truth was that the cracks had already begun to open up in his recently patched-up relationship with Somerset, who had been sounding out conservative support in order to bolster his position at court. It is noteworthy that Somerset's return to the political arena had coincided with the council's grudging acceptance to attempt a reconciliation with Stephen Gardiner, still imprisoned in the Tower. On 8 June Somerset visited him there, offering him pardon on condition that he accepted the 1549 Prayer Book, which Gardiner readily accepted, though he admitted he 'would not have made it so myself'.[55] This was good enough for Somerset, but not for Dudley, who was insistent that Gardiner apologize for his 'notorious and apparent contempt' and dug his heels in, arguing that the bishop should sign a deliberately provocative confession of his guilt. When the new charges were laid before him at a new meeting – this time with Dudley present – Gardiner was adamant that no apology would be given: 'I should sooner ... tumble myself desperately into the Thames'.[56]

Amidst this confusion and disagreement, Dudley confronted Somerset's servant Richard Whalley over his master's recent overtures to Gardiner and the conservatives. Evidently distressed at Somerset's conduct and showing 'most plainly the inward grief of his heart with not a few tears', Dudley railed against Somerset for his 'lack of good consideration in the order of his proceedings' for it seemed that the duke was aspiring 'to have the self and same overdue an authority to the despatch and direction of the proceedings as his Grace had, being Protector'. 'What meaneth my Lord in this wise to discredit himself?' Dudley implored. 'Why will he not see his own decay herein? Thinks he to rule and direct the whole council as he will, considering how his late governance is yet misliked?' If Somerset thought that his close relationship with Edward would ensure his position, Dudley urged Whalley to make him see otherwise: 'Neither is he in that credit and best opinion with the King's Majesty, as he believeth, and is by some fondly persuaded.' Dudley was probably right. Edward had been furious over Gardiner's disobedience, writing in his diary how 'I marveled that he would not put his hand to the confession'; Somerset's support for Gardiner's freedom must have driven a wedge between Edward and his uncle, for it would soon become apparent in the case of his sister Mary that the bond of faith mattered more to the king than any family ties. This Dudley had the perspicacity to realize; by throwing his lot in with the reformers, he was only following the course that Edward himself had chosen to take. Yet Dudley knew that factionalism amongst a divided council and the

'No painting ever boasted greater': Holbein's mural of Henry VIII, whose puffed-up poise next to his father Henry VII created the iconic image that defined Henry's reign. On the other side of the monument, a demure Jane Seymour beside Henry's mother Elizabeth is barely noticeable.

The image of royal supremacy: Henry through Holbein's eyes.

The reality: by the time Edward was born, years of over-indulgence and persistent injury had left Henry prematurely aged, barely able to walk.

PARVVLE PATRISSA, PATRIÆ VIRTVTIS ET HÆRES
  ESTO, NIHIL MAIVS MAXIMVS ORBIS HABET.
GNATVM VIX POSSVNT COELVM ET NATVRA DEDISSE,
  HVIVS QVEM PATRIS, VICTVS HONORET HONOS.
ÆQVATO TANTVM, TANTI TV FACTA PARENTIS,
  VOTA HOMINVM, VIX QVO PROGREDIANTVR, HABENT
VINCITO, VICISTI. QVOT REGES PRISCVS ADORAT
  ORBIS, NEC TE QVI VINCERE POSSIT, ERIT.   Ricard Morysini Car—

ttle one, emulate thy father and be the heir of his virtue': even as a baby, the young Edward was
ady being prepared for greatness.

) Jane Seymour's fierce loyalty to the Tudor regime and determination to provide Henry with
nale heir more than made up for her plain looks.

As this cameo makes clear, Henry was a devoted father to his son – when he could spare the time.

Edward's early childhood was one of carefree abandon. Here he is seen playing with a pet monkey that possibly belonged to Henry's fool, Will Somers.

Henry Howard, Earl of Surrey. Foolish, vain and unstable, his attempts to control a dying Henry cost him his life. It was argued in his trial that this picture – the broken pillar supposedly representing the Tudor commonwealth – proved his designs upon the crown.

Sir John Cheke, the Cambridge scholar who became Edward's tutor – and one of his greatest influences – in 1544

Edward at Ashridge house. The pose is deliberately reminiscent of his father's. Little could he have known that he would be king within a year.

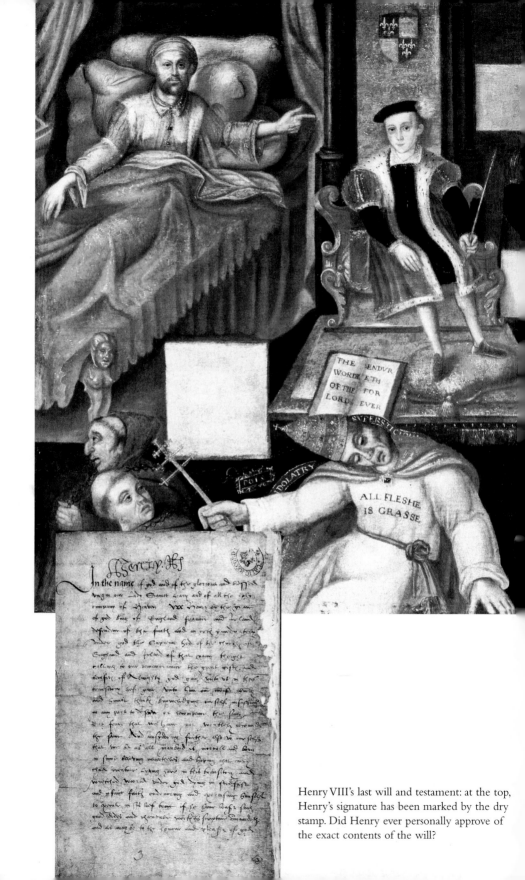

Henry VIII's last will and testament: at the top, Henry's signature has been marked by the dry stamp. Did Henry ever personally approve of the exact contents of the will?

In this allegory of Edward's reign, painted during Elizabeth's reign, a dying Henry points towards the future of the Tudor dynasty. Edward's council look on as beneath Edward, the Pope is crushed by the word of God. Outside, images are being torn down. The blank spaces were probably left to insert commentary.

'Remember what you promised me . . .' William Paget, Henry VIII's private secretary and the political brain behind Somerset's seizure of power. Dubbed the 'master of practises', Paget ruthlessly deserted Somerset during the coup d'état that brought him down in October 1549.

Edward Seymour, Duke of Somerset and Edward's uncle; he was appointed Lord Protector within days of Henry's death, despite Henry's original wish that the kingdom be ruled by a council of equals.

Edward

Edward's signature: under the influence of his tutor Roger Ascham, Edward developed a calligraphic hand similar to that of his sister Elizabeth.

Edward on the cusp of manhood. This portrait was sent to the French court in 1552.

Princess Mary, Edward's elder half-sister and daughter of Katherine of Aragon and Henry VIII. Her stubborn refusal to adhere to the religious changes of the Edwardian reformation frequently brought her at loggerheads with her younger brother.

teenage Princess Elizabeth, Edward's half-sister and daughter of Anne Boleyn and Henry VIII. Here ...e stands in front of the curtains of her bed-chamber – perhaps where Sir Thomas Seymour came upon ...er 'bare-legged'.

Of person rare strong limbes & manly shape,
of nature framed to serue on seas & lande
of Frindshipe firm in good state & ill happe
in peace hedde and in warre skill greate bould hande
on horse on fote in perill or in playe
none coulde excel though many did asaye
A subiecte true to Kinge & seruant greate
frind to Gods truth & enimye to romes deceite
Sumptuos abroad for honnor of the lande
temperate at home yet keepte great state
and gaue more mouthes more meate
then some aduanst one higher steps to stand
yet against nature reason & iust lawes
his bloud was spilt iustless weut iust cause

Thomas Seymour, Somerset's younger brother, who grew increasingly bitter at his success.
s attempts to win Edward's favour ended in disaster – and his eventual execution.

i) Katherine Parr, Henry VIII's sixth wife, who married Sir Thomas Seymour shortly after the
ng's death. A keen reformer, she was close to both Edward and Elizabeth.

Thomas Cranmer, Archbishop of Canterbury and the architect of the Edwardian Reformation.

An allegory of Edward's reign, from John Foxe's *Acts and Monuments*, 1570. As images burn, Catholics flee to the continent with their relics. Edward can be seen in the bottom left corner, delivering a bible to his subjects.

John Dudley, later Duke of Northumberland. His Machiavellian scheming saw Somerset deposed as Protector and his rivals swept aside.

Thomas Wriothesley, Earl of Southampton. A conservative opponent of Somerset's regime, his attempts to win power in the winter of 1549 were crushed by Dudley's ruthless manoeuvrings.

A woodcut from Foxe's *Acts and Monuments* showing Hugh Latimer preaching from a pulpit before the court and Edward, who can be seen in the top left window.

A seventeenth-century woodcut of the Duke of Somerset's execution on Tower Hill. As the crowds look on, the executioner holds up the severed head.

below) The frontispiece of the controversial 1549 Book of Common Prayer, which received universal disdain from Protestants and Catholics alike. Here, Edward can be seen as the archetypal model of kingship, taking advice from his council.

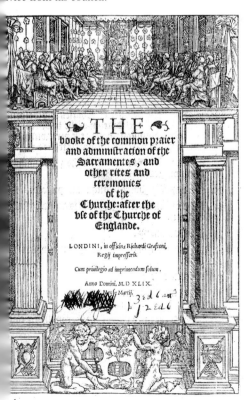

Edward VI opening Parliament in March 1553. Though formulaic, the drawing gives an impression of Edward's maturity.

For lakke of 1551 of my body. To the L Fran
ceses heires masles, and her to the
L Janes heires masles, To the L katerins heires
masles, To the L Maries heires masles, To
the heires masles of the daughters which she
she shal haue hereafter. Then to the L Mar
gets heires masles. for lakke of such issu,
To theires masles of the L Janes daughters
To theires masles of the katerins daughters
and so forth til yow come to the L mar
gets daughters heires masles.

Edward's 'devise for the succession'. Altered to allow Jane to accede to the throne, the crucial change is in line four, where 'L Janes heires masles' becomes 'L Jane and her heires masles'.

Jane Grey
QUEEN of ENGLAND
Proclaimed
on 10 July, 1553,
Executed
on 12 Feb, 1554.

Lady Jane Grey; Edward's ill-fated cousin who was suddenly propelled into becoming England's shortest-reigning monarch. An engraving from a painting presumed lost.

threat of a repeat of the stand-off that had taken place the previous October would be in no one's best interests. For now, Somerset had received his first warning; by 'taking private ways by himself, and attempting such perilous causes', Dudley told Whalley, 'he will so far overthrow himself as shall pass the power of his friends to recover'.[57] Whether Somerset chose to listen would be another matter.

Somerset's manoeuvrings were not the only problem Dudley and the council faced. Mary had remained in a heightened state of anxiety since Dudley's rise to power, and was probably all too aware that it would only be a matter of time before the council prohibited her household from hearing mass. This indulgence, the council quite justifiably claimed, was being abused, since Mary had felt it her duty to provide mass for everyone and anyone who came to her house seeking it. By the middle of April the council resolved to limit the service to the servants of her chamber. Warned by a friend that this would soon be the case, Mary summoned the Imperial ambassador der Delft at the end of April to her residence at Woodham Walter, near Maldon, Essex.

She asked Van der Delft what she should do, but it was quickly obvious to him that she had already settled upon her course of action. 'They are wicked and wily in their actions, and particularly malevolent towards me, I must not wait till the blow falls,' she told him.[58] There could be no more delays. With the emperor's assistance, she must leave the country. Van der Delft was hesitant. What if Edward were to die? Her absence would deprive her not only of the Crown, but also 'religion would be set aside for good without any hope of mending it'. 'If my brother were to die, I should be far better out of the kingdom,' she insisted, 'because as soon as he were dead, before the people knew it, they would despatch me too.' She hoped the emperor would not leave things too late: 'I fear I may tarry too long; and if the Council were possessed of the same foresight that the late King my father had, I should be too late now even to save myself.' As she imagined what might happen – first she would be ordered inland away from any port, then deprived of her servants, reducing her to 'utmost destitution'; 'they will deal with me as they please' – Mary grew increasingly hysterical and confused – if she left, what would happen to her household? 'But if in your opinion I had better go,' she turned to Van der Delft, by now no doubt baffled that Mary had now managed to persuade herself that the idea had been his in the first place, 'so be it in God's name, for I know no danger in going that will not be as great or even greater at any other time.'[59]

Van der Delft was in a difficult position. Previously, he had told the emperor, he had always dissuaded her from thoughts of escape, fearing 'that the good lady through her own incompetence might fall into a worse evil'.[60] Now he considered that she be 'evacuated' as swiftly as possible. Once she was safe, then the 'righteous' might be encouraged to rise on her behalf. About to be recalled on grounds of his own ill health, he prepared a plan of escape. If the time and route were planned correctly Mary might join his ship in disguise. Alternatively, a boat might be sent to Maldon for the purpose of trading grain, upon which Mary might escape unnoticed and be taken out to an Imperial ship at anchor off the coast. Over the next month, with the emperor eventually persuaded of its necessity, plans for Mary's escape were finalized with the help of the emperor's sister, Mary of Hungary, who had become deeply involved in the scheme.[61] Preparations were set in place and the timing set for early June, when Van der Delft was to be recalled. To avoid any later accusations of complicity in the scheme, his replacement, Jehan Scheyfve, was told nothing: the agent responsible would be Jehan Dubois, secretary to both Van der Delft and Scheyfve. Meanwhile, Mary moved back to Woodham Walter, two miles from sea, with the excuse that her residence at Beaulieu, a further four miles inland, was in need of cleaning and repair.

Two Imperial warships commanded by one Cornelius Schepperus arrived off the coast of Maldon on 30 June. That same day Dubois, in his guise as a merchant selling grain, reached Harwich. The passage to Maldon was a difficult one, unable to be navigated in the dark, so he left the next morning on a flat calm sea.

Arriving at Maldon on 2 July and with his boat moored at sea, Dubois wrote to Mary's household officer Robert Rochester in 'simple Latin', notifying him of his arrival. His men had brought the corn to town, but had found no one to receive them. He urged Rochester to act fast. Schepperus would soon be arriving with the warship off Stansgate, whilst other ships were waiting ready and prepared. The tides were even in their favour, and would remain high until two o'clock. Now was the time to act: 'By that hour or immediately afterwards all ought to be here.' Any longer delay and they would recede, leaving them in danger of being beached on the grey silt of the riverbank. 'I will sell my corn at once, and will be ready tonight. Please let me know your intentions. There would be danger were there to be many women.'

At this point the sound of his men returning interrupted him in his thoughts. The news was unpromising, for Rochester was being difficult and urged delay. Dubois continued to write: there was no better opportunity than now, yet he was afraid that their cover could be blown at any moment. 'However, I will yield to a better opinion, and I pray God to inspire you now, for the Emperor has done all he could.'

Within the hour Dubois's messenger returned with an answer. Rochester wanted to meet in the secluded graveyard of St Mary's church, under the pretence of bargaining for the corn. Dubois met Rochester there an hour later, who secretly ushered him into a nearby house and into the garden where they paced up and down in conference.

Rochester was getting cold feet. There was, he believed, 'no earthly possibility' of his mistress's escape without great risk. A nightly watch had been posted on every road around her house. Even those within her household 'which was not so free of enemies to her religion as she imagined' could not be trusted. And what pressing reason was there for her to leave? She remained free to live as she liked; her escape would only cause 'a mighty scandal'. Above all, were Edward to die, she would lose her right to the throne. He asked for Dubois's advice, who remarked he was but a 'nobody to advise one way or the other in a matter of so great importance'. Dubois would do whatever Mary commanded and would leave as quietly as he had arrived, though that would astonish him 'beyond measure' given her previous disposition. But if that was to be the case, he would need letters to discharge him of his duty.

Startled, Rochester began to backtrack. 'I beg you do not judge me thus; for I would give my hand to see my Lady out of the country and in safety, and I was the first man to suggest it. And if you understand me, what I say is not that my Lady does not wish to go, but that she wishes to go if she can.' 'The thing is now a question of Yes or No,' Dubois retorted, 'and you have the choice; you must be good enough to make up your mind and be quick about it, if it is to be done at all.' Soon Scepperus's ships would be sighted, risking discovery. As for his talk of the succession, he reminded him that this had been the emperor's own argument against the plan, which Mary herself had dismissed in letters dictated to him.

'You say well,' Rochester replied, seemingly ignorant of Dubois' plea, 'but this is not a matter to be hurried ... and as for what you say of my Lady's words, they were that she wished to stay if she could, but to have all things in readiness.'

'Yes, but you are putting the wrong interpretation on them,' Dubois answered, his frustration seething. His temper was not much improved when Rochester announced that Mary first wished to see him. Refusing for fear of discovery they parted, Rochester departing with one of his servants, promising to send for him when he knew his mistress's intention. Dubois meanwhile continued to go about his business in his guise as merchant, getting customs clearance for his corn, only narrowly avoiding a brush with the local officials when they were told that the cargo had been sold to Mary's household, since they held 'my Lady's grace' in as high esteem as the king himself.

When word finally arrived from Woodham Walter at one o'clock in the morning, Dubois was escorted to the house where he found Mary in agitation, having packed 'some of her property in great long hop-sacks'. Probably wondering with horror how these would assist her in her necessary hasty escape, Dubois 'made so bold as to say that if she once crossed the water she should lack for nothing, and that her effects did not matter so much; the great thing was to bring her person to safety, and that was the point on which she must now make up her mind'.

But Mary was not ready to leave, and requested two more days to prepare. Hand in mouth, Dubois agreed. He now faced significant difficulties that needed to be resolved almost immediately: Schepperus would need to be warned not to arrive that night, instead to withdraw his ships to avoid detection; he himself would need new cover for remaining. Suddenly, however, they were interrupted by Rochester's agent with news that the townsmen were intending to seize Dubois's boat, having become suspicious of the Imperial ships lying off the coast. His requests to take Mary immediately were straight away quashed by Rochester: 'It is impossible, for they are going to double the watch tonight, and, what is more, post men on the church tower, a thing that has never been done before ... all we can do is to see to getting you out of this.' One senses that the entire alarm had been orchestrated by the Comptroller for the purpose of thwarting his mistress's escape; his servant had never turned up at a rendezvous in Antwerp that had been arranged, and he had told Dubois 'he was quite persuaded the King could not outlast the year; for he and others knew his horoscope to say so'. It is clear that Mary was hardly in control of the situation. Her only response to the situation was to repeat endlessly 'What shall I do? What is to become of me?' Eventually deciding to return in ten days time when the alarm had died down, Dubois left to return to his ship, sailing back out to Schepperus's ship at two o'clock that morning.[62]

There would be no further attempt at an escape. On 13 July the council, having discovered news of the plot, were 'greatly scandalised and displeased'. Sending Sir John Gates into Essex with a band of horsemen, as Edward recalled, 'to stop the going away of the Lady Mary, because it was credibly informed that Scipperus should steal her away to Antwerp', five hundred soldiers were further stationed at every port in the area and Somerset, together with Lord Russell, was ordered to prepare a force of eight hundred men to be sent to the coast.[63] The opportunity had been wasted and Mary had squandered the only chance to flee that apparently she had desperately so wished. She now would have to face the consequences of her faith alone.

With Dudley's ascendancy and Edward's growing commitment towards the reformed faith, the year had seen the pace of religious change quicken. Three acts passed through Parliament in January 1550 ordering the suppression of all service books other than the 1549 Prayer Book and Henry VIII's Primer, together with the final destruction of any remaining religious statues: 'All books called antiphoners, missals, scrayles, processionals, manuals ... primers in Latin or English, cowchers, journals ...' and so continued the long list of ancient and priceless works of medieval theology that were to be 'abolished, extinguished and forbidden for ever'. A second law permitting the reform of the Canon Law eventually came to nothing, but the third ushered in a new ordinal, used for the ordination of new priests, but which also set down a new structure for Edward's Church. Replacing the eight orders of the medieval Church, a threefold division into bishops, priests and deacons was instituted. What was most significant, however, was the trans-formation of the role of priest, whose job it had once been to offer sacrifice and divine grace, but now whose primary function was 'to preach the Word of God and to minister the holy sacrament'.

Crucially, the balance of power on the ecclesiastical benches was shifting towards the reformers, as the conservative clergy that had once acted as a brake upon Somerset's early reforms lost seven sees out of twenty-seven through the combination of forced retirements, death and confrontation with a government that now simply refused to compromise. Their replacements were eager to implement reforms in their dioceses. Upon his appointment as Bishop of London, Nicholas Ridley ordered all altars to be taken out of churches and replaced by communion tables, to 'move the simple from the superstitious opinions of the popish mass, unto the right use of the Lord's Supper'.[64] Trouble was avoided by dismantling altars in St Paul's at night, but soon the process was under way everywhere, where spontaneous action on the part of vicars and curates often selling altars as gravestones drew the government ever closer into the web of Reformation.

For some, however, the pace of reform could not go fast enough. One of these enthusiastic evangelicals was John Hooper, who had been imprisoned under Somerset for disobedience but now found himself, as an ally of Dudley's, presented to the see of Gloucester. Yet Hooper had been a harsh critic of the new ordinal, whose oath upon the saints he considered to 'promote the kingdom of Antichrist'.[65] Demanding that he would accept the bishopric only upon the condition that he might dispense with the Episcopal vestments and 'popish ceremony' of the consecration, he began a protracted battle with Cranmer over the issue. Eventually the matter was passed up to Edward himself – a sign of the young king's central role in the Reformation – who sent for Hooper on 20 July, informing him that he would need his Episcopal robes at court – elsewhere, and in his own diocese, he could do as he pleased. After some hesitation, Hooper agreed. They both then went through the service of consecration, until Edward noticed that the last sentence of the oath – 'So help me God, all saints and the holy evangelists' and growing 'much excited' exclaimed: 'What wickedness is here, Hooper? Are these offices ordained in the name of the saints, or of God?' Before Hooper could comment, Edward had struck the offending sentence through with his pen. 'This was a Henry VIII in the making,' one historian has written. 'Seldom has there been a more immediate demonstration of the meaning of the Royal Supremacy in the Tudor Church.'[66]

Two days after stepping in to resolve the crisis with Hooper, Edward left for his summer progress, starting from Greenwich where he crowned Gilbert Dethick Garter King-of-Arms, according to the ancient ritual by pouring a cup of wine over his head. He then travelled to Hampton Court, then to Windsor and Guildford, before travelling back via Oatlands and Woking through to Richmond, returning back to London in October. As his riding and stamina improved, his journeys lengthened, and it was decided, Edward proudly noted, that he would be capable of travelling to Windsor 'in one day'.[67]

At the same time, the instability of the early summer months continued, fuelled by high prices and the anticipation of a poor harvest. The Imperial ambassador reported how a 'great number of staves, batons and ammunition' had been sent to parts of the country. Lord Russell and the Lord Warden Cheyney were dispatched to their counties, as was Dudley, as lieutenant of Warwickshire, 'to enquire of by oaths of good and lawful men of our country'.[68] There were rumours that the earl was to be made the Duke of Gloucester and warden of the North. In fact he had fallen ill, confined to his bed. 'God were more mercifuller unto him,' wrote one courtier, 'if he were restored to his health, for at this present he is very sick and lyeth at Canterbury.'[69]

Dudley's health eventually recovered, but there were even greater challenges to be faced, particularly amongst the conservative Northern nobility, who had taken objection not only to the pace of the Reformation in religion, but also to Bishop Gardiner's treatment. By September Scheyfve reported that a quarrel had broken out between Derby and Shrewsbury against Dudley and William Paget over their local jurisdiction. Together with the Earl of Arundel, both earls had apparently intended to propose in the forthcoming Parliament the strict observance of Henry's will 'on all points, as regards religion and in all other respects, until the present king comes of age'.[70]

In the capital, the government had repeatedly attempted to rid its streets of the soldiers who had loitered there since their demobilization from Boulogne. By September, the City rulers heard that they planned to muster at Finsbury Fields, forming 'several companies in London and come out of several lanes and streets ... and set upon the citizens and their houses and take there such booty and spoil as they can lay hand upon' and vowing that they would 'turn all England up so down at their pleasures'. On 25 September a nightly watch was ordered.[71]

Of all this Edward was probably oblivious. Throughout the summer and autumn months, his journal demonstrates a growing interest in foreign affairs, including the adventures of the pirate Andrea Doria upon the Mediterranean sea.[72] But from the end of October the journal falls strangely quiet. The reason for this was that Edward had fallen gravely ill. Bedridden, his mysterious illness puzzled everyone 'and his recovery was despaired of. Even the physicians had given him up. The news was kept very secret'. On 4 November warrants were issued by the Privy Council for white cloth from Holland, 'to be employed for the King's majesty's use to a little bed for his own lying' and 'one yard of crimson taffeta to be employed about the said little bed'.[73] The reformers hoped and prayed; with Edward's life, the future of the Reformation lay in the balance.

Behind the scenes, news that the king's life was in danger only created greater instability as the rivalry and division between Somerset and Dudley deepened even further. The death of Somerset's mother – Edward's grandmother – became the occasion for new tensions between Somerset and Dudley when the earl refused her the right, as traditionally had been expected of a member of the royal family, to an official period of mourning and a state funeral. Somerset made a cautious objection, which was rejected by the council announcing that 'private men should reserve their own sorrows to their own houses'.[74] The rebuff was a barbed attack upon Somerset's loss of influence and power, which the duke did not take lightly. By early November the Imperial ambassador Scheyfve was reporting that 'There are deep causes of discord among the members of the council. Some take Warwick's [Dudley's] side, others my Lord of Somerset's.' Somerset was 'doing his utmost to acquire friends, and especially to win over the people, which he has not tried to do before'. Meanwhile, he had heard from a 'safe source' that Dudley was about to 'cast off his wife' to marry Elizabeth, with whom he had been having 'several secret and intimate personal communications' – 'by these means he will aspire to the crown,' he added.[75]

While the ambassador's reports turned out to be exaggerations, they had been coloured by the uncertainty surrounding the king's health. By the end of November this had improved enough that Edward had returned to his studies, and even had time to enquire after the French reformer Jean Calvin's health in whose teachings he had begun to take 'a great interest'.

With Edward's health restored, stability returned to the corridors of power, and by December any discord between Somerset and Dudley seems to have been resolved. This was in everyone's best interest, the English ambassador at Brussels Sir John Mason told William Cecil, for their new concord made him 'rejoice even at the bottom of my heart; for in so doing consisteth their own healths, and the upright administration of the commonwealth'.[76] To many, however, Somerset had become a different character. The Duchess of Suffolk had written to Cecil in October complaining of Somerset's 'ingratitude' over a suit of her cousin's. 'I could blame my lady [the Duchess of Somerset] for my lord's fault,' she added in a postscript, 'but I think he has been warned too late to fall again into that evil.'[77] The reformers detected a change in Somerset's commitment to the gospel. He 'had become so lukewarm in the service of Christ as scarcely to have anything less at heart than the state of religion in this country'.[78] Yet his old followers continued their attempts to persuade him to act the 'good' duke. William Gray, a servant of Somerset's, wrote to him with advice in the form of a New Year's gift. Sensing that 'the papists be rank on the treble hand ... But never more lustier then they are now' he urged Somerset to 'further God's word as much as you may' and

> Remember poor suitors who doth sustain great wrong
> Speak & dispatch them, they busy too long
> They be deferred from morrow to morrow
> Their silly poor hearts like to break for sorrow
> Yet come from them daily to know the lords pleasure
> Their answer is made 'The lords be not at leisure'
> They walk up and down at the chamber door
> Make room for the rich, and keep back the poor.[79]

Even if Somerset had wanted to, it seems as if he would have been hard pressed to distance himself from the 'commonwealth men' whose attitudes and ideas he had so disastrously followed. Others were sceptical that Somerset would ever forgive the wrongs inflicted upon him. His friend Richard Morison was confident that the duke would 'not forget good turns so lately done to him', telling Sir Nicholas Throckmorton that 'imprisonment and such a throng of faults forgiven him would have made him a new heart if his old had been anything set upon revenging'. Throckmorton disagreed, and was adamant that Somerset would be unable to forgive those that had brought him down.[80]

With Edward fully recovered, the pace of religious change quickened. The destruction of altars that had taken place earlier in the year now became official, and in November letters were sent to bishops ordering them 'to pluck down the altars' and in their place to erect communion tables. Those that refused to enforce the instructions were sent to the Fleet prison. Elsewhere there was reluctant obedience; the curate Robert Parkyn, blaming 'Edward Seymour and the Earl of Warwick [Dudley], two cruel tyrants and enemies to God and holy Church', reported that altars were removed 'from Trent northwards' in December, whilst in Winchester conservatives argued this new step had been orchestrated by the king's wicked advisers: 'But when he cometh once of age, he will see another rule, and hang up an hundred of such heretic knaves!'[81]

This new burst of reform was matched by an equally uncompromising stance upon Mary's right to hear mass in her household, which she claimed to have been promised to her by Somerset. Throughout December tensions between Mary and the council had continued to mount, with their exchanges following the familiar pattern of accusation and denial. Now the council sought to target her chaplains, issuing warrants for their arrest for practising mass. Mary refused to serve them – claiming that she had no idea of their whereabouts – which prompted a lengthy rebuke from the council that read more like a Protestant sermon. Matters did not improve at Christmas when Mary paid a visit to court, only to be confronted by Edward himself who challenged her to admit the truth – had she been allowing her household to hear mass? After attempts to explain her situation failed, Mary burst into tears, the sight of which caused Edward himself to weep, asking Mary to dry her tears 'saying he thought no harm of me'.

Mary departed with the impression that all was resolved, and felt confident enough to reel off a letter to the council two weeks later, in spite of suffering from an 'attack of catarrh in the head', stoutly reminding them again of their promise that she be allowed to practise mass in her own household: 'God knows the contrary to be the truth, and you in your own consciences know it also.'[82] She pledged her full support to Edward but was hardly veiled in her antipathy towards the council whom, owing nothing 'beyond amity and good-will', she castigated for their changes in religion, 'desiring that all may be left as the late King his father left it, until his Majesty has reached the age to judge for himself' and ending curtly: 'Take this as my final answer to any letters you might write to me on matters of religion.'

But of course this could never be the case, for the situation had grown too serious to be left alone, with the council's lenience and Mary's disobedience setting a poor example towards Edward's subjects who had been forced to accept religious reform wholesale – why should the princess be treated any differently? Yet Mary could hardly have expected what was to follow when a letter from Edward himself, partly written in his own hand, arrived on 28 January 1551. Its contents shook Mary to the core, for it shattered the mainstay of her argument that she had held on to for so long, that Edward was simply too young to understand complicated religious doctrine, and was instead being the victim of the persuasions of his evil councillors.

In fact, Edward's response proved how wrong Mary had been to underestimate her brother. It is from about this time that a change in the council's stance towards Mary can be detected; previously they had seemed content to allow the dispute to rumble on, but now a new sense of urgency filled the air. From now on there was to be no compromise, for Edward had taken a personal interest in the affair – perhaps prompted by Mary's visit to court the previous month – and was no longer happy to let the matter lie.

'Knowledge was offered to you, and you refused it,' Edward wrote damningly, drawing on his own limited experience within the classroom: 'We might ourselves chide you for this; for we acquire knowledge daily in our schooling, and we learn those things we have no knowledge of, nor are permitted to say ... we will not learn them because we do not believe them to be good.' Though she was his sister, he told her, he would not tolerate the abuse of his office as king:

> We have suffered it until now, with the hope that some improvement might be forthcoming, but of none has been shown, how can we suffer it longer to continue? It is our duty to watch over the welfare of each one of our subjects as each ought to watch over himself. You would be angry to see one of the servants of your household, of those nearest to you, openly disregarding your orders; and so it is with us, and you must reflect that in our estate it is most grievous to suffer that so high a subject should disregard our laws. Your near relationship to us, your exalted rank, the conditions of the times, all magnify your offence. It is a scandalous thing that so high a personage should deny our sovereignty; that our sister should be less to us than any of our other subjects is an unnatural example; and finally, in a troubled republic, it lends colour to faction among the people.[83]

He admitted he was young but he knew – and would have done six years ago – when a subject was breaking his law. And despite his age, he was adamant that he had been invested with the same authority as their father had, 'without diminution of any sort, either culled from the Scriptures or drawn from universal laws'. 'Do you not understand that of necessity this must trouble us?' Edward pleaded, demanding Mary 'correct' her behaviour with the implicit, but nevertheless real, threat: 'Our natural love for you is great without doubt; therefore do not seek to diminish it.'

Mary was stunned, writing back somewhat hysterically to her brother that his words 'have caused me more suffering than any illness even unto death'. Protesting her loyalty, still she clung to the promise that she might hear mass alone. She did not deny that Edward was 'indeed gifted with understanding far beyond that possessed by others at your age', but she begged him to weigh up both sides of the question and suspend any judgement on spiritual matters 'until you reach riper and fuller years, and then with better knowledge and understanding your Majesty will exercise your freedom to decide'.[84]

What Mary simply failed to grasp was that Edward had already made up his mind. And no one, not even his royal sister, would persuade him to change it.

9

HIDDEN CONSPIRACIES

In desperation, Mary did all that she could think of. On 30 January 1551 – the same day that she replied to Edward – she sent another letter hastily scrawled on a half-sheet of paper to Francesco Moronelli, a former servant of the late Van der Delft (who had died after returning to the Netherlands) who had travelled in secret to Newhall to visit the princess. Once she had made Moronelli promise that if she were ever in trouble, he would travel to Flanders to tell the emperor's ministers that help was urgently needed. Now she wrote in panic: 'Francisco, you must make great haste concerning the message, for since your departure I have received worse and more dangerous letters than ever before from the King himself . . . I request and command you to burn this note directly after you have read it.'[1]

Hearing of the news, the Imperial ambassadors went into diplomatic overdrive, demanding that the promise that had once been made be honoured. Yet Mary and her ambassadors failed to realize that with a new player on board, the rules of the game had changed. Their pleas now faced a stony silence from the council. Three years had elapsed since the original promise, countered Dudley. 'Though the King was young in feeling and knowledge,' William Paget added defensively, 'he already wished to understand and take a share in the State affairs of his kingdom.' There was little that the ambassadors could say or do; they were hardly in a position to deny Edward's growing independence, and when Scheyfve finally hinted this, the council branded him 'a man much unbroken and rude' and he was thrown out of the council chamber.

It was under these circumstances that Mary decided to resort to her tactics of December and confront Edward in person. Meanwhile, there had been reports that Elizabeth had been favourably received at court in a deliberate demonstration of favour 'to show the people how much glory belongs to her who has embraced the religion and is become a very great lady'.[2] Edward himself had welcomed her warmly, dining with her on Epiphany, the highest court ceremony of the whole year. Later they watched bear-baiting together, where Elizabeth appeared more like a consort than his half-sister.

Mary's visit was a gamble. She herself recognized the danger, fearing that she would be arrested at court and forced to embrace the new religion, but it seemed a risk worth taking. As she arrived at the city gates on 15 March the enthusiasm of the people who came out into the streets in droves to welcome her cheered her spirits, though the absence of the council to greet her seemed ominous.

Mary had a point to make, and she knew exactly how it needed making. She had gone too far to pull back from her demands of religious freedom; whether she truly believed her own words to the Imperial ambassadors that she would die for her faith, it was too late to flee the realm to safety. So as she rode into London, accompanied by fifty knights wearing velvet coats and chains of gold and followed by her train of around four hundred gentlemen and ladies, she had made sure that each one held aloft 'a pair of beads of black' – their rosaries, as badges of their faith. The symbolism must have been immediately recognized by those who looked on as she made her way through the capital, but the stunt was much more than an exercise in public relations. For Mary's followers were also her retainers, men and women who had pledged their allegiance – and their lives – to their mistress. Their presence was a visual demonstration of Mary's private power, which she now intended to show in force; in terms of lands and wealth, she was the fifth wealthiest magnate in the country, but her claim to the throne made her far more dangerous a threat. Mary held the power that, with the emperor's backing, could force the kingdom into civil war. With division in the royal family, omens presaging doom were seen: in the sky, three suns supposedly appeared so that men could not 'tell which was the true sun' whilst other reports recorded how the earth had been felt to shake throughout the city.

Two days later, when Mary rode to court at Westminster, her following had grown, and she came 'with many noble men of lords and knights and gentlemen and ladies and gentlewomen'.[3] When she arrived at the gates, however, she was brought back down to earth when she found herself greeted by a single household officer. Led into the Presence Chamber where she found Edward surrounded by twenty-five members of the council, she was received kindly. Mary, having made 'all due reverences', excused herself for the delay in her visit owing to 'her indisposition', to Edward, who expressed his sorrow, though acerbically remarking that 'God had sent him health' but illness to her.

Walking with her in conversation, Edward led his sister into the Privy Chamber where, separated from her entourage of ladies, she found herself alone, surrounded by the council. There the pleasantries ended. Edward spoke first, desiring 'to remind her of the letters that both he and his Council had sent'. The council then launched into their attack, declaring Edward 'no longer intended that she should practise the old religion'. Mary returned to the promise given to the emperor, to which Edward replied that 'he knew nothing about that, for he had only taken a share in affairs during the last year'. 'In that case,' Mary responded sharply, Edward himself 'had not drawn up the ordinances on the new religion'. Without answering, the council then warned her of the danger 'if she, sister to the King and heiress to the Crown, observed the old religion'. The ordinances must apply, 'without exception of persons'.

Mary begged them to await the emperor's reply on the matter. When they failed to answer her, she persevered, professing her loyalty as the king's sister and subject. And turning to face Edward directly, said: 'Riper age and experience will teach Your Majesty much more yet.' 'You also may have somewhat to learn. None are too old for that,' Edward snapped back. Mary answered that it would be hard to change her religion 'in which the King, her father, bred her and left her at his death, both because of her age and inclinations and devotion'.

Again the councillors interjected. Had Henry lived, he would have overthrown 'all the Holy Father's constitutions and drawn up others like those now in force'. This Mary refused to discuss, adding only she wished that everything had remained as it was at the time of Henry's death. The council changed tack. Under the terms of Henry's will, they remarked, she became their subject. Replying that 'she had carefully read the said will', Mary countered that this applied only in the matter of her marriage. Had not Henry also ordered 'two masses to be said for him every day, and four obsequies every year, and other ceremonies' which they had failed to observe? On the back foot, they replied that they 'felt themselves bound by the will, and obliged to execute its provisions, in so far as they were in no way harmful to the King, their master'.

Mary continued her attack. She was quite sure, she told them, 'that the late King had never ordered anything in the least prejudicial to the King her brother because of the paternal love he bore him'. 'It is reasonable to suppose that he alone cared more for the good of his kingdom than all the members of his Council put together.'

This was too much for Dudley to bear. 'How now, my Lady!' he shot back. 'It seems your Grace is trying to show us in a hateful light to the King our Master, without any cause whatever.' This Mary denied, and returned quickly to the question of her mass. Even if there had been no assurance, she told Edward, she hoped that as his sister, he 'would have shown her enough respect to allow her to continue in the observance of the old religion, and to prevent her from being troubled in any way'. And as was always the way with Mary, she ended her argument with one final deliberate provocation. 'Might it please him to take away her life rather than the old religion, in which she desired to live and die'? she asked Edward who, stunned by the remark, replied that 'he wished for no such sacrifice'. Their meeting broke up unresolved. As Mary departed, she begged Edward not to listen to those who spoke ill of her 'whether about religion or anything else' and assured him that she would always remain his obedient sister. Edward replied 'he had never doubted of that' and there the audience ended.[4] Mary's greatest mistake was to assume that her innocent little brother's mind was being poisoned by courtiers; but just as the matter of her mass touched Mary's conscience, Edward was just as passionate on the issue, since her disobedience threatened to make a mockery of his own royal supremacy. Later Edward wrote in his diary how 'I had suffered her mass against my will' but now, unless Mary changed her ways he 'could not bear it . . . her example might breed too much inconvenience'.[5] It would only be a matter of time before the stalemate was broken.

This came sooner rather than later, with the news two days later that Emperor Charles V was threatening outright war if his cousin Mary was to be denied her right to hear mass. The king now came under pressure from his own councillors to change his mind.[6] The situation had now become far too serious for the council to bear, for what had previously been a domestic matter was on the point of blowing up into a crisis of international proportions – one that they had neither the resolve nor the finances to deal with. Recognizing the immediate need to back down, they encountered an unforeseen obstacle in Edward himself, who point blank refused to obey 'any king or Kaiser's entreaty'. Thinking that their Protestant credentials would sway Edward into submission, Cranmer and Nicholas Ridley were chosen to reason with the king. 'There were good kings in the old testament,' they argued, 'that had suffered hill altars, and yet were praised for good kings.' But again Edward stuck fast, answering them 'roundly' with a speech, based solidly on the Scriptures, that evidently impressed all who heard it. 'It is not two days since that we had in our Psalms,' Edward recalled, 'a complaint of God against his people, that they had broken his covenant, that they turned their backs, that they fell from him as their forefathers did . . . when God heard this he was wrath, and took sore displeasure at Israel.'[7] And in a crushing reference to Charles's incessant ill-health, told them that he was not afraid of a man 'liker to die himself every day then to do us any great harm, how much so ever he mean it'.

After 'long debating' of the matter, it was all too clear that Edward would not budge. He would 'spend his life, and all he had', he told them, 'rather than agree and grant to what he knew certainly to be against the truth'. Yet still the bishops continued to press, until, realizing that they would 'by no means have his nay', Edward burst into tears, prompting the bishops, 'seeing the king's zeal and constancy', to do likewise.

Cranmer was impressed by the forming Protestant zeal that he saw before him. As he left the royal chamber, he passed Cheke. Seizing the royal tutor by the hand, he said: 'Ah! Master Cheke, you may be glad all the days of your life, that you have such a scholar, for he hath more divinity in his little finger, than all we have in all our bodies.'[8]

Edward's tears had not been wasted, for despite the council's suggesting otherwise, Mary received no concessions. The king wrote of the confrontation in his journal that the bishops 'did conclude to give license to sin was sin' though for the moment, they agreed it was best to 'suffer and wink at it for a time'. The ambassador Nicholas Wotton was sent to the Imperial court to reason with the emperor, yet despite this temporizing, two days later the council made the extraordinary move of sending two gentlemen who had twice heard mass in Mary's household over the previous few days, to the Fleet prison.[9] And in April, Mary's chaplain Mallet was committed to the Tower. Another of her chaplains, the poet Alexander Barclay, was so despondent that he left her service to accept a benefice under Cranmer.[10] Had Edward got his way after all? For the moment, it seems, an air of truce had settled. War was not an appealing prospect for Charles V, whose hands were full with matters in Germany. He urged conciliation. 'If they may be brought to consent,' he wrote to Scheyfve, 'that she may hear mass privately in her own house, without admitting any strangers, let her be satisfied with that; for her conscience cannot be hardened by submission to outside violence.'

Nevertheless the episode had proved deeply disturbing for the young king. He had discovered his entire council ranged against him; Richard Morison later wrote how they had grown suspicious of his abilities, 'that they still charged men of his chamber, as though the King had learned things of others; yea, because his talk was always above some of their capacities, they therefore thought it rather stirred up in him by gentlemen of his Privy Chamber than grown in himself'. To prevent him being briefed in advance, Edward had been sent for suddenly 'in such haste as though his realm had been already upon the sacking' and not informed about what business was to be discussed. In what had been the first test of his own kingship he had managed to retain his authority, but only just. In his frustration, the Imperial ambassador Simon Renard had heard gossip from the court how Edward had 'plucked a falcon, which he kept in his private chamber, and torn it into four pieces, saying as he did so to his governors that he likened himself to the falcon, whom every one plucked; but that he would pluck them too, thereafter, and tear them in four parts'.[11]

Meanwhile the council had other matters upon their mind as disturbances that threatened the fragile sense of order became a regular occurrence.[12] A tract written the previous October set out the mounting problems that they faced: religious division was rife, printers were printing pamphlets 'be it never so foolish so seditious or dangerous for the people to know' whilst players travelled the country perfoming plays 'to the danger of the King and his council' encouraging the people to 'tell tales, deviseth lies, spread rumours of the King, his councillors, and ministers, discoursing of the affairs of estate at their liberty'.[13] The winter months provided some respite from commotion, but by April and as the summer neared, the government grew nervous, sending the Lords Lieutenants – members of the council with direct military responsibility for the regions – into their counties and issuing letters to all justices ordering them to strictly enforce laws against vagabonds, illegal games and seditious gatherings.[14] Rumours, fuelled by the migration of exiled European Protestants into the country, circulated that forty to fifty thousand foreigners had come to London, causing the price of food and accommodation to rise, and there was talk of a rising against them. 'The people have rather welcomed the idea,' the Imperial ambassador believed. But foreigners were not the only ones threatened with violence, and the ambassador thought that English merchants and rich burgesses were susceptible to attack, though it was Dudley who was said to be 'hated by the commons and more feared than loved by the rest' who was the obvious target.[15] Sensing the growing mood of disenchantment, John Hooper's wife wrote to her husband: 'We are much disturbed by apprehension of riots; for there is great danger of them ... by reason of the dearness of provisions and other things, although there is great plenty of wheat and other grain: but on whom the blame is laid you know better than I do.'[16]

All this acted as the backdrop to events on the stage at court, for the fissure between Dudley and Somerset had begun to split apart once more. Dudley did nothing to calm the situation, deciding instead to humiliate Somerset in a series of moves designed to degrade the duke's position and honour. First depriving him of his separate dining table at court, Dudley planned to reduce Somerset's pre-eminent status as the king's uncle even further by adding the words 'on his mother's side' into his title ready for the feast of the Order of the Garter on St George's Day. But perhaps the most galling moment for the duke came when, despite the council's orders preventing the state funeral he had wished for his mother, Dudley ordered the exact opposite for Edward's Chamberlain, Lord Wentworth, who was to be buried on 7 March in a state funeral at Westminster Abbey 'with a great company of lords and knights' as mourners, together with 100 children and a 'great dole'.[17]

Meanwhile, as if to infuriate Somerset ever further, Dudley's own loyal followers were rewarded handsomely. On 5 April Sir Thomas Darcy was created Lord Chamberlain and promoted to the House of Lords as Lord Darcy of Chiche. Three days later Sir John Gates was made vice-chamberlain and captain of the guard, receiving £120 worth of land. Dudley himself consolidated his own position on 17 April, appointing himself to the highest position of honour, that of earl marshal, a position formerly held by the duke. 'It seems that what was taken from the Duke has been given to the Earl,' Scheyfve noted pointedly.[18]

Dudley's provocation proved too much for Somerset to bear. Sir Richard Morison urged William Cecil to convince the duke not to attempt the impossible and meddle with Dudley — 'the mastiff himself', but soon rumours of a fall-out between Somerset and Dudley in open council were followed by a series of clashes between their followers; a servant of Somerset's was imprisoned for declaring that 'his master was better qualified to govern than Warwick [Dudley], and, besides, ought to be preferred to him because he was the King's uncle' whilst on 16 February Somerset's servant Richard Whalley, who the previous summer had been urged by Dudley to convince his master not to meddle in state affairs, was examined in council 'for persuading divers nobles of the realm to make the Duke of Somerset Protector at the next parliament'. Whalley denied everything, and though the Earl of Rutland gave evidence against him 'affirming it manifestly', nothing could be proved and Whalley was released under a recognizance of £1,000.[19]

An anonymous letter from a nobleman – probably the Earl of Shrewsbury – suggests that Somerset *was* up to something, for its contents describe how he had been approached by a man (perhaps Whalley) who 'practised with me to feel my disposition in friendship towards the duke of Somerset and Dudley'. Shrewsbury wanted nothing more to do with the conversation, and despite admitting that he had heard rumours of growing division between the two, said that he hoped 'my said lords were too wise to do so, considering the great inconvenience that might come thereof ... I was fully persuaded the same rumours to be untrue and surely great pity it were and as I think not a little damage and disquietness to the whole realm would grow thereof, if any such thing should chance'.[20]

Shrewsbury was probably acting through fear, for he already under-stood what it meant to cross Dudley, having recently received a letter from his servant that made some mention of 'the truth of the matter betwixt the earl of Warwick [Dudley] & your lordship'. In this, the servant had described how his own home had been raided by Dudley's men and 'by commandment of my lord of Warwick, my closet was broken up and all my books so handled and tossed together ... with wet and evil handling are so evil and rent'. Shrewsbury was obviously a threat that Dudley felt needed dealing with, but what did he have to hide? Together with the Earl of Derby, he had been described by the Imperial ambassador as 'powerful and popular, not only with the people, but secretly with many prominent personages'.[21] Could one of these 'prom-inent personages' have been Somerset?

Whilst Dudley continued to bolster his Protestant credentials, winning praise from reformers who considered him 'the thunderbolt and terror of the papists', Somerset had been forced to look elsewhere for support. It has been previously mentioned how he had begun to turn towards the conservatives; by championing the causes of Mary and Bishop Gardiner he had won himself new and unexpected supporters, including the Earl of Derby, who had remained resolutely attached to the Catholic faith, actively voicing his opposition to the new Prayer Book in Parliament. The year before it had been rumoured that Derby, Shrewsbury and the Earl of Arundel had been planning to organize a movement within Parliament to force Dudley to adhere to the terms of Henry VIII's will, no doubt to ensure that no further religious change would take place until Edward reached his majority. By August 1550, Derby's defiance rankled Dudley so much that, according to the Imperial ambassador Scheyfve's reports, the council had ordered Derby to meet with Dudley in Newcastle, apparently under the pretext that they wished 'to make some change in the government and give him a share in it'. But fearing a trap, Derby refused: 'It is rumoured that Lord Warwick's [Dudley's] object in going to Newcastle,' Scheyfve added, 'was to seize the person of my Lord Derby by force and take him to London by sea.'[22]

Dudley's actions merely pushed Derby further into Somerset's fold; their new-found allegiance was sealed with the marriage of his son Lord Strange to one of Somerset's daughters. Their common cause was either to restore Somerset as Protector or Princess Mary as regent and turn the clock back on the Reformation. By April 1551 the Imperial ambassador Scheyfve had heard whispers that Somerset 'would not object to abandoning the new religion and taking up the old again'; other councillors were of the same opinion, he added, 'only nobody dares unmask as yet'. No details of their plans survive, though the rumours suggest that Somerset was to seize London whilst Derby and Shrewsbury would raise the North in rebellion. Mary's involvement, though impossible to prove, should not be discounted either, for amidst her protracted struggles with Edward and the council, a man named Bennett of Ware was examined, confessing that 'my Lady Mary would go westward to the earl of Shrewsbury'. Whatever was planned and whoever was involved, Dudley was taking no chances and ordered his ally the Earl of Westmorland to return back to his lands in the North with instructions to stand ready 'in all events'.[23]

Dudley was all too aware that Somerset was planning some kind of attack, and sought to guard himself as best he could against any prospect of vengeance. Back in February he had ordered the creation of the 'gendarmes' – a mounted guard of 850 cavalry, divided into twelve trained bands and paid out of the royal coffers (at the cost of £18,000 [£3.4 million] per annum) 'for the surety of his Majesty's person as for the stay of the unquiet subjects, and for other services in all events'. The decision was passed by the council only after lengthy discussion, for it was obvious that with ten of the bands led by Dudley's supporters, its purpose was more to act as the earl's own private army. In London an armed patrol, to the number of seven or eight hundred horse, was raised, and the mayor and aldermen were ordered to have 'a vigilant regard to the order of the City; first, for their nightly watch; then for the correction of vagabonds; thirdly for the repulsion of strangers coming into the realm; fourthly for the reformation of disorder in churches that an unity may be had'. They carried out their duties with vigour; seventeen vagabonds were whipped across the City, all 'suspect persons' were arrested and the city gates locked shut.[24] Across the country, commissions appointing councillors with direct military action over their counties were issued and letters sent to all justices of the peace commanding strict execution of laws against vagabonds, illegal games, unlawful assemblies and the spreading of rumours.

The precautions proved worthwhile. On 16 April Edward's diary recorded that a conspiracy had been discovered in London, intending to encourage the entire city to rise on May Day. The day before plans 'to bring people together to Chelmsford and then to spoil the rich men's houses if they could' were foiled and the rebels seized.

In fact the conspiracy was far more serious than Edward could ever have known or imagined. According to Scheyfve, the two conspiracies were linked. While 'a gathering of ruffians and serving men' were to 'excite the people to revolt' a force of peasants totalling ten to twelve thousand in number would assemble to march on London. But there is more to be told than this, for when a man was discovered near Dudley's house at midnight on 16 April, his bloodied sword in hand, it seems likely that an assassination attempt against Dudley had been foiled.[25]

Was Somerset involved in a plot to bring down his rival? On 19 April bills and books 'of slanderous devices against the Council' stirring the city to rebellion were discovered and presented to the council.[26] A month later one Tracy – probably Richard Tracy, a writer of Protestant tracts who remained a close acquaintance of Somerset's – was interrogated upon accusations of treason.[27] With rumours flying around that Somerset had already rebelled, Shrewsbury and Derby quickly reneged on any plans they had made to travel to London and support the duke, requesting permission to be absent from the Feast of the Garter on 23 April.[28] When summoned by the council to repair to court, they refused, reportedly adding that 'If the Council ... were governing the kingdom well, they were very glad to hear it, and if not, they would not say what might not hereafter come to pass'.[29] Somerset's attempt to topple Dudley had been thwarted; its failure would eventually prove to be the duke's final undoing.

Despite evidence that some kind of rising or assassination had been planned, for the moment no arrests were made. In fact, a concerted effort was made to dispel any talk of rebellion, and in a deliberate show of unity, the council banqueted together for four successive days between 23 and 26 April. As Edward sensed in his diary, the aim was 'to show agreement among them, whereas discord was bruited, and somewhat to look to the punishment of talebearers and apprehending of evil persons'; watching the whole charade, the Imperial ambassador Renard observed how the council deliberately 'loaded one another with caresses'. Despite this, he wrote, 'England is in a very divided and factious condition'.[30] A proclamation was issued appealing for calm, its preamble complaining that the 'precious jewel' of God's word was being abused by 'licentious behaviour, lewd and seditious talks'. Vagabonds and 'masterless men' were to be sent home to the places of their birth and were given four days to depart. Any 'tale, rumour or talk' concerning the king, his council or magistrates was forbidden. Printers were prohibited to publish anything in English without a warrant signed by the king or six members of the council. Another proclamation in May ordered the destruction of 'slanderous and wicked bills' cast abroad in streets and fastened at 'privy corners ... to the slander and infamy of many godly and well-disposed persons and defacing of their well-doings in the commonwealth'. It ordered that they be destroyed immediately; those who discovered them and left them standing would be punished as if they were the author.[31]

The situation at court remained fraught. One reformer wrote that Dudley seemed 'wonderfully occupied and distracted; especially in this dangerous and turbulent crisis of the state, than which I know not whether any more troublesome or dangerous ever before existed', and by June the strain of the previous months was clearly showing, when the earl himself wrote to the council that he would 'rather be dead than live such a life as this two or three years they have been in'.[32] Even as far away as Rome news sheets were being circulated that the northern lords had attempted a revolt against Dudley, that Londoners were struggling to cope amidst thousands of religious refugees and there was continual 'chopping and changing in the Council'.[33] For the Venetian ambassador

Daniel Barbaro it was clear that 'everything is going daily from bad to worse'. Nothing remained in its place save 'the reputation of the present King, who is of a good disposition, and the whole realm hopes the best from him'. Edward, it appeared to him, was handsome, affable and of 'becoming stature' and was beginning to interest himself 'about public business'. In bodily exercise, literary study and linguistic ability he 'appears to surpass his comrades and competitors'. It seemed that Edward was ready to assume the reins of power.[34]

Edward's studies had accelerated, with the king now composing one-thousand-word essays both in Latin and Greek every two weeks. Their topics varied, ranging from discussing the benefits of peace to whether adulterers should be put to death, though their purpose seems to have been to train Edward in the rigours of oratory, forcing him to weigh up both sides of the argument before coming to his conclusion in truly regal fashion, signing off 'I have finished. Edwardus Rex'. John Cheke and his French tutor Jean Belmain remained as Edward's principal influences, though at some stage, probably in early 1551, Edward developed a somewhat mysterious relationship with the clerk of the council William Thomas, who seems to have become his political tutor – unofficially at least. Managing to slip the tight security net around the king, Thomas managed to supply in secret a lengthy list of eighty-five questions concerning the duties of a prince to Edward.[35] Edward showed a keen interest in Thomas's work and requested that Thomas provide him with further information, sending him 'notes of certain discourses' – probably his homework – to apply himself to. Edward first wished to hear Thomas's opinions on the reformation of the coinage, but in secret and without the knowledge of the council, much to Thomas's commendation. Once completed, Thomas delivered his discourse 'sealed ... as it were a thing from the Council', to which Thomas assured Edward: 'no creature living is or shall be privy either to this or to any of the rest through me. Which I do keep so secret to this end, that your Majesty may utter these matters as of your own study; whereby it shall have the greater credit with your council'.[36]

The clearest evidence of Edward's growing interest in state affairs survives in a remarkable document, a discourse on the reform of abuses both within the Church and the State. Written entirely in Edward's own hand during 1551, it gives an impression of the king's own understanding of how his kingdom should operate, and at first, as one historian has argued, seems to suggest that Edward was influenced by the 'thought and aspirations of the commonwealth party' – arguing for merchants to be only allowed land up to the value of £100 and for no man to own more than two thousand sheep or two farms.[37] Yet having criticized almost every group in society for its greed and idleness, Edward's principal concern was for his own class – the nobility whose 'maintenance ... is ill looked to', arguing that 'The most part of true gentlemen (I mean not these farming gentlemen, nor clerking knights) have little or nothing increased their rents; yet their housekeeping is dearer, their meat is dearer, their liveries dearer, their wages greater, which thing at length, if speedy remedy be not had, will bring that state into utter ruin'. And Edward's attitude to the genuine poor seems to have been in sharp contrast to the charity expressed in Latimer's teaching: 'The vagabonds ought clearly to be banished,' he wrote, 'as is the superfluous humour in the body, that is to say, the spittle and filth.'

In fact, in his gloom there was little good Edward could find to say about his nation. He continued:

> slack execution of the laws has been the chiefest sore of all. The laws have been manifestly broken, the offenders punished, and either by bribery or foolish pity escaped punishment. The dissention and disagreement, both for private matters and also in matters of religion, has been no little cause, but the principal has been the disobedient and contentious talking and doing of foolish and fond people, which for lack of teaching have wandered and broken, wilfully and disobediently, the laws of this realm. The lawyers also, and judges, have much offended in corruption and bribery ... What shall I say of those that buy and sell offices of trust, that impropriate benefices, that destroy timber, that – not considering the sustaining of men ... turn till-ground to pasture, that use excesses in apparel, in diet, and in building; of enclosures of wastes and commons; of those that cast false and seditious bills – but that thing is so tedious, long and lamentable to entreat of the particulars that I am weary to go any further in the particulars.[38]

Having told the worst, Edward looked for a remedy. Continuing his medical analogy, these 'sores' now needed 'medicines or plasters' to cure them. Edward drew up his eight-point plan:

1. Good education.
2. Devising of good laws.
3. Executing the laws justly, without respect of persons.
4. Example of rulers.

5. Punishing of vagabonds and idle persons.
6. Encouraging the good.
7. Ordering well the customers.
8. Engendering friendship in all the parts of the commonwealth.

Of these, education was the most important. 'Youth must be brought up – some in husbandry, some in working, graving, gilding, joining, printing, making of cloths,' Edward wrote, 'even from their tenderest age, to the intent they may not, when they come to man's estate, loiter as they do nowadays ... but think their travail sweet and honest', adding that 'I wish that artificers and others were commanded to bring up their sons in like trade or else have some places appointed them in every good town where they should be apprentices ... those vagabonds that take children and teach them to beg should, according to their demerits, be worthily punished.' The law should be reformed so that 'the superfluous and tedious statutes were brought into one sum together and made more plain and short, to the intent that men might the better understand them', but would only be effective if properly backed up by the authority of the nobleman and justices: 'I would wish that after this Parliament were ended, the noblemen, except a few that should be with me, went to their countries and there should see the statutes fully and duly executed.'

Whereas the passages dealing with secular matters are entirely written in Edward's own voice and seem independent of any other influence, Edward's understanding of religious matters appears to have been derived in part from the reformer Martin Bucer's masterpiece *De Regno Christi*, which had been presented to Edward as a New Year's gift at the start of the year.[39] Edward had shown a close fondness for Bucer, writing to him admiringly in 1550, and treating him almost as a second father. 'Since we have received nothing from our first parents wherein we may glory,' Edward wrote in a telling statement of how he had come to view the tyranny and excesses of Henry VIII's reign, 'I am compelled, reverend father, since I have been called, by Divine Goodness and your agency and ministry, to this connection in Christ and a partaking of the gospel, daily to give thanks' to God for his 'infinite and unbounded (though undeserved) bounty towards me'.[40] Yet Bucer, who had fallen ill some months before, died shortly after his work had been presented to the king. One of the most moving passages in Edward's diary records his funeral at Cambridge when 'all the whole university with the whole town bringing him to the grave, to the number [of] 3,000 persons; also there was an oration of Mr. Haddon made very eloquently at his death ... three sermons made the people wonderfully to lament his death. Last of all, all the learned men of the university made their epitaphs in his praise, laying them on his grave'.[41]

Edward's genuine affection for Bucer is reflected in his Privy Purse accounts that show a payment of £20 for 'Mr Bucer his relief in sickness'. It was not the only act of charity Edward was accustomed to, for in addition to providing alms worth £447 17s 1d (£85,700), Edward also gave £36 17s 7d (£7,056) to one Alexander Ginzam 'for the finding of his two sons', £6 13s 5d to Margaret de la Rose for 'her loss by fire', and even tended to his father's fool, William Sommer, to whom he paid £39 16s 10d (£7,623) for 'diverse and sundry needs'.[42]

Yet Edward was not solely preoccupied in acting the 'godly imp'; he was, after all, a Tudor king who had inherited the full splendour of his father's court. Like his father, he enjoyed both listening to and playing music, with his music tutor Philip van Wilder being paid 116s 8d (£1,116) 'for ribbing and for lyming his majesty's lute cases'. Edward also maintained a considerable orchestra which included eighteen trumpeters, seven vial players, four sackbuts, a harpist, a bagpiper, a drummer, a rebeck player and eight minstrels.[43] Edward also spent his time being entertained by troupes of players, including those belonging to Somerset, Northampton and the Duchess of Suffolk, the choirboys of St Paul's and Philip Hoby's own lute player, whom he rewarded with £10.

But it was in the field that Edward had already begun to follow his father's favourite pursuits. Hunting was a regular pastime, with an Italian observer noting that 'he does it so as to have an excuse to ride, because his men, out of fear for his life, often seem to keep rather a tight rein on him in this area'.[44] The parish priest of Barkham, Berkshire, recorded how the following year, in 1552, Edward had hunted 'in the bear wood in the forest of Windsor and there did his grace kill a great buck'.[45] Edward had also become a keen archer, with £84 6s spent on 'divers kinds of artillery, quivers, strings, racks for crossbows, staves for back swords'. His diary entry of 14 May 1551 recalls how he enjoyed watching others shoot, witnessing '100 archers, two arrows apiece, all of the guard, afterward shot together, and they shot at an inch board, which some pierced quite and stuck in the other board; divers pierced it quite through with the heads of their arrows, the boards being very well seasoned timber'.

That summer the Imperial ambassador noted how Edward was 'beginning to exercise himself in the use of arms, and enjoys it heartily'. At the beginning of April, he mounted his horse in full armour and 'rode two or three miles each time, and also charged the target to exercise and show himself to the people'. That month he took part in his first tournament, issuing a challenge that, with sixteen of his chamber, he 'should run at base, shoot, and run at ring' with seventeen gentleman servants of the court. He won the first challenge but lost the shooting match.[46] The following month he took part in a 'great triumph' at Greenwich. On one side, Edward and his company were dressed in black and white, his footmen wearing hats, cloaks and carrying banners and spears of the same colours. On the other, Somerset's son the Earl of Hertford, 'with a great company of lords and knights, all young men' dressed in yellow, ran at the ring and at tourney with swords 'five or six times with other lords'.[47] Edward despondently recorded the outcome in his diary:

> The challenge at running the ring performed, at which first came the King, sixteen footmen, and ten horsemen, in black silk coats pulled out with white silk taffeta; then all lords having three men likewise apparelled, and all gentlemen, their footmen in white fustian pulled out with black taffeta. The other side came all in yellow taffeta. At length the yellow band took it twice in 120 courses, and my band tainted often – which was counted as nothing – and took never – which seemed very strange – and so the prize was of my side lost.[48]

The French ambassador attempted to soothe Edward's pride, telling him that he had 'borne himself right well, and shown great dexterity', to which Edward replied hopefully 'that it was a small beginning, and as time passed he hoped to do his duty better'. He stuck to his word. By June, Sheyfve reported that Edward 'practises the use of arms every day on horseback, and enjoys it greatly. They say he intends to exercise himself against the coming of the French, when jousts and other sports are to take place'. Edward did not confine his sporting activities to the field, for the Venetian ambassador noted how he delighted 'in every sort of exercise, drawing the bow, playing rackets, hunting and so forth, indefatigably'. At Greenwich, Hampton Court and Whitehall there were tennis courts, bowling alleys and tiltyards on hand for Edward's amusement, and with the court attendant earning of 7 shillings 6 pence (£71–75) for every time Edward played tennis – which was no less than

293 times in the year – he ended up with the rather grand wage of £109 14s (£20,989).[49]

On 7 July 1551 a sudden outbreak of the sweating sickness erupted in London, last seen in 1528. Edward noted that it was 'more vehement' than previously. The disease's occurrence had first been detected in Shrewsbury in April, but soon incidences had quickly spread elsewhere. Edward described its symptoms in his diary: 'If one took cold, he died within three hours, and if he escaped, it held him but nine hours, or ten at the most. Also, if he slept the first six hours, as he should be very desirous to do, then he raved and should die raving.'[50] The first sign of the disease was a pain in the back or shoulder, which spread to the entire body, followed by bouts of flushing and wind. There was little chance of survival. All the doctors could recommend was for the patient to be kept awake for at least twelve hours and given 'a whey posset of ale and milk and collecting sorrel leaves and sage with other herbs which brought on a sweat which expelled the evil'. John Caius, who wrote a manual about the disease, blamed its rapid hold on a lack of fish in the diet. Men were nowadays 'too unwisely fine, and womanly delicate', he insisted, 'the old manly hardness, stout courage & painfulness of England is utterly driven away. Instead whereof, men . . . receive womanliness and become nice, not able to withstand a blast of wind, or resist a poor fish. And the children be so brought up, that if they be not all day by the fire with toast and butter, and in their furs, they be straight sick.'[51]

Casualties were immediate and spared neither the rich nor poor. Lord Cromwell in Leicestershire, Lord Powis in Woolwich, and the stout captain Sir John Luttrell succumbed early. By 10 July Edward was removed from Westminster to Hampton Court 'with very few with me' as the location of infection began to creep nearer to court. On the 11th Edward noted that 120 had died that day alone. Two days later Sir Thomas Speke, who had been taken ill at the court, was found dead from the sweat. Edward also mentioned that another, unnamed, groom of his chamber had succumbed. By the time the ravages of the disease had passed, it had drastically affected the upper ranks of society; one observer noted that it had killed 'many merchants and great rich men and workmen . . . young men and old'.[52]

On 16 July the disease claimed its most prominent victims. Henry and Charles Brandon, Edward's close school companions, died in their beds in Cambridgeshire. According to the Imperial ambassador, Edward was devastated, though he made little show of his sorrow at court. Later, perhaps as a means of dealing with his grief, he devoted the subject of one of his orations to mourning the death of friends.[53]

Meanwhile the disease continued its ravaging course across London, the chancellor's department estimating that 872 had perished between 8 and 19 July.[54] Mass graves had to be dug to accommodate the bodies. To avoid the spread of disease, the burials were carefully orchestrated, with commandments sent out prohibiting any burial between the hours of six in the evening and six o'clock in the morning. As a warning, a bell was rung three quarters of an hour before the next burial in order to clear the streets.[55]

The effect of the sweat was immediate. 'Terror-stricken inhabitants of London were flying in all directions,' reported the Imperial ambassador, whilst Hooper had noticed that the sweat 'being hot and terrible enforced the people greatly to call upon God, and to do many deeds of charity'. Hooper himself considered the disease 'a most remarkable token of divine vengeance' since it seemed to affect only Englishmen, 'following us, as the shadow of the body' even abroad, with 'none other nation infected therewith'. However, it was noticed by one chronicler that 'as the disease ceased, so the devotions quickly decayed'. Others placed the blame elsewhere. After matins at St Martin Ludgate on 11 July, Margaret Harbottle stood up to denounce the curate: 'He and such as he is was the occasion that God did plague the people so sore, because that they would not suffer them to pray upon their beads . . . and that men did die like dogs because they cannot see their maker borne about in the streets as they have seen it in time past.'[56]

As if the devastation brought by the sweating sickness was not enough hardship for the people to bear, its onslaught coincided with the council's decision to revalue the coinage after years of its debasement, the process by which the precious metal content of coins was reduced, despite retaining their face value. The idea was very much Henry's baby, for it had first begun in 1542 and continued throughout the 1540s when Henry, desperate for a quick injection of cash, decided to reduce the silver content of the coinage from 11.1oz per 12oz to 4oz by 1546. Effectively, debasement became a licence to print (or rather coin) money, for within five years Henry had raised a massive £450,000 (£121.7 million). There were of course downsides, but it was only now during his son's reign that the administration really had to face up to these. The number of coins in circulation had doubled, causing hyperinflation. And the poor quality of the new coins fooled no one, containing so much copper that they shone red; the poet John Heywood wrote how they 'blush for shame' whilst the preacher Hugh Latimer had poured scorn upon the 'pretty little shilling' that he had mistaken for a groat.

Dudley realized that such a deleterious method of economics could not continue, and became determined to restore the value of the coinage. But not before one last indulgence, reducing the silver content to 3oz and raising funds of £120,000.

The problem came not so much in the principle, but in the method whereby the process was reversed, by 'calling down' the coinage. A proclamation on 8 May announced that from August every shilling would now be valued at ninepence and the groat, worth fourpence, would now be worth threepence. This was a relatively easy way of gradually revaluing the coinage whilst new coins with a much higher silver content (near to the pre-1542 levels) would be produced to replace the old. The real issue lay in the timing – specifically in announcing the timing at all – for predictably few were now enthusiastic to accept the old coinage knowing its value would shortly decrease by 25 per cent. Rumours began to spread that their value would be further reduced, and soon shillings were being refused at half their value. Those in the know got out as soon as they could: 'Most poor men were much grieved,' one chronicler wrote, 'for their whole substance lay in that kind of money, where as the richer sort, partly by friendship understanding the thing beforehand, did put that kind of money away.'[57] The poor, meanwhile, had just become poorer than ever.

On 8 July the council finally bowed to pressure and did what it should have done all along, announcing the immediate implementation of the new coinage values. But the uncertainty remained, and despite a further proclamation in July to the contrary, proved entirely justified when the value of the shilling was further reduced to sixpence on 16 August. Such arbitrary treatment of men's pockets was not easily forgiven, and reports of murmurings against the council were soon rife; Isaac Herne, a shoe-maker from Wokingham, was brought before the council, alleged to have encouraged five others to 'rise and make a rebellious assembly' with the words: 'If you will you may now assemble a good company together then we will have the rents of farms and prices of victuals to be brought lower again as they were in King Richard's time.'[58]

At court, however, it was a different story as events focused upon a possible alliance between England and France, to be sealed with a new marriage treaty. In April the Marquess of Northampton had travelled to France to bestow the Order of the Garter on the French king Henry II, and at the same time brought up the question of Edward's age-old marriage contract with Mary Queen of Scots, which the French refused 'saying both they had taken too much pain and spent too many lives for her'. Instead they proposed that Edward marry Henry II's daughter Elizabeth, and after some protracted haggling over the price of a dowry a new treaty was signed. Edward was also granted the French honour of the Order of Saint-Michel, at which he was delighted, though the council wrote back that 'His Majesty's French speech being not natural to him, cannot so abundantly express the joy of his heart'.[59]

The French envoys, led by Jacques d'Albon, Marshal de Saint-André, duly arrived on English shores to present Edward with the honour, reaching the capital on 11 July. There, Edward recorded, they were 'saluted with all my ships being in the Thames, fifty and odd, all with shot well furnished and so with the ordinance of the Tower'.

Because of the threat of the sweating sickness, Saint-André and his retinue of four hundred were lodged at Richmond before finally arriving at Hampton Court on 14 July to greet Edward at nine o'clock in the morning. Edward's description of their reception is one of the longest in his diary; as its enthused passages reveal, Edward was clearly captivated by Saint-André's visit and the entertainments arranged. Determined to impress, a series of lavish spectacles had been organized, including a magnificent banquet that was put on at a specially erected banqueting house in Hyde Park, measuring 62 feet by 21 feet and built at a cost of £450 9s 7d, accompanied by a firework display. On 19 July Saint-André had supper with Edward and afterward 'saw a dozen courses'; on the following day, Edward recalled, 'he came to see mine arraying and saw my bedchamber and went a-hunting with hounds and saw me shoot and saw all my guard shoot together. He dined with me, heard me play on the lute, ride, came to me in my study, supped with me, and so departed.' Saint-André dined with Edward again on 26 July, afterwards watching a display of 'the strength of the English archers'. According to one French source, Edward remained charming throughout, even joking with the envoys about the miserable state of English food, though when the topic of religion cropped up, Edward went silent, answering only that he 'must consult with my Council before giving your lordship an answer'.

Edward was invested with the Order of Saint-Michel on 16 July.

Entering his Presence Chamber, the French envoys were taken aback by Edward's magnificent attire, describing him as 'an angel in human form'. It was impossible, one observer wrote, 'to imagine a more beautiful face and figure, set off by the brilliance of jewels and robes, and a mass of diamonds, rubies and pearls, emeralds and sapphires – they made the whole room look as if lit up'.[60] All this was deliberate, for the council had gone to the trouble to make sure that new caps were made specifically for the occasion, one white velvet cap being garnished with forty-eight rubies and countless pearls and decorated with a diamond brooch. Edward had become something of a jewel collector himself, and in May 1551 he purchased from the Continent the famous Burgundian jewel named 'The Three Brothers' that he gloatingly described in his diary as 'a very fair jewel ... four rubies marvellous big, one orient and great diamond, and one great pearl' for 100,000 crowns.[61] The purpose of such magnificence was to create an overall impression of wealth and power, with the court acting as an expression of Edward's divine authority. To achieve this, protocol was strictly observed; a Florentine visitor noted how Edward usually dressed in red and white, wearing a violet cap that was unique, for 'nobody would venture to wear a hat of that colour'. The French envoys were impressed that Edward's guard wore specially embroidered 'E's on their coats, though most foreign observers considered many rituals to border on the ridiculous. Even Elizabeth, wrote one Italian, had been seen to 'kneel down before her brother five times before she sat down'.

During their stay, the envoys had been lavished with expensive gifts of gold plate totalling a massive sum of £8,200, which to Edward's relish was raised by melting down 'church stuff, [such] as mitres, golden missals and primers ... and relics'. Edward was determined that his generosity would remain unrivalled, certainly intending to outdo the French, whose gifts to the English envoys had only totalled a few hundred pounds, which Edward noted somewhat indignantly as 'all about one scantling'.[62] Other gifts were more personal and far removed from the circus of the gift-giving process; when Edward wrote in his diary at Saint-André's departure 'I gave him a diamond from my finger worth by estimation £150 both for [his] pains and also for my memory', it seems he did so with genuine affection.

Saint-André left for France soon after, and the court painter William Scrots busied himself painting Edward's portrait to be sent over the Channel the following year as a present for Edward's new bride-to-be,

Elizabeth. Still only six years old, she was enchanted by the image of the English king who was to be her husband, rising each morning to wish him 'good day'. The portrait survives, and can still be seen in the Louvre today. Wearing a doublet of intricately patterned blue velvet, with his new plainly designed Order of the Garter around his neck, Edward stands with his slim white legs proudly on display, gloves in one hand and bejewelled rapier at his side. The pose is familiar, yet unlike all previous portraits of Edward, this one is markedly different: for whereas before Edward's manly posturing and oversized clothes struggled to hide the body of a child beneath, now image and reality stood together as one.

10

THE DESTRUCTION OF
THE DUKE

With the new French alliance arranged and Edward's marriage to Henry II's daughter Elizabeth firmly in place, Dudley now felt confident enough finally to resolve the problem of Mary's disobedience. The revival of the Hapsburg–Valois conflict – the intermittent rivalry between the ruling houses of France and the Empire – also meant that Emperor Charles V had his hands tied and would be unlikely to be able to come to the rescue of his cousin Mary. The only sticking point was any possible resistance at home. Mary had her supporters, notably Somerset and the Catholic earls of Arundel, Derby and Shrewsbury, who seem to have voiced their opposition to her treatment back in the spring. Dudley decided to keep his enemies close, and on 9 August Arundel and Derby were drafted on to the council for one day only for an extraordinary meeting of the council at Richmond where it was resolved to prohibit the saying of 'any Mass or other Divine Service' within Mary's household. Dudley's plan was to prove that he meant business: by ensuring that Arundel and Derby signed up to his latest round of attacks upon Mary, he had forced them to show their hand, leaving them with the only choice to rebel or remain in discomforting silence.

On 23 August three officers of Mary's household – Rochester, Englefield and Waldegrave – were charged with disobedience and sent to the Tower. With the unified agreement the council now turned to Mary. When a deputation led by Lord Rich visited her at the end of August, ordering that her chaplains desist from saying mass in the future, they were welcomed by a defiant and somewhat histrionic performance from Mary who told them that rather than 'use any other service ... I will lay my head on a block and suffer death'. Blaming the council for making her ill ('if I shall chance to die, I will protest openly that you of the Council to be the causes of my death') she again refused to acknowledge that Edward had any part to play in her treatment, naively insisting that she would obey no religious change until he reached eighteen. But with the emperor's support having evaporated, Mary was in no position to call the shots; grudgingly, she caved in and her protests died down. For the next two years her household heard no mass as Mary alone continued to console herself with her own private devotions behind closed doors. The Imperial ambassador Scheyfve continued his protests, but the mood at court had changed. Dudley insisted that Edward be informed personally, being 'now so old that he wished to concern himself with all the public affairs of the kingdom'. Having visited the king, Dudley replied that Edward 'was quite determined that the laws and statutes that had been decreed and issued in his kingdom should be obeyed inviolably by everyone'.[1]

Dudley's attack upon Mary may have been premeditated by the situation abroad, but the actual reasons for its launch struck far deeper. Ever since Somerset's aborted assassination of the earl, the Imperial ambassador believed that Dudley had been 'meditating revenge' upon his rival. How he was going to achieve this, however, remained far from clear, for it was probably likely that Dudley knew something had taken place in April, but lacked the evidence to prove it one way or the other. Somerset was again becoming a nuisance, and having opposed the French match from the start, had ordered Lord Strange, the eighteen-year-old son and heir of the Earl of Derby, and a close companion of the king, to encourage Edward to marry his own daughter Jane instead. Absent from court for most of the summer, Somerset was left in the dark over much of the business at council, protesting to a friend how it was 'strange that those things should come before the Council, and I not hear of it. I am of the Council also'.[2] Increasingly isolated, soon he was relying on Lord Strange to keep him informed of what was going on at court, as Edward later recalled, willing Strange 'to be his spy in all matters of my doings and sayings and to know when some of my Council spoke secretly with me'.[3] Added to this, Somerset had taken advantage of his popularity amongst the people to suggest that the country's social and economic problems were solely the responsibility of Dudley and that the policy of debasement had been carried through against his advice, causing a great 'murmur' amongst the commons.[4]

Somerset's position was becoming untenable, yet his high authority and degree still marked him out as 'King of the King'.[5] Dudley needed some means of entrapping the duke if he was to bring him down. A final assault upon Mary provided the perfect vehicle. Ever since his release,

Somerset had taken the opportunity to side with the princess over the religious freedoms that he himself had granted her during his time as Protector. It was probably no coincidence that Somerset's planned attack on Dudley had taken place shortly after Edward's showdown with Mary; then the duke had managed to galvanize the members of the conservative nobility, outraged by the princess's treatment, into supporting his scheme. With Derby's support secured at the 9 August meeting, this time it would be a different story. As the attacks upon Mary grew increasingly degrading – Dudley refused to recognize her royal title as princess, calling her 'the King's Sister' – Somerset made the suggestion that her household be able to hear mass, provoking a furious outburst from Dudley. 'The mass is either of God or the Devil,' he retorted. 'If it is of God, it is but right that all our people should be allowed to go to it; but if it is not out of God, as we are taught in the Scriptures, why then should not the voice of this fury [i.e. the mass] be proscribed to all?'[6] According to Edward, the meeting on 9 August that resolved to take action against Mary had been only agreed 'at length' – had Somerset been reluctant to sign the agreement?

Dudley had pushed Somerset too far; during the end of August and after Mary's confrontation with Lord Rich, Somerset met with the Earl of Arundel to discuss how finally to bring about his rival's downfall. As their plans continued to be set throughout the autumn, Dudley realized that he would need to act fast, particularly given the fact that the emperor's sister, Mary of Hungary, was making disconcerting noises about organizing an invasion to free Edward from 'the hands of his pernicious governors'.[7] Dudley needed to send out a message – both to the remaining conservative faction at home and to Mary's allies abroad – that he meant business. Within two weeks Somerset was once again in the Tower.

The final pieces fell into place on 7 October 1551, when Dudley was visited by Sir Thomas Palmer, a former associate of Somerset's but who had now drawn in close league with Dudley. The evidence for their meeting comes entirely from Edward's diary, but it seems that Palmer divulged to Dudley how Somerset had planned to 'raise the people'. A banquet had been planned at which Dudley and Northampton were to be assassinated, the method of execution being 'to cut off their heads'. Four days later, Palmer had further confessed that Somerset's follower, Sir Ralph Vane, 'had 2,000 men in readiness'. Another supporter, Sir Miles Partridge, was to raise London with the help of certain 'apprentices', seizing the Great Seal and the Tower of London. Alexander Seymour, a distant relative of Somerset's, and Lawrence Hammond, possibly a Yeoman of the Guard, were also to ensure that 'all the horse of the gendarmerie should be slain'. Whether Palmer's accusations were true or false remains to be seen, but for the moment it provided Dudley with all the evidence he needed to destroy his greatest enemy.

First Dudley needed to bolster his support. This he did with the creation of new peerages – the same tactic he had used before, in the winter of 1549, when he planned to destroy Wriothesley. In an age of ruthless ambition, loyalty could be easily bought: Henry Grey, the Marquess of Dorset, became the Duke of Suffolk; William Paulet, Lord St John, was promoted to Marquess of Winchester; and William Herbert, having been created Lord Herbert the previous day, was now raised to Earl of Pembroke. Dudley awarded himself a dukedom, becoming the Duke of Northumberland. In one sense, the giving of titles in fact merely reflected the existing political situation of Dudley's – now North-umberland's – dominance; he was now undoubtedly the most important nobleman in the land, holding three of the five great offices of state.[8] One chronicler at least considered a different motive. Relating that none of the council dared to tell Somerset 'to come or go because he was a Duke' it being 'contrary to usage among lords for a man of lower rank to order one of higher rank to do something against his will', the promotions would provide an opportunity for Dudley, as Duke of Northumberland and therefore now his equal, to finally mount a chal-lenge upon Somerset. Already Scheyfve had detected something was amiss. 'I have heard from a trustworthy source,' he wrote, 'that the Duke of Somerset is again going to be arrested, and that the plot is being very secretly woven by the Earl of Warwick [Dudley]and his party'.[9]

The ceremonies took place at Hampton Court, and seem to have been marred only by a disagreement between the now ennobled Dudley and Lord Grey of Wilton – a supporter of Somerset's – who took exception to the fact that one reason announced for Dudley's promotion was his gallant conduct in leading the campaign in Scotland back in 1547, something that Grey denied, saying that the accolade belonged to Somerset instead. Despite this outburst, the new peers sojourned for dinner, Dudley – now referred to by all as Northumberland★ – now even sitting at the same table as Somerset. What they spoke of, the records do

★ As he will be referred to from this point on.

not reveal. Yet beneath the ceremony and symbolism, Fortune's wheel had begun to turn. Northumberland had lain in wait for his rival to be exactly where he wanted. Now the time was right.

When Somerset was commanded to delay a planned journey to the North, he began to grow suspicious, yet his fears were allayed by William Herbert, whose complicity in the whole affair had been sealed with his promotion to Earl of Pembroke, who told him that 'on his honour that he should have no hurt'. By 14 October, however, Somerset grew further unsettled. Sending for his former secretary William Cecil, he told him that he suspected 'some ill'. Cecil's cryptic remark, that 'if he were not guilty he might be of good courage; if he were, he had nothing to say but to lament him', left Somerset with no better idea of what was going on, but he knew he needed to act fast if he was to save his neck. Dispatching a letter 'of defiance' to Cecil, he summoned Thomas Palmer to his chamber. Palmer denied that he had made any accusation against Somerset and, confident that his innocence would be restored, Somerset let him go.

But the treachery that Palmer had set in motion had by now gathered a pace all of its own. Significantly, the following day the court moved from Hampton Court to Westminster. The palace was fast becoming the official seat of government, where business could to be transacted at ease. It was, however, to be the setting for another purpose. As Edward recalled cryptically, 'it was thought this matter easier and surelier be dispatched there'.

The next day Northumberland struck. Somerset simply had no time to prepare for what was to come. Edward is our best witness as he watched the events unfold:

This morning none was at Westminster of the conspirators. The first was the Duke, who came, later than he was wont, of himself. After dinner he was apprehended. Sir Thomas Palmer [was taken] on the terrace walking there. Hammond, passing by Mr. Vice-Chamberlain's door, was called in by John Peers to make a match at shooting, and so [was] taken. Newdigate was called for as from my Lord his master and taken. Likewise were John Seymour and Davy Seymour. [Sir Thomas] Arundel also was taken, and the Lord Grey, coming out of the country. Vane, upon two sendings of my Lord was not stout, and if he could get home he cared for none of them all, he was so strong. He was discovered hiding beneath the straw in a stable at Lambeth. These went with the Duke to the Tower this night, saving Palmer, Arundel and Vane, who were kept in chambers here, apart.[10]

The same day the council sent out a circular to the justices throughout the country declaring how the 'Duke's evil heart and discontented nature hath prevailed in him to be so great a troubler and shame to his country, and to such a peril, as we could none otherwise avoid than thus in doing our duties'. Further arrests followed over the next few days. The Duchess of Somerset, the keeper of their chamber, William Crane and his wife, were sent to the Tower for their complicity in the supposed conspiracy, as was one James Wingfield 'for casting out of bills seditious'. Soon joining them were the duke's closest supporters.[11]

On 17 October the Imperial ambassador Scheyfve was informed of the conspiracy. 'The machination seemed so extraordinary to me,' he wrote to the emperor, 'I could not understand what could have driven the Duke to it.' Northumberland replied that he 'failed to imagine what it could have been; for the Duke had enjoyed the greatest reputation and authority with the Council, and had possessed a huge fortune of 30,000 to 40,000 angels a year'.* The plot, he told him, 'had long been in preparation, and the Council had suspected it, but their great zeal for the repose of the realm had caused them to wink at it for the time until they should be able to learn more about it'. With fresh evidence that Somerset was 'about to put his wicked undertaking into execution', they had decided to strike first. Scheyfve then asked after Edward, whom he had heard had 'become very thin and weak during the last season', adding, 'he must be deeply distressed'. He 'might well think so,' Northumberland replied. 'It was only natural.'

Soon Somerset's allies found themselves alongside him in the Tower. At first commanded to keep his house, William Paget was carried to the Tower on 21 October accompanied by an armed guard. Arundel and Lord Grey of Wilton followed shortly. Arundel had been reluctant to visit court, but was seized after the council had letters drawn up in Edward's hand ordering him to be present for an official visit of Mary of Guise. As he was taken away, in a pointed jibe at Northumberland's tainted ancestry, he remarked that 'Neither he nor any of his family had ever been traitors but all knew who had'.[12]

The case of Somerset's ally, the Lord Chancellor Richard Rich,

---

* A coin worth ten shillings.

proceeded along somewhat different lines. When he had sent back a letter for the execution of a commission on 1 October, refusing to seal it 'because there were but eight hands [signed] to it', he received a sharp letter from Edward that the council 'maketh not our authority'. In response, Rich probably thought it politic to remain away from court, citing illness which apparently became so developed that he eventually resigned from his position on 21 December.[13]

The seventeenth-century historian Thomas Fuller told another story of Rich's demise. According to this account, the chancellor had been present at a meeting of the council to discuss Somerset's arrest, and 'though outwardly concurring with the rest, began now secretly to favour the Duke of Somerset, and sent him a letter, therein acquainting him with all passages at the Council-board'. Rich promptly sent his reply to Somerset through a courier. When the courier returned more quickly than expected, Rich asked where 'the Duke' was when he had received the letter. 'In the Charterhouse,' came the reply. Rich's heart sank: the Charterhouse was one of the London residences of Northumberland, to whom the letter had been accidentally delivered. Amusing as it is, the story seems an unlikely one. In fact, Rich was not recorded as being present at a council meeting between 29 August 1551 and 27 November 1552.[14]

The episode is of some significance, however, when assessing Edward's own developing authority. On 12 October he turned fourteen, an age that was conceptually important for a Tudor king; in 1526 it had been the age when his cousin, James V, had been declared to have reached his majority.[15] With Edward about to reach this milestone, Rich's interventions had called into question not only the procedure of government, but the new position of the king on the cusp of adulthood. Edward had already recorded in his diary on 14 August that it had been 'appointed that I should come to, and sit at, Council, when great matters were in debating or when I would'.[16] This would now be taken further. On 10 November it was asserted at a meeting of the council that it was of 'some derogation to his Majesty's honour and royal authority' for the council to sign bills on Edward's behalf – as had been the procedure since the 1549 coup against Somerset – since Edward was now perfectly capable and old enough to sign them himself.[17]

These moves have been considered as 'rather sinister' by historians, who have argued that instead of giving Edward any more say in the affairs of the realm, in fact they became the means by which Northumberland was now finally able to bypass the council and control affairs entirely through Edward's hands.[18] The council itself was evidently concerned at the developments, ordering that all such bills passed through the king's hands be minutely detailed in a docket book. Yet their worst fears were realized when, on 14 December, in place of his actual signature, Edward allowed the use of the dry stamp wielded by none other than North-umberland's stooge John Gates, 'to seal all such warrants as shall pass under the king's privy seal without other more special warrant'.[19] It must have seemed that the charade of Henry VIII's will was repeating itself all over again.

With Somerset behind bars, was Edward becoming a puppet at the hands of his new master? If this was the case, Edward certainly believed that he was holding the strings, for we can catch very definite glimpses of his growing impertinent sense of authority and majesty developing. Recording in his diary the letter he had sent to Lord Rich, Edward wrote how he had 'marvelled that he would refuse to sign that bill or deliver that letter that I had willed any one about me to write', reasoning that 'it should be a great impediment for me to send to all my Council and I should seem to be in bondage'.[20]

The Imperial ambassador also recorded how Edward refused to sign a document passed by the council, 'at which the Duke of Northumberland grew angry, believing the King to have been influenced in this by Somerset'. Edward's kingship may not have been entirely his own, but then to what extent had Henry VIII's, who had been more than content for the dry stamp to be applied in his absence?

Yet Edward seems to have lacked his father's boredom for the tedium of administration − or at least it all seemed still very exciting to his enquiring mind − throwing himself into whatever tasks he might be assigned. Cheke had even grown concerned about the pressure being put on the young king by the attentions of visiting preachers and dignitaries keen to present Edward with books and gifts − that year his accounts include works of Calvin, a French translation of Isocrates and a 'book in French of civil policy' presented by 'Archevile the Frenchman' − telling a party of reformers that they might best approach the king through him. 'The people's esteem of His Majesty,' he told a friend, 'will destroy him − and then his Reformation will be overthrown.'[21]

Meanwhile, amidst the arrests and uncertainty at court, security both in the Tower and around the city was increased. On 20 October the Mercers Company forbade any mention of Somerset's arrest, whilst the watch over the gates of London was ordered to continue from six in the morning to six at night, remaining so until 23 November. 'This town is being so closely watched,' Scheyfve grumbled, 'that no one dares discover himself ... as soon as anyone utters a word in favour of any of the prisoners, he is arrested; which angers the commons greatly.'[22]

On 22 October 1551, the guilds of London assembled in their halls, where Somerset's plots were revealed in full; he had intended to seize the Tower and destroy London before sailing to the Isle of Wight.[23] Few seem to have believed the accusations. 'It has proved impossible to persuade the people or impress it upon them,' Scheyfve considered, 'for they believe him to be a good man wrongly accused of this conspiracy, and think the origin of the matter is to be sought rather in the Duke of Northumberland's covetousness and fear of Somerset,' before smugly adding: 'It seems that God wishes to punish him and his wife, as they were the instruments of the introduction of the new religion into England.'[24] Arundel's arrest had 'caused more discontent than ever among the commons, for the Earl is very popular with all men'. Even the merchants who had been a strong base of support for Northumberland in 1549 were openly branding him 'a tyrant, hating him, and declaring that Somerset was innocent'.[25] Viewing the 'great unrest', Scheyfve believed 'serious trouble is still to be feared': 'Indeed the matter is kept alive by the hatred borne towards the Duke of Northumberland and his party by many lords, and, above all, by the commons, who are saying quite openly that the Duke of Somerset is being unjustly accused, and that the other party deserves punishment much more than the prisoners.' Already people had begun to say that 'it would be better for the King's security that he should be under the protection of the Sheriffs and the City authorities of London than in the hands of Northumberland and his following'. Tensions remained high, eventually erupting in a fight at St Paul's on 1 November, when Northumberland's servants attempted to seize the chain of office from the sheriff of London.[26]

But not all were convinced of Somerset's innocence. Former allies now sought to distance themselves from their patron, whom they found changed since his imprisonment, becoming 'so ungrateful a man'. Some had hoped that chastisement 'would have made him a new heart' but had found instead that his desire for revenge was simply too great, being unable to forget how he had been treated. Others wrote to Northumberland himself, urging him not to give the duke yet another chance.

Meanwhile the interrogation of the prisoners got under way in the Tower. By 26 October there were fresh revelations. Edward recorded that William Crane had confessed 'the place where the nobles should have been banqueted and their heads stricken off was the Lord Paget's house, and how the Earl of Arundel knew of the matter as well as he'. Crane's evidence was damning. He deposed that Somerset and Arundel had met in the grounds of Somerset House, five days before Somerset left for his tour of the Home Counties in August, though another servant admitted that Arundel, wearing a black cloak, had frequently come to Somerset Place and had used Sir Michael Stanhope 'to be the trusty messenger'. Here Arundel and Somerset had discussed 'the reformation of the estate of the realm' and agreed that Northumberland and the Marquess of Northampton should be sent to the Tower and a new Parliament called to ensure that religious affairs 'should stand as it now doth'. The meeting ended with Arundel promising 'to take such part as he did', but Somerset was nervous, and made him swear a further oath of allegiance.

Somerset's enthusiasm continued to pale. William Crane admitted the duke had told him how he 'would no further meddle with the apprehension of any of the Council' and had commanded the duchess to tell Stanhope 'to meddle no more in talk' with Arundel, admitting he was 'sorry he had gone so far'.

When confronted with evidence of his participation in Somerset's conspiracy Arundel readily submitted. 'My Lords, I cannot deny that I have had talk and communication with the Duke of Somerset, and he with me, touching both your apprehensions; and, to be plain, we determined to have apprehended you, but, by the passion of God for no harm to your bodies.' They had talked once, he admitted. The initial plan had been to arrest Northumberland, Northampton and Pembroke at the council. But after he had been shown a confession supposedly signed by Somerset, he sighed and, lifting his hands into the air, said 'They knew all': 'For my part,' he begged, 'I meant no hurt to your bodies; but we would have called you to answer and reform things.' The council stepped up their enquiries. Desperate for further proof, they ordered the Lieutenant of the Tower to allow the examiners free access to the prisoners; he himself was to assist their enquiries by 'putting the prisoners, or any of them, to such tortures as they shall think expedient'.[27] In the Tower, Somerset was interrogated by Northumberland himself. The questions put to him revealed the full range of accusations Northumberland had stacked against him: when did he intend to arrest

Northumberland? Had anyone given him 'advice to promise the people their mass, holy-water, with such other'? To whom had he spoken of taking the Isle of Wight or fortifying the harbour at Poole? To whom had he spoken about publishing a proclamation against the council, 'to understand that they went about to destroy the Common Wealth, and had also caused the King to be displeased with the Lady Mary's Grace?' Sadly, Somerset's answers do not survive.

Preparations for the trial soon got under way. On 16 November 'good and substantial full juries of knights and esquires of the best sort' were arranged to review the charges. On 23 November Paulet was appointed High Steward and ordered, ominously, to proceed in accordance with the fateful trials of those other unfortunate peers executed for treason during Henry's reign – the Duke of Buckingham and the Marquess of Exeter. Besides the council, twenty-two lords were summoned to sit as jurors, though the Earl of Shrewsbury, claiming poor health, was a notable absentee.

On the night of 30 November 1551, Somerset was informed that his trial would begin the following morning. Stripped of his Order of the Garter, he remained defiant, declaring he 'would confess nothing'. The next day security remained tight. Armed officers, their swords visible but not drawn, were placed in strategic positions, whilst that night a double watch was kept, with every householder ordered to 'see to his family and keep his house'. In order to prevent a large crowd gathering, Somerset was brought from the Tower to Westminster by boat at five in the morning. Despite this, two men drowned in the Thames as they sought to catch a glimpse of the duke as he passed under London Bridge.

The trial lasted from eight o'clock until three. The charges were read out:

> Edward Duke of Somerset ... did on 20 April ... at his mansion house, called Somerset Place, in the Strand, compass and imagine, with other persons, to deprive the King of his Royal Dignity; and to seize the King's person: and, at his, the Duke's, will and pleasure to exercise Royal Authority.
>
> That the Duke, in order to carry his traitorous intentions into effect, together with Michael Stanhope, Miles Partridge, Thomas Holcroft, Francis Newdigate, and other persons, assembled for the purpose of taking and imprisoning John now Duke of Northumberland ... Furthermore, that the said Duke of Somerset ... compassed to obtain possession of the

Great Seal, and also to obtain possession of the Tower of London, and of the treasure, jewels, and munitions of war therein contained.

And furthermore, that the said Duke, of his own authority, incited the citizens and inhabitants of London to rebellion and insurrection against the King, with drums and trumpets, crying out in English 'Liberty, Liberty,' and for the purpose also of robbing and destroying such of the other citizens and inhabitants, as would not follow his will.[28]

Somerset was defiant; he 'has never given evidence of a better mind than on this occasion,' the Imperial ambassador Scheyfve reported.[29] Denying every charge that was laid against him, he challenged each witness called before him, arguing that their evidence was either insufficient or false, declaring 'all ill he could devise' of the principal witness, Thomas Palmer. The best account we have of the trial is in Edward's own hand, set down in his diary:

> For the banquet: first he swore it was untrue and required more witnesses; when Crane's confession was read, he would have had him come face to face. For London: he meant nothing for hurt of any lord, but for his own defense. For the gendarmery: it were but a mad matter for him to enter-prise, with his 100 against 900. For having men in his chamber at Greenwich . . . it seemed he meant no harm, because, when he could have done harm, he did not.[30]

Edward seems to have been hardly convinced by Somerset's defence, writing to Barnaby Fitzpatrick how he had 'barely answered' the charges, believing Someset 'seemed to have confessed' to charges of felony. However, Edward can hardly be taken at his word, having probably been fed a description of the trial by Northumberland's acolytes, with the new duke himself being presented as magnanimous and merciful to his foe, not allowing 'for any charges relating to him to be taken as treason'. A different, and more hostile, version of Northumberland's participation in the trial relates how Northumberland had feigned sadness in the hope that his actions would be seen 'to proceed from modesty'. Instead the move backfired, since it was assumed he simply lacked the proof to convict Somerset of treason.[31] The lords' discussion was heated. North-ampton was 'contentious with many' whilst some questioned whether it was legal at all for Northumberland, Pembroke and Northampton to be involved in the proceedings since many of the charges directly concerned them, while others wondered that such 'a mean action' should be taken as treason.

Crowds had gathered outside Westminster Hall, their chants of 'God save the Duke' so loud that they could be heard within the hall, leaving the lords 'much perplexed and astonished'. When the final verdict was read out, Somerset was found not guilty of treason. Upon the words of acquittal, the guardsman of the hall, not expecting further verdict, left with his axe pointing downwards, traditionally taken by the awaiting crowds outside as a sign of the defendant's innocence. At once scenes of jubilation erupted: 'There was such a shout of men and women, for they thought that he had been quit, for they threw a hundred caps on high for gladness.' According to Scheyfve, Edward himself heard the tumult and asked what it meant. Told that Somerset had been acquitted, he replied 'he had never believed Somerset could be a traitor'. That day, he wrote in his journal how: 'The people, knowing not the matter, shouted half a dozen times so loud that from the hall door it was heard at Charing Cross plainly, and rumours went that he was quit of all.'

Messengers were dispatched with the news which was quickly 'scattered through the town, to the great joy and satisfaction of all'. When Matthew Colhurst, Somerset's auditor, heard of his master's acquittal he caused bonfires to be lit and bells rung for hours, handing out bread and drink in celebration. The next day he sent his servant through the streets to give twopence each to the poor, 'where he never gave 1d in his life before'.[32]

All was premature, for the sentencing had not finished. Somerset, though innocent of the crime of treason, had been found guilty of committing felony under legislation passed to prevent the gathering of unlawful assemblies. The duke must have known his fate before the sentence of death by hanging was pronounced. A silence struck the court as he fell to his knees. Thanking the court for his trial, he requested pardon from Northumberland, Northampton and Pembroke, asking that his wife, children, servants and debts be taken care of. Edward's accounts of the trial, recorded in his journal and in a letter to Barnaby Fitzpatrick, recorded how he confessed he 'meant to destroy' them 'although before he swore vehemently to the contrary', though such statements – probably fed to him by Northumberland's agents – should be treated with caution. According to another report, Northumberland heard Somerset's pleas in silence before replying: 'Duke of Somerset, you see yourself a man in peril of life and sentenced to die. Once before I saved you in a like danger, nor will I desist to serve you now, though you may not believe me. Appeal to the mercy of the King's Majesty, which I doubt not he will extend to you. For myself, gladly I pardon all things which you have designed against me, and I will do my best that your life may be spared'.

As Somerset was led back to the Tower, the crowd were divided: 'The one cried for joy that he was acquitted, the other cried out that he was condemned.'[33] Was Somerset guilty? No less an authority than the jurist Edward Coke considered that the indictment against him was insufficient and faulty, whilst some historians have branded the evidence contrived and the trial a travesty, entirely concocted by Northumberland, 'the subtlest and most devious disciple of Machiavelli'.[34] Importantly, Northumberland himself would later confess that he had 'procured his death unjustly' and had regretted his actions ever since, for 'nothing had pressed so injuriously upon his conscience as the fraudulent scheme against the Duke of Somerset which would never have come to pass without his authority and favour'.[35]

But, as has been shown, a conspiracy *was* planned during April 1551. The questions put to Somerset during his interrogation were both specific and related to the events of April and the testimonies of the duke's other associates. According to the Imperial ambassador Scheyfve, Somerset admitted during the trial that he had 'talked with some of his familiars and friends about finding means to abase the Northumberland, but not to kill him; and he considered he had had ample cause for so doing'. To Edward, all this was proof enough that Somerset had 'seemed to confess he went about their death'.[36] Somerset also seemed to have confessed to the charge that he sought to marry Edward to his daughter, reportedly mentioning that 'history showed that the Kings of England had usually married in the country, and that he would have done nothing without the Council's consent'. Piece by piece, there was sufficient evidence to suggest that Somerset was a man too dangerous to be kept either free or alive.

Two days after the trial, the duke seems to have finally cracked. Edward recorded in his diary how Somerset, now placed in the Tower, had admitted to hiring a Frenchman named Berteville to kill Northumberland. The episode is mysterious and remains unexplained. Earlier Berteville had been arrested and confessed under examination, but was released on 1 November, when the council had curiously paid off his debts and provided him with a house. Had a deal been struck to ensure Somerset's conviction? Interestingly, Berteville's involvement was not discussed during the trial, and was perhaps held back to later convince those who doubted the duke's conviction. For Edward, the news seems to have been evidence enough of his guilt.

The negative reaction to Somerset's arrest had shocked Northumberland, with the Imperial ambassador considering that he had been 'greatly deceived' to believe there had been sufficient evidence to convict Somerset: 'This tends to diminish Northumberland's prestige and give him pause, showing him that it is not so easy to govern according to his whim.' Northumberland now faced the dilemma of whether to execute the fallen duke, and at what cost – when Edward was old enough to rule would he possibly take revenge? He spent time with Somerset in the Tower, so much so that Pembroke and Northampton began to grow suspicious. 'It seems he is sorely puzzled at present,' the Imperial ambassador wrote, 'and does not know how all this is to end.'[37]

Northumberland's woes and spiralling popularity were not helped by an unfortunate flaw in the die of the new coinage which many believed showed Northumberland's emblem of the bear's ragged staff – a clear sign that the new duke had in mind to take over the kingdom. Added to this, prophecies began to circulate that Edward did not have long to live.[38]

Security was further heightened. From 10 December 1551 the mayor sent his deputies each Sunday to warn preachers at St Paul's Cross not to read out any writings or bills presented to them, and the writer and his printer of a seditious tract printed as a New Year's gift were punished. When one William Thompson sang a lewd ditty, the council ordered the mayor to investigate if it was of his own composition; if it was, he was to be set in the pillory and have both his ears cut off.[39] Order was promptly restored with a blatant show of the council's military power, for on 7 December their new private army, the gendarmery, assembled for the first time, parading past Edward in St James's Park. They 'will serve to intimidate the people,' Scheyfve wrote, 'and will be ready to strike if there is any sign of revolt'.[40] It numbered a thousand men dressed in the liveries of the nobility. Edward watched, no doubt impressed, for he proudly wrote in his diary that they were 'all well-armed men, some with feathers, staves and pencels of their colours, some with sleeves and half coats, some with bards and staves . . . The horses all fair and great', whilst he boasted in a letter to Barnaby that the new guard were 'so horsed as was never seen, I dare say, so many good horses, and so well-armed men. We think you shall see in France none like.' The Imperial ambassador was less impressed, finding the guard 'lightly armed and only middling-well accoutred, neither armour or horses being remarkable ... the troops were clumsy and unseasoned'.[41]

That winter the court was a hive of activity. Tournaments and banquets followed each other in quick succession with Edward holding open court and table 'which had not yet been done in his time'.[42] Edward's thoughts were clearly preoccupied. He wrote to Barnaby that 'this last Christmas hath been well and merrily passed'. Edward's diary entries are concerned solely with the tournaments and entertainments that were staged, drawing up lists of the challengers and defendants – on 3 January 1552 eighteen men, including Northumberland's three sons, 'ran six courses apiece at tilt against the challengers, and accomplished their courses right well'. Again on the 6th there were more challenges, a play and 'a talk between one that was called Riches, and the other Youth, whether [one] of them was better' which developed into a mock tournament. Edward even took part in directing the 'plays and pastimes' that Christmas, which were frequently altered 'to serve his majesty's pleasure and determination'.[43] According to one chronicler, the revels were 'of the council's appoint-ment' intended to distract Edward from thoughts of his uncle's execution and 'to remove fond talk out of men's mouths'. Such a strategy seems to have worked, with Edward even snubbing the Imperial ambassador in mid conversation as he became absorbed in the entertainments around him. Yet relying on his contacts at court, Scheyfve had heard from trustworthy sources that Edward 'is grieved and sombre about the impris-onment of his uncle' but 'had been so carefully primed with evil accounts of the said Somerset that he shows no feeling for him'.[44]

Throughout Christmas, many still held out hope for Somerset's pardon. 'Thou shalt see another world ere Candlemas,' Thomas Holland predicted. 'The Duke of Somerset shall come forth of the Tower, and the Duke of Northumberland shall go in.'[45] Northumberland had other plans. Fearing that the duke's supporters might attempt to question and overturn his sentence in Parliament, he resolved to execute the duke before it reconvened on 23 January. Others were on side to force his hand, not least the French ambassador de Gye, who had found Somerset frustratingly resistant to the alliance between England and France that he was attempting to forge, including the projected marriage between Edward and Henry II's daughter Elizabeth. He was said to have 'used certain persuasive arguments' to persuade Edward, at first reluctant to agree to his uncle's execution, that Somerset had to die, 'showing him that an example was required in so serious a matter, that many disturbances had cropped up in the kingdom during Somerset's administration and Protectorate, and, above all, that he was so popular that the commons had become less devoted to the Crown'.[46]

Yet Edward knew what fate held for his uncle. Somerset had been condemned by law, and had to face justice: 'Let the law take its course,' he is reported to have remarked. According to Scheyfve, he wrote to the duke on 21 January, informing him that he would receive the more merciful execution of beheading. The same day the warrant for his execution was issued, signed by Edward's own hand.[47] That night, Somerset came to terms with his fate. Inside a book of devotions he had taken to the Tower, he wrote the following words:

> Fear of the Lord is the beginning of wisdom.
> Put thy trust in the Lord with all thine heart.
> Be not wise in thine own conceit, but fear the
> Lord and flee from evil.

> From the tower, the day before my death ... E. Somerset.[48]

At eight o'clock in the morning of 22 January 1552, Somerset was brought out of the Tower. Surrounded by an entourage of armed guard, he was led to Tower Hill. Despite Northumberland's attempts to prevent an audience being present by moving the time of execution three hours ahead, a huge crowd had already gathered. Some still held out hope that the king's pardon might grant the duke a last reprieve, others came to pay their last respects to a man they considered their hero.

When he had reached the scaffold, Somerset knelt down on both knees. Raising his hands, he commended himself to God. A nobleman standing nearby recognized the gesture as one that he had frequently used in his household. After reciting 'a few short prayers', he stood to face the east of the scaffold. Emotionless at the sight of the axe's blade, he displayed an 'alacrity and cheerfulness of mind' as he bowed and addressed the crowd:

> Masters and good fellows, I am come hither to die; but a true and faithful man as any was unto the King's Majesty and to his realm. But I am condemned by a law whereunto I am subject, and are we all, and therefore to show obedience I am content to die; wherewith I am well content, being a thing most heartily welcome unto me; for the which I do thank

God, taking it for a singular benefit as ever might have come to me otherwise. For, as I am a man, I have deserved at God's hand many deaths; and it has pleased his goodness, whereas He might have taken me suddenly, that I should neither have known Him nor myself, thus now to visit me and call me with this present death as you do see, where I have had time to remember and acknowledge Him, and to know also myself, for the which I do thank Him most heartily. And, my friends, more I have to say to you concerning religion: I have been always, being in authority, a furtherer of it to the glory of God to the uttermost of my power; whereof I am nothing sorry, but rather have cause and do rejoice most gladly that I have so done, for the mightiest benefit of God that ever I had, or any man might have in this world, beseeching you all to take it so, and to follow it on still; for, if not, there will follow and come a worse and great plague.[49]

Suddenly a thunderous sound burst out across the skies. The crowd began to scatter in fear and confusion; some ran into nearby houses, others dived into the Tower ditch. Many fell to the ground and grovelled, clinging to their poleaxes and halberds crying, 'Jesus save us, Jesus save us' and 'This way, they come that way, they come, away, away, away!' Those present described the sound as being like gunpowder stored in an armoury exploding, the noise of 'some great storm or tempest' or the sound of the galloping charge of cavalry. An observer recorded how Somerset stood amazed, 'looking when any man would knock me on the head'.[50]

Sir Anthony Browne circled beneath the scaffold on his horse, attempting to calm the crowd. The message quickly spread: 'The king, by that messenger, had sent his uncle pardon.' Caps and cloaks were thrown into the air as the reassembled crowd began to chant, 'Pardon, pardon is come; God save the king.'

But there was no pardon. Shouts of rejoicing soon returned to sorrow and tears. 'I do not think that, in so great slaughter of dukes as hath been in England within these few years,' one onlooker recalled, 'there were so many weeping eyes at one time.'

Somerset had remained quiet, standing on the same spot of the scaffold, his cap in hand. With a 'grave countenance' he made a sign to the crowd with his hand as if to quiet them:

There is no such thing good people, there is no such thing. It is the ordinance of God thus for to die, wherewith we must be content, and I pray you be quiet for I myself am quiet and make you no stirring and I pray you now let us pray together for the King's majesty to whose Grace I have been always faithful, true and most loving subject, desirous always of his most prosperous success in all his affairs and ever glad of the furtherance and helping forth ward of the common wealth of this realm.[51]

His speech was interrupted by shouts of 'Ye, ye, ye'. Upon mention of the king's name a cry of 'Amen' rose up from those gathered below.

It was a time for old wounds to be healed. Wary of his reckoning before God, Somerset looked for forgiveness: 'I have had oftentimes affairs with divers men, and hard it is to please every man, therefore, if there be any that hath been offended and injured by me, I most humbly require and ask him forgiveness, but especially Almighty God, whom, throughout all my life, I have most grievously offended; and all others whatsoever they be that have offended me, I do with my whole heart forgive them.'

Once again he urged for silence. 'Now I once again require you, dearly beloved in the Lord, that you will keep yourselves quiet and still, lest, through your tumult, you might trouble me. For albeit the spirit be willing and ready, the flesh is frail and wavering, and, through your quietness, I shall be much more quiet.'

For Antonio de Guaras, a Catholic and hostile observer and newcomer to the spectacle of an English public execution, the request was scarcely believable. Would there be no sign of struggle, one last attempt for freedom? Surely, he later wrote, 'if he had cast himself from the scaffold, or struggled with the executioner, assuredly he had not died there, being held of no chains or bonds, it being the custom to exempt noblemen from these when they are led to the scaffold ... the guard of halberdiers and the others would have connived at his escape on account of the favour of the people'. Somerset, he declared, clearly showed a 'want of spirit'.[52]

The duke turned to kneel. Cox presented him with a scroll containing his confession; without hesitation Somerset read it aloud and returned to his feet. Having shaken hands with everybody on the scaffold he rewarded the executioner with a few coins, set aside in the hope that he would deliver a blow both quick and painless. Taking off Somerset's gown, the executioner turned the stiff collar around in order not to hinder the stroke of the axe. Somerset's cheeks, the observer noted, began to turn visibly red.

As the axe fell the crowd groaned. The corpse was thrown on to a cart and taken away to be buried in the Tower. Throughout the day, crowds came to the execution site to talk about the duke, lamenting and bewailing his death. Those near to the scaffold 'washed their hands in his blood'; others mopped it up with their handkerchiefs.[53]

Further down the river at Westminster, Edward wrote only one line in his journal that day: 'The Duke of Somerset had his head cut off upon Tower Hill between eight and nine o'clock in the morning.' For some historians, these chilling words have characterized his personality, accusing him of displaying a lack of 'personal warmth' and 'boyish affection'. Another account tells a different story. It relates that upon hearing news of his uncle's death, Edward 'gave no token of any ill distempered passion' since he thought it 'not agreeable to majesty openly to declare himself'. The tournaments and revels that had been part of the Twelfth Night festivities had been staged, it pointed out, 'to dispel any dampy thoughts, which the remembrance of his Uncle might raise'. However, if Somerset's name was ever mentioned Edward would 'often sigh and let fall tears' saying

> that his Uncle had done nothing, or if he had it was very small and proceeded rather from his wife than from himself, and where then said he was the good nature of a Nephew? Where was the clemency of a Prince? Ah how unfortunate have I been to those of my blood, my mother I slew at my birth, and since have made away two of her brothers, and happily to make away for others against myself, was it ever known before that a King's Uncle, A Lord Protector one whose fortunes had much advanced the honour of the realm, did lose his head for felony; for a felony neither clear in law, and in fact weakly proved. Alas so how falsely have I been abused? How weakly carried? How little was I master of mine own judgement, that both his death and envy thereof must be laid upon me.[54]

His rival destroyed, Northumberland's power now went unfettered as he turned his attention to Somerset's supporters. On 27 January Sir Ralph Vane, Sir Thomas Arundell, Sir Miles Partridge and Sir Michael Stanhope were indicted for their parts in the conspiracy. Vane, ever fiery in temperament, answered to the charges 'like a ruffian'. The jury had been understandably reluctant to convict Arundell, who had been a prisoner in the Tower since January 1550 and had only been released three days before Palmer's first confession. But locked in a room together from noon until the following morning, without food or water, they eventually submitted.[55] On 26 February Stanhope and Arundell were beheaded, with Vane and Partridge suffering the baser death of hanging from a nearby gallows. They went to their deaths proclaiming their innocence to the last. Their bodies, placed in new coffins, were buried in the Tower.[56]

The Earl of Arundel and Paget escaped this fate, but both their political careers were effectively terminated. Arundel never came to trial, but after he had confessed his part in the conspiracy he was fined and eventually set free in December 1552. Not even Northumberland could find any evidence upon which to pin down Paget on charges of treason, so the charges were dropped and instead altered to those of corruption and embezzlement of public money. Paget's offence was minor – probably no less crooked than that of other members of the council, but he knew full well his real offence had been to have remained too close a friend of Somerset's. According to Edward, furious that Paget had abused his princely authority, Paget 'confessed how he without commission did sell away my lands and greater timber woods, how he had taken great fines of my lands to his said peculiar profit and advantage, never turning any to my use or commodity . . . For these crimes and others he surrendered his office and submitted himself to those fines that I or my Council would appoint.' There were further humiliations to follow. Shortly before the annual feast of the Order of the Garter, Paget was stripped of his garter, as Edward recalled 'chiefly because he was no gentleman either on his father's side nor mother's side'. Traditionally the move has been seen as entirely part of Northumberland's policy of vengeance against Paget, but if this was the case, Edward was in full agreement. His drafts for the new Order of the Garter specifically laid out that those 'attainted of . . . negligence and notable crime' should be removed from their stalls and Paget was 'well content' to hand over his garter, 'seeing it was the king's pleasure it should be so'.[57] Fined a further £5,000 and ordered to renounce all his stewardships and keeperships, Paget was ordered to depart to his Staffordshire estates. He accepted the fine with grace, but when it came to leaving London, he pleaded 'with the effusion of many tears' to be allowed to remain – his wife, Lady Paget, suffered from a 'stitch in her side' that required the attention of a London doctor, as did his own complaint, a fistula which he told the council 'rots as he goes', and finally convinced them to allow him to stay.[58]

Somerset's death shook not only the political landscape, but the hopes of the reformers. Both Cranmer and the preacher Nicholas Ridley had appealed to Northumberland to save Somerset's life, with Ridley earning

Northumberland's 'high displeasure ... for shewing his conscience secretly, but plainly and fully'. Uncertain times lay ahead, with the reformers in a difficult position. Horrified at Somerset's death, they could hardly complain for fear of jeopardizing their cherished project of reform of the Church. Some, in hope that Edward might step forward to reform the kingdom, looked to the day when he would come of age: 'At this time many that bore affection to the Duke talked that the young King was now to be feared,' one chronicler wrote. But it was perhaps Henry's erstwhile queen, Anne of Cleves, in a letter to her brother, who best summed up the mood: 'God knows what will happen next.'[59]

AN EMERGING KING

With Somerset dead, Northumberland's dominance of Edward was complete. Northumberland seems to have held an incredible, almost mesmeric, sway over Edward, who by all accounts regarded him 'in the place of a father'. No more clearly was this felt than by the Imperial ambassador who, snatching a moment to speak with Edward in early January over the perennial question of his sister's mass, observed how the king kept his eye constantly upon Northumberland and 'got up to withdraw because of the signs the Duke of Northumberland made to him'. Other observers noticed that Northumberland's influence over Edward was derived in part from his obsequious flattery of the king, designed to convince him into believing that he was completely in control of affairs.[1]

Perhaps more importantly, the appointment of Northumberland's 'intimate friend' and confidant Sir John Gates to the king's Privy Chamber in 1550 provided the duke with the best opportunity to get beneath Edward's skin. Gates was noted by a French observer as 'the principal instrument which he used in order to induce the King to something when he did not want it to be known that it had proceeded from himself'. Gates not only held the dry stamp of Edward's signature, allowing him to sign on behalf of the king, but was continually at Edward's side, allowing him unique access to report everything said in private back to Northumberland. Northumberland's careful manipulation of the Privy Chamber – essentially the men closest to the king – had allowed him to graft himself to Edward, controlling his thoughts whilst at the same time allowing him the semblance of greater power and freedom. 'All of the others who were in the Chamber,' the Frenchman considered, 'were creatures of the Duke.' Sir Henry Sidney, Northumberland's son-in-law, had 'acquired so great an influence near the King that he was able to make all of his notions conform to those of the Duke'. One wonders also whether William Thomas, the clerk of the council whose secret correspondence with Edward had proved so influential upon the developing mind of the young king, may not also have been merely an agent of Northumberland's, whose subtle purpose was solely to plant ideas into Edward's mind whilst fostering a mirage of independence. Northumberland himself was not averse to using the same tactic, paying secret visits to Edward at night, 'unseen by anyone, after all were asleep' so that Edward would come into the council chamber the following day and propose matters of business 'as if they were his own; consequently, everyone was amazed, thinking that they proceeded from his mind and by his invention'.[2]

Yet the sheer strength of the royal will meant that little could be done if Edward wanted things his way. The poetical autobiography of one of Edward's Privy Chamber gentlemen, Nicholas Throckmorton, certainly gives the impression of a king whose personal whims could not be denied. As a favourite of Edward's who was treated with 'special grace' above all others, Throckmorton was well placed to observe the mechanics of court politics from the inside. As he grew closer to the king, Edward, being 'wearied much with Lords', spent increasing amounts of time with him 'most merrily' in play. Then one day Edward decided that Throckmorton should be knighted on the spot, abruptly declaring that he kneel to receive his honour. Knowing what Northumberland might think of the whole charade, Throckmorton thought it best to run away. Edward gave chase and, finding Throckmorton hiding behind a chest, dubbed him a knight.

As a result of Edward's favour, Throckmorton's position at court rose considerably: 'My joys did flow: The King me fancied daily more and more. For as his years so did my favour grow ...' Despite being accused 'with false reports' by others jealous of his success, they were unable to dislodge Throckmorton from Edward's favour. In his own words, he remained:

> In childish cradle of security
> I rocked myself asleep; devoid of care;
> For why? I was the King's familiar.

Shortly after Somerset's death, however, Throckmorton recalled how Edward had begun to frown upon Northumberland for his part in the execution, a fact picked up by an Italian visitor who reported how Edward had turned on Northumberland whilst out at archery practice, taunting that he had 'aimed better when you cut off the head of my uncle Somerset'. Paranoid that Throckmorton's influence was poisoning Edward's mind against him, Northumberland 'sought at once to pull me down':

> He much misliked our secret conference,
> The privy whisperings that the King did use;
> He thought they little made for his defence,
> And that, alone, the King I did abuse
> With tales. But sure of me he did misdeem,
> Who thought I drew not yoked in his team.[3]

When Edward discovered that Throckmorton had accrued significant debts whilst at court, he offered him lands and an income. Throckmorton at first refused, but was encouraged by his friends to 'take time, while there was: and while the iron was hot to strike the stroke'. Edward's generosity, which had once got him into severe trouble in his dealings with his uncle Sir Thomas Seymour, seemingly showed no bounds.

These incidents may have been both exaggerated and apocryphal (Edward makes only one mention of Throckmorton in his diary) yet they reflect closely a similar story told by the aforementioned Italian visitor. When Edward rewarded his servant with a castle, his councillors did not dare to oppose his wishes in public, but later spoke with the servant, offering him money instead. When the servant reported back to Edward asking for a less valuable present, Edward demanded to know why his will had not been obeyed. After the reason had been explained, Edward 'with childish grief' was almost in tears: 'But to yourselves and your friends,' he answered, 'whatsoever you have importuned me for, has always been given advisedly and expediently, nor was utility or royal honour then an obstacle, neither will I permit those things to be given by you, which it is my will and my duty to bestow from myself.'[4]

Edward's letters to Barnaby Fitzpatrick, still ensconced in France, reveal to us his self-assured and confident nature. They also illustrate Edward's tastes and the strength of his religious outlook. On 28 February Edward willed Barnaby 'not to live too sumptuously as an ambassador, but so as your proportion of living may demean you ... because we know how many will resort to you, and desire to serve you. I told you how many I thought convenient you should keep.' If he was 'vehemently procured' he might 'go as waiting on the king, not so intending to the abuse nor willingly seeing the ceremonies, and you look on the mass; but in the mean season read the Scripture or some good book, and give no reverence to the mass at all'. Edward ordered Barnaby to stay close to the English ambassador, William Pickering, 'and to be instructed by him how to use yourself. For women, as farforth as you may, avoid their company. Yet if the French king command you, you may sometimes dance, so measure be your mean. Else apply yourself to riding, shooting or tennis, with such honest games – not forgetting, sometimes, when you have leisure, your learning; chiefly reading the Scripture. This I write, not doubting but you would have done so though I had not written, but to spur you on to do so.'[5]

There could be no denying that Edward had begun to take upon himself a greater share in the government of the realm. Edward's surviving political papers attest his detailed attention to its business. In January 1552 Edward had drafted 'Certain points of weighty matters to be immediately concluded on by my council', which he delivered personally to the Marquess of Winchester in the Privy Chamber at Greenwich.[6] Edward's diary best demonstrates this growing sense of independence. Not only are its entries fuller and more aware of the detailed business of government, but its language suggests Edward was taking a prominent position within it. On 3 March Edward wrote that 'it was agreed that for better dispatch of things certain of the council, with others joined with them, should overlook the penal laws and put certain of them in execution. Others should answer suitors; others should oversee my revenues and the order of them, and also of the superfluous, and the payments heretofore made, others should have commission of taking away superfluous bulwarks.' 'I did deny after a sort the request to enter into war,' he noted on 28 March; in Parliament on 15 April, 'I signed a bill containing the names of the acts which I would have pass'. Other changes were more subtle but no less significant. 'The Council' had become 'my Council' confirmed by the Imperial ambassador's report in late March that Edward was 'usually' present at council meetings 'especially when state business is being transacted' and had begun attending before Somerset's arrest.[7]

But it was the reorganization of the council's administration mentioned in Edward's 3 March journal entry that pointed to a new stage in the king's own political involvement. Under these plans, one of the new commissions set up was a council 'for the State' composed of members of the Privy Council with the responsibility 'to attend matters of the state', meeting Edward once a week on Tuesday afternoons 'to hear the debating of things of most importance'. This was more than another commission. Merging a core group of men from the Privy Chamber, the Privy Council and the royal household together, its focus was around the king, briefing him on all matters of policy in preparation for his own impending majority.[8]

Despite every sign that Edward was maturing into a king able to seize fully the reins of power, there is no surviving evidence for his involvement in the formulation of the second Book of Common Prayer, authorized in April 1552, and brought into use from 1 November. This book was to act as a clarification to the 1549 Prayer Book, which, despite acting as a compromise between Protestantism and Catholicism, was most probably intended only as a temporary measure and had pleased no one, especially the reformers, who shirked at any mention of the mass in the text. 'I am so much offended with that book,' wrote the reformer John Hooper, 'that if it be not corrected, I neither can nor will communicate with the church in the administration of the supper.'[9] At the same time, as the reformers embedded themselves as bishops in their new sees, they had been horrified to discover the state of parish religion; attendance at church was poor, half of the priests Hooper met could not recite the Ten Commandments and most were continuing to use forbidden ceremonies. Many had simply found ways to work around the 1549 Prayer Book whilst retaining the essentials of their Catholic belief; the noblewoman Lady Marney, whose will requested that she be buried with full Catholic pomp, including masses being sung for her soul, could see no contradiction that on the day of her burial she wanted sung 'such service as is set out or appointed by the King's book [i.e. the Prayer Book]'. Meanwhile, despite the smashing of images, the whitewashing of churches and the toppling of altars, destruction could never amount to conversion and the formation of a Protestant nation. Reforms had not been followed through with preaching and discipline, the reformer Martin Bucer told Edward in person in 1550, only 'by means of ordinances which the majority obey very grudgingly, and by the removal of the instruments of ancient superstition'.[10]

Something needed to be done, and a uniform order imposed upon every church. In doing so, the new revised Book of Common Prayer made a decisive break with the past. Ceremonies that had been retained in the old service and had been condemned by Protestants were now removed, and the baptism, confirmation and burial services rewritten – with an end to any possibility of prayers for the dead, the way communities viewed their world order was transformed drastically. In the communion service, many prayers were omitted and the former structure of the mass removed. Any hint of transubstantiation – that the bread and wine actually transformed into the body and blood of Christ – was removed, with emphasis being placed instead on remembrance of Christ's sacrifice: 'Take and eat this, in remembrance that Christ died for thee, and feed on him in thy heart by faith, with thanksgiving.' All mention of the Virgin Mary, saints and prophets now disappeared, as did all vestments except for the priest's surplice, and music was reduced to a bare minimum, whilst in a final coda, a 'black rubric' – tagged on after the book had gone to press – was forced to deny that kneeling at the communion suggested adoration.

The 1552 Prayer Book was the high-water mark for Edward's Reformation, marking 'the greatest single achievement of Edward's reign'.[11] Its legacy would live on into our own times, for it was the model for the Elizabethan Book, which was only slightly changed in 1662 and became the liturgy for the Church of England for the next four centuries. Whether the 1552 Prayer Book was Cranmer's final word on the Reformation, however, seems unlikely, for as he moved the Church of England cautiously step by step towards the model that John Calvin had set in Geneva, reformers would later maintain that he would have 'drawn up a book of prayer a hundred times more perfect than this that we now have' if only he had not faced the opposition of others.[12]

The new direction that Edward's Church was taking was confirmed in a statement of doctrine, the forty-two articles of faith, issued early the following year. Going further than ever before, the articles affirmed the Protestant doctrines of justification by faith alone, and even a belief in predestination, whilst finally declaring transubstantiation 'repugnant to the plain words of scripture' and the ceremonies of the mass as 'fables and dangerous deceits'. At the same time new inventories were ordered to be prepared for authorities to gather in what was left of the Church plate, bells and vestments that remained unsold, ready to be melted down in one final spoliation, to pay for a government that was teetering upon the brink of bankruptcy.

Though Edward may not have put his hand to the 1552 Prayer Book, he continued to maintain a strong interest in the reformed faith and its application. In one celebrated story, Edward sent for Bishop Nicholas Ridley after he had heard his sermon exhorting the rich to charity. Meeting him alone in the great gallery at Westminster, Edward commended Ridley on his sermon, but wanted to know how he could do more: 'I am in the highest place, and therefore I am the first that must make answer to God for my negligence if I should not be careful therein, knowing it to be the express commandment of almighty God to have compassion of his poor and needy members...' He understood that Ridley had been in contact with others about 'what ways are best to be taken' and wanted him to 'say your mind' about what should be done. Ridley urged Edward to write a letter to the mayor asking for his support, which Edward immediately agreed to, making the bishop wait until the letter had been written and signed before sending him away with it. With the wheels set in motion, Ridley and the city fathers devised a plan for the royal palace of Bridewell to be used to house the able-bodied poor and re-founded as Christ's Hospital, first instituted as a 'place of correction for the idle and vagabond'.[13]

All this seems to be evidence of Edward's direct involvement in the business of government. But the future of Bridewell had been in consideration long before Ridley's sermon. The City authorities had already been in contact with the council and a series of committees, drawing up schemes, had been arranged. Indeed the enterprise of London hospitals had been a slow birth, dating back to around 1544. Nor was Edward's assent the final push that the reform measures needed. Ridley later pleaded with Cecil how the matter 'hath lain too long abroad ... without lodging in the streets of London both hungry, naked and cold'; still nothing was done, despite the citizens of London appealing once more to Edward that for this deed Christ would 'crown your grace with an everlasting diadem'. Still, Edward would need to be lying on his deathbed before he made the gift of Bridewell to the City and plans were still being drawn up and discussed for its foundation in 1557.[14]

However, on 2 April, Edward 'fell sick of the measles and the small-pox'. He made a swift recovery, writing to Barnaby on 12 April that: 'We have a little been troubled with the small pox, which hath letted us to write hitherto; but now we have shaken that quite away.'[15] Elizabeth wrote shortly after, declaring her joy for Edward's 'good escape out of the perilous diseases': 'For I do now say ... that a disease is to be counted no sickness that shall cause a better health when it is past than was assured afore it came. For afore you had them, every man thought that that should not be eschewed of you that was not scaped of many, but since you have had them, doubt of them is past and hope is given to all men that it was a purgation by these means for other worse diseases which might happen this year.'[16]

Edward seems to have recovered swiftly, and returned to the world of the court and the next chapter of the Garter ceremonies that he had worked so studiously upon, participating in the new ceremonies in person. By 28 April the Imperial ambassador was reporting that Edward was 'very cheerful' and in 'the most favourable countenance possible'. On 12 May he was seen riding from Greenwich Park to Blackheath, shooting at arrows and running the ring. On 16 May he inspected the muster of the gendarmerie again.[17]

From 30 May there is evidence that Edward was now directly participating in government, signing warrants for payment by his own hand rather than the collective signatures of the council. When, on 8 June, the lords of the council warned the mayor and aldermen of London in front of a thousand at the Guildhall of 'their slothfulness' in tolerating high prices for victuals and the craftsmen for 'their willfulness', Edward recalled in his diary how 'if upon this admonition they did not amend, I was wholly determined to call in their liberties as confiscate'.[18]

Edward was on the threshold of power, and he knew it. Roger Ascham recalled how during his calligraphy lessons with the king, Edward 'would oft most gently promise me one day to do me good'. Ascham brushed aside the remark: 'Your Majesty will soon forget me when I shall be absent from you.' Yet Edward was insistent. 'I do not mistrust these words because they were spoken of a child,' wrote Ascham, 'but rather I have laid up my sure hope in them because they were uttered by a King.'[19]

If more proof were needed that Edward, inching his way through adolescence, was on the cusp of inheriting his kingship and its duties, the decision that he should leave the environs of London for the first time to make his first official 'progress' of his country – essentially a royal tour – of his country confirmed it. Of course for the Tudors this meant travelling no further than the southern counties of England, but its geographical limitation should not obscure the fact that for the first time the English nation outside London would be given the opportunity to see their king. It was also a mark of improving stability – there had been few reports of trouble so far – that the council felt comfortable about leaving the capital whilst they accompanied Edward on his tour.

On 15 July Edward began his progress, first travelling to Guildford then to Petworth the following day. Yet by 24 July the sheer size of Edward's massive following, numbering some four thousand horse, had begun 'to eat up the country'. Finding 'little meadow nor hay all the way' the large numbers of bands that had been arraigned were sent home, and the progress continued with a select band of 150. On 25 July Edward travelled to Cowdray, the house of Sir Anthony Browne, where he recorded in a letter to Barnaby Fitzpatrick that 'we were marvellously, yea, rather excessively banqueted'. Edward next journeyed to Halnaker, near Chichester – 'a pretty house', Edward recorded. On 2 August he travelled to Warblington, a 'fair house' belonging to Sir Richard Cotton, then Waltham, 'a fair, great old house' currently in the possession of the Marquess of Winchester. 'In all these places we had both good hunting and good cheer.'

Next Edward visited Portsmouth, where he viewed the naval defences of the city. 'We found the bulwarks chargeable, massy, well rampaired, but ill-fashioned, ill-flanked, and set in unmeet places,' he wrote to Barnaby, 'the town weak in comparison of what it ought to be ... the haven notable, great, and standing by nature easy to be fortified; and for the more strength thereof we have devised two strong castles on either side of the haven, at the mouth thereof; for at the mouth of the haven is not past ten score over, but in the middle almost a mile over; and in length, for a mile and a half, able to bear the greatest ship in Christendom.'[20]

Edward arrived at Southampton on 14 August. 'The citizens had bestowed for our coming great cost in painting, repairing, and rampairing of their walls,' he wrote of his visit. 'The town is handsome, and for the bigness of it as fair houses as be at London. The citizens made great cheer, and many of them kept costly tables.' His route then took him through Hampshire into Dorset and on to Wiltshire. At Salisbury he was received by twenty-four aldermen in crimson gowns, and forty-eight 'other honest men' in violet, all on horseback, and presented with a gilt cup filled with £20 in gold.[21]

Edward wrote to Barnaby on 22 August, apologizing for his lengthy delay in writing since 'we meant to have something worth writing, ere [before] we would write anything'. In contrast to Barnaby's own experiences on the battlefield in France, Edward was hard pushed not to boast of his enjoyments. 'For, whereas you have all been occupied in killing of your enemies, in long marchings, in painful journeys, in extreme heat, in sore skirmishings, in divers assaults; we have been occupied in killing of wild beasts, in pleasant journeys, in good fare, in viewing of fair countries, and rather have sought how to fortify our own than to spoil another man's.'

On 28 August he arrived at Wilton, the home of William Herbert,

Earl of Pembroke, where he was entertained 'with great magnificence ... served in vessels of pure gold'. When he came to leave, Pembroke presented him with a camp bed, decorated with pearls and precious stones. Stopping at Winchester on 5 September where he was presented with a book of verses by Winchester scholars, Edward arrived at Reading on 13 September. The town's borough records noted how he was received by the mayor 'in his best apparrel'. Edward 'most gently stayed his horse' and ceremonially received the town's mace and accepted a gift of two yokes of oxen costing £15, before finally reaching the end of his progress, at Windsor Castle, on 15 September.[22]

On 24 September Edward wrote to Barnaby that he was 'in good health', though there was still concern over the spread of the sweating sickness. 'I hear of no place where any sweat or plague hath reigned,' he continued, 'but only in Bristol and in the country near about. Some suspected it to be among a few in the town of Poole ... but I think rather not; for I was within three miles of it and less, and yet no man feared it.' Barnaby had now been away for the better part of a year, and as the summer drew to a close, Edward had begun to miss his friend. He wrote to him, declaring that 'for divers other causes ... which you shall the perfectlier know at your coming hither' he should return home, 'considering the dead time of the year for wars draweth near' and requested that Barnaby ask his leave from the French king Henry II. But Barnaby was unwilling; about to be put into the field with a commission in the army, he did not want to seem lazy or afraid by refusing. Edward replied: 'We like your opinion very well ... Nevertheless, as soon as this business is once overpast, you ... may take some occasion to ask leave for this winter to come home ... in such manner and form as we have written in our former letters ... Therefore, we commit you to God.' It was arranged that Barnaby would return in December; by then his new campaign would have ceased.[23]

Northumberland was glad that Edward's progress had finally ended, for there was serious business to return to 'in these troublesome days'. Furthermore, Northumberland's illnesses had returned, causing him to fall into depression. He was 'so troubled with the falling of the uvula that I am forced to keep my chamber for it is now a fortnight since it began to fall and continueth worse and worse so that I can scarcely eat any meat for it.'[24] His condition was probably an ulcerous stomach; medical recipes prescribed to him were intended to 'stop inward bleeding' and 'restore corrupted blood' but others also sought to remove 'the bloody fluxe' from the lungs.[25] Whatever the exact nature of his complications, North-umberland had become a shadow of his former self. He had grown tired of the power and authority he had sought so hard to win, and bore the burden of responsibility with a heavy heart. He now wrote from his bed 'as ill at ease as I have been much in all my life':

His Majesty's choice of Councillors is, in my opinion, very well appointed, all save myself, who neither hath understanding nor wit, meet for the Association, nor body apt to render his Duty any ways, as the will and heart desireth. And as it is a most great grief to me to think it, so I cannot but lament it, that it is my chance to occupy a room in this common weal, meet for a man of much wit and gravity: But as Christ in the Gospel did allow the mite or farthing of the poor woman, wherein she showed the good zeal and will that was in her; so I trust the same Christ, through the work of his Grace, will put in the heart of his majesty to accept the earnest will and good heart that remaineth in me, though there be no other thing, as indeed I . . . am driven to confess.[26]

He knew that he remained unpopular, but cared little for public opinion. 'If I should have past more upon the speech of people than upon the service of my master,' he wrote to William Cecil, 'I needed not to have had so much obloquy of some kind of men. But the living God . . . shall be my judge at the last day with what zeal, faith and truth I serve my master.' And in one of the most poignant passages, he reflected on the duty of his 'poor father', Edmund Dudley, Henry VII's faithful servant:

who, after his master was gone, suffered death for doing his master's commandments, who was the wisest prince of the world living in those days, and yet could not his commandment be my father's charge after he was departed this life; so, for my part, with all earnestness and duty I will serve without fear, seeking nothing but the true glory of God and his Highness' surety: so shall I most please God and have my conscience upright, and then not fear what man doth to me.[27]

Once again the surfacing of rumours and plots seemed ominous. In September a tailor, William Lowe, was set in the pillory for saying 'The king of England is a cuckold's son and a bastard born'.[28] The case of Elizabeth Huggons, a servant to the Duchess of Somerset, was naturally viewed with greater suspicion. According to her informer, Mrs Huggons blamed the Duke of Somerset's death 'to no man but my Lord of Northumberland, who she thought was better worthy to die than he'.

Edward, she declared, was an 'unnatural nephew' for allowing it, and she wished she had the 'jerking of him'. Examined in the Tower, she denied the charges against her, but admitted that she thought that 'those which were the procurers of the Duke of Somerset's death, his blood would be required at their hands, even like as the Lord Admiral's blood was at the Duke's hands, for she thought if the said duke had lived one hundred years, he would never have given such occasion'. She remembered that she had said, 'The world doth condemn the Duke of Northumberland for my Lord of Somerset's death, even as they did the Duke of Somerset for the Lord Admiral his brother's death' but had meant only 'the voice of the people'. She remained a prisoner in the Tower until the following June.[29]

More serious were the activities of one Hawkins, who had been caught sending out seditious bills and counterfeiting Cranmer's signature, in the hope of raising a rebellion. Arrested and examined in the Tower, Hawkins refused to co-operate, feigning madness. Northumberland looked to round up his conspirators, whom Hawkins refused to name. 'It should be well done in my opinion,' he ordered, 'that some discreet persons were furtherwith appointed to have the examination of him and either by fair means or foul to cause him to declare his counsellors or supporters', adding that 'this to be in the mean time kept very close and secret'. Yet Northumberland remained merciful to others less threatening, including one John Borrough who, having accused the duke of 'conveying [stealing] the King's majesty's coffers', was spared any further punishment, since he was 'of a good house and not so much in default as others, and a young man of tall personage and peradventure sufficiently punished by this long imprisonment'.[30]

Northumberland wrote anxiously to the council, requesting them to be vigilant and keep watch to prevent disturbances before they arose, beseeching them to do their duty to 'be ready, not only to spend our goods, but our lands and lives, for our master and our country'. But yet he seemed helpless to prevent their incessant desire for the accumulation of wealth, 'the flattering of ourselves with heaping riches upon riches, house upon house, building upon building'.[31]

The problem of order was not the only one the country faced. With the country's debts still unresolved and mounting, Northumberland was warned that England's credit on the foreign markets was in danger of falling 'as low as the credit of the Emperor' who was currently offering a 16 per cent return on any loan without success.[32] Northumberland was determined to 'play the good physician' in order to address the problem which, he wrote to the council, 'having all this while been put off by the best means ... is grown to such an extremity ... it has so long been suffered to fester, for lack of looking into time'. But when a report revealed that in the decade since 1542 the country's military expenditure had nearly totalled £3.5 million (£684.6 million), it was clear that a new Parliament would be needed to pass a subsidy to remedy debts which Northumberland acknowledged were 'for one great part he was left by his highness father our late sovereign lord' but above all had been

> augmented by the wilful government of the late Duke of Somerset who took upon him the protectorship and government of his own authority, and his highness being by the prudence of his said father left in peace with all princes, suddenly by that man's unskilful protectorship and less expert in government was plunged into wars whereby his majesty's charges was suddenly increased to the point of 120 to 140 thousand pounds a year over ... these things being now so onerous and weighty to the king's majesty.[33]

Meanwhile the Imperial ambassador Scheyfve reported that Edward was healthy and 'takes riding exercise and fences daily, without forgoing his studies, which are multiple, and concern especially the new religion, in which he is said to be proficient. He has begun to be present at the Council and to attend to certain affairs himself'.[34] Much to the ambassador's dismay, Edward's own determination to assert the values of his faith was clearly witnessed when he first agreed to stand as godfather to Scheyfve's newly born son, only to change his mind upon hearing that the ambassador intended to have his child christened according to the Catholic rite, telling him that he would send a present but would be unable to attend himself since 'he was firmly resolved that his laws and constitutions should be obeyed within his realm ... a different course of conduct would be against his conscience'.[35]

Despite his formal education having ended on his fourteenth birthday, Edward continued his studies, always observing his appointed hour of study. His abilities were by now so advanced that, according to the sixteenth-century historian John Foxe, writing almost ten years later, Cranmer wept for joy at Edward's skill in translating Greek and Latin. To this Foxe added somewhat glibly: 'To recite here his witty sentences, his grave reasons, which many times did proceed from him, and how he would sometimes, in a matter discoursed by his council, add thereunto, of his own, more reasons and causes, touching the said matter, than they themselves had or could devise, it was almost incredible in that age to see, and tedious here to prosecute.'

Edward was able to recite the names of all the ports, havens and creeks, not only in England, but also in Scotland and France, and even 'what coming in there was; how the tide served in every haven or creek; moreover, what burden, and what wind, served the coming into the haven'. Edward's memory was perhaps even photographic, with Foxe recording how he was able to remember 'the names of all his justices, magistrates, gentlemen that had any authority' and also 'their house-keeping, their religion, and conversation'.[36]

To what extent is this evidence true, or merely a reflection of Foxe's own hopes – in the words of one historian, 'the product of his own wishful thinking'? Foxe was clearly drawing on other manuscript evidence, whilst Edward's own papers and orations demonstrate his remarkable talents. The breadth of Edward's learning is also illustrated in the other surviving seventy-two books that belonged in his library, comprising works in six languages, twenty-seven being classical texts, with thirty-three modern works concerned primarily with the reformed religion.[37]

It was during late October that Edward met Hieronymus Cardano, an Italian physician and astrologer, whose later account of their meeting is the most contemporary, and possibly most objective, account of Edward's abilities. Edward had apparently grown weak and the council wished for Cardano to discover the nature of his illness and cast his horoscope. Received by the king, Cardano found Edward to be 'of a stature some-what below the middle height, pale-faced with grey eyes, a grave aspect, decorous and handsome' adding that 'he was rather of a bad habit of body, than a sufferer from fixed diseases. He had a somewhat projecting shoulder-blade: but such defects do not amount to deformity'. Con-versing with him in Latin, Edward asked Cardano about his recent book which had been dedicated to him. There then ensued a debate upon the nature of comets, during which Cardano considered Edward 'spoke Latin as politely and fluently as I did' but was reserved in his judgement of Edward's own reasoning, commenting that Edward had 'began to love and favour liberal arts and sciences, before he knew them, and to know them before he could use them'. He also noted that Edward seemed old before his time, and 'carried himself like an old man; and yet he was always affable and gentle, as became his age'. Nevertheless, the Italian was obviously impressed: 'It might seem a miracle of nature, to behold the excellent wit and forwardness that appeared in him, being yet but a child. This I speak not rhetorically, to amplify things, or to make them more than truth is; yea, the truth is more than I do utter.'[38]

Edward's own interest in astronomy is readily evident in one of his orations, a lengthy defence of the practice written in 1551 against those 'who hold that this is not useful to the body, nor the mind, nor the State, a view which ought, not undeservedly, to be affected by much cursing', arguing 'what is more natural than understanding of the principles, the sky, the constellations, the stars, the planets through the courses of which our bodies ... and all grasses, flowers, trees, grains, wines and all others are governed and ruled?' He owned various astronomical instruments including 'a little pillar of astronomy of white bone' and had delivered to him a dial of ivory 'with diverse conclusions of Astronomy' for his own use. In November 1549 he ordered for two cases of instruments of astronomy 'with dials of white bone' to be delivered, giving one to his friend Lord Strange, whilst in 1551, he was presented with a quadrant by John Cheke, accompanied by an instruction manual written by Oliver Holinshed, who admitted that 'I doubt not but your highness have so travailed in the study of the mathematical sciences, that you know right well the use of the common instruments thereof'.[39] Yet Edward's keen interest in the stars was almost entirely founded on the strength of his faith; in his own words: 'Astronomy proclaims the works of God, from which he is revealed to men, For the skies describe in detail and reveal heaven, the invisible ... glory of God and his power over the whole world.'[40]

Cardano also found Edward to be short-sighted and a little deaf. This may have been caused by the difficulty of straining to understand the Italian's pronunciation of Latin, but that Edward suffered problems with his eyes seems to be confirmed in that he owned a pair of spectacles and 'a glass to read with' and was treated with a concoction that 'profiteth much all manner of sore eyes' made from red fennel, sage and herbs, the powder of fifteen peppercorns, white wine, three spoonfuls of honey and five 'of the water of a man-child that is an innocent' to be applied with a feather.[41]

Cardano and Edward met again several times, with Cardano becoming more impressed at every meeting: 'This boy,' he wrote, was 'filled with the highest expectation ... on account of his cleverness and sweetness of manner ... in his humanity he was a picture of our mortal state; his gravity was that of kingly majesty, his disposition worthy of so great a prince. This boy of so much wit and promise was nearing a comprehension of the sum of things.' Cardano then cast Edward's horoscope, a process that occupied him for a hundred hours. Calculating his life expectancy, he predicted a long life for the king, warning that at the ages of 32, 34 and 55 he would suffer from various illnesses, including 'skin disease and a slight fever' and 'languor of mind and body'.

Time would prove that Cardano could not have been more wrong, for Edward would be dead within a year. Later, explaining away his mistake, Cardano excused himself on the grounds that in a court dominated by Northumberland and his men, he had been allowed too little time with his subject and had been unable to observe the directions of the sun and moon.[42]

12

PROMISE UNFULFILLED

Edward returned to Greenwich on 23 December 1552 to celebrate the Christmas festivities, where once again George Ferrers was appointed to run the ceremonies as Lord of Misrule, throwing himself into the preparations for the celebrations with his usual vigour. Others showed equal enthusiasm, with Sir George Howard, brother of Henry's ill-fated Queen Katherine, staging a 'triumph of Cupid' on Twelfth Night in which even members of the council took part. Everyone seemed content except Northumberland. His health remained poor and he had grown weary of the court and its sycophants whom he described as the 'multitude of cravers' who hung continually around him. In his most pained letter to William Cecil, he lamented how

> when others went to their sups and pastimes after travail, I went to bed with a careful heart and a weary body; and yet abroad no man scarcely had any good opinion of me. And now, by extreme sickness and otherwise constrained to seek some health and quietness, I am not without a new evil imagination of men. What should I wish any longer this life, that seeth such frailty in it? Surely, but for a few children which God hath set me, which also helpeth to pluck me on my knees, I have no great cause to desire to tarry much longer here. And thus, to satisfy you and others whom I take for friends, I have entered into the bottom of my care, which I cannot do without sorrow.[1]

The introduction of the new Prayer Book had been shrouded in controversy, and the radical Scottish preacher John Knox's complaints that it continued to sanction idolatry resulted in a significant dispute with Cranmer. At first Northumberland had been content to allow Knox, whom he had nominated for the bishopric of Rochester, to speak out, hoping he 'would . . . be a whetstone, to quicken and sharp the Bishop of Canterbury, whereof he hath need'. But first appearances had been deceptive. Knox refused the appointment and after a meeting in

December, Northumberland dismissed him 'because I love not men which be neither grateful nor pleasurable'. The preacher even had the temerity to question Northumberland's own religious views: 'I have for twenty years stood to one kind of religion,' Northumberland complained to William Cecil, 'in the same which I do now profess; and have, I thank the Lord, past no small dangers for it.'[2]

Nevertheless, there was a sense that the worst of the country's troubles was over, and for once the year had begun without crisis. Most of the king's foreign loans – which in 1551 had totalled £130,000 (£24.8 million) – had been repaid, the coinage had been restored, and a major report into the royal finances had been submitted, detailing the levels of corruption and waste, but also suggesting new means for reform.[3]

Relations had also been repaired with Edward and his sister Mary, and in February the princess accepted an invitation to come to court for the first time since their stand-off two years earlier, in March 1551. Her reception at court on 10 February was impressive, and it was reported that she was 'more honourably received and entertained with greater magnificence' than ever before. Met by Northumberland and a hundred horsemen on the outskirts of the city, when she arrived at court she was greeted by the council at the outer gate, who bowed their heads 'as if she had been Queen of England'.

Yet behind the smiles and reverences, the change in the council's attitude belied something altogether more serious, for when Mary was taken inside to visit her brother, she found him bedridden, having fallen sick in early January with a cough. Nevertheless, although Edward received her kindly, entertaining her with 'small talk', ten days later his condition had not improved and he was still confined to his chamber. The Imperial ambassador believed that his condition was aggravated by a physical defect since his right shoulder was lower than his left: 'He suffers a good deal when the fever is upon him, especially from a difficulty in drawing his breath, which is due to the compression of the organs on the right side.' Edward's illness had been deteriorating daily, and the doctors feared the worst, informing the council that the king might not hold out long against serious illness. 'Some make light of the imperfection,' Scheyfve continued, 'saying that the depression in the right shoulder is hereditary in the house of Seymour, and that the late Duke of Somerset had his good share of it among the rest.' It had been reported that Edward had suffered a strain hunting a year ago, aggravating the defect. 'No good will he ever do with the lance,' the ambassador added, before concluding rather smugly that 'I opine that this is a visitation and sign from God.'[4]

During Lent a mood of anxiety grew around the court. Noblemen rode through the capital surrounded by their armed guard, whilst preachers used their Lenten sermons to denounce members of the household who had criticized the new faith, warning of the desolation of plagues that would follow. The omens were clear. An anonymous prophecy told of 'much sorrow' to come, presaging the Thames would run with blood. Worse still, Edward would disappear, never to be found. A dog had been found, carrying a piece of a dead child in its mouth. All this was taken very seriously by the audience, who listened to the preacher John Bradford remind them how the Duke of Somerset had 'became so cold in hearing God's word that, the year before his death, he would not disease himself to hear a sermon'. Then God's judgement had brought Somerset to his knees; now Edward's illness was a sign of his wrath.

All this was too much for Northumberland and the council, who reacted furiously by dropping Cranmer's treasured scheme of reforming the canon law and threatening the preachers with further punishment 'if they did not teach the true doctrine and word of Christ'.

Parliament opened on 1 March, though the opening ceremony was a low-key affair conducted at Whitehall on account of Edward's illness, the king wearing his Parliament robes and sitting under the cloth of estate while the Lord Chancellor made a brief speech. Parliament was then temporarily suspended to reconvene at Westminster the next day, 'because the King was sickly'.[5] There survives in the register book of the royal herald, Gilbert Dethick, a drawing of the scene. Edward sits upon his throne, sceptre in hand. Beneath him sit his subjects, the bishops on one side, the lords on the other. Though somewhat formulaic, it shows Edward fully participating within the model of Tudor governance – the king ruling through Parliament. It would also be the last living portrait of Edward.

Before Parliament had opened, rumours had circulated of a bill being passed, declaring that Edward had arrived at his majority and giving Northumberland greater 'facility and scope to execute his designs in safety', but these came to nothing. In fact the duke had favoured delaying Parliament until 'after the harvest time' when there would be fewer opportunities for 'murmurings and grudgings'.[6] Behind the gossip, however, there was a hint of truth, for Edward was becoming ever more closely associated with the business of government. Producing memoranda for council discussions, he worked with the council's secretary, William Petre, in January to formulate a set of articles 'for the quicker, better, and more orderly dispatch of causes by His Majesty's Privy Council'.[7] These were strongly influenced by Paget's earlier procedures, but now Edward's presence was strongly felt: kept fully informed of all council business, he was free 'to hire the debating of any matters' at his pleasure, sanctioning their resolution in both public and private affairs. Though Edward was still not yet attending full council meetings, rather the once weekly 'Council for the estate' that had been created for him in March 1552, the boundaries between the council's authority and the king's own were becoming increasingly blurred, and further moves were being taken to restructure the polity in preparation for an adult male monarchy. Most tellingly, Edward's personal signature, rather than the collective signatures of the council, can be found on existing warrants for payments from this time, suggesting that Edward was now participating in everyday financial affairs, essentially running his own kingdom.

Edward had arrived at the threshold of power, yet by now he was too weak to cross it. By 17 March, now weakened and thin, he had still not left the confines of his room, for the slightest change in his environment – or so the doctors believed – would place his life at risk. By April, hopes were raised when Edward's condition improved with the spring weather, allowing him to play in Westminster Park, and it seemed that by following a careful diet and programme of exercise his health was on the mend. Yet this proved to be a false dawn. By the end of the month it was clear that Edward was again growing weaker and the year's Garter celebrations would need to be postponed. His doctors were perplexed, struggling to find a cure for his symptoms: 'The matter he ejects from his mouth is sometimes coloured a greenish yellow and black, sometimes pink, like the colour of blood.'[8]

On 11 April Edward was moved to Greenwich, where it was hoped that the clean air would aid his recovery. For a while this seemed to have worked, and a joyful Northumberland wrote to William Cecil on 7 May with news that the doctors had no doubt of a thorough recovery, since the king was 'fully bent' to follow their advice and was expected to 'take the air' soon. Mary wrote to Edward, congratulating him on his recovery from his 'rhume cough'. Edward had sent her a token, 'not a little to my comfort'. She had, apparently, been praying to God, 'according to my most bounden duty, to give your Majesty perfect health and strength, with long continuance in prosperity to reign'. Her letter strikes a humble tone, far removed from her previous letters of defiance, yet while she undoubtedly expressed genuine love and concern, Mary more than anyone must have realized the gravity of the situation.[9]

A few days later Edward's condition deteriorated again, and on 12 May Scheyfve wrote that Edward was still 'indisposed, and it is held for certain that he cannot escape'. His doctors were convinced he was suffering from 'a suppurating tumour' of the lung, made worse by a hacking cough and constant high temperature with fever. As his condition deteriorated, ulcers – possibly bed sores – had spread across his swollen body.

A mood of uncertainty clouded the air as rumour-mongers were ruthlessly punished. One man had his ear nailed to the pillory for declaring that Edward was dead, whilst another was set in a pillory at Reading on 27 May and had both his ears cut off, wearing a paper hat with the words: 'FOR LEWD AND SEDITIOUS WORDS TOUCHING THE KING'S MAJESTY AND THE STATE.'

The council continued to conduct their business with as much normality as was possible, shrugging off any suggestion that Edward was in fact dying, but the signs were all there that something was seriously amiss. The council's secretary William Cecil travelled armed and only at night, making frequent trips across the river to Greenwich; ammunition and artillery were seen being carted from the Tower to some unknown destination; jousts organized to be held on 1 May had been postponed until Whitsuntide. Meanwhile in London, members of the council 'down to the very secretaries' were buying up armour, and carpenters had been seen 'working ceaselessly' on board the royal fleet.

Other members of the nobility had already left the capital, in preparation for the troubles that lay ahead. Northampton, too, had set off for Windsor 'under colour of going to hunt and of carrying out a bet', but in fact he had gone to victual and prepare Windsor Castle for the worst. Lord Cobham had also set out for Romney Marsh, a convenient landing spot for troops to guard against the threat of foreign invasion.

Confined to his room, Edward spent his days being cared for by the Chief Gentlemen of the Privy Chamber, perhaps passing the time playing board-games with the counters that he kept in his desk.

It was at this stage or earlier that Edward turned his hand seriously to a document he had probably been considering for some time: his 'Devise' for the succession of the Crown. In this, Edward sought to divert the succession and disinherit his sisters. This was both remarkable and revolutionary. Edward was abandoning his family, turning against the traditional laws of inheritance and his late father's wishes. Instead, he would create a new dynasty, one founded upon the true faith. Whatever the future held, Edward was determined that his dream of establishing an evangelical realm would survive beyond him.

Edward had probably made a start on the original draft early in the year. His writing is bold and clear – hardly the work of someone with an advanced debilitating illness – and Edward made it perfectly clear that he might still marry and have heirs of his own. Possibly he had been thinking of taking the problem of the succession to Parliament, for the initial purpose of the document seems to have been to secure against a female succession, no doubt an anathema to the young king and the male-dominated Tudor society he ruled. In any case, it seems that Northumberland was unaware of the king's intentions, for written and corrected in his own hand, the 'Devise' reads very much as of Edward's own making. An anonymous French source believed the Chief Gentleman of the Privy Chamber, John Gates, to be 'one of the principals who induced the King to make out his will to the prejudice of the Lady Mary' but it also included mention of John Cheke and Thomas Goodrich, the Bishop of Ely, as encouraging the king to make his will.[10] This should not be taken as evidence that Edward was browbeaten into writing his own sisters out of the succession; rather that the king took the widest possible counsel in drawing up plans for a new evangelical dynasty.

According to the original draft, if Edward died childless, the Crown would now descend through the male heirs of Frances, Duchess of Suffolk, the daughter of Henry VIII's younger sister Mary. The line of succession would then continue through the male heirs of Frances's daughters, Jane, Catherine and Mary. Mary and Elizabeth, on the other hand, were to be effectively bought out of the succession. If they would follow the advice of his executors 'and will be bound to live in quiet order' they would both receive an annuity of £1,000. And if they married according to the council's wishes, they would further receive a gift of £10,000 on top of the sum set out in Edward's bequest.

The only problem was that there were no male heirs. Moreover, it had been some time since Frances last gave birth to a child. For the moment, Edward's heir remained unborn.

All the more crucial, then, that Jane and Catherine be married off as soon as possible. For Jane, Northumberland could think of no better suitor than his own fourth surviving son, Guildford. The following day, on Whit Sunday, 21 May, they were married at Durham Place, the duke's London residence, 'with a display truly regal'. Edward's presence had been expected, but he supplied the robes for the celebrations in his absence. Over the next few days other marriages were solemnized: Lord Herbert, the eldest son of the Earl of Pembroke, took the hand of Jane's sister, Lady Catherine Grey and Lord Hastings, the son of the Earl of Huntingdon married Northumberland's daughter, Lady Catherine Dudley, whilst further arrangements were made for Northumberland's brother, Sir Andrew Dudley, to marry Lady Margaret Clifford, Jane's cousin and co-heiress of the royal blood.[11]

These marriages, so 'suddenly knit', fooled no one and were 'much murmured at'. To outsiders, not realizing what Edward's plans were, it was blatant that Northumberland was planning something. 'Certain wise men thought more than they spake of these combinations,' William Harrison declared in his *Universal History*, 'but ye common sort spake more than either ... first crying God save ye king and defend him from his enemies.'[12]

A few days after the marriages and celebrations at Durham Place, however, there was a dramatic turn of events. His condition worsening, Edward must have realized that there was no time to wait for Frances or Jane to become pregnant; he would have to choose his heir apparent now. With a few strokes of the pen, where the original line of succession in the 'Devise' had read 'To the Lady Fraunceses heirs males' followed by 'For lack of such issue to the Lady Janes heirs males', it now read: 'To the Lady Fraunceses heirs males, *if she have any* such issue *before my death* to the Lady Jane *and her* heirs males.'[13] By default, the Crown would be Jane's.

Few knew of Edward's decision, let alone Jane. For those that did, the news came as a shock. For centuries it was assumed that the 'Devise' was doctored by Northumberland, pressuring Edward into changing the line of succession in favour of Northumberland's new daughter-in-law, Jane. Yet Edward's detailed revisions demonstrate that he had thought very deeply over the nature of the English succession. Indeed his first drafts to exclude his sisters may have seemed entirely natural to the Tudor eye. Until then no woman had succeeded to the throne. Women could, however, transmit their claims to their male descendants, hence Edward's original plan to trace his new dynasty through the female line. Most important of all, Edward could never countenance the spectre of a Catholic ruler undoing the work that his reign had achieved.

By the end of May, Edward's situation was growing desperate. He was wasting away daily without any sign of improvement. Scheyfve speculated that he had at most two months to live. 'He cannot rest except by means of medicines and external applications; and his body had begun to swell, especially his head and feet', and he had heard that Edward's hair was to be shaved off ready for plasters to be placed on his head.[14]

Scheyfve's intimate knowledge of Edward's illness came from the secret dispatches of John Banister, a twenty-year-old medical student whose father was a minor official in the royal household. On 28 May he sent a report chronicling the ceaseless deterioration of the king:

> He does not sleep except when he be stuffed with drugs, which doctors call opiates ... first one thing then another are given him, but the doctors do not exceed twelve grains at a time, for these drugs are never given by doctors (so they say) unless the patient is in great pain, or tormented by constant sleeplessness, or racked by violent coughing ...
>
> The sputum which he brings up is livid, black, fetid and full of carbon; it smells beyond measure; if it is put in a basin full of water it sinks to the bottom. His feet are swollen all over. To the doctors all these things portend death, and that within three months, except God of his great mercy spare him.
>
> Today the Duke called the doctors together and asked them what the king's chances were. With one voice they answered that since this season of the year is kindest to him but yet does nothing to improve him, so likewise when autumn comes it will end his life. The Duke told them not to slacken their efforts nor to cease to pray to God that He should prosper their treatment; meanwhile, he said, you will all be paid your fees every month, at a rate of 100 crowns.[15]

By 11 June, Scheyfve reported back that Edward's health was worsening, despite rumours spread by the council that he was on the mend. 'The people do not believe the said rumours, as the King does not show himself, but no one dares to voice any comments, at least not openly.' Confusion had spread across the courts of Europe as ambassadors struggled to dispel the stories of Edward's imminent demise, telling the emperor that Edward was 'but a little sick of a cough, the lewd people had devised and reported that he was dead'. Writing from Brussels, Sir Richard

Morison had heard that Edward was 'very sick', his stomach swollen with a 'post hume' that would need to be cut away.[16]

Edward had resolved in his own mind that Jane would succeed him, but in order that the legal ends be properly tied up, on 12 June the judges of the King's Bench were summoned by the council to discuss the matter of the succession. Shown Edward's 'Devise' and commanded to turn it into a legal will, they were evidently dumbfounded and requested more time to consult. Conferring together, however, they considered 'the danger of treason' in overturning the legal succession too great and two days later explained their refusal to the council. Northumberland flew into a rage. Denouncing the Lord Chief Justice as a traitor, he challenged them to the contrary, shouting that he 'would fight in his shirt with any man living'. The judges' attempt at a compromise – that Mary should be allowed to succeed upon the promise of making no alteration to religion – was sharply rejected, and the meeting broke up unresolved.[17]

The next day the judges returned to face Edward himself. He demanded angrily to know why his wishes had not been obeyed, to which they explained that to do so 'would put the Lords and us in danger of treason'.

Despite his evident weakness, Edward 'with sharp words and angry countenance' addressed the room. He was convinced that Mary 'would provoke great disturbances' and would leave 'no stone unturned' in her efforts to gain control of the throne. More importantly, 'it would be all over for the religion whose fair foundation we have laid'. He had therefore resolved to 'disown and disinherit her together with her sister Elizabeth, as though she were a bastard and sprung from an illegitimate bed':

> For indeed my sister Mary was the daughter of the king by Katherine the Spaniard, who before she was married to my worthy father had been espoused to Arthur, my father's elder brother, and was therefore for this reason alone divorced by my father. But it was the fate of Elizabeth, my other sister, to have Anne Boleyn for a mother; this woman was indeed not only cast off by my father because she was more inclined to couple with a number of courtiers rather than reverencing her husband, so mighty a king, but also paid the penalty with her head – a greater proof of her guilt. Thus in our judgement they will be undeservedly considered as being numbered among the heirs of the king our beloved father.[18]

He demanded that his cousin Jane be his heir, and that the judges upon their allegiance draw up the letters patent of his will. Those standing near huddled around the judges, menacing that to refuse would be treason. Such arm-twisting tactics got their way, and the Lord Chief Justice – who later claimed he was 'in great fear as ever I was in my life' – caved in, though not before a promise of pardon under the Great Seal had been granted.[19]

The letters patent were duly drawn up in Edward's presence. Edward put his signature to the document in six places and between 15 and 21 June over a hundred signatories – comprising the major figures in the council and of the nobility, judges and prominent London officials – were gathered, their support bought with gifts of land and office. For his obedience, the Earl of Arundel was pardoned for his earlier plotting against Northumberland and discharged of his fine. Significant grants were also made to Edward's close Privy Chamber attendants, suggesting the king's guiding hand in their dispersal.[20]

A separate document was also produced and signed, binding them to uphold the new succession unto death. Cranmer refused to sign. To do so, he argued, would be to perjure his oath sworn upon Henry's will. He was not the only councillor to have made that sacrifice, came the reply. 'I am not judge over any man's conscience but mine own only,' the archbishop retorted.[21] He demanded to speak to his godson alone but this was refused. Instead he met Edward in open council, and faced with the news that the judges had legitimated the devise, could say little when the king hoped he 'would not be more repugnant to his will than the rest of the Council were'.

Such a spirited defence, made in retrospect, belied Cranmer's own separate agenda, for he had already declared both Mary and Elizabeth illegitimate before, in nullifying their mother's marriages to Henry VIII. Besides, there were greater prizes to be had for his compliance. The additional provisions of Edward's will ordered its executors to ensure not only that the new religious settlement remain unaltered but also commanded them to go further and 'diligently travail to cause godly ecclesiastical laws to be made and set forth, such as may be agreeable with the reformation of religion now received within our realm, and that done shall also cause the canon laws to be abolished'. The incentive was too great: Cranmer's great project stood to be realized. He signed 'unfeignedly and without dissimulation'.[22]

If the archbishop did have genuine reservations, he was not alone. One judge, Sir James Hales, refused to sign despite being a committed Protestant, whilst the Earl of Arundel, though agreeing to the patent, refused to put his hand to the undertaking. And of those who had put their signatures to the letters patent, there was soon regret; Justice John Gosnold soon repented of his actions whilst the Imperial ambassador reported on 4 July that Shrewsbury, Winchester, Cheyney, Bedford and Arundel had taken objection to the letters patent.[23]

Meanwhile Northumberland looked across the seas towards an alliance with France to shore up his fragile position. Relations with France had been strong since Edward's betrothal to the French king Henry's daughter Elizabeth, but Northumberland needed more than mere gestures of friendship. If Edward's plan was to succeed, he knew that a sizeable military force would be needed to ensure a smooth transition of power. Henry II – looking for allies in support of his war against the Empire – was keen to take full advantage of the situation, sending a special mission to the English court to register his support for Northumberland and curry favour. The plan certainly worked, for Northumberland even allowed the French ambassadors a private audience with Edward; except that Edward – confined to his bed – was not present. After dinner, when it was announced that the king would receive them, they were merely led into the ante-chamber where Northumberland and certain members of the council were waiting. No mention was made of Edward; in any case the ambassadors did not feel it was their place to ask. A brief discussion ensued, with the meeting breaking up less than an hour after it had begun. As it came to an end, Northumberland turned to the ambassador and asked with genuine emotion in his voice: 'What would your lordship do in my case?'

However, Edward did continue to receive visitors into early June, rewarding Sir Thomas Gresham with an annuity of £100 and promising that 'he would hereafter see me rewarded better, saying I should know that I served a King'.[24] He even maintained his studies, with Sir John Cheke writing on 7 June that he had delivered books to Edward: 'How kindly and courteously he received them, and how greatly he esteems them.' Yet his tutor knew the king 'debilitated by his long illness' was running out of time. He could but hope that 'should a longer life be allowed him ... I prophesy indeed, that, with the Lord's blessing, he will prove such a king, as neither to yield to Josiah in the maintenance of true religion, nor to Solomon in the management of state, nor to David in the encouragement of godliness.'[25] Deep down, Cheke knew this was unlikely to be the case.

Edward's efforts in persuading his councillors to agree to his devise had taken their toll. With the letters patents signed, he gave up any hope of recovery. Another violent fever lasting twenty-four hours left him unable to walk. The fever returned again on 14 June, though this time it was more violent. By now the doctors, evidently clueless to his condition, had decided he was beyond recovery; the best their medical expertise could suggest was to turn to the stars, believing that on 25 June – the point of the full moon – 'he must decline to a point at which his life would be in the gravest danger, nay that he might die before that time, because he is at present without the strength necessary to rid him of certain humours which, when he does succeed in ejecting them, give forth a stench'. Unable to keep any food down, Edward was now living entirely on the medicines and restoratives prescribed to him. In pain, his legs had swelled so much that he was confined to lying flat on his back and it was reported that he 'says he feels so weak that he can resist no longer, and that he is done for'. 'I am glad to die,' he whispered to Cheke.[26]

Away from the Privy Chamber, the council met daily in a secluded chamber where even secretaries were forbidden. Rumours of Edward's imminent death continued, though these were admittedly 'widely varying'. 'His doctors dare reveal nothing,' Scheyfve wrote.

> Only two of them are in attendance on his person; the other three, when they go to visit the King, examine his urine and excrements, but are not allowed to approach him. The King's ordinary attendants are unable to stir abroad, so that it is exceedingly difficult to obtain any information as to his state, especially as in these days mothers no longer trust their sons, and there is every appearance that the circle will be made still narrower. Up to the present there seems to be no sign of improvement, so the general conviction is that he cannot escape, and has been poisoned.[27]

On 19 June, the council ordered a prayer for Edward's recovery to be said daily in the King's Chapel.[28] Posted up in the city, it caused 'great astonishment'. 'It is now thought that this has been done to ascertain the people's temper,' Scheyfve believed. Meanwhile, appearances at court were kept up as normal. On Sunday 18 June the French ambassador Noailles had an audience with the council, finding them in apparent good humour. The king's health was improving, they announced – over the last few days his fever had left him and he had been regaining strength daily. In celebration, the court had been 'decked out' and the sound of trumpets and other musical entertainment during dinner had returned. Noailles did not believe a word.

Outside, it was difficult *not* to believe that something was amiss. Night watches of the city doubled and the opening times of its gates were restricted. Prisoners in the Tower were kept more closely confined and the guard increased, whilst the nobility were summoned from their counties back to the capital. Military preparations continued unceasingly; when twenty warships suddenly appeared by the banks of the Thames, the French ambassador, growing ever suspicious, demanded to know what was going on. Yet Northumberland denied all, replying disingenuously that they were intended for a mission to the Spice islands.[29]

Despite these scenes of desperation, Northumberland still clung to the hope that Edward might survive just a few more months so that his 'devise' might be ratified by Parliament, which he had ordered to commence on 18 September. This was hopelessly optimistic. On the same day the Imperial ambassador was informed that the king would not last three days. 'It is firmly believed that he will die tomorrow, for he has not the strength to stir, and can hardly breathe. His body no longer performs its functions, his nails and hair are dropping off, and all his person is scabby.'[30] On 25 June, Edward was so ill that it seemed certain he would die. But he made a brief recovery, or at least an appearance of one, so that 'no one knows what the hour may bring forth'. Rumours of his death continued unabated, despite a ruthless crackdown by the council upon offenders; on 30 June a post was set up in Cheapside where a man, tied by a collar of iron around his neck, was whipped by two men for 'pretended visions and for opprobrious and seditious words'.[31]

Realizing that the situation in England was playing entirely to their diplomatic advantage, the French pressed for ever closer union, urging a beleaguered Northumberland to commit himself to a war against the emperor Charles V in return for French support for Jane's imminent accession.[32] Yet the duke remained 'close lipped and reserved in everything', refusing to act without the council's consent. All he would disclose was that 'they had provided so well against the Lady Mary's ever attaining the succession, and that all the lords of the Council are so well united, that there is no need for you, Sir, to enter into any doubt on this score'.

When the French ambassador attempted to tease more information from him through flattery, adding that the French king and people would be greatly pleased 'if the crown should fall to him himself',

Northumberland gave thanks 'very humbly', but added with false modesty he was 'too unworthy of such an estate' and would 'consider himself unfortunate to think of it'.[33]

News of Edward's condition had spread across the courts of Europe. At Brussels some reports even suggested he was already dead, whilst in Antwerp wagers were being placed on the timing of the king's death. On 25 June, the anxiety of the English ambassador at the Imperial Court, Sir Philip Hoby, was hardly quelled by a 'very dark' letter he had received from Cecil that he wished 'might have been both more pleasant and more plainer to me than it is'. 'I pray God our wickedness have not caused God to turn his face aside from us,' he replied, 'and to plague us with the most gravest and greatest Plague that could come to England, even the taking away of our King.' Hoby informed Cecil that the emperor, in anticipation of Mary attempting to seize the throne, had sent three ambassadors to act on her behalf as councillors: 'if England should be ruled by such Councillors as they be (the living Lord defend it from coming to pass, as I trust he will) Woe! Woe! may be said to England; for then would it come to utter ruin and destruction; and those that favour God's Word in England, in worse case, than those that were in the time of Sodom and Gomorrah: God be merciful unto us and deliver us from such plagues.'[34] 'We do assure you, thanked be to God! His majesty is alive,' the council replied, 'whatsoever evil men do write or spread abroad . . . the recovery out of his sickness shall shortly appear to the comfort of all good men . . .' As if to add credence to their persuasions, it was signed by no fewer that twenty-two of its members.[35]

Hoby was correct on at least one count. News of the French mission had prompted Charles V to send his own delegation of three ambassadors on 23 June, headed by Simon Renard, in an attempt to ensure Mary's succession to the Crown. Diplomacy was to be their weapon of choice. No matter how desperate Mary's plight, he instructed, to send a 'strong expedition' would be impossible. Instead, they were to remind the council of the emperor's goodwill, of the fact that 'the French are England's ancient enemies' and to allay any fear of Imperial intervention. Mary would marry an English suitor, and should be persuaded to make any promise necessary to ensure her succession, even a guarantee of religious freedom. Threats would be of little use. Only the English people themselves could place Mary upon the throne.[36]

As Edward lay dying, the battle lines had begun to be drawn. Earlier in the summer a 'marvellous strange monster' had been born: twin girls, joined at the waist, facing east and west. To many it was an omen that England would be ruled by two queens.[37] Knowing what was in store, the regime sought to blacken the names of the king's sisters. On 2 July the traditional prayers for Mary and Elizabeth were omitted from the service at St Paul's and Nicholas Ridley denounced them both as bastards, at which the audience were 'sore annoyed'.[38] Mary did not need any further hints to convince her that her freedom was under threat. Under the cover of darkness, she left Hunsdon on 4 July, claiming that she intended to visit her physician whose illness seemed life threatening. Instead she aimed for Swanston Hall in Cambridgeshire, far away from the council's, and Northumberland's, reach.

To reassure the crowds assembling nervously at Greenwich, Edward made his final appearance, peering out from his window on Saturday 1 July. The sight of his thin and wasted body only confirmed the worst, for those watching from below looked on horrified, saying 'he was doomed, and that he was only shown because the people were murmuring and saying he was already dead, and in order that his death, when it should occur, might the more easily be concealed'. Thinking Edward would show himself the next day, a large crowd gathered. But they were disappointed: the king, they were told, would appear the following day. However, the weather was poor, and the wellwishers were informed that 'the air was too chill' for an appearance.

Writing to the emperor on 4 July, Scheyfve was under no illusions about Edward's fate. 'Sire, the King is very ill today and cannot last long. He will die suddenly, and no one can foretell whether he will live an hour longer, notwithstanding his having been shown to the people, for that was done against the physicians' advice.'[39]

His predictions were correct. Two days later, between eight and nine o'clock on the evening of 6 July 1553, Edward lay dying. Surrounded by his two Chief Gentlemen of the Privy Chamber, Sir Thomas Wroth and Sir Henry Sidney, his groom Christopher Salmon and his doctors, Dr Owen and Dr Wendy, he raised his eyes upwards to whisper:

Lord God, deliver me out of this miserable and wretched life, and take me among thy chosen: howbeit not my will, but thy will be done. Lord I commit my spirit to thee. O Lord! thou knowest how happy it were for me to be with thee: yet, for thy chosen's sake, send me life and health, that I may truly serve thee. O my Lord God, bless thy people, and save thine

inheritance! O Lord God save thy chosen people of England! O my Lord
God, defend this realm from papistry, and maintain thy true religion; that
I and my people may praise thy holy name, for thy Son Jesus Christ's
sake!⁴⁰

Sensing their presence, he turned his face towards them.

'Are you so nigh? I thought ye had been further off.'

'We heard you speak to yourself, but what you said we know not,'
they replied.

'I was praying to God.'

Sidney took the boy in his arms. Edward's last words were: 'I am faint;
Lord have mercy upon me, and take my spirit.'

Whilst Edward had lain dying, Noailles reported that those who whispered that the king had been poisoned had been placed in the Tower.
Scheyfve, too, had heard others call Northumberland a 'great tyrant'
who was poisoning the king. Rumour now exploded into open con-
demnation. Machyn's backdated diary entry for 6 July declared that
'the noble King Edward the VI ... was poisoned, as everybody says,
where now, thank be to God, there be many of the false traitors brought
to their end, and I trust in God that more shall follow as they may be
spied out',⁴¹ and Robert Parkyn was certain his death 'was through
poisoning'.

The finger was pointed instantly at Northumberland.⁴² John Burcher
wrote to Bullinger on 16 August, declaring how 'That monster of a man'
had had the king poisoned. 'His hair and nails fell off before his death,
so that, handsome as he was, he entirely lost all his good looks. The
perpetrators of the murder were ashamed of allowing the body of the
deceased king to lie in state, and be seen by the public, as is usual:
wherefore they buried him privately in a paddock adjoining the palace,
and substituted in his place, to be seen by the people, a youth not very
unlike him whom they had murdered.'⁴³ An Italian observer also recorded
how there had been 'suspicions here and there thrown out, that he
[Edward] was either gradually carried off by some slow poison administered long before, or even, as poison worked slower than the expectation & desire of Parricides [Northumberland] that he was secretly
destroyed by violence & the dagger'.

Conspiracy theories abounded. Julius Terentianus, an Italian who had
accompanied the reformer Peter Martyr to England, blamed Catholics

wishing to incite hatred against Northumberland: 'If I may say what I think, I believe the papists themselves to have been the authors of so great wickedness, for they have expressed no signs of sorrow, and no inquiry has been made respecting so great a crime.'[44] Scheyfve, on the other hand, believed that Edward had been poisoned by Northumberland in an attempt to frame Mary. Had not he fallen ill on the same day the princess had last visited him – 'and that the same ailment has continued to prey upon him ever since'? 'This fact is all the more suspicious,' he explained, 'because it seems the Duke and certain of his party used urgent and unwonted persuasions to induce the Lady Mary to come to visit the King. If she was in the King's presence before he felt unwell, it may come to pass that all the blame will be visited upon her.'[45]

The controversy surrounding the nature of Edward's death continued well into Elizabeth's reign. William Baldwin, writing in 1560, described in *The Funeralles of King Edward VI* how 'Great hath been the doubt among many, ever since the death of our late virtuous sovereign ... by what means he died, and what were the causes of his death.' Over twenty years later Osorius, Bishop of Sylves in Portugal, renewed the charge that Edward had been poisoned in a letter to Elizabeth, prompting a vicious reply from Walter Haddon.[46]

Rumours of Edward's poisoning no doubt extend from the uncertainty surrounding the final months of his reign, compounded by the secrecy surrounding the king's seclusion. Edward's symptoms were so complicated that the royal doctors George Owen and Thomas Wendy sought additional medical expertise. Northumberland's own physician, a professor at Oxford University, and a doctor from London were summoned, swearing an oath that they were 'strictly and expressly forbidden, under pain of death, to mention to anyone private details concerning the King's illness or condition'. Scheyfve reported that an unknown woman had also been admitted to tend Edward 'who professes to understand medicine, and is administering certain restoratives, though not independently of the physicians'.[47] The Italian writer Giulio Raviglio Rosso described how she had come forward 'with an offer to cure him, provided he was altogether entrusted to her care'. Despite the doctors' advice to the contrary, she was admitted to treat Edward, with little success, 'bringing the King to the verge of his life, through the restringents that she employed, which in a brief space of time puffed up his limbs, and burthened his person much more than before'. She was promptly removed and the doctors returned, but it was too late. Later in the seventeenth century the Jesuit Matthew Pattison extended the story, claiming that the apothecary who 'poisoned' Edward drowned himself 'for the horror of the offence and disquietness of his conscience', whilst the laundress who washed the dead king's shirt 'lost the skin of her fingers'.[48]

The exact cause of Edward's death has remained a matter of debate. The surgeon who later opened up Edward's chest found that 'the disease whereof his majesty died was the disease of lungs'. Hayward recorded that he had a 'tough straining cough' which became more violent as he slowly weakened, whilst William Baldwin described how Edward developed a 'crasy Cold' after drinking from an infected cup after a game of tennis.[49]

What is the likely truth? To understand the nature of Edward's illness, we must look back to April 1552. Then, Edward described in his journal how he fell ill with what he described as 'the measles and the smallpox'.[50] Edward made a quick recovery, but this brief illness was significant, and probably responsible for his eventual demise. Modern research has shown that measles can suppress natural immunity to tuberculosis, reactivating the bacteria that can survive intracellularly within healthy lung tissue. The large cavities described by surgeons opening Edward's lungs after his death, 'which had in them two great ulcers, and were putrified', are typical of such a reactivation, and may be still seen in adolescents today. Edward was probably in close contact with at least one person who had tuberculosis, most likely before his contraction of measles than after. Epidemiologic studies have shown that exposure to tuberculosis would only need to be brief, perhaps even fleeting. If this was the case, it was only a matter of time after Edward had contracted measles that he would succumb to the disease. His swelling legs, failing pulse, the loosening of his finger and toenails and changed skin colour, signs that contemporaries took to be the work of poison, were secondary symptoms of the disease, resulting both from septicaemia and cyanosis, the blueish purple discolouration of the skin and mucous membranes resulting from a deficiency of oxygen in the blood.[51]

Edward's death was lamented across the nation and beyond, where many considered it to have been a measure of divine punishment. The reformer John Calvin believed that England had 'been deprived of an incomparable treasure of which it was unworthy'. 'By the death of one youth,' he wrote, 'the whole nation has been bereaved of the best of fathers.'[52] Looking back in 1563, John Foxe movingly wrote in his *Acts and Monuments* how Edward 'was taken from us, for our sins no doubt'; 'this godly and virtuous imp ... was cut from us'. 'He would have reformed such a commonwealth here in the realm of England ... But the condition of this realm, and the customable behaviour of English people ... deserved no such benefit of so blessed a reformation, but rather a contrary pledge of deformation ...'[53] Public eulogies came instantly:

> This King to others was a lamp of light,
> Whose fame of right must want an ending day!
> A foe to none! A friend to every wight;
> The sky did gape to catch his soul for prey.
> For age he might deserve a riper end:
> Death calls the best, and leaves the worse to mend.[54]

Sir Richard Morison had celebrated Edward's birth in joyous prose. Now he lamented the death of his 'young, innocent and blessed King' whom God had taken from Englishmen for their sins: 'Our noble King is dead. Which of us is there but sin might draw us to the bar, and prove us guilty of his death?'

Looking back upon Edward's reign, he wistfully remembered how 'greater change was never wrought in so short space in any country sith [since] the world was'. 'It was such a time as ours can hardly dream on, when they are asleep, sure never in England, or if elsewhere to see none such as long as they be awake.' The dream over, he could only imagine 'What a King should England have had if God had given him his father's age.'[55]

Some refused to believe the news that Edward could have died so young. In November, three men were summoned before the Privy Council 'for their lewd reports touching that the late king should yet be alive', and in January 1554 Robert Robotham, 'of the wardrobe of the robes' was committed to the Fleet for claiming that Edward was still alive.[56] Pretenders soon emerged, claiming Edward's crown. William Constable was thrown into the Marshalsea prison for declaring himself to be the king, spreading seditious bills that remained in circulation until January 1556.[57] Another named Mantell was still practising his deception into the late 1570s. As late as 1587 William Francis of Hatfield had heard 'there was one in the Tower which saith he is King Edward'. He himself believed Edward had been sent into Germany, and knew the man that carried him 'in a red mantle' away on board a ship named *The Harry*.

When told that Edward had been interred where 'they use to bury kings' Francis refused to believe it: 'There was a piece of lead buried that was hollow, but there was nothing in it.'[58] Troops fighting in the Netherlands swore they had seen Edward there in charge of an army, others believed him to be in Spain, and in 1599 a 'vagrant' reported that Edward had been conveyed to Denmark, where he had married the queen 'and now is king there'.[59]

13

NEMESIS

'Libertatem adeptus sum morte Regis, et ex misero aulico factus liber et mei juris.'
[At the death of the king I obtained my liberty, and was freed from this miserable court.]
William Cecil's private journal, 6 July 1553[1]

For the whole of the next day Edward's death was kept secret. However, the news soon leaked out and before long it had spread throughout the court. Having denied what was clearly inevitable just days before, the council wrote to the ambassador Sir Philip Hoby at Brussels on 7 July confirming the news – a 'great heap of infelicity' – and explaining that 'the disease whereof he died was of the putrefaction of the lungs, being utterly incurable'.[2]

Preparations were made ready for Jane's arrival at the Tower of London to be crowned queen, though the ceremony would not take place for another four days; warships had been spotted sailing to the mouth of the Thames, whilst troops were stationed everywhere 'to prevent the people from rising in arms or causing any disorder'.[3] Everything seemed to be going to plan. The next stage in securing the new line of succession was to apprehend Mary, but when a small force commanded by Lord Robert Dudley arrived at her residence at Hunsdon, they discovered she had fled. Instructions were hurriedly dispatched to lieutenants and justices across the country, notifying them of Mary's escape and ordering them to prepare to muster troops at an hour's notice and to maintain continual watches.[4]

In fact, after having secretly departed from Hunsdon on 4 July, Mary had travelled to Swanston Hall, Cambridgeshire, before heading towards Norfolk and finally arriving at Euston Hall, Thetford. Here she was informed of Edward's death by her goldsmith.[5] Uncertain whether to believe the news, she hurried on to her palace at Kenninghall. There, having received confirmation, she consulted with her household officers and summoned the entire household, informing them of her brother's death. 'The right to the Crown of England,' she told them, 'had therefore descended to her by divine and by human law ... through God's high providence.' She appealed for their help, 'as partners in her fortunes'. She would fight for her crown. Roused by her words, they 'cheered her to the rafters and hailed and proclaimed their dearest princess Mary as queen of England'. Over the next few days she set to work gathering further support from nearby supporters.[6]

'This attempt should have been judged and considered one of Herculean rather than of womanly daring,' one Suffolk gentleman later commented, who witnessed Mary's rebellion at first hand. But was Mary really responsible for her own actions? Already her comptroller Rochester's steady-handed influence and guidance had proved invaluable during the farcical episode of her bungled escape. And so it seems to have been the case here. As early as March Northumberland had been attempting to gain her favour – she had been granted the castle and park of Framlingham in May, and in June received a diamond and pearl pendant from the king.[7] The reason for all this, the Venetian ambassador later recalled, was to persuade her 'without any doubt, she would be Queen'. When in a gesture of striking generosity Northumberland sent Mary her full arms as Princess of England, as she had borne them in Henry's reign, this only raised the ambassador's suspicions.

Mary, on the other hand, trusted Northumberland implicitly. Fortunately, her household officers did not – they decided that if their mistress were to stand any chance of succeeding her brother, she would need to be kept in the dark and worked 'by secret means'. So when they told her to continue befriending the duke, Mary followed their advice 'to the letter', fooling Northumberland into thinking he could obtain possession of Mary at any time.[8] Nor should the influence of the Imperial ambassadors on Mary be discounted. Warning her not to trust the first news she received of Edward's death in case she fall into the trap of treasonously proclaiming herself queen whilst the king still lived, she closely heeded their advice.

Her decision to contest the Crown was, however, entirely her own, for Mary knew her rights. Disinherited once before by her own father, she was not about to allow history to repeat itself. Now she faced another struggle – not only to retain a title that was rightfully hers, but to protect her Catholic faith from obliteration.

She would receive little support from her Imperial friends, however, who in fear of their lives had kept to Scheyfve's house for five days. Writing to Charles V, they insisted that Mary had no chance of gaining widespread support 'because of religion' – Northumberland's hand was simply too strong. 'All the forces of the country are in the Duke's hands, and my Lady has no hope of raising enough men to face him, nor means of assisting those who may espouse her cause.' In a contest between might and right, the former would always win through. 'The actual possession of power' was all that mattered, 'especially among barbarians like the English.'[9]

Meanwhile, amid the confusion, few knew of Edward's death; even fewer that Jane was about to be crowned queen. On 8 July the Lord Mayor and city dignitaries were brought before the council to be informed of the king's death. Shown the will, to which they were required to affix their signatures, they vowed to keep the new succession secret. The next day every officer in the Tower was sworn to protect Jane as queen. For the moment, everything was neatly going to plan.

At three o'clock in the afternoon of 10 July 1553 Jane was brought from Richmond and crowned in the Tower. As she embarked from her barge on the Thames, the curious gathered to catch a glimpse of their new queen. 'She has small features and a well-made nose,' recalled one observer, 'the mouth flexible and the lips red. The eyebrows are arched and darker than her hair, which is nearly red. Her eyes are sparkling and reddish brown in colour. I stood so near her grace that I noticed her colour was good but freckled. When she smiled she showed her teeth, which are white and sharp.' Jane wore a dress of green velvet with long sleeves embroidered with gold; beside her, dressed in white and gold, her husband Guildford Dudley doted on her with 'much attention'. His height stood in stark contrast to her own tiny frame – to compensate, she walked on stilts hidden beneath her dress.

Walking in procession under a cloth of estate, her mother Frances, the Duchess of Suffolk, bore the train. Behind them followed her ladies-in-waiting, the council and several members of the nobility. In contrast to the splendour of Edward's coronation, little ceremony was accorded to the proclamation of Jane as queen; a peal of guns echoing across the city was the only indication that an event of significance had taken place. An hour later, at seven o'clock in the evening, two heralds and a trumpeter told the news of Edward's death and proclaimed Jane queen in front of thousands of Londoners, who by all reports apparently stood silently astonished, their faces 'sorrowful and averted'.[10]

When one man named Gilbert Potter lambasted the crowd for their lack of defiance, he was promptly seized and both his ears severed 'at the root' the following morning. His example was to be a lesson to all. But one pamphlet, written as a letter to Potter and scattered in the streets, celebrated his sacrifice on behalf of Mary, urging others to do the same and to fight with their lives for the princess.

Then, on 11 July, the council received a letter from Mary. Her defiance reverberated throughout. Mourning her brother's passing, she made clear that the Crown was hers only. Her claim, backed by an Act of Parliament and her father's will, was self-evident: 'You know,' she appealed, 'the realm and the whole world knoweth; the rolls and records appear by the authority of the king our said father, and the king our said brother, and the subjects of this realm; so that we verily trust that there is no good true subject, that is, can, or would, pretend to be ignorant thereof.' She announced her intention to openly proclaim and publish her title as the rightful Queen of England.

It was strange, she thought, that she had not been told of her brother's death. Yet she was willing to give the council the benefit of the doubt, and hoped that she would be secure in their loyalty. But she would not be taken for a fool, for she knew exactly what had been going on behind her back: 'We are not ignorant of your consultations, to undo the provisions made for our preferment, nor of the great bands, and provisions forcible, wherewith ye be assembled and prepared – by whom, and to what end, God and you know, and nature cannot but fear some evil.' She was ready to pardon their doings, hoping to avoid any bloodshed and violence that civil war might cause. She hoped that they too would see reason. Yet behind such generosity shone her determination to claim the Crown and she was prepared 'to use the service of others our *true* subjects and friends' to seize it. And she had every faith that God, 'in this our just and right cause', was on her side. She expected them to follow suit.[11]

It had been a bold move. Privately she was less sure. Before he delivered the letter to the council, she had instructed her messenger to deliver a verbal message to the Imperial ambassadors: without the emperor's support, she saw 'destruction hanging over her'. But there would be no help forthcoming. That same day, Ambassador Scheyfve received a letter from Charles V, casting his cousin to the fates.[12]

By all reports the council were astonished to receive Mary's letter; on hearing it read out, the duchesses of Northumberland and Suffolk began to weep.[13] 'I am truly sorry that it was your lot to be so immature and thus rashly to throw yourself away in this embassy,' Northumberland told Mary's messenger as he ordered him to be seized and sent to the Tower. But Mary's boldness had paid off, for hearts and minds had begun to turn.

The council's reply was quickly drafted by Sir John Cheke. They refuted her 'supposed title, which you judge yourself to have'. Rather, Jane was their 'sovereign lady queen': their duty and allegiance was to her and no other. Mary, through her parents' divorce, had been rendered illegitimate – a fact borne out by 'sundry acts of parliaments remaining yet in their force' – and she should cease her attempts 'to vex and molest' the queen's subjects from their true faith and allegiance, 'wherein you may be otherwise grievous unto us, to yourself, and to them'. Another circular to the justices was also hurriedly prepared, denouncing Mary's claim. Cecil apparently refused to draft the document; Northumberland wrote it himself, its hasty scrawl ordering them to 'assist us in our rightful possession of this kingdom and to extirp to disturb, repel and resist the fained and untrue claim of the Lady Mary bastard . . .'[14]

It was decided that the Duke of Suffolk, together with certain other noblemen, should travel to Norfolk, apprehend Mary and bring her back to London. But that night, Jane was so upset by the prospect that 'with weeping tears made request to the whole council that her father might tarry at home in her company'. Suffolk, for his part, on the advice of his wife, apparently feigned fainting fits and 'attacks of giddiness'.[15] The council resolved that Northumberland should go instead, persuading him that his military expertise made him the best man for the job.

'Well, since ye think it good,' the duke replied, 'I and mine will go, not doubting of your fidelity to the Queen's majesty, which I leave in your custody.'

The following morning Northumberland's retinue met outside his residence at Durham Place. Carts were seized and made ready, laden with munitions, artillery and field guns. Drums were sounded to muster men, recruited on the promise of ten pence a day wages. After all the preparations had been finished, Northumberland sat down to dine with the council, where he addressed them, urging them to remain loyal to Jane and himself. Above all, it was 'God's cause' that they fought for, and the 'fear of papistry's re-entrance' that had led them to sign their names pledging their lives to Edward's Devise. 'Think not the contrary,' North-umberland warned, 'but if ye mean deceit, though not forthwith yet hereafter, God will revenge the same. I can say no more; but in this troublesome time wish you to use constant hearts, abandoning all malice, envy, and private affections.'

'If ye mistrust any of us in this matter,' one councillor replied, 'your grace is far deceived; for which of us can wipe his hands clean thereof? And if we should shrink from you as one that were culpable, which of us can excuse himself as guiltless? Therefore herein your doubt is too far cast.'

'I pray God it be so,' Northumberland answered.[16]

The next morning Northumberland departed with over six hundred men. His troops were well equipped with cannon and field guns taken from the Tower and had considerable military experience, with many mustered from the yeomen of the guard and the gentlemen pensioners who trusted Northumberland's reputation as a soldier.[17]

As Northumberland and his troops rode through Shoreditch on their way out of the capital, the streets fell eerily silent. 'The people press to see us,' he remarked, 'but not one sayeth God speed us.' Possibly they mused on Mary's fate: 'We believe that my Lady will be in his hands in four days,' the Imperial ambassadors grudgingly wrote back to Charles V.[18]

Meanwhile courts across Europe were coming to terms with Jane's accession, including the acceptance of her husband, Northumberland's son, Guildford, as king. At Brussels, the emperor's cousin Don Diego congratulated the English ambassadors Sir Philip Hoby and Sir Richard Morison on gaining 'so noble and toward a prince': 'Whether the two daughters be bastard or no, or why it is done, we that be strangers have nothing to do with the matter,' Diego remarked. 'You are bound to obey and serve her majesty, and therefore it is reason we take him for your king.'[19]

Elsewhere across the country, news of Jane's accession came as a shock to many. In Cornwall, she was proclaimed at a general assize in front of the gentry of the county, 'who nevertheless came not for that purpose or knew of any such thing towards at their coming thither, nor in heart favoured the same'.[20] Many towns were uncertain whether to proclaim Jane or Mary queen. When the sheriff of Norfolk and Suffolk, Sir Thomas Cornwallis, received Northumberland's orders to proclaim Jane, he gathered the leading men of the counties together at Ipswich where, after they had 'earnestly discussed the perils of the situation', had her proclaimed 'not without murmurs of discontent and great indignation from the common people' on 11 July, yet the same day Mary's servant, Thomas Poley, on her 'especial order' proclaimed Mary queen in the marketplace before hurriedly fleeing the town.[21]

In London, life returned to normal, and the city began to collect contributions for its customary present to the new monarch. But an air of suspicion remained, and when the Goldsmiths' Company held their general assembly on 14 July, it was advised that none should 'talk or meddle with the Queen's affairs but that it is honest and faithful' and a watch was ordered by the city authorities to prevent arms leaving the city.[22]

The scarcity of evidence rarely affords us a glimpse into the thoughts and minds of the ordinary man of Tudor England, but one document – a petition of one Richard Troughton to the Privy Council – allows just that: a record of his own experiences of the turbulent month of July and his attempts to rouse support for Mary in Lincolnshire. Troughton's narrative indicates what those outside the Tudor court understood and believed about its politics. His own hatred of Northumberland stemmed back to the execution of Somerset, but Troughton knew of the duke's father, Edmund Dudley, who 'was a traitor and he was a very villain' and would have killed Henry VIII. He now believed Northumberland had taken Edward's life, and 'feared he would go about to destroy the noble blood of England'. And he was confident that 'over a hundred thousand men would rise' on Mary's behalf, believing 'her grace should have her right, or else there would be the bloodiest day for her grace that ever was in England'.[23]

Sending his infantry in front and cavalry behind, Northumberland's army made its way towards Cambridge. The duke met his sons and five hundred men at arms at Ware, where Mary was proclaimed bastard, before travelling to Swanston Hall, where she had stayed a few nights previously, which they set about destroying, earning Northumberland 'the deepest hatred in the surrounding countryside'. Having then joined forces with Lord Clinton, Northumberland arrived in Cambridge on Saturday 14 July, where he dined with university officials, and the next day heard the vice-chancellor preach from the university pulpit, urging obedience to the new regime.[24]

Mary, meanwhile, was one step ahead. With her council sending out messengers to notify the gentlemen in the surrounding countryside of her situation, supporters had begun to flock to Kenninghall. The most notable of these was Henry Radcliffe, one of the sons of the Earl of Sussex, whom John Huddleston had intercepted on his way to deliver letters to the council from his father. Mary was 'thoroughly delighted', since the letters that Radcliffe was carrying gave details of the council's plans against her. The elder earl, who had been falsely persuaded by Robert Dudley that Edward remained alive, soon hastened to join her upon hearing of his son's capture, pledging his support 'that he would uphold her cause in the future'.[25] Sir Richard Southwell brought with him a welcome supply of provisions, money and armed retainers: 'nothing at that time could have been more opportune or desirable'. Others soon followed: Sir John Mordaunt, the eldest son of Lord Mordaunt, the serjeant at law, Thomas Morgan and Sir William Drury amongst 'other distinguished young men'.

Her forces growing by the hour, Mary realized that Kenninghall was simply too small to withstand a siege or accommodate her increased household. On 12 July, determined to fight to the very last, she decided the best course was to move to Framlingham, the ancient seat of the Howards and easily the strongest castle in Suffolk.[26] But as she began her journey the revolution had already begun as, one by one, cities and towns refused the council's edict to proclaim Jane queen. That same day Bury became the first town to proclaim Mary queen, amidst rumours that she had sent a messenger to Northumberland declaring that she 'would give him his breakfast, dinner, and supper' (in other words, his just deserts). News of the town's decision spread fast, and in Lincolnshire it inspired Richard Troughton to travel around the county spreading the news, singing as he rode to stir up support for her cause. Calling in at the home of a local gentleman, Sir John Harrington, they celebrated with beer and wine until Harrington, by now 'very merry', thought it necessary to take out his book of Statutes, 'and laid it open, upon the board, that every man might read it; And had noted the substance of the Statute for the declaration of the Queen's Majesty's right to the Crown of England ... and so, pointing to it with his finger, said never a word.'

Other cities soon followed suit. In disbelief at Edward's death, Norwich had at first refused to proclaim her, but by the 13th the city had not only proclaimed her queen but also sent weapons and men. Coventry had also declared for Mary, despite its strong Protestant links, whilst in Gloucester the mayor commanded twenty-four soldiers to be sent to Framlingham to fight against Northumberland. Others, whilst not rejecting Jane's authority out of hand, refused to take up arms against a daughter of Henry VIII, even including the gentleman pensioner Edward Underhill, whose heady commitment to Protestantism had earned him the nickname of the 'hot gospeller' and had named his new-born son Guildford after Northumberland's son and the new queen's consort, asking the new rulers to stand as godparents at his christening.[27]

Mary reached Framlingham at around eight o'clock on the evening of 13 July. Already a crowd of local gentry and justices had gathered amongst the 'country folk' in a deer park beneath the castle. One had even come 'laden' with the most recent tax collection. Soon the retinues of the earls of Sussex and Bath had joined the forces. In total, annuities given as a reward to 134 men who served at Framlingham came to £2,234 13s 4d (£500,000).[28] But Mary was particularly keen to gain the support of the local magnate Thomas, Lord Wentworth, who had already declared his support for Jane. Sending her servants to negotiate, she delivered the stern message that 'he should take a good care for himself and for his family not to forsake the queen's cause, which would be to the perpetual dishonour of his house'. Wentworth needed little thought before making his answer: though he had pledged his support for Jane by oath, 'his inner conscience constantly proclaimed that Mary had a greater right to the throne' and he resolved to join her as soon as possible.

Back in London, nobody could be certain of what might happen. In paranoia, even the French ambassador Noailles feared that North-umberland had made a deal with Charles V to hand Mary over to be married as the emperor pleased, perhaps to his eldest son – 'a thing which is more to be feared than a thousand others which might happen in this affair'.[29] In desperation he had presented the council with further 'honest and fine offers' from Henry II, pledging his military support. North-umberland thanked him for these 'honest, great, and generous offers' saying that he hoped for the support of French troops 'when the occasion presents itself', whilst a letter was sent from the council to the French court: 'We shall never forget this great friendship in so difficult times, although we doubt not but that the estate and power of this realm shall, by God's goodness, prevail against all manner of practices or attempts, either by the Emperor or any other, either foreign or outward enemies whatsoever the same be.'[30]

With the French alliance firmly shored up, a message was sent to the Imperial ambassadors threatening them with expulsion if they attempted any communication with Mary. But when the ambassador Simon Renard bluffed that the council had been misled by the French, whose spies had informed him they were offering their support to Northumberland only in order to place Mary Stuart on the throne, he was taken seriously and urged to remain.[31]

Meanwhile morale in the Tower was sinking fast. William Cecil later claimed that he resolved to flee the realm but was persuaded by Cheke to stay.[32] Meanwhile, Russell had apparently become 'broken withal', declaring that he had always been opposed to Edward's Devise. Plotting soon broke out, with William Cecil and William Paulet, the Marquess of Winchester, devising a plan to gain Windsor Castle and levy men from the west on behalf of Mary. One by one, members of the council who had put their own hand to Edward's Devise and had pledged their lives to Northumberland, were beginning to desert him. Yet Renard's bluff had been closer to the truth than he could have imagined. Earlier Northumberland had dispatched his cousin Sir Henry Dudley to the French court to ask for the troops that Henry II had promised. Dudley reached Compiègne on 18 July, and according to the Imperial ambassadors, received a promise from Henry that he would fight in person if the emperor became involved in English affairs.[33] He then travelled to Guisnes, carrying letters to the governors of Calais and Guisnes to allow the French in 'with an armed force on the pretence of assisting the said duke'. However, he was arrested upon his arrival on 26 July. Examined in mid August, he confessed that 'the Duke had promised to hand over to the French Calais, Guisnes, and Hammes, the English possessions on the mainland, and Ireland'.[34] Was Northumberland intending to betray his country to the French in order to cling on to power? Rumours at the time abounded. 'They say that he made a close league with France,' a Spanish merchant resident in London recorded, 'and great promises to deliver Calais and Guisnes to him in return for his alliance', whilst a man was placed in the pillory for saying that the deputy of Guisnes, Lord Grey, 'should have betrayed the town'.[35] Desperation knows no bounds.

By now there was news of risings on behalf of Mary in Oxfordshire and Buckinghamshire.[36] Little is known about these insurrections, though one author believed they had been sparked off by the Earl of Huntingdon confiding to his brother Sir Edward Hastings that Northumberland was intending to assassinate Mary. Hastings was mortified, and revealing the plot to Sir Edmund Peckham, both resolved to raise Buckinghamshire against the duke.[37]

The greatest turning point, however, was yet to come. Before Northumberland's departure, he had dispatched six ships containing around nine hundred men towards Yarmouth in an attempt to arrest Mary, but they had been hastily prepared, with men of little naval experience pressed into service.[38] To ensure his orders were obeyed, Northumberland had removed the ships' captains, placing his retinue in charge of the fleet, his servant Gilbert Grice being in charge of the 200-ton *Greyhound*. However, a storm scattered the ships, and forced the *Greyhound* to seek shelter in Lowestoft Road. There Grice went ashore to discover news and muster men, but found himself arrested by suspicious townsmen. The *Greyhound* then lay at anchor for two days whilst the ship's master, Hurlock, received enticements from both sides, Grice sending him three gold rings, requesting he come ashore and speak with him. Eventually Mary's servant Pooley was allowed on board, but was unable to convince the crew to take sides, and the *Greyhound* cast anchor in search of the rest of the squadron, entering Orwell Haven and coming to rest in Harwich Water. By now, desperate for wages, the mariners had broken open Grice's chest and distributed the money amongst themselves.[39]

Hearing the news of the *Greyhound*'s arrival, Mary's household officer, Sir Henry Jerningham, travelled to inspect the ship. There he was greeted by the mariners who, by now fed up with their scant wages and poor conditions on board, asked him whether he would arrest their captains.

'Yea, marry,' Jerningham replied.

'Ye shall have them, or else we shall throw them to the bottom of the sea,' came their ecstatic response.

Yet no arrests were necessary, for the captains too agreed to serve Mary 'gladly'. In Framlingham, Mary found the news 'wonderful joyous'.[40] She now found herself with a ready supply of ordnance to combat the duke. However, the decision of the ships to defect to Mary was hardly the mutiny that many commentators have made it out to be. Many of the crew had found themselves hastily thrown together, under the control of an unknown and inexperienced captain. Their resolve had been tested to extremes by the storm, yet they held out from declaring for Mary until it was clear that their other comrades would not take up arms against them.

Back at the Tower, news of the ships' defection struck morale badly, with one observer describing scenes of general pandemonium, and how 'each man then began to pluck in his horns'. In a last-ditch attempt to muster further support, the council wrote to the justices across the country again on 16 July, informing them that the 'bastard daughter' of Henry VIII was encouraging men 'by all ways and means she can' to

rebel 'through the council of a number of obstinate Papists'. The threat
Mary posed was now a very real one. If the Crown descended to Mary,
they wrote, foreigners would rule the land, resulting in 'the bondage of
this Realm to the old servitude of the Antichrist of Rome, the subversion
of the true preaching of God's word, and of ancient laws, usages and
liberties of this Realm'.[41]

Such words masked their own reservations at their own actions – one
ambassador noticed how council appeared anxious, some even remarking
that Mary's rising was a punishment from God. A letter addressed to Jane
had been found in St Paul's and its author rounded up and thrown into
the Tower.[42]

The nobility had become prisoners in their own fortress, with
Suffolk refusing to allow them to leave the Tower.[43] When Pembroke
and Sir Thomas Cheyney tried to depart they were forbidden, whilst
the Marquess of Winchester's attempt to escape to his London house
was quickly foiled, and the Tower gates suddenly bolted shut and their
keys taken to Jane.

Stalled in Cambridge, Northumberland had begun to grow uneasy.
News of the ships' defection had come as 'great a heart-sore' and had
weakened the morale amongst his camp who had already begun to desert
him. On 18 July he took the decision to move to Bury, twenty-four
miles away from Framlingham, yet having sent messages to the council
for further aid, he received certain 'letters of discomfort' which prompted
his sudden return to Cambridge where he wrote 'somewhat sharply' to
the council demanding the reinforcements and ammunition he desperately needed. He received no reply.

Worse still was to come. As the duke prepared to set out for Bury
again the next day, news broke of the Earl of Oxford's defection. The
council wrote to Rich, who had departed into Essex in order to raise
troops against Mary, informing him of the 'grievous' news, and encouraging him to remain loyal.[44] But it was too late: Rich too was already on
his way to Framlingham.

On the same day members of the ruling elite in Sussex proclaimed
Mary queen. Jane, on the other hand, they considered 'a queen of a new
and pretty invention'. They would to send a letter to London, advising
them to recant their proclamation of Jane 'or else'. 'It is most necessary
that we brave ill', came the defiant message.[45]

Amid this desperate news, Arundel had begun to consider his position.
Through marriage, he had great attachment to the Grey household.[46]

Nevertheless, it was clear that Northumberland had failed. Arundel decided that he could no longer support Jane, telling Cecil that 'he liked not the air'. He resolved to raise the matter with Pembroke. It was a risky decision; Pembroke's own son was now married to Jane's sister, Catherine Grey. But he knew Pembroke and Northumberland had quarrelled before, and decided to take the gamble. Conferring together, they decided to call a meeting of the council and aldermen at Pembroke's residence, Baynard's Castle on the banks of the Thames. The reason for this, they claimed, was to give an audience to the French ambassador, since 'the Tower was not fit to him to enter into at that season'. Once everyone had gathered in the hall, Arundel rose from his chair. Northumberland, he told them, was a 'thirster of blood', 'a man of very small or no conscience at all ... I do not doubt but you shall have good cause to concur with me in opinion, and to show how little I ought to esteem the Tyrant'. The duke had imprisoned him for almost a year, 'practising my death by many wicked devises'. Yet he did not come to seek revenge: 'I am only hereto induced for the safety of the common wealth and liberty of this kingdom, whereto we are bound no less than to ourselves, both by the law of God and nature, as likewise through remorse of conscience, seeing the Lady Mary's right, lawful successor to this Crown, by another possessed, and thereby all we like to be deprived of that liberty which we have so long enjoyed under our lawful Kings and Princes'. He was convinced that Northumberland was attempting to become 'Lord of this land':

> I think you conceive that neither zeal of religion, or desire of the common good, moved him hereunto, but only an ambition to reign: for, to bring a free state into servitude, cannot be termed the common good, neither can you say there is any religion in him, who hath violated his faith against his Prince ... You shall see at last, when he is once possessed of the kingdom, that he will make reason obey his appetite, abandoning the first, and embracing the second, from whence will grow injustice, violence, rapine, seductions, cruelty and all kinds of villany. Yea, yourselves shall be thereby so weakened as you cannot possibly after remedy the same.

Mary meanwhile 'shone with goodness'; they could expect justice, pity and 'mercy and mild government' from her. It was true that Northumberland was accompanied by his forces, but this could all change: 'those forces be at our commandment, if we trust ourselves and agree in one, especially at this present, when you see the greater part of his army hath forsaken him, together with the general discontentment that this whole land conceives to see one raised to the Crown that hath no right thereunto, and her deprived to whom it appertains by succession.'

If they worried about breaking their oath, 'having already acknowledged Jane, showing thereby your variableness in that kind', he urged them to reconsider. They risked making themselves slaves, he warned, for continual turmoil and civil war threatened:

> Consider that now the factions are divided, some biding with Mary, others with the Duke, which be the utter overthrow of this Land; for you shall see brother against brother, uncle against nephew, father in law against son in law, cousin against cousin, and so from one unto another, you shall see those enemies that be of the same blood. Thus will they weaken the strength of this kingdom by such a dangerous division, which at last will be an occasion to draw foreign forces into this Land, so as, in short time, we can expect no other than to have ourselves, our substance, our children and wives, a prey to the soldiers, with the utter ruin of our nobility.

He ended by urging them to abandon Northumberland's cause, 'being contrary to all reason, unjust, and fit to breed infinite mischiefs and inconveniences': 'Take from the Tyrant his authority, depriving him of his forces, and giving the title of this Crown to whom it by all right belongeth,' Arundel's voice bellowed. 'Herein you shall do justice, and be accounted both pitiful to men and pious towards God, who will never forsake you in so glorious an enterprise.'

No sooner had he finished than Pembroke shot up: 'For my own part,' he said, 'I allow all that which he hath said, and I bind myself to maintain the quarrel against any man that shall speak the contrary.' And laying his hand upon his sword, said: 'If my Lord of Arundel's persuasions cannot prevail with you, either this sword shall make Mary Queen, or I will lose my life.'[47]

Scenes of jubilation followed. As the meeting broke up, Pembroke, Arundel, Shrewsbury, the Lord Warden Cheyney, the Lord Mayor, Sir John Mason and Sir John Cheke hastened to Cheapside. A crowd had already assembled, perhaps already briefed of the news. Before them, a herald proclaimed Mary queen.

'Great was the triumph,' one observer recalled, 'for my time I never saw the like, and by the report of others the like was never seen'. The number of caps that were thrown up at the proclamation were 'not to be told'. The Earl of Pembroke threw away his own cap full of angelets.★ People threw money from windows whilst old men were seen leaping and dancing 'as though besides themselves'. Some wept with joy whilst others, desperate to spread the news, ran through the streets crying 'Long live Queen Mary!' As the news spread, some stood astonished, silent in disbelief and fear. It had been forbidden to speak in Mary's favour, under the penalty of death.[48] Now there were bonfires 'without number': 'What with shouting and crying of the people, and ringing of the bells, there could no one hear almost what another said, besides banquetings and music and singing in the street for joy.' From a distance, thought Scheyfve, it must have looked as if Mount Etna was erupting.[49]

Struggling to pass through the crowds, the lords rode to St Paul's where they heard — for the first time in years — Te Deum with the full blast of organs. In declaration of loyalty to the new queen they ordered the letter M to be hastily stitched on to the livery coats of their retainers.[50] Bonfires burned as banquets set up in the street, accompanied by singing, music and drinking, continued through the night. Only one man was arrested for speaking against the new queen. Later, when the scenes of celebration came back to haunt those present, John Knox poignantly reminded them that those whose voices openly spoke out against her went unheard 'when fires of joy and riotous banquetings were made at the proclamation of Mary ... the stones and timber of those places shall cry in fire, and bear record that the truth was spoken.'[51]

The sound of church bells rung from every parish church continued until ten o'clock. Cheering on those in celebration around bonfires, Arundel and Paget made their way at full speed toward Mary, with news of her proclamation as queen. Hearing the news from the Tower, Suffolk ordered his men to lay down their arms. He was 'but one man' he told them. It was time to concede defeat.

The news soon reached Northumberland. At five o'clock he came to the market cross in Cambridge where he proclaimed Mary queen; with no herald near by, he proclaimed her style himself. As men threw up their caps in joy, he held his arm aloft, waving his white staff of office. Witnesses remarked there were tears of sorrow in his eyes. Casting off his weapons, he urged his followers to do the same. He told one observer that he believed Mary to be a 'merciful woman' whom he would sue for pardon.

'Be you assured,' replied the observer, 'you shall never escape death,

★ A gold coin worth 3s. 9d.

for if she would save you, they that now shall rule will kill you.'[52]

Turning away from the scenes of celebration, Northumberland returned to his lodging in tears.

Within the hour a herald arrived, sent by the council, with letters announcing their instructions: Northumberland was to disarm his troops immediately and remain outside the capital until further ordered. 'If he do not,' they warned, 'we will not fail to spend our lives in subduing him and his.'

As his troops disbanded, an alderman of the town attempted to arrest the fallen duke, but his pride remained. 'Ye do me wrong to withdraw my liberty,' he protested. 'See you not the council's letters, without exception, that all men should go whether they would?'[53]

Meanwhile back at Framlingham, as Arundel and Paget raced through the countryside to bring her the news, Mary remained oblivious to the events that had taken place in the capital, proclaiming her the nation's rightful heir. On 20 July, still awaiting Northumberland's onslaught, Mary took the opportunity to inspect her troops, now armed and ready to fight on behalf of their queen. Once the standards had been unfurled, the army stood ready, its battle lines drawn up and armed with pikes, lances, bows, guns and loaded cannon.

At four o'clock, Mary rode out to inspect her army, but soon got into difficulty when the white horse she was riding reared up, forcing her to dismount and inspect her troops on foot. Despite this untimely disturbance, Mary commanded the total respect of everyone present, her soldiers offering her such reverence that one observer wondered even 'whether they could have given greater adoration to God if he had come down from Heaven'.

Mary spent time speaking to each division 'with exceptional kindness and with an approach so wonderfully relaxed . . . that she won everyone's affections'. After the inspection, which had lasted three hours, Mary was treated to a mock charge of her cavalry thundering across the field, before she retired back into the confines of the castle.

Upon her return, Mary found Arundel and Paget waiting for her. They carried with them a fawning letter from the council in London, hoping to convince her of their change of heart: 'Our bounden duties most humbly remembered to your most excellent Majesty . . .' it began, and so on.[54]

For the moment, Mary did not care. Overjoyed, her first act was to arrange with her chaplains for a crucifix to be erected in the chapel and for mass to be said in thanksgiving. No one could now prevent her from practising her religious devotions as she wished. God had given her the victory against Northumberland and his stalwarts of Protestantism. The suddenness of her victory, she believed, could not be taken as anything else. It was a sure sign of God's favour that she must lead his Church back to Rome.[55] For now, she ordered Arundel to ride to Cambridge to arrest Northumberland and to bring him back to the capital as a traitor to be placed in the Tower.

The following day Arundel arrived at Cambridge to perform the task of arresting the man to whom he had promised his body and blood. As the earl approached him in his chamber, Northumberland fell on his knees. He begged for mercy. 'Consider I have done nothing but by the consents of you and the whole council.'

'My Lord, I am sent hither by the Queen's majesty, and in her name I do arrest you.'

'And I obey it,' Northumberland replied. 'I beseech you, my Lord of Arundel, use mercy towards me, knowing the case as it is.'

'My Lord', Arundel responded, 'you should have sought for mercy sooner; I must do according to my commandment.'[56]

Across the country, news of Mary's proclamation was greeted with scenes of celebration. At Grantham, a messenger burst into Richard Troughton's house and announced the news 'with his mouth sounded like a trumpet three times'. Troughton immediately ordered bonfires to be lit so that 'all the Queen's tenants might praise God for his marvellous victory and miracle', ordering small children to carry wood to the fire in particular 'for a remembrance thereof'. After distributing meat and drink, he ordered them to kneel and 'give thanks to God . . . and so I said certain psalms, and prayed God save the Queen'. Robert Parkyn at Chester-le-Street recalled that priests were commanded by the gentry to say the Latin mass with its full Catholic rites. In Northampton, Sir Thomas Tresham proclaimed Mary queen, being carried aloft by the crowd; only Sir Nicholas Throckmorton dared to object and would have been lynched had he not escaped in fear of his life. Elsewhere, the news was slower to spread: in Dover, Mary was not proclaimed until 29 July, whilst in distant Kilkenny, Jane was proclaimed on 27 July and Mary not until 20 August.[57]

Back in the Tower, Jane sat down to write. She had never wanted the Crown, but against the will of her father the Duke of Suffolk her resistance had been futile. She had once told her tutor Roger Ascham that whenever she was with her parents, 'whether I speak, keep silence, sit, stand, or go, eat, drink, be merry or sad, be sewing, playing, dancing or doing anything else, I must do it, as it were, in such weight, measure and number ... or else I am so sharply taunted, so cruelly threatened, yea, presented sometimes with pinches, nips, and bobs, and other ways ... so without measure misordered, that I think myself in hell'.

Now she wrote to her father, informing him of her decision to abdicate the throne. 'Out of obedience to you and my mother, I have grievously sinned and offered violence to myself. Now do I willingly, and obeying the motions of my own soul, relinquish the Crown, and endeavour to solve those faults committed by others, if, at least, so great faults can be solved, by a willing and ingenuous acknowledgement of them.' She had entered the Tower as queen; from now, she would become its prisoner.

News of Mary's proclamation astounded the Imperial ambassadors. Only the day before they had written desperately to the emperor, begging for his assistance. Now, it was surely a 'miracle', they wrote, 'a work of the Divine Will'. Renard could hardly believe he was not dreaming.[58]

Writing to Henry II, the French ambassador Noailles grudgingly accepted defeat with no less amazement. 'The atmosphere of this country and the nature of its people are so changeable that I am compelled to make my dispatches correspondingly wavering and contradictory ... I have witnessed the most sudden change believable in men, and I believe God alone has worked it.'[59]

Those who had supported Jane now looked to hide if not absolve their guilt. In the margin of his copy of Jane's proclamation, William Cecil added the words *Jana non Regina*. Any support for Jane across the country had always been blended with a desire to protect self-interest. The leading members of the borough of King's Lynn, who had given her their support, had benefited from the Reformation, receiving three hundred acres of chantry lands, which they were perhaps understandably reluctant to sacrifice. Others were hesitant to come down on one side or the other. Receiving a copy of Mary's letter, the corporation of Great Yarmouth had hesitated to proclaim Mary and sent three of their officers to Norwich to seek advice. Arriving in time to hear Mary being proclaimed at the marketplace there, they rushed back to deliver their news. Only then did they proclaim Mary queen. But there was evidently a greater power struggle taking place, which the borough's officers later sought to hide. An entry for 11 August in their surviving Assembly Book, crossed through with the accompanying note that 'This is erased with the consent of the whole Assembly, 6 October, 1556', indicates that leading townsmen had been removed from their offices for opposing Mary. At Boston, the pages of the borough's minute book for July 1553 have been conveniently torn out, though we know that the mayor and aldermen appeared on the pardon roll at Mary's coronation in October.[60]

Meanwhile Mary prepared to travel back to London to take control of the kingdom she had fought for and won. Leaving Framlingham on 24 July, she travelled to Ipswich, where she was given eleven pounds' worth of gold by the bailiffs of the town and a golden heart inscribed with the words 'The Heart of the People' by some 'pretty little boys'. As she made her slow journey towards the capital, courtiers raced to become the first to pay their respects – and earn their pardon – from the new queen.[61]

At Newhall Mary was presented with a purse of crimson velvet containing £500 in half sovereigns by the city authorities of London. Finally, at Wanstead, she was joined by Elizabeth and her retinue. Here Mary planned her entrance into London, though she was nervous, being 'among people so inconstant and so easily led astray'.[62]

But first the capital celebrated the return of the fallen. On 30 July Northumberland was brought back on horseback, a prisoner riding alongside his captor Arundel. As they made their way towards the Tower, Londoners filled the streets to watch. Despite a proclamation ordering citizens to allow the prisoners to pass by peacefully, an armed guard of four thousand men struggled to hold back the crowds.[63] There were cries of 'Death to the traitors and long live the true Queen!' as volleys of stones were thrown. As they made their way past Bishopsgate, one man broke free from the cordon. It was Gilbert Potter. With his sword in hand, he shouted insults at Northumberland, taunting and threatening him: 'Behold the free tongue of an honest citizen, as you have disfigured the head of an innocent man by the mutilation of his ears, so shall you be dragged to the punishment due to treason & parricide, according to your deserts.'[64]

Northumberland turned to Arundel. 'Ought this most impudent fellow be allowed to afflict me while no accusation has yet been laid against me?'

'Be of good courage,' Arundel replied. 'Although I cannot stop the tongues of men accusing you, yet I will stop their hands from injuring you.'[65]

Along the route the taunts continued, the 'mockers striving to outdo each other'. At the front of the crowd, women waved red handkerchiefs at the duke, stained with Somerset's blood.

The atmosphere in the capital remained tense and uncertain. On 21 July a watch was ordered and any suspected 'adherents' of Northumberland stopped and arrested at the city gates.[66] On 29 July a man was set in the pillory for speaking against Mary and several preachers, 'Scotsmen in particular' – perhaps the followers of the preacher John Knox – were reported to be 'going so far as to say that men should see Antichrist come to life, and popery in the land'. Despite Paget's persuasions, Mary remained sceptical of the council that had attempted to disinherit her. On 1 August the Earl of Rutland was arrested, whilst when Pembroke was commanded to wait upon her at London, he brought fifteen men instead of the prescribed ten, earning himself 'a rebuke': 'Some say he is fled,' one gossip wrote, 'but the truth I know not, he hath not been seen since Thursday night neither can his men tell where he is.'[67]

At seven o'clock in the evening of 3 August 1553, riding upon a palfrey the gold-embroidered trappings of which reached to the ground, Mary made her entrance into the capital. It was to be her triumphal procession and a demonstration of the victory that she believed had been ordained by God. Accompanied by a thousand retainers dressed in velvet coats, she wore 'a gown of purple velvet, French fashion', her kirtle shining with gold and pearls, and hanging around her neck a necklace of gold pearls. Affirming the legitimacy of her succession, she was followed by Elizabeth and her 180 ladies-in-waiting. Bringing up the rear were her throng of supporters from Northampton, Buckinghamshire and Oxfordshire, numbering over three thousand and dressed in green, red, blue and white.

As the mayor welcomed her at the city gates hung with streamers, he kissed the sceptre 'in token of loyalty and homage' and placed it in her hands. Mary thanked him, remarking how the city had always been good to her. As she passed on streets freshly gravelled, one bystander remarked that the sound of trumpets, bells 'so long disused' and guns echoed like thunder.[68] Rich cloths and tapestries hung from buildings and between them, images of the Virgin Mary and other effigies of saints, now proudly restored from their hiding places, peered out from windows. On every crossroad, the banners proclaimed the same message: '*Vox populi, vox Dei*' – 'The voice of the people [is] the voice of God.'[69]

As she neared the Tower, another peal of ordnance rang out. At the Tower gate a line of prisoners had been arranged. They knelt begging for mercy. Mary knew them well: Norfolk, Gardiner, Bonner and the Duchess of Somerset. She kissed each one. 'These are my prisoners,' she declared, and with that they were free.

Five days later, and over a month since his death, on 8 August 1553 Edward was buried at Westminster. His body had been embalmed and placed in a sealed lead coffin before being taken to Whitehall by river. The night before, a procession transferred the body to the abbey led by 'a great company' of children dressed in surplices, singing clerks and twelve of Henry VIII's bedesmen from the Greyfriars Church. Edward's former servants, wearing black, carried banners that proclaimed his ancestry. Among them were the Welsh dragon, the badge of Owen Tudor, the Lancastrian emblem of the greyhound and the standard of the lion, that of his father. Three heralds followed, one carrying his helmet and crest, another his shield, sword and garter and the last his coat of armour. Nine henchmen dressed in black and each carrying a banner rode upon a chariot pulled by 'great horses trapped with velvet to the ground'.[70]

Behind them came the coffin, covered by a canopy of blue velvet upon a chariot decorated with cloth of gold pulled by seven horses. Upon it lay the effigy of Edward, fashioned by the Italian sculptor Nicholas Bellin, wearing his crown and garter collar and holding a sceptre and his garter ribbon tied around the leg. Standards of the garter, the rose and the Seymour families surrounded the coffin.

As the cortège passed along its route Londoners watched weeping and lamenting; 'at his burying was the greatest moan made for him of his death as ever was heard or seen' one later wrote.[71]

Inside the abbey a hearse surrounded by thirteen branched pillars bearing lit tapers had been draped with black velvet, and the walls and aisles covered completely with black cloth.[72] The service was presided over by Cranmer according to the Protestant rite of the 1552 service. Mary had prevaricated over whether to allow her brother this much, but was persuaded to settle upon a compromise. Refusing to attend, instead she marked Edward's departure with three days of requiems in the Tower of London.[73]

In the abbey the remnants of Edward's court gathered. Many had been present to witness his christening – Edward's tutor and almoner Richard Cox was released from his recent detention to attend – now they came to pay their final respects. The one notable absentee was Northumberland. Though also absent from the ceremony, the Imperial ambassador considered the funeral was conducted 'with small ceremony', forgetting this was exactly what the young king would have wanted. The occasion was spoilt only by Mary's appointment of George Day, Bishop of Chichester, as preacher; according to one observer, his sermon 'prepared the way for papistry just like an advance raiding party'.[74]

Lowered into a vault of white marble, beneath the altar constructed for Henry VII's tomb, Edward's body soon lay forgotten.[75] Today, beneath the feet of eager tourists queuing to see the graves of Elizabeth or Mary, Queen of Scots, a simple plaque laid into the marble tiles of the chapel floor is all that marks his grave.

Despite initial fears that Mary would seek immediate revenge on all those that had sought to disinherit her, pardons were granted to all who had sworn an oath to Jane. Mary could have hardly done anything else, given that the entire ruling order had ascribed to it. Nevertheless, as the chronicler Richard Grafton remarked, the general pardon was 'interlaced with so many exceptions as they that needed the same the most, took smallest benefit thereby'.[76]

Women, once pawns, had become brokers. Lady Exeter and Mary's gentlewoman Mistress Clarencius pleaded with the queen to save Northampton's life: through his sister Queen Katherine Parr he was, after all, a member of the royal family.[77] Northumberland's wife Jane even wrote in desperation to Paget's wife Anne, to speak on her behalf with the two women. She was partly successful, and secured her sons' lives. But little could be done for her husband.[78]

On 18 August Northumberland, his eldest son the Earl of Warwick and the Marquess of Northampton were brought to trial before their peers at Westminster Hall. A huge stage had been erected, 'very majestic and richly tapestried, and in the midst of it a rich canopy, and under this a bench with rich cushions, and carpets at its foot'. Norfolk presided for the queen as Lord High Steward. The prisoners entered, making three bows before taking their places. The lords, an observer noted, beheld Northumberland with 'a severe aspect', the greatest courtesy paid to him being the touch of a cap. The duke was called first. Protesting his faith and obedience to the queen, he confessed to his crime. He did not intend to defend himself, but wished to ask the court their opinion whether he could be charged for treason for 'doing an act by the authority of the Prince and council, and by warrant of the Great Seal of England, and doing nothing without the same'. And was it just, he added, that he should be judged by men equally as guilty as him?[79]

The lords merely retorted that his use of the Great Seal had been illegal; rather it was 'the seal of a usurper'. As for his second point, so long as no attainder had been passed against them, they were fit to pass judgement.

Northumberland declared his repentance 'using few words'. He stood condemned by the law. He requested Norfolk to be his means to the queen for mercy, and asked for the 'favour of such a death as was executed on noblemen, and not the other', beseeching care be taken of his children 'in respect of their age'. He asked that he might be permitted to hear confession 'for the settling of his conscience'. Lastly, he requested to speak with four of the queen's council 'for the discovery of some things which might concern the state': 'Thus I beseech you all to pray for me.' Many were in tears; out of compassion or in grief 'for their own sakes for the stain they had contracted by the offence they had committed against the Queen' one observer was unable to tell.[80]

Next to follow, Northampton put up a spirited defence, claiming that he had deliberately absconded to go hunting during Jane's brief reign. But there were to be no excuses, and the verdict was a mere formality – all were found guilty. The next day Sir Thomas Palmer, Sir John Gates and Sir Andrew Dudley came to face justice. Palmer alone was defiant, accusing his judges of 'being worse traitors than him', though again the verdict was never in doubt.[81]

That Sunday, Dr Watson preached at St Paul's Cross accompanied by 120 of the guard armed with bills and weapons to avoid any of the previous week's disturbances, when daggers had been thrown at the pulpit. Urging the congregation to disregard their old preachers, he wished them 'to have no new faith, nor to build no new temple, but to keep the old faith, and re-edify the old temple again'. He highlighted the contradictions in the twists and turns of religious policy during Edward's reign: 'there hath been in his time that he hath seen twenty catechisms & every one varying from other in some point & well he said they might all be false but they could not all be true'. They must return to the scripture, set down in Hebrew and Latin, rather than in English, since he doubted that the translation was correct. They had 'followed men's traditions and had gone astray' he told them, and called upon them 'to come home again and re-edify the old temple'. The Reformation was over. Only days later, one observer reported how 'altars and masses are in building faster than ever they were put down'.[82]

At eight o'clock the next day, ten thousand people gathered at Tower Hill. The scaffold had been made ready and straw and sand had been strewn on the platform, ready to soak up the blood of the condemned. The Tower guard marshalled the crowds, creating a lane for Northumberland's final walk from his cell to the block. Even the executioner, having sharpened the axe's blade, was prepared. But then came a sudden announcement, ordering those present to return to their homes. The prisoners had earned a temporary reprieve, for Northumberland had declared his wish to hear mass.

For the new regime, it was an opportunity not to be wasted. Before the mass had even begun, fifteen London merchants were ordered by the council to observe the ceremony. To bring the point home, that same day a priest and a barber had their ears nailed to the pillory for seditious words spoken during the uproar at St Paul's Cross.[83]

In the Tower, the chapel of St Peter ad Vincula was prepared accordingly. Then the duke, together with Northampton, Sir Andrew Dudley, Sir John Gates and Sir Thomas Palmer were led through the courtyard. If they had looked up they might have seen Jane, as one observer did, gazing down from her cell. The ceremony was performed with full Catholic rites. As he came to receive the sacrament, Northumberland turned to the audience:

> I let you all to understand that I do most faithfully believe this is the very right and true way, out of the which true religion you and I have been seduced these sixteen years past, by the false and erroneous preaching of the new preachers, the which is the only cause of the great plagues and vengeance which hath light upon the whole realm of England, and now likewise worthily fallen upon me and others here present for our unfaithfulness. And I do believe the holy sacrament here most assuredly to be our Saviour and Redeemer Jesus Christ; and this I pray you all to testify, and pray for me.[84]

He had regretted ever having pulled down the mass: 'If it had pleased God to have granted him life & had remained in Authority,' he remarked, 'he would have put it down himself ever one year had come to an end, and added that to win the hearts of the Citizens of London because they loved new things he would not before do it.'[85]

Kneeling, he asked for forgiveness. Amongst others standing by were Somerset's sons.

Whether Northumberland's 'conversion' to Catholicism was genuine or not, it was the last possible card he could play to earn Mary's pardon and cheat death. Religion had once before saved his career; now he hoped it would save his life. Later that evening he wrote to Arundel, grovelling: 'Alas, my good Lord, is my crime so heinous as no redemption but my blood can wash away the spots thereof? An old proverb there is and that most true that a living dog is better than a dead lion. Oh, that it would please her good Grace to give me life, yea the life of a dog, that I might but live and kiss her feet.' It was signed, 'Once your fellow and loving companion, but now worthy of no name but wretchedness and misery. J.D.'[86]

They were the last words he was ever to write.

There was to be no reprieve. The next morning the prisoners were led from their cells to hear mass. Northumberland seized the opportunity to snatch a word with Gates: 'God have mercy upon us for this day shall end both our lives; and I pray you forgive me whatsoever I have offended, and I forgive you with all my heart, although you and your counsel was a great occasion hereof.'

'Well, my Lord,' Gates replied, 'I forgive you as I would be forgiven; and yet you and your authority was the original cause of all together; but the Lord pardon you, and I pray you forgive me.'[87]

Arriving at Tower Hill, Northumberland was the first to proceed to the scaffold. Throwing off his gown of grain-coloured damask, he leant upon its east rail. He confessed how he had 'been an evil liver, and have done wickedly all the days of my life; and, of all, most against the Queen's highness'. Asking for their forgiveness, he fell on to his knees, claiming he was not the only 'original doer' of his treason. There were others, but he refused to name them: 'for I will hurt now no man'. Instead, he placed the blame for his fall elsewhere – upon the 'false and seditious preachers' who had persuaded him to denounce 'the Catholic faith and true doctrine of Christ'. Exalting the one true faith, he rounded upon the arrogance of those who had believed Edward's reign heralded a new start: 'For I pray you, see, since the death of King Henry the Eighth, into what misery we have been brought; what open rebellion, what sedition, what great division hath been brought throughout the whole realm; for God hath delivered [us] up to [our] own sensualities, and every day [we] wax worse and worse'.[88]

He asked for the forgiveness of those he had offended. He thanked Mary in particular for her mercy, for 'where as I was with force and arms against her in the field, I might have been rent in pieces without law, her Grace hath give me time and respect to have judgement'.

It was an impressive display. Northumberland had acted the model of repentance and many were apparently 'turned with his words'. The speech was later printed by the government in English, French and Latin, to be distributed across Europe in a concerted effort to persuade Protestants to return to the Catholic fold.

The duke then recited a prayer and the psalm *De Profundis*.[89]

Out of the deep I have called unto thee, O Lord; Lord hear my voice. O let thine ears consider well the voice of my complaint. If thou, Lord, wilt be extreme to mark what is done amiss, O Lord, who may abide it? For there is mercy with thee; therefore shalt thou be feared. I look for the Lord; my soul doth wait for him. In his word is my trust. My soul fleeth unto the Lord before the morning watch, I say, before the morning watch.

If he still held out for a last gasp reprieve, it was clear there would be none.

Taking off Northumberland's jerkin and doublet, the executioner handed him the neckerchief. He placed his head on the block. It was all over with one stroke of the axe.

Sir John Gates was next to approach the scaffold. Acknowledging his offence, he asked the people to pray for him and, refusing a neckerchief, his head fell on the third blow of the axe. Thomas Palmer was the last to be executed. He leapt on to the scaffold, now covered with the blood of his comrades. Throwing his cap into the crowd he shouted:

'God give you all good morrow!'

'Good morrow!' a few shouted back.

'I do not doubt that I have a good morrow, and shall have I trust a better good even.'

With a smile, he spoke of a common Christian faith. He remained resolute in his personal conversion to Protestantism. When in the Tower he had a vision of Christ 'sitting at ye Right hand of God the father in glory and majesty ... whose power is infinite'. He knew then, he said, that eternal life beckoned:

I say god is such a one that without thou will sit down and behold the greatness above: the sun & moon, the stars above the firmament, the course of the sun, the moon, stars and clouds, the earth with all that in them is and how they be all preserved, thou shalt never know god ... The world is altogether vanity, for in it is nothing but ambition, flattery, foolish or vainglory, pride, discord, slander, boasting, hatred and malice.[90]

There is perhaps no more fitting remark to describe the feelings of a man who had experienced life at Edward's court. Before his own eyes, he remarked, he had seen and heard his friends and colleagues die before him. Death was no longer to be feared. 'Neither the sprinkling of the blood or the shedding thereof, nor the bloody axe itself, shall not make me afraid.' He turned to the executioner: 'Come on, good fellow – art thou he that must do the deed? I forgive thee with all my heart.'

Laying his head upon the block, Palmer joked how its shape fitted his neck well, before adding, 'I pray thee strike me not yet, for I have a few prayers to say, and that done, strike in God's name ...'

His prayers over, he desired every man to pray for him. In one stroke he was dead.

The spectacle finished, the audience drifted slowly away. The three bodies were loaded upon carts and taken away to be buried in the chapel of St Peter ad Vincula. There their bones still lie, alongside the bodies of Somerset, Thomas Seymour, Katherine Howard and Anne Boleyn.

SELECT BIBLIOGRAPHY

Manuscript Sources

BRITISH LIBRARY

Additional MSS
Cottonian MSS
Cottonian Charters
Egerton MSS
Harleian MSS
Lansdowne MSS
Lansdowne Rolls
Royal MSS
Salisbury MS Vol. 150; M 485/39

PUBLIC RECORD OFFICE

SP 1: State Papers Henry VIII
SP 10: State Papers Edward VI
SP 15: State Papers Edward VI
 Addenda
SP 68: State Papers Foreign Edward VI
C 66: Patent Rolls
E 36: Treasury of Receipt,
 Miscellaneous Books
E 101: Exchequer, King's
 Remembrancer, Various Accounts
E 315: Court of Augmentations,
 Miscellaneous Books and
 Proceedings
E 351: Exchequer, Pipe Office,
 Declared Accounts
LC 2: Lord Chamberlain's Office,
 Robes and Special Events
PROB 10: Prerogative Court of
 Canterbury, Filed Wills

PROB 11: Prerogative Court of
 Canterbury, Registered Copy
 Wills
REQ 2: Court of Requests
 Proceedings
Rolls Chapel Series MS A 2
STAC 3: Star Chamber, Proceedings,
 Edward VI

INNER TEMPLE LIBRARY

Petyt MS 538 vol. 47

COLLEGE OF ARMS

Herald's MSS
M Series MSS

CORPORATION OF LONDON
RECORDS OFFICE

Journals
Letter Books
Repertories

LONGLEAT, MANUSCRIPTS OF THE
MARQUESS OF BATH

Seymour Papers
Thynne Papers
(This material is included by kind
permission of the Marquess of
Bath, Longleat House, Warminster,
Wilts.)

BODLEIAN LIBRARY, OXFORD

MS Tanner 464
MS Ashmole 857, 861, 1730
MS Rawlinson D 1070

CAMBRIDGE UNIVERSITY LIBRARY

Dd.9.31 (William Gray's 'sayings' for

Edward Seymour, Duke of
Somerset)

BIBLIOTHEQUE NATIONALE,
PARIS

MSS Francais (Anciens fonds) 15888

Primary Sources

Acts of the Privy Council of England, eds. J. R. Dasent *et al.* (n.s., 36 vols.; London 1890–1964). [APC]

Adams, S., Archer, I. W., Bernard, G. W. (eds.), 'A "Journall" of Matters of State. . .' and 'Certayne Briefe Notes of the Controversy betwene the Dukes of Somerset and Duke of Northumberland', in *Religion, Politics and Society in Sixteenth Century England* (*Camden Society*, 5th Series, Vol. 22, 2003), pp. 52–137.

Beer, B. L., 'A critique of the Protectorate: an unpublished letter of Sir William Paget to the Duke of Somerset', *Huntington Library Quarterly*, 34 (1971), pp. 277–83.

Beer, B. L., and Jack, S. M. (eds.), *The Letters of William, Lord Paget of Beaudesert, 1547–1563, Camden Miscellany*, 25 (Camden Society, 4th ser., 13; London, 1974), pp. 1–142. [Paget Letters]

—— (ed.), '"The Commoyson in Norfolk, 1549": a narrative of popular rebellion in 16th century England', *Journal of Medieval and Renaissance Studies* 6 (1976), pp. 73–99.

Burnet, G., *History of the Reformation of the Church of England*, ed. N. Pocock (7 vols.; Oxford, 1865).

Cairns, C. S. (ed.), 'An unknown Venetian description of King Edward VI', *Bulletin of the Institute of Historical Research* 42 (1969), pp. 109–15.

Calendar of state papers, foreign: Edward VI, Mary, Elizabeth I, eds. J. Stevenson *et al.* (23 vols.; London, 1861–1950). [CSP Foreign]

Calendar of the Carew manuscripts . . . at Lambeth, 1515–1624, eds. J. S. Brewer and W. Bullen (London, 1867).

Calendar of state papers, domestic series, 1601–1609; with addenda, 1547–1565, ed. M. A. E. Green (London, 1870). [CSP Domestic]

Calendar of state papers and manuscripts, relating to English affairs, existing in the archives and collections of Venice. . . , eds. R. Brown *et al.* (9 vols.; London, 1864–98).

Calendar of the patent rolls preserved in the Public Record Office, Edward VI, ed. H. C. Maxwell Lyte (6 vols.; London, 1924–9). [CPR]

Cheke, Sir John, *The hurte of sedicion howe greveous it is to a common welth* (STC 5109, 5110; London, 1549).

Clifford, H., *The Lie of Jane Dormer, Duchess of Feria*, ed. J. Stevenson (London, 1887).

Collier, J. P. (ed.), Trevelyan papers prior to AD 1558, *Camden Miscellany* (2 vols.; Camden Society, 1st ser., 67; London, 1857).

Corrie, G. E., *Sermons by Hugh Latimer . . . Sermons and Remains of Hugh Latimer. . .*, (Parker Society, 1844, 1845).

Cox, J. E., *Works of Archbishop Cranmer* (2 vols. Parker Society, 1846).

Ellis, H. (ed.), *Hall's Chronicle* (London, 1809) [Hall's Chronicle]

—— *Original letters, illustrative of English history . . . from autographs in the British Museum and . . . other collections* (1st ser., 3 vols.; London, 1824).

Feuillerat, A. (ed.), *Documents relating to the revels at court in the time of King Edward VI and Queen Mary* (Louvain, 1914).

Foxe, John, *The acts and monuments of John Foxe and a life of the martyrologist, and vindication of the work*, ed. G. Townsend (8 vols.; London, 1843–9).

Gorham, G. C., *Gleanings of a Few Scattered Ears* (London, 1857).

Grafton, R., *A Cronicle at large . . .* (London, 1569) [Grafton's Chronicle]

Guaras, Antonio de, *The accession of Queen Mary: being the contemporary narrative of a Spanish merchant resident in London*, trans. and ed. R. Garnett (London, 1892).

Harington, John, *Nugae Antiquae: being a miscellaneous collection of original papers, in prose and verse; written during the reigns of Henry VIII, Edward VI, Queen Mary, Elizabeth, and King James*, ed. Thomas Park, 2 vols. (London, 1804).

Haynes, S. (ed.), *A collection of state papers . . . left by William Cecill Lord Burghley* (London, 1740) .

Hayward, John, *The Life and Raigne of King Edward the Sixth*, ed. B. L. Beer (Kent, Ohio, 1993).

Holinshed, R., *Chronicles, & c.*, ed. H. Ellis (6 vols; London 1807–8).

Howell, T. E. (ed.), *Cobbett's complete collection of state trial . . .* (24 vols; London, 1809–28).

Hughes, P. L., and Larkin, J. F. (eds.), *Tudor royal proclamations* (3 vols.; New Haven and London, 1964–9). [TRP]

Hume, M. A. S. (trans. and ed.), *Chronicle of King Henry VIII of England. Being a contemporary record of some of the principal events of the reigns of Henry VIII and Edward VI* (London, 1889).

Jordan, W. K. (ed.), *The chronicle and political papers of King Edward VI* (Northampton, 1966). [Chronicle]

Kempe, A. J. (ed.), *Loseley manuscripts* (London, 1835).

Kingsford, C. L. (ed.), 'Two London chronicles from the collections of John Stowe', *Camden Miscellany*, 4 (Camden Society, 3rd ser., 18; London, 1910), pp. iii–59.

Knighton, C. S. (ed.), *State papers of Edward VI. Calendar of state papers domestic series of the reign of Edward VI 1547–1553* (London, 1992).

Lefevre-Pontalis, G. (ed.), *Correspondance Politique de Odet de Selve, Ambassadeur de France en Angleterre, 1546–1549* (Paris, 1888).

Letters of the Fifteenth and Sixteenth Centuries from the Archives of Southampton, ed. R. C. Anderson, Southampton Record Society, vol. 22 (Southampton, 1921).

Letters and papers, foreign and domestic, of the reign of Henry VIII, 1509–1547, eds. J. S. Brewer, J. Gardiner and R. H. Brodie (23 vols. in 38; London, 1862–1932). [LP]

Letters, despatches, and state papers, relating to the negotiations between England and Spain, preserved in the archives at Vienna, Brussels, Simancas and elsewhere, eds. M. A. S. Hume, R. Tyler et al. (15 vols. in 20; London, 1862–1954). [CSP Spanish]

The Lisle Letters, ed. M. St. C. Byrne (6 vols; Chicago, 1980).

Lodge, E. (ed.), *Illustrations of British history, biography, and manners, in the reigns of Henry VIII, Edward VI, Mary, Elizabeth and James I, exhibited in a series of original papers* . . . (3 vols.; London, 1838 edn).

MacCulloch, D. (ed.). 'The Vita Mariae Angliae Reginae of Robert Wingfield of Brantham', *Camden Miscellany*, 28 (Camden Society, 4th ser., 29; London, 1984), pp. 181–301. [VM]

Madden, F. (ed.), 'The petition of Richard Troughton . . . to the privy council . . .', *Archaeologia*, 23 (1831), pp. 18–49. [Troughton]

Malkiewicz, A. J. A., 'An eye-witness's account of the coup d'etat of October 1549', *English Historical Review*, 70 (October, 1955), pp. 600–609.

Memoires de la vie de Francois Scepeaux, sire de Vieilleville, xxvi–xxvii of *Collection complete de memoires relatif a l'histoire de France*, ed. C.-B. Petitot (Paris, 1822).

Muller, J. A. (ed.) *The Letters of Stephen Gardiner* (Cambridge, 1933).

Nichols, J. G. (ed.), 'The diary of Henry Machyn, citizen and merchant-taylor of London, from 1550–1563', *Camden Miscellany* (Camden Society, 1st ser., 42; London, 1848). [Machyn]

—— (ed.) 'The Life of Henry Fitzallan, last Earl of Arundell', *Gentleman's Magazine*, 104 (1833).

—— (ed.) 'The chronicle of Queen Jane and two years of Queen Mary, and especially of the rebellion of Sir Thomas Wyat', *Camden Miscellany* (Camden Society, 1st ser., 48; London, 1850).

—— (ed.) 'Chronicle of the Grey Friars of London', *Camden Miscellany* (Camden Society, 1st ser., 53; London, 1851).

—— 'The Second Patent Appointing Edward Duke of Somerset Protector', *Archaeologia* 30 (1844).

—— (ed.) *Narratives of the Reformation* (Camden Society, 1st ser., 77; 1859).

—— *The literary remains of King Edward VI* (Roxburghe Club, 2 vols.; 1857). [LR]

—— *The Legend of Nicholas Throgmorton* (London, 1874).

Parkyn, Robert, 'Robert Parkyn's narrative of the Reformation', ed. A. G. Dickens, *English Historical Review*, 62 (1947), pp. 58–83.

Pocock, N. (ed.), *Troubles connected with the Prayer Book of 1549* (Camden Society, n.s., 37; London, 1884).

Pollard, A. F. (ed.), *Tudor Tracts, 1532–1588* (London, 1903).

Ponet, J., *A shorte treatise of politike power, and of the true obedience which subiectes owe to kynges and other civile governours, with an exhortacion to all true naturall Englishe men* . . . (STC 20178; Strasbourg, 1556).

Robinson, H. (ed.), *Original letters relative to the English Reformation* . . . *chiefly from the archives of Zurich, Parker Society* (2 vols.; Cambridge, 1846–7). [OL]

Rymer, T., and Sanderson, R. (eds.), *Foedera, conventions, litterae* . . . (20 vols.; London, 1727–35).

Scudamore, R., (ed.) S. Brigden, 'The letters of Richard Scudamore to Sir Philip Hoby', *Camden Miscellany*, 30 (Camden Society, 4th ser., 39; London, 1990), pp. 68–148. [Scudamore Letters]

Smith, Sir Thomas, *De republica anglorum*, ed. Mary Dewar (Cambridge, 1982).

State papers published under the authority of His Majesty's commission. King Henry the Eighth (11 vols.; London, 1830–52).

Statutes of the realm, eds. A. Lunders, T. E. Tomlins, J. France, W. E. Taunton and J. Raithby (11 vols.; London, 1810–28).

Stow, J., *The Annales of England* (London, 1605)

Strype, J., *The life of the learned Sir Thomas Smith, kt. DCL. Principal secretary of state to King Edward the sixth, and Queen Elizabeth* ... (Oxford, 1820).

—— *The life of the learned Sir John Cheke, kt. First instructor, afterwards secretary of state, to King Edward VI* ... (Oxford, 1821).

—— *Ecclesiastical memorials, relating chiefly to religion, and the reformation of it, and the emergencies of the Church of England under King Henry VIII, King Edward VI, and Queen Mary I* (3 vols. of 6; London, 1822).

Tawney, R. H., and Power, E. (eds.), *Tudor economic documents* (3 vols.; London, 1963 edn).

Tytler, P. F. (ed.), *England under the reigns of Edward VI and Mary* ... (2 vols.; London, 1839).

Vertot, A. and Villaret, C., *Ambassades de Messieurs Noilles en Angleterre* (5 vols.; Leyden, 1763).

Vincentius, P., *Historical Narration of certain events that took place in the Kingdom of Great Britain in the month of July, in the year of our Lord, 1553*, ed. J. P. Berjeau (Bell and Daldy, 1865).

Vowell, John, *The Description of the Citie of Excester*, ed. H. Tapley-Soper *et al.*, (Exeter, 1919–47).

Werdmueller, O., *A Spyrytuall and Moost Precyous Pearle*, trans M. Coverdale (RSTC 25255, 1550).

Wriothesley, C., *A Chronicle of England during the reigns of the Tudors from 1485 to 1559, by Charles Wriothesley, Windsor Herald*, ed. W. D. Hamilton (2 vols.; Camden Society, n.s., 11, London, 1875–7).

Secondary Works

Adair, E. R., 'William Thomas: a forgotten clerk of the privy council', in Seton-Watson (ed.), *Tudor Studies*, pp. 133–60.

Alford, S., *Kingship and Politics in the Reign of Edward VI* (Cambridge, 2002).

Allison, K. J., 'The sheep–corn husbandry of Norfolk in the sixteenth and seventeenth centuries', *Agricultural History Review*, 5 (1957), pp. 12–30.

Alsop, J. D., 'The revenue commission of 1552', *Historical Journal*, 22 (1979), pp. 511–33.

—— 'Protector Somerset and warrants for payment', *Bulletin of the Institute of Historical Research*, 55 (1982), pp. 102–108.

—— 'Latimer, the "commonwealth of Kent" and the 1549 rebellions', *Historical Journal*, 28 (1985), pp. 379–83.

—— 'A regime at sea: the navy and the 1553 succession crisis', *Albion*, 24 (1992), pp. 577–90.

Beer, B. L., 'London and the rebellions of 1548–1549', *Journal of British Studies*, 12 (1972), pp. 15–38.

Beer, B. L. and Nash, R. J., 'Hugh Latimer and the Lusty Knave of Kent: the commonwealth movement of 1549', *Bulletin of the Institute of Historical Research*, 52 (1979), pp. 175–8.

Beer, B. L., Northumberland. *The political career of John Dudley, Earl of Warwick and Duke of Northumberland* (Kent, Ohio, 1973).

—— *Rebellion and riot. Popular disorders in England during the reign of Edward VI* (Kent, Ohio, 1982).

Beresford, M. W., 'The poll tax census on sheep, 1549', *Agricultural History Review,* 1 (1953), pp. 9–15.

—— 'The poll tax census on sheep, 1549', *Agricultural History Review,* 2 (1954), pp. 15–29.

Berkman, J., 'Van der Delft's Message. A Reappraisal of the Attack on Protector Somerset', *Bulletin of the Institute of Historical Research*, 53 (1980).

Bernard, G. W., 'The downfall of Sir Thomas Seymour' in *The Tudor Nobility*, pp. 212–40.

—— 'New perspectives or old complexities?', *English Historical Review,* 115 (2000), pp. 113–20.

—— *The power of the early Tudor nobility. A study of the fourth and fifth earls of Shrewsbury* (Brighton, 1985).

—— (ed.), *The Tudor Nobility* (Manchester and New York, 1992).

Bindoff, S.T., 'A kingdom at stake, 1553', *History Today*, 3 (1953), pp. 642–8.

—— *Kett's Rebellion* (London, 1949).

—— *Tudor England* (London, 1950).

—— (ed.), *The History of Parliament. The House of Commons, 1509–1558* (3 vols., London, 1982).

Braddock, R.C., 'The character and composition of the duke of Northumberland's army', *Albion*, 6 (1974), pp. 342–55.

—— 'The duke of Northumberland's army reconsidered', *Albion*, 19 (1987), pp. 13–17.

Brigden, S., *London and the Reformation* (Oxford, 1991 edn.).

—— 'Henry Howard, Earl of Surrey, and the "Conjured League"', *Historical Journal*, 37 (1994), pp. 507–37.

—— *New Worlds, Lost Worlds* (London, 2000).

Bush, M. L., 'The Lisle–Seymour land disputes', *Historical Journal*, 9 (1966), pp. 255–74.

—— 'Protector Somerset and requests', *Historical Journal*, 17 (1974), pp. 451–64.

—— 'Protector Somerset and the 1549 rebellions: a post-revision questioned', *English Historical Review,* 115 (2000), pp. 103–12.

—— *The government policy of Protector Somerset* (London, 1976).

Chapman, H., *The Last Tudor King: A Study of Edward VI* (Bath, 1958).

Cornford, M. E., 'A Legend concerning Edward VI', *English Historical Review,* 23 (1908).

Cornwall, J., *Revolt of the Peasantry* (London, 1977).

Davies, C. S. L., 'Slavery and Protector Somerset: the Vagrancy Act of 1547', *Economic History Review,* Second series 19 (1966).

De Molen, R. L., 'The Birth of Edward VI and the Death of Queen Jane', *Renaissance Studies* 4 (1990).

Dewar, M., *Sir Thomas Smith: A Tudor Intellectual in Politics* (London 1964).

Dickens, A. G., 'Some Popular Reactions to the Edwardian Reformation in Yorkshire', *Yorkshire Archaelogical Journal* 34 (1939).

Dowling, M., *Humanism in the Age of Henry VIII* (Beckenham, 1986).

Duffy, E., *The Stripping of the Altars: Traditional Religion in England, c.1400–c.1580* (New Haven and London, 1992).

Elton, G. R., *Policy and Police* (Cambridge, 1972).

—— 'Reform and the "Commonwealthmen" of Edward VI's reign', in *The English Commonwealth, 1547–1640,* ed. P. Clark, N. Tyacke (Leicester, 1979).

Emmison, F. G., 'A Plan of Edward VI and Secretary Petre for Reorganizing the Privy Council's Work, 1552–3', *Bulletin of the Institute of Historical Research,* 31 (1958), pp. 203–10.

Gammon, S. R., *Statesman and Schemer. William, First Lord Paget – Tudor Minister* (Newton Abbot, 1973).

Graves, M. A. R., *The House of Lords in the Parliaments of Edward VI and Mary I* (Cambridge, 1981).

Guy, J., *Tudor England* (Oxford, 1988).

Haigh, C. A., *English Reformations* (Oxford, 1992).

Harbison, E. H., *Rival Ambassadors at the Court of Queen Mary* (Princeton, 1940).

Herbert of Cherbury, Edward Lord, *The Life and Raigne of King Henry the Eighth* (1649).

Hoak, D. E., *The King's Council in the Reign of Edward VI* (Cambridge, 1976).

—— 'Rehabilitating the Duke of Northumberland: Politics and Political Control, 1549–1553', in *The Mid-Tudor Polity,* ed. J. Loach and R. Tittler (London, 1980), pp. 29–51.

—— 'The King's Privy Chamber, 1547–1553', in *Tudor Rule and Revolution,* ed. D. J. Guth and J. W. McKenna (Cambridge, 1982), pp. 87–108.

—— 'The secret history of the Tudor court: the king's coffers and the king's purse, 1542–1553', *Journal of British Studies,* 26 (1987), pp. 208–31.

—— 'The coronations of Edward VI, Mary I, and Elizabeth I, and the transformation of Tudor Monarchy', in R. Mortimer and C. S. Knighton (eds.), *Reformation to Revolution: Westminster Abbey 1540–1660* (Stamford, 2002).

Houlbrooke, R. A., 'Henry VIII's wills: a comment', *Historical Journal*, 37 (1994), pp. 891–9.

Ives, E. W., 'Henry VIII's will – a forensic conundrum', *Historical Journal*, 35 (1992), pp. 779–804.

—— 'Henry VIII's will: the protectorate provisions of 1546–7', *Historical Journal*, 37 (1994), pp. 901–14.

Jack, S. M., 'An unknown draft of the October 8th letter from the Council at Windsor to the Council at London', *Huntington Library Quarterly*, 46 (1983), pp. 270–75.

—— 'Northumberland, Queen Jane and the financing of the 1553 Coup', *Parergon* (1988), pp. 137–48.

James, H., 'The Aftermath of the 1549 Coup and the Earl of Warwick's Intentions', *Bulletin of the Institute of Historical Research*, 57 (1989).

James, S. E., *Kateryn Parr: The Making of a Queen* (Ashgate, 1999)

Jordan, W. K., *Edward VI: the young king. The protectorship of the duke of Somerset* (London, 1968).

—— *Edward VI: the threshold of power. The dominance of the duke of Northumberland* (London, 1970).

King, J. N., 'Protector Somerset, patron of the English Renaissance', *Papers of the Bibliographical Society of America*, 70 (1976), pp. 307–31.

Knighton, C. S., 'The principal secretaries in the reign of Edward VI: reflections on their office and archive', in C. Cross, D. Loades, J. J. Scarisbrick (eds.), *Law and government under the Tudors* (Cambridge, 1988), pp. 163–75.

Land, S. K., *Kett's Rebellion: The Norfolk Rising of 1549* (Ipswich, 1977).

Loach, J., *Edward VI*, ed. G. Bernard and P. Williams (London, 1999).

—— and R. Tittler (eds.) *The Mid-Tudor Polity* (London, 1980).

—— '"A Close League with the King of France": Lady Jane Grey's Proclamation in French and its part in a planned betrayal', *Proceedings of the Huguenot Society* 25 (1991).

—— 'The Function of Ceremonial in the Reign of Henry VIII', *Past and Present*, 142 (1994).

Loades, D., *John Dudley, Duke of Northumberland, 1504–1553* (Oxford, 1996).

—— *Mary Tudor: A Life* (Oxford, 1989).

MacCulloch, D., *Thomas Cranmer* (London, 1996).

—— 'Kett's Rebellion in Context', *Past and Present*, 84 (1979).

—— *Tudor Church Militant: Edward VI and the Protestant Reformation* (London, 1999).

—— and Fletcher, A., *Tudor Rebellions* (4th edn., London, 1997).

Miller, H., 'Henry VIII's unwritten will: grants of lands and honours in 1547', in E. W. Ives, R. J. Knecht, J. J. Scarisbrick (eds.), *Wealth and Power in Tudor England* (London, 1978), pp. 87–105.

Murphy, J., 'The illusion of decline: the Privy Chamber 1547–1558' in *The English Court*, ed. D. Starkey (London, 1987).

Parry, G. J. R., 'Inventing "The good duke" of Somerset', *Journal of Ecclesiastical History*, 40 (1989), pp. 370–80.

Prescott, H. F. M., *Mary Tudor* (London, 1962).

von Raume, F., *The Political History of England* (London, 1837).

Ravensdale, J. R., 'Landbeach in 1549: Kett's Rebellion in Minature' in *East Anglian Studies*, ed. L. M. Munby (Cambridge, 1968).

Richardson, W. C. (ed.), *The Report of the Royal Commission of 1552* (Morgantown, 1974).

Rose-Troup, F., *The Western Rebellion of 1549: an account of the insurrections in Devonshire and Cornwall against religious innovations in the reign of Edward VI* (London, 1913).

Rowse, A. L., *Tudor Cornwall* (London, 1941).

Russell, F. W., *Kett's Rebellion in Norfolk* (London, 1859).

Scarisbrick, J. J., *Henry VIII* (Berkeley, 1968).

Shagan, E. H., 'Protector Somerset and the 1549 rebellions: new sources and new perspectives', *English Historical Review*, 114 (1999), pp. 34–63.

Slack, P. (ed.), *Rebellion, Popular Protest and the Social Order in Early Modern England* (Cambridge, 1984).

Slavin, A. J., 'The Fall of Lord Chancellor Wriothesley: A Study in the Politics of Conspiracy', *Albion* 7 (1975).

Smith, L. B., *Henry VIII: The Mask of Royalty* (London, 1971).

—— 'The Last Will and Testament of Henry VIII: a question of perspective', *Journal of British Studies* 2 (1962), pp. 14–27.

Speight, H. M., 'Local Government and the South-Western Rebellion of 1549', *Southern History* 18 (1996).

Starkey, D., *The Reign of Henry VIII: Personalities and Politics* (London, 1985).

—— *The English Court* (London, 1987).

—— *Six Wives: The Queens of Henry VIII* (London, 2003).

Strype, J., *Annals of the Reformation* (London 1708–09)

Thurley, S., 'Henry VIII and the Building of Hampton Court', *Architectural History* (1988).

Tittler, R. and Battley, S. L., 'The Local Community and the Crown in 1553: the Accession of Mary Tudor Revisited', *Bulletin of the Institute of Historical Research*, 57 (1984), pp. 131–9.

Williams, P., *The Later Tudors: England 1547–1603* (Oxford, 1995).

Youings, J., 'The South-Western Rebellion of 1549', *Southern History* 1 (1979).

UNPUBLISHED DISSERTATIONS

Bryson, A., 'The great men of the country: the Edwardian regime, 1547–53', PhD dissertation, University of St Andrews (2001).

Jones, A. J., '"Commotion Time": the English Risings of 1549', PhD dissertation, University of Warwick (2003).

Sturge, C., 'The Life and Times of John Dudley, Earl of Warwick and Duke of Northumberland 1504–1553', PhD dissertation, University of London (1927).

NOTES

Introduction

1. Richard Morison, *A Comfortable Consolation* (1537), B v r.
2. See J. Youings, *The Dissolution of the Monasteries* (London, 1971).
3. Richard Hooker, *Of the Laws of Ecclesiastical Polity* (1593).
4. LR I, ccxxvii.
5. See the most recent treatments in MacCulloch, *Tudor Church Militant*; Alford, S, *Kingship and Politics in the Reign of Edward VI*.
6. Cooper, *Chronicle*, p. 355.
7. MacCulloch, *Tudor Church Militant*; MacCulloch, *Cranmer*, chapters 9–13.

1. Marriages, Birth and Death

1. LP X 351, p. 134.
2. LP X 901.
3. LP X 1047 (printed in *Lisle Letters* III, p. 306)
4. LP XI 8 (p. 9).
5. LP XII (i) 1267; *Wriothesley's Chronicle* I, p. 64.
6. J. Rowlands, *Paintings of Hans Holbein* (Oxford, 1985), p. 225.
7. *State Papers* I, pp. 551–2; LP XII ii, 77.
8. This became the subject of a contemporary ballad:

   > The queen in travail pained sore
   > Full thirty woeful hours and more,
   > And no ways could relieved be,
   > As all her ladies wished to see.

   Though hours were soon supplanted by days! An anonymous Spanish chronicler referred to a three-day labour, whilst the Register of the Order of the Garter implies a difficult two-day labour. Strickland, *Lives of the Queens of England* II, p. 282; Hume, p. 72; Anstis *Register of the Most Noble Order of the Garter* (1724) II, p. 410.
9. LP XII ii, 680, 839, 861, 871, 911. *Wriothesley's Chronicle* I, p. 65.
10. *Wriothesley's Chronicle* I, pp. 66–7.
11. BL Cotton MS Nero C x, fo. 1; LP XII ii, 911. Some slipped through in

advance: Henry, Lord Fitzalan (later Earl of Arundel) wrote to Cromwell on 7 October informing him he had received 'the joyful tidings that the Queen was delivered of a prince'. LP XII ii, 893.

12. BL Harleian MS 282, fo. 211; LP XII ii, 890.

13. LP XII ii, 894.

14. Margaret's ordinances are in BL Harleian MS 6079, printed in John Leland, *Derebus Britannicis Collectanea*, ed. Thomas Hearne (London, 1774) IV, 179–84.

15. Ceremony described in College of Arms, MS M6, fos. 23–26v.

16. For instance, as surviving town records reveal, with bonfires in Shropshire and the ringing of bells at Bridgnorth Fair. Gunn, S. J. 'War, dynasty and public opinion in early Tudor England' in Bernard, G. W.; Gunn, S. J., (ed.), *Authority and Consent in Tudor England* (Aldershot, 2002), 131–49; p. 140.

17. *State Papers* I, 571.

18. LP XII ii, 911, 923.

19. LP XII ii, 988.

20. LP XII ii, 977.

21. 'All this night she hath been very sick,' the Earl of Rutland wrote to Thomas Cromwell, 'and doth rather appaire [worsen] than amend'; BL Cotton MS Nero C x, fo. 2.

22. LP XII ii, 971; there has been surprising confusion over the exact date of Jane's death. See DeMolen, pp. 380–83; College of Arms Heralds MS 1, 11, fo. 37, printed LP XII ii, 1060.

23. Loach, *Edward VI*, p. 7.

24. *State Papers* V, viii, 1–4.

25. PRO E 36/120, fo. 58; PRO Rolls Chapel Series MS A 2, fo. 30: 'He should be killed that never was born, and nature's hand or man's hand brought it to pass, or soon would bring it to pass.' For the ballads, see Strickland II, 282–3, Child, *The English and Scottish Popular Ballads* III, 372–6, V 245.

26. Vatican Archives Add. MS 15,387, printed in N. Pocock, *Records of the Reformation: The Divorce 1527–1533* (Oxford 1870), II, 564.

27. N. Sanders, *Rise and Growth of the Anglican Schism* (1585), ed. Lewis, 138.

28. *Lisle Letters* IV, no. 1024, p. 425.

29. Hall, *Chronicle*, p. 825; LP XII ii, p. 339

30. Morison, *Comfortable Consolation*, sig. Avir.

31. Foxe, *Actes and Monuments*, V, p. 148. Foxe speculates that the verse was penned by Armagal Waad. A strikingly similar poem circulated in English:

    Phoenix Jane dies, a Phoenix borne, wee're sad,

    That no one age two Phoenixes e're had.

    J. N. King, *English Reformation Literature* (Princeton, 1986), p. 165, quoting Bodl. MS Eng poet E 14, fo. 97v. I am grateful to Dr Tracey Sowerby for providing this information.

32. LP XII ii, 1075.

33. LP XII ii, 1030.

34. BL Harleian MS 2194, fo. 20r; LP XII ii, 1004.

35. *Chronicle*, p. 3.

36. LP XIII (i), 1011.

37. LP XIII (i), 1290, 1538. The sister-in-law of Sir William Sidney, chamberlain of the household, she was offered the post through his recommendation. His letter of support to Cromwell reads much like a modern-day reference. Sidney was 'right well assured of her good demeanour, able ness, honesty, and truth': 'I doubt not there shall be found no want of diligence nor scarcity of good will towards the accomplishment of that which unto her office and duty shall appertain at all times.' LP XIII ii, 524; W. C. Richardson, *The Report of the Royal Commission of 1552*, p. 83.

38. In January 1538 a sinister discovery was made in a London churchyard. Around a half-buried bundle protruding from the ground, a crowd gathered to watch as the parish clerk dug it up to discover a wax statue of a child inside, two pins driven through its body. Soon news of the discovery had reached Cromwell, who dispatched an investigation team. Depositions from witnesses pointed to the involvement of a carpenter named Pole. Cromwell had been keeping an eye on Pole for some time. His books had been confiscated before, though whether his surname (the same as Henry's attainted royal cousins) or merely his mischievous behaviour rankled the secretary we do not know. The story ends here, but shortly afterwards a kitchen porter at the Catholic Corpus Christi College, Oxford, was accused of telling a tale how another wax figure was discovered, a knife struck through its body. This time the figure clearly represented the prince. PRO E 36/120, fo. 71 [LP XIII (i), 41]; LP XIII ii, pp. 360, 505.

39. SP 1/153, fo. 4 [LP XIV ii, 11].

40. SP 1/153, fo. 38 [LP XIV ii, 73].

41. SP 1/153, fos. 56–57 [LP XIV ii, 102].

42. Sir William Sidney was appointed chamberlain, Richard Cox, later Edward's tutor, was made almoner and Sir John Cornwallis steward. *Lisle Letters*, V, p. 79.

43. BL Cotton MS Vitellius C x, fo. 65; Thurley, S. 'Henry VIII and the Building of Hampton Court: a Reconstruction of the Tudor Palace', *Architectural History* (1988), 1–51, p. 31.

44. London was out of bounds. Neither Edward's Privy Chamber nor anyone holding office in his household was to go there, especially in the summer when this 'contagious place' was at its most infectious. Journey was only permitted by special licence, and once completed, a period of quarantine was to be enforced. If anyone fell ill, then immediately 'without tracte or delay of time' they were to be removed from the prince's lodgings. The poor were also of troublesome concern, for the lame and the sick – looking for alms and perhaps even hoping for a miracle at the sight of the royal child – had begun to loiter outside the palace gates. A spot was appointed 'a good way from the gates' where they might receive payment from the

almoner and, once the weekly alms had been doled out, quickly depart. 'If any beggar shall presume to draw near the gates,' Henry warned, 'then they be appointed to be grievously punished to the example of others'.

45. LP XIII i, 323, 338, 402, 1011.

46. Madden, *Privy Purse expenses of the Princess Mary* (1831), pp. 52, 61, 64, 69, 85.

47. *State Papers* I, p. 586.

48. Folger MS Z. d. 11.

49. Bod. MS Tanner 464 iv, fo. 55.

50. BL Royal MS App 89, fo. 39, printed LR, cclxiii–cclxiv; The following year Henry's presents had not improved (though they were becoming more costly, including a pair of flagons weighing 178½oz); Mary's pious tastes were apparent in her gift of a brooch of gold set with a ruby 'with the image of Saint John Baptist' whilst Elizabeth, again choosing the personal touch over costly plate or jewellery, sent 'a braser of needlework of her own making'; BL Additional MS 11,301, fo. 11, printed LR, cclxv.

51. *CSP Spanish* V, p. 509.

52. LP XIX ii, 871; Muller, *Letters of Stephen Gardiner*, pp. 161–2.

53. LP XIV ii, 12.

54. LP XVI 380.

55. Kaulek, *Correspondance politique de MM de Castillion et de Marillac* (Paris, 1885), p. 302; LP XVI 1297.

56. LP XVIII i, 904; Kaulek, pp. 350–54, 408–10.

57. SP 1/243, fo. 292 [LP Add. I ii 1535].

58. Moving to Hunsdon in January in 1543, one neighbour was required to surrender his house to lodge the rest of Edward's household since there was not sufficient room 'without pestering the house in this troublous season of winter'. SP 1/244, fo. 205 [LP Add I ii, 1636]; Clifford, *Jane Dormer, Duchess of Feria*, p. 59.

59. This was termed a 'void'. See Starkey, *Elizabeth*, p. 31.

60. Henry also owned a cameo of Edward's face in agate. BL Egerton MS 2679, fo. 6.

61. Holinshed, *Chronicle*, p. 816.

62. LP XVII 1221, 1233.

63. J. Wormald, *Mary, Queen of Scots* (London, 1988), pp. 58–9.

64. *State Papers*, I,764; LP XIX I, 864.

65. Roger Ascham, *The Schoolmaster* (1570), pp. 6–7.

66. Neville Williams, *Henry VIII and His Court* (New York, 1971), p. 236; LP XXI i, 8, printed *State Papers*, X, 822.

67. Williams, *Henry VIII and His Court*, p. 237.

68. These included not only his cousins on his father's side, Henry and Charles Brandon, the younger sons of the Duke of Suffolk, and on his mother's side Edward and Henry Seymour, the sons of his uncle Edward, Earl of Hertford, but also the heirs of the earls of Arundel, Shrewsbury, Bath, Derby and

Ormond, SP1/195, fo. 262. Partly this was Henry's wish; the children had been 'appointed to attend upon' Edward, but Cox also urged the king's secretary William Paget to have his son grow up with Edward so that he might 'after do him service'. And Ormond at least owed his place to the petitions of his father, keen 'that my son and heir might attend upon my lord Prince's grace, and be brought up in his right noble court'. On corporal punishment, see LR, lxx–lxxv; the Duke of Richmond's gentlemen usher even prevented his fellow pupils being hit in his presence, reasoning 'it was improper to unbreech boys before so great a prince'. Henry VI, however, does not seem to have be spared the correction of punishment; a writ of 1428 authorized chastisement 'as it had been customary to restrain and chastise other princes of like age, as well in this kingdom as elsewhere'. Rymer, *Foedera*, X, p. 399.

69. SP 1/195, fos. 261–2.
70. LR, lxxix; Chapman, *The Last Tudor King*, p. 71.
71. BL Harleian MS 1419A, fos. 133–5.
72. RSTC 2419 sig. Aiiii; cited Loach, *Edward VI*, p. 152.
73. BL Harleian MS 5087, fo. 7, printed RL, p. 14.
74. LP XXI i, 136, printed LR, no. 26.
75. LR I, pp. 16–17.
76. BL Harleian MS 5087, no. 33.
77. LR I, pp. 37–8; LP XIX ii, p. 110.
78. LR I, pp. 21–2; RL, p. 15.
79. BL Harleian MS 1419A, fos. 86, 254–5v; BL Harleian MS 7376, fo. 37v, cited Loach, *Edward VI*, p. 136 (These were probably destroyed in February 1551, when 'all superstitiouse bookes, as masse bookes, legends and suche like' were purged from the royal library, retrieving large quantities of gold, silver and 'garnytures'; APC III, 2240).
80. Scepeaux, *Memoires*, I 341; BL Additional MS 46348, fos. 217–217v; BL Harleian MS 611, fo. 22.
81. Cox to Cranmer, 13 January 1546.
82. RL, p. 6.
83. Renaissance Humanism was a European intellectual movement that focused upon the values of human reason, beauty and virtue. It was highly influenced by the rediscovery of Latin and Greek classical texts. BL Harleian MS 5087.
84. BL Harleian MS 5087, fo. 11.
85. LR I, pp. 9, 31.
86. Clifford, *Life of Dormer*, p. 59; Chapman, *The Last Tudor King*, p. 107.
87. LR I, xcvii–c; BL Harleian MS 611, fo. 14r.
88. LR I, pp. 22–3; RL p. 16.
89. For retinues, see LP XXI i, 1384 (p. 695); Hall, *Chronicle*, p. 867; Holinshed, *Chronicle*, p. 859.
90. LP XXI ii, 571; G. Lefevre-Pontalis (ed.), *Correspondance politique de Odet de Selve* (Paris, 1888), p. 105 (no. 121).
91. LP XX ii, 726.

2. Last Will and Testament

1. PRO E 315/160, fo. 133v.
2. Hamilton Papers II, no. 237.
3. PRO SP 1/227, fo. 97 [LP XXI ii, 555(1)].
4. PRO SP 1/227, fo. 129 [LP XXI ii, 555(18)].
5. Selve, *Correspondance*, pp. 23, 50–51; *CSP Spanish* VIII, p. 556; SP 1/221 fo. 181–2 [LP XXI (i), 1263]; LP XXI ii, 555 (7ii).
6. LP XXI ii, 605.
7. MacCulloch, *Cranmer*, p. 358; OL I, p. 41; Foxe V, p. 692.
8. SP 1/227, fos. 18, 82 [LP XXI ii, 509, 548]; BL Stowe MS 396, fo. 8.
9. BL Harleian MS 297, fo. 255v; SP 1/227, fos. 103–4 [LP XXI ii, 555(4); Herbert, *Life and raigne*, p. 564.
10. SP 1/227, fos. 123–4 [*State Papers* I, pp. 891–2]. For a more detailed treatment of Surrey's downfall, see S. Brigden, 'Henry Howard, Earl of Surrey, and the "Conjured League"', *Historical Journal* 37 (1994), pp. 504–37.
11. PRO E 23/4/1, printed T. Rymer *Foedera* XV, 110–117 and Howells, *State Trials*, 743–54. An earlier will, dated 13 December, has been proved to be a copy; Inner Temple Petyt MS 538/47, fos. 398–406; Guy, *Tudor England*, pp. 198–9; Ives, 'Henry VIII's Will', pp. 780–81. I am grateful to Professor Dale Hoak for his communication with me on this issue.
12. Foxe V, p. 691; VI, 163–4, 170, 177, 181.
13. E 23/4/1, fo. 11v.
14. *CSP Spanish 1547–49*, pp. 340–41; *APC 1542–47*, p. 566.
15. J. P. Collier (ed.), *The Egerton Papers*, pp. 41–9, cited Miller, pp. 94–5.
16. *CSP Spanish 1547–49*, p. 30.
17. Walter Lord Hungerford had been executed in 1540 for attempting to predict the king's death by the use of magic.
18. Foxe V, p. 689.
19. SP 10/8/4; BL Cotton MS Titus F III, fos. 277–279v; printed Strype, *Ecclesiastical Memorials* II ii, 429–37.
20. SP 10/1/1; printed Tytler I, 15–16.
21. SP 10/7/8.
22. SP 10/1/2; printed Tytler I, 17–18.
23. *CSP Spanish 1547–49*, p. 6.
24. BL Additional MS 71009, fo. 45r.
25. *APC 1547–49*, p. 5.
26. PRO E 101/426/3, fos. 6, 23.
27. Society of Antiquaries MS 123, fo. 1r.
28. This was recorded in an inventory of Edward's possessions as a 'Tablet of gold with phisonemyes of kinge henrie theight and Quene katherin garnished wt tenne emeralds and twoo Agathes', BL Harleian MS 611, fo. 14r.

29. BL Harleian MS 5087, no. 34; printed LR I, pp. 38–9, RL II, p. 25.

30. BL Harleian MS 5087, no. 35; printed LR I, pp. 39–40, RL II, p. 26.

31. Elias Gruffyd, *Calais Chronicle*, p. 54.

32. Details of Henry's funeral preparations can be found in Strype, *Ecclesiastical Memorials*, II ii, p. 289; and J. Loach, 'Ceremonial in the reign of Henry VIII', pp. 56–68.

33. SP 10/1/5; printed Muller, 253–254, Tytler I, 21–2.

34. 'Certayne Brife Notes', in I. Archer, S. Adams, G. W. Bernard (eds.), *Religion, Politics and Society in Sixteenth Century England* (Camden Society, 5th Series, 22), p. 124.

35. Grafton also noted that Somerset's advancement 'was well allowed of all the noblemen saving of Thomas Wriothesley'; *Grafton's Chronicle* II, 499–500.

36. *APC 1547–49*, pp. 7–8; College of Arms, MS I 7, fo. 29; LR, lxxxvii.

37. College of Arms, MS I 7, fo. 29, printed LR, lxxxvi–lxxxvii.

3. A Second Josiah

1. Strype, *Ecclesiastical Memorials*, VI, p. 277; Hume, p. 154.

2. Strickland, *The Queens of England*, Vol. II, p. 443.

3. Bodl. Ashmole MS 857, fo. 431.

4. *Chronicle*, p. 4.

5. *CSP Spanish 1547–49*, p. 47.

6. Loach, 'Ceremonial', p. 44.

7. College of Arms, MS I 7, fo. 32, printed LR, cclxxviii–cccviii.

8. LR, ccxci.

9. Hoak, 'The Coronations', p. 117.

10. PRO SP 10/1/7. Oxford was also given the furniture used by Edward the night before his coronation. This included a bed nine-feet square, with valences of crimson cloth of gold, embroidered with the royal arms and fringed with gold and silver lace. PRO E 101/427/2; Loach, 'Ceremonial', p. 47.

11. For the text of the *Liber*, see L. G. Wickham Legg, *English Coronation Records* (London, 1901), pp. 81–130; see also Schramm, *English Coronation*, pp. 170–71, 211–12, and H. G. Richardson, 'The coronation in medieval England', *Traditio* XVI (1960), 111–75.

12. Wickham Legg, *Coronation Records*, p. 230.

13. Schramm, *English Coronation*, p. 217; Hoak, 'The Coronations', p. 148.

14. J. E. Cox, *Works of Archbishop Cranmer*, II, pp. 126–7.

15. TRP I no. 257, p. 381.

16. Ratcliff, *English Coronation Service* (1936), p. 115.

17. Feuillerat, *Revels*, pp. 3–8. The entire costs of the coronation came to £442 10s (£132, 765) compared to the grand costs of £1,039 9s 7d (£311, 878) for Henry's funeral.

18. *CSP Spanish 1547–49*, p. 48; *Chronicle*, p. 5.
19. *CSP Spanish 1547–49*, p. 48.
20. *CSP Spanish 1547–49*, pp. 19–20.
21. BL Additional MS 48126, fo. 15v.
22. BL Harleian MS 249, fos. 16–17; *APC 1547–49*, pp. 48–59; Burnet, *Reformation*, II, 57–8, V, 137–9.
23. *APC 1547–49*, p.56.
24. *CSP Spanish 1547–49*, pp. 50, 91–2, 340.
25. *CSP Spanish 1547–49*, pp. 91–2.
26. *APC 1547–49*, pp. 67–74.
27. BL Additional MS 35838, fos. 48–9.
28. Strype, *Ecclesiastical Memorials*, II ii, Appendix B.
29. Hoak, *King's Council*, p. 102.
30. *CSP Spanish 1547–49*; De Selve, p. 111.

4. Milder Climates

1. PRO SP 1/228, fo. 55 [LP XXI ii 710].
2. Foxe VI, p. 61; *APC 1547–49*, pp. 25–6; *Documentary Annals* I, pp. 53–4.
3. *CSP Spanish 1547–49*, pp. 49–50, 52; Stowe, *Annales*, p. 594; Foxe VI, p. 35.
4. Bush, *Government Policy of Protector Somerset,* pp. 66–70; Brigden, *London and the Reformation,* p. 424; Foxe V, p. 547; Dowling, *Humanism in the Age of Henry VIII* (London, 1986), pp. 240–41; Harrington, *Nugae Antiquae* I, p. 43; BL Royal MS D III, fo. 3r.
5. BL Royal MS 17 D XIII, fo. 2r. See also BL Royal MS 17 C V, fos. 3r, 4v; Royal 17 C IX, fo. 2; OL I, p. 258.
6. TRP I, no. 281, p. 387; PRO E 101/426/5; *Wriothesley's Chronicle,* Vol. I, p. 184; MacCulloch, *Cranmer*, p. 369.
7. *CSP Spanish 1547–49,* p. 122.
8. Haynes, *State Papers*, pp. 90, 92.
9. De Selve, pp. 152–5; Vertot I, 102–3; *CSP Spanish 1547–49,* p. 340; James, *Kateryn Parr*, p. 291.
10. James, *Kateryn Parr*, p. 404.
11. James, *Kateryn Parr*, p. 413.
12. Bodl. Rawlinson MS D 1070/4.
13. James, *Kateryn Parr*, p. 404.
14. PRO SP 10/1, fo. 41; SP 10/6/22, fos. 57r–58v; Bodl. Rawlinson MS D 1070/4.
15. BL Lansdowne MS 1236, fo. 26, printed Ellis, *Letters*, 1st Series, Vol. II, p. 149.
16. LR I, pp. 46–7.
17. *Chronicle*, p. 6.
18. Hayward, *Edward the Sixth*, pp. 197–8.

19. HMC Salisbury I, p. 51; Bodl. Rawlinson D 1070/4.

20. BL Cotton MS Titus B ii, fos. 79–81; Patten, *Expedition*, p. 82.

21. *State Papers* V, pp. 371–3 [LP XIX i, 319]; LP XVII 1090, 1249, XIX i, 348; *CSP Spanish 1547–49*, p. 196; De Selve, p. 262.

22. Patten, p. 125. For a list of different estimates, see Jordan, *The Young King*, p. 260.

23. BL Harleian MS 5087, fo. 17; BL Lansdowne MS 1236, fo. 16.

24. *APC 1547–49*, p. 517; *Wriothesley's Chronicle* I, p. 186.

25. PRO SP 10/6/10, fos. 24v–25r; SP 10/6/13, fo. 35.

26. BL Hatfield MS M485/39, Vol. 150, fo. 112 (Haynes, *State Papers*, p. 75).

27. MacCulloch, *Tudor Church Militant*, pp. 72–4.

28. *Greyfriars Chronicle*, p. 54.

29. *APC 1547–49*, p. 137.

30. *APC 1547–49*, pp. 147, 149.

31. 1 Edw. VI c.1, printed Gee and Hardy, *Documents Illustrative of English Church History* (London, 1896), pp. 322–8; TRP I, 296.

32. *CSP Spanish 1547–49*, p. 221; *Wriothesley's Chronicle* I, p. 187.

33. C. S. L. Davies, *Peace, Print and Protestantism* (London, 1976), pp. 265–6. On slavery, see 1 Edward VI, c. 3., 3 & 4 Edward VI, c. 16., and discussion in Davies, 'Slavery and Protector Somerset; the Vagrancy Act of 1547' *Econ. Hist. Review*, pp. 533–49.

34. Nichols, *Archaeologia* XXX (1844), pp. 480–81.

35. SP 10/6/10; BL Hatfield MS M485/39, Vol. 150, fo. 51 (Haynes, *State Papers*, p. 74); PRO E 351/2932; BL Lansdowne MS Roll 14.

36. PRO E 351/2932.

37. BL Hatfield MS M485/39, Vol. 150, fo. 115 (Haynes, *State Papers*, p. 76) PRO SP 10/6/13; SP 10/6/14; SP 10/6/26; SP 10/6/7.

38. PRO SP 10/6/12; SP 10/6/15.

39. PRO SP 10/6/7; SP 10/6/12; BL Hatfield MS M485/39, Vol. 150 fo. 93v (Haynes, *State Papers*, p. 105).

40. Bernard, 'The Downfall of Sir Thomas Seymour', p. 227.

41. Haynes, *State Papers*, p. 91; BL Harleian MS 249, fos. 37–37v; BL Additional 48023, fo. 350v. Bernard, 'Downfall', p. 226.

42. PRO SP10/6/13 (9).

43. BL Hatfield MS M485/39, Vol. 150, fo. 85 (Haynes, *State Papers*, p. 100).

44. PRO SP10/6/22; SP10/6/21; BL Hatfield MS M485/39, Vol. 150, fo. 80v (Haynes, *State Papers*, p. 96).

45. PRO SP10/6/19; SP10/6/22.

46. *Greyfriars Chronicle*, p. 56.

47. King, *English Reformation Literature*, pp. 88–9, 127, 129, 287; Haigh, *English Reformations*, pp. 168, 173.

48. TRP I 299; VAI II, p. 184; Duffy, *Stripping of the Altars*, p. 457.

49. Cranmer, *Remains*, p. 510; BL Additional MS 5751, fo. 37.

50. Duffy, *Stripping of the Altars*, p. 462.

51. Dickens, *Reformation Studies*, pp. 295–6.
52. Duffy, *Stripping of the Altars*, p. 458.
53. *Fourth Report of the Deputy Keeper of Public Records* (London, 1843), App. II, pp. 217–19; TRP I, no. 303.
54. PRO STAC 3/1/49.
55. Loach, *Edward VI*, p. 58.
56. R. H. Tawney & E. Power, *Tudor Economic Documents* III, p. 63.
57. TRP I 427–9; CPR I 419–20.
58. Muller, *Letters*, p. 427.
59. Thomas Lanquet, *An epitome of cronicles* (1549), Aii; Foxe VI, p. 290; Brigden, pp. 491–2; Bush, pp. 73–83 and 'Protector Somerset and Requests', HJ XVII (1974), pp. 451–64. BL Harleian MS 284, fo. 31, printed Tytler, I 75. For other evidence of Somerset's interference in the suits of the poor, HMC 11th Report App.VII 95, PRO Req 2/14/32, 135; 2/15/88, 2/16/9, 2/17/79, 2/18/73, 2/18/114.
60. PRO SP 10/8/4; Strype, *Ecclesiastical Memorials* II ii, pp. 429–37.
61. See W. R. D. Jones, *The Tudor Commonwealth, 1529–1559* (1970); Elton, G. R., 'Reform and the "Commonwealthmen" of Edward VI's Reign', in *The English Commonwealth, 1547–1640*, ed. P. Clark *et al.* (Leicester, 1979).
62. BL Harleian MS 6989, fo. 146.
63. Cooper, *Annals of Cambridge* (Cambridge, 1842–1908) II, p. 34.
64. Strype, *Ecclesiastical Memorials* VI, 333; Loach, p. 64; Tyacke N., 'Introduction: re-thinking the "English Reformation"' in Tyacke, N. (ed.) *England's Long Reformation* (London, 1998), p. 18; SP 10/4/33, fos. 53–54v.
65. PRO SP 10/4/26.
66. *Chronicle*, p. 10.
67. C. S. Cairns, 'An Unknown Venetian Description of King Edward VI', *BIHR*.42 (1969), pp. 110–15; p. 114.
68. De Selve, p. 284.
69. BL Vespasian D XVIII, fo.19; OL I, p. 321.
70. F. A. Gasquet, *Edward VI and the Book of Common Prayer* (London, 1890), p. 177.

5. The Downfall of the Lord Admiral

1. Haynes, *State Papers*, p. 62; SP10/4, fo. 14.
2. PRO SP 10/4/40; SP 10/5/1.
3. Haynes, *State Papers*, p. 104.
4. Hearne, *Sylloge Epistolarum*, pp. 151–2, 165–6.
5. PRO SP 10/5, fo. 2.
6. PRO PCC:19 Populwel; James, p. 332.
7. College of Arms, MS RR 21/C, fos. 98–9 printed Strickland, p. 463.
8. Strickland, p. 463.

9. PRO SP 10/6/12.

10. PRO SP 10/6/9.

11. PRO SP 10/6/9; Strype, *Ecclesiastical Memorials* II i, p. 188.

12. BL Hatfield MS M485/39, Vol. 150, fos. 81v, 84, 119–120; Haynes, *State Papers*, pp. 97, 98–9, 77–9); SP 10/6/7.

13. SP 10/6/22, fos. 57r–58v.

14. Haynes, *State Papers*, pp. 98–9.

15. PRO SP 10/6/15, fos. 41r–41v.

16. PRO SP 10/6/16, fo. 44.

17. PRO SP 10/6/17i.

18. PRO SP 10/6/17, fo. 47.

19. PRO SP 10/6/17i, fo. 47v.

20. Haynes, *State Papers*, pp. 87, 76.

21. Haynes, *State Papers*, pp. 87–8.

22. PRO SP 10/6/8.

23. Haynes, *State Papers*, p. 108.

24. PRO SP 10/6/1, fo. 1r.

25. *CSP Spanish 1547–49*, p. 332. OL II, p. 648.

26. PRO SP 10/6/2; *CSP Spanish 1547–49*, p. 340; Haynes, *State Papers*, p.106.

27. BL Hatfield MS M485/39, Vol. 150, fo. 91 (Haynes, *State Papers*, p. 102).

28. Haynes, *State Papers*, p. 90.

29. BL Hatfield MS M485/39, Vol. 150, fo. 78 (Haynes, *State Papers*, p. 95).

30. *APC 1547–49*, 246–7.

31. *APC 1547–49*, 246–7; LR I ccxxi.

32. *APC 1547–49*, 256–8, 260; BL Lansdowne MS 94, fos. 15–15v.

33. G. E. Corrie, *Sermons and Remains of Hugh Latimer*, pp. 161–5; LR I, cxxiii–iv.

34. Elias Grufydd, *Calais Chronicle*, p. 60.

35. Harington, *Nugae Antiquae*, ii, 328–9.

36. *Chronicle*, pp. 10–11.

37. Ellis, II ii, 256; Leti, *Historia Elizabetta*, I, 201.

38. Corrie, *Sermons...*, pp. 161–5.

39. Nichols (ed.), *The Legend of Sir Nicholas Throckmorton* (London, 1874), p. 17.

40. De Guaras, p. 84; OL II, 735; Tytler I, p. 136.

41. Vertot, *Ambassades* I 140; BN Fonds Francais 15888, fo. 186v.

42. BL Additional MS 48023, fo. 351v; Additional MS 48126, fo. 6v.

43. BL Harleian MS 2194, fo. 21v.

44. OL II, 535–6.

45. See MacCulloch, *Cranmer*, pp. 410–21; Williams, *Later Tudors*, pp. 44–5.

46. Seymour Papers IV, fo. 102.

47. Beer, 'Critique', *Huntington Library Quarterly* XXXIV (May 1971), pp. 277–83.

48. BL Cotton MS Titus F III, fo. 273; Strype, *Ecclesiastical Memorials* II I, pp.34–5; *Paget Letters*, pp. 19–20.

49. *Paget Letters*, pp. 22–5.
50. Corrie, *Sermons of Hugh Latimer*, p. 98.
51. LR I i, xx; cxxvii.

6. Commotion Time

1. G. E. Corrie, *The Works of Hugh Latimer* (Cambridge 1844), I 230.
2. *Statutes of the Realm* IV, 95–8; Hales 'Defence', lxi–lxii; TRP I, 451–3.
3. Thynne MS, fos. 104–105v.
4. Jones, p. 99; Hudd 'Two Bristol Calandars'; Sawyer, *Memoirs of Bristol* II, pp. 230–32; APC II, p. 421; STAC 2/19/106.
5. PRO SP 10/8/41.
6. TRP I 461–2, 462–4.
7. Elias Gruffyd, *Calais Chronicle*, p. 61.
8. PRO SP 10/7/35, fos. 91–91v.
9. CSP *Spanish 1547–49*, p. 395.
10. Foxe V, p. 736; Even the boys of Bodmin School divided themselves into factions – those supporting the old religion and those who stood for the new – their mock battles turning ugly when they ended up blowing up a calf and all being beaten.
11. On 6 June two local gentlemen, Humphrey Arundell and John Winslade, raised a thousand men near Bodmin. The events surrounding the rising are shadowy, but a sense of frustrated ambition may have been a factor in their decision to rebel. Arundell was a member of the Arundell of Lanherne family, known as the 'Great Arundells', but had failed to win a place on the magistrate's bench, whilst Winslade, a wealthy squire, had seen his influence wane in recent years. With no resident magistrate in the town, their rising soon spread unchecked. Arundell dispatched a band to seize the stronghold of St Michael's Mount, which was surrendered after brief resistance. At Tremanton Castle, the elderly Sir Richard Grenville was tricked into opening its gates; once the rebels had 'laid hold on his aged unwieldly body' threatening 'to leave it lifeless', he gave in, allowing the castle to be promptly sacked. Marching east along two routes, one across Bodmin moor, the other through Liskeard, the rebels reached Plymouth where the town surrendered, but not before the rebels had burnt a 'steeple' containing the town's official papers. See Younings, 'South Western Rebellion' and Speight, 'South Western Rebellion'.
12. John Hooker, *The Description of the Citie of Excester*, Devon and Cornwall Record Society (1919), p. 61.
13. Petyt MS 538, vol. 46, f. 435, printed Pocock, *Troubles*, p. 23.
14. Cox, II, pp. 163–87.
15. The articles are conveniently printed in Fletcher and MacCulloch, *Tudor Rebellions* (4th edition), pp. 139–41.

16. Petyt, MS 548, vol. 46, fo. 444, printed Pocock, *Troubles*, pp. 40–41.

17. See E. H. Shagan, 'Protector Somerset and the 1549 Rebellions; New sources and new perspectives', *EHR*, cxiv (1999)

18. PRO SP10/8/4; Strype, *Ecclesiastical Memorials* II ii, pp. 429–37.

19. TRP I, no. 341, pp. 475–6; PRO SP 10/8/24; Hales, 'Defence' lvi; I. S. Leadam, *The Domesday of 1517–1518* (1897) ii, 656–66; HMC Salisbury I 54, APC II 199; Loach, *Edward VI*, pp. 68–9.

20. In Cambridge warning was given on 9 July that students 'should go to their books & talk of no news concerning uprising'. The following day a hundred rebels gathered to the sound of a drum, pulling down the fences of a close. Pacified by the mayor and university officials who reported the incident to Somerset, his reply seemed almost to blame both parties, requesting that any unlawful enclosures be destroyed: 'we will that ye endeavour your number to show themselves some good examples of obedience' he wrote, 'that learning, virtue and godliness be not slandered, but that by your conformity and temperance the difference may be tried betwixt the ignorant and the learned, the rude and the taught'. Cecil stepped in as an intermediary for the rebels, requesting their pardon from Somerset, which was granted 'being moved with pity upon this their first offence'. Repeat offenders, however, would face the King's 'princely power and sword ... as a scourge to rebels'; CCCC MS 106, fo. 490r; Cooper, *Annals of Cambridge* II, p. 37.

21. Inner Temple Library Petyt MS 538/46, fo. 438; Pocock, *Troubles*, pp. 22–4.

22. Pocock, *Troubles*, pp. 1–2.

23. Pocock, *Troubles*, p. 14.

24. Robert Kett owned two manors worth an annual value of £50. Whilst the value of his goods and movable property has been estimated to have been as high as 1,000 marks, a tax assessment in 1543 of his goods placed him among the ten richest residents at Wymondham. Tanners were often particularly wealthy and of high social standing in the community; Kett seems to have been no exception. Cornwall, *Revolt of the Peasantry*, p. 139.

25. One gentleman, Roger Woodhouse, who offered two cartloads of beer, was stripped naked by the rebels, 'cruelly tugged' and thrown into a ditch. Another found his goods and dovehouse spoiled. Many were rounded up and imprisoned in Mount Surrey as passions ran high and struggled to be contained. Gentlemen brought before the tree of Reformation to the cries of 'Hang him' and 'Kill him' were taunted with death threats as they were cast in locks and chains and Richard Wharton, a bailiff of the Duke of Norfolk, was captured and pricked with 'spears and other weapons on purpose to kill him'.

26. BL Harleian MS 304, fo. 75. They represent a moderate and conservative attitude of those just beneath the ruling circle of local government, protesting against the mismanagement of their superiors, the local gentry. Five articles looked back to a golden age, the first year of the reign of Henry VII in 1485,

when enclosure legislation gave renewed protection against aggressive landlords and the rebels' attacks upon their self-interest were matched with a concern for justice and good governance, to ensure 'good laws, statutes and proclamations' that had been ignored by their JPs. The over-riding sense of order is no more clearly felt in the document being signed by forty-five rebel deputies, each of whose name seems to represent their own specific geographical and administrative area.

But it is Article Sixteen, striking in its language and tone, that has aroused most interest and debate: 'We pray that all bond men may be made free for God made all free with his precious blood shedding.' On its face, it appears to be a radical assertion of social equality on the basis of Christian idealism. The article does, however, bear a possible link with the Twelve Articles of Memmingen drawn up in the German Peasants' War of 1525. A comparison between the two lists of demands reveal striking similarities, with both demanding changes in religion and society, asking for the clergy to be chosen by their parishioners, preach the gospel and limit tithe payments. The need to reduce rents, restore rights to common land and the freedom of river fishing were also concerns raised by both. It has also been argued that the clause represents a celebration of the fall of the Duke of Norfolk, whose oppressive landlordship and retaining of bondage on his estates had prompted his tenants to petition Somerset for manumission, rather than any underlying coherent philosophy. See MacCulloch, 'Kett's Rebellion in Context', p. xx.

27. PRO C1/1231/65; STAC 3/4/7; *CPR Elizabeth I* V, p. 1073, cited MacCulloch, 'Context', pp. 44, 47.

28. Historical Manuscripts Commission (HMC), Rutland Papers I, p. 42

29. APC II, 301–2.

30. BL Harleian MS 5087.

31. Holinshed, *Chronicles*, p. 988.

32. Cox, *Works*, II, 195.

33. Brigden, *London and the Reformation*, pp. 493–7.

34. To avoid an attack from the Thames, watermen were ordered to leave their boats on the north bank of the river: CLRO *Repertory* 12, fos. 97v, 102v, 104v, 105v; *Letter Book* R, fo. 12r.

35. Stow, *A Survey of London*, ed. C. L. Kingsford (Oxford 1908–27), p. 131.

36. Inner Temple Library Petyt 538/46, fo. 438; Pocock, *Troubles*, pp. 27–8.

37. Archbishop Holgate put the figure at ten to twelve thousand. Capturing a local Chantry commissioner, together with his brother-in-law, they dragged the prisoners into a wood and murdered them, stripping their bodies of clothes and money and 'left them naked behind them in the plain fields for crows to feed on'. Offered pardon, they refused but soon after the ringleaders were rounded up and eventually executed at York on 21 September. A. G. Dickens, 'Some Popular Reactions to the Edwardian Reformation'.

38. Inner Temple Library Petyt MS 538/46, fo. 439, printed Pocock, *Troubles*, pp. 30–34.

39. Hooker, p. 94.

40. PRO E368/327.

41. CLRO Repertory 12, fos. 104v, 110r, 111r, 115r, 116r, fo.118r.

42. Strype, *Ecclesiastical Memorials* II (ii), p. 425.

43. BL M904/1, fos. 24–5, Jones, pp. 282–3; HMC Rutland, p. 36; *CSP Spanish 1547–1549*, p. 424; PRO SP 46/124, fo. 73; Cooper, *Chronicle*, fo. 346r.

44. See also Southerton, 'Commoyson', pp. 41–2.

45. Russell, *Kett's Rebellion*, p. 148.

46. *Scudamore Letters*, p. 88.

47. PRO LR 2/118 fo. 80r.

48. *Scudamore Letters*, p. 88; Russell, *Kett's Rebellion*, p. 227.

49. PRO E 351/221.

50. PRO PCC 19 Stevenson; MacCulloch, 'Kett's Rebellion in Context: A Rejoinder', p. 75.

51. Clifford, pp. 60–62.

52. BL Lansdowne MS 1236, fo. 28.

53. *CSP Spanish 1547–1549*, p. 375.

54. *CSP Spanish 1547–1549*, p. 382.

55. APC II, p. 291; Foxe VI, p. 7.

56. Foxe VI, p. 10–11; *CSP Spanish 1547–1549*, pp. 406–8; PRO SP 10/8/51; SP 10/8/53.

57. PRO SP 10/8/30.

58. Burnet, *Reformation*, VI, pp. 283–4.

59. *CSP Spanish 1547–1549*, p. 405.

60. 'de Mario vel Marianis valde me angit, immo prope exanimat': Tytler I, p. 185.

61. The intrigue deepens with the involvement of Paget's own brother, Robert Paget, as an acknowledged ringleader in the western rebellion. Somerset decided to single him out for particularly severe treatment, writing to Russell that 'considering his offences ... we think him an evil instrument of this commonwealth and to have deserved death with the worst'. Russell hesitated to carry out his orders, earning an unusual rebuke from Somerset that considering the matter was 'touching our honour, for as we have been credibly informed divers have not left unspoken that we should consent to [the] death of our own brother and now would wink at him'. Whether Robert Paget suffered the fate Somerset demanded, or whether he earned a reprieve courtesy of his well-connected brother, remains unclear: Gammon, *Statesman and Schemer*, p. 159. Roger Woodhouse was another who attempted to scout out the rebels' support as they moved to Mousehold Heath, offering them three carts laden with beer and provisions. In return he was beaten up. But Woodhouse seems to have had interesting connections with Southwell; a year later, one Norwich resident recalled that Sir Richard Southwell, Sir Thomas Woodhouse and Mr Roger Woodhouse had gone around with a large 'band of men' about them: 'he took him not for the King's friend'. As Woodhouse

had left a local church he had been overheard saying, 'by God's wounds he would have some of the Church goods, for he was a parishioner, and his friends gave things to it'. Other gentry were suspected of giving Kett their support, including Thomas Godsalve, who was accused of being 'a maintainer and a great setter forward' of the rebels, and Sir Nicholas L'Estrange, who denied that he was 'the beginner of the commotions in Norfolk'. Other conservatives also took the opportunity to sound out the rebels. William Rugge, the Bishop of Norwich, was indicted for treason for comforting the rebels. Kett had sent for him, and Rugge had immediately obeyed his command. Five of the bishop's servants later confessed that he had conferred with Kett alone in his bed chamber three times. Rugge remained at the camp, providing it with victuals and money. When he realized that the rebel defeat was inevitable, his attempt to buy Warwick's support with a gift on the morning after the battle proved futile. Walter Rye (ed.), *Depositions taken before the Mayor and Aldermen of Norwich 1549–67* (Norwich 1905). [Norwich Depositions]

62. Tytler I, p. 191.
63. SP10/8, fos. 27–30v. Printed Russell, *Kett's Rebellion*, pp. 202–203.

7. Coup d'Etat

1. BL Royal MS 17 A XVII.
2. Paget, *Letters*, pp. 76–8.
3. HMC Cecil I, 322. Undated.
4. *CSP Spanish 1547–49*, pp. 445–8, 454–5.
5. Hume, pp. 185–6; 'Eye Witness Account', pp. 603–605.
6. APC II, 330–32.
7. APC II, 328–9.
8. PRO SP 10/9/1; Tytler I, 205; SP 10/9/2–9.
9. 'Certayne Brife Notes' p.129; Grafton, *Chronicle* II, p.522.
10. *Chronicle*, p. 17; 'Certayne Brife Notes', p. 130.
11. PRO SP 10/9/11; Tytler I, pp. 209–10. The author was probably Sir Thomas Smith: Van der Delft later wrote that the council had interviewed 'Dr. Smith whom they taxed with the proclamation made at Windsor against the council of which he was the author'. *CSP Spanish 1547–49*, p. 459.
12. PRO SP 10/9/12; Tytler I, pp. 210–11; *APC 1547–49*, p. 331.
13. APC II, pp. 330–31.
14. PRO SP 10/9/10; Pocock, p. 94.
15. PRO SP 10/9/33; Tytler I, 248–51.
16. *CSP Spanish 1547–49*, pp. 445, 449.
17. HMC Rutland, p. 36.
18. Seymour Papers IV, fos. 106, 108, 112.
19. *Wriothesley's Chronicle* II, pp. 24–5.
20. *CSP Spanish 1547–49*, p. 459.

21. BL Hargrave MS 134; Harleian MS 1749, fos. 174v, 253; Foxe, pp. 289–90; CLRO Rep. 12(1), fo. 151v; CLRO Journal 16, fo. 37–37v.
22. *CSP Spanish 1547–59*, p. 456.
23. Hume, p.187; *CSP Spanish 1547–49*, p. 457.
24. PRO SP 10/9/14, fos. 15–15v.
25. Ellis II, pp. 166–8; Tytler I, pp. 215–16.
26. PRO SP 10/10/18 fos. 48–48v.
27. Inner Temple Library, Petyt MS, Vol. 46, fo. 466v; Tytler I, p. 231.
28. Bodleian Rawlinson MS D 1087, fos. 16v–17v.
29. PRO SP 10/9/23, fos. 30r–30v; Pocock, pp. 90–92; Tytler I, pp. 217–19.
30. BL Cotton MS Caligula B VII, fo. 407; Burnet V, pp. 275–6.
31. Bodleian Rawlinson MS D 1087, fos. 17v–18r; John Stow, *The Annales of England* (1615), p. 598.
32. SP 10/9/23; Tytler I, pp. 220–22.
33. SP 10/9/26; Tytler I, pp. 223–7.
34. 'What hath my lord done to any of these noble men? Or others? that they should thus rage and seek the extremity to him and his that never had thought in the like towards any of them ... I have ever loved and trusted you, for that I have seen in you a perfect honest friend to my lord who hath always made the same account and assuredly bare you his good will and friendship as you yourself hath best trial. God have given you a great wisdom and a friendly nature. I know you may do much good in these matters being a wise man. How can God be content with this disorder to danger the King and all the realm in seeking extremities? Oh, that I could bear this as I ought to do with patience and quietness, but it passeth all frail flesh to do. For knowing so well my lord's innocency in all these matters that they charge him with all, they be so untrue and most unfriendly credit that surely it hath been some wicked person or persons that first sought this great uproar ... Good Master Comptroller, comfort my lord as I trust you do, both with counsel and otherwise, for I much fear he is sore grieved at the heart, first for the king and the realm, and as greatly to see these lords' friendships so slender to him as it doth appear and specially of some, albeit he hath pleasured them all. Alas, that ever any Christian realm should be so slandered': Paget, *Letters*, p. 135.
35. BL Cotton Caligula B VII, fo. 410, printed Ellis, p. 173–5; *Paget Letters*, p. 80.
36. STC 7828; *Chronicle*, p. 17; see also *CSP Spanish 1547–1549*, p. 459.
37. BL Harleian MS 353, fo. 77.
38. Ibid.
39. *Chronicle*, p. 18; BL Cotton Caligula B VII, fo. 408, printed Ellis, pp. 169–71.
40. 'Certayne Brife Notes', p. 133.
41. *CSP Spanish 1547–49*, p. 461.
42. BL Cotton Caligula B VII, fo. 410, printed Ellis, p. 171–2; and Burnet V, p. 282; Tytler I, pp. 241–3.
43. He apparently entered at St Giles in the field 'at his desire, for because he

would not come by the place that he had begun and pulled down divers churches and the cloister in Paul's to build it' At Cheapside he told the crowd 'he was as true a man to the king as any was there, even proudly'. *Greyfriars Chronicle*, p. 64.

44. BL Titus B ii 49, fos. 91–94. BL Hatfield MS M485/39, Vol. 137; HMC Cecil I, no. 320; BL Harleian 284, fos. 16r–17v.

45. PRO SP 10/9/41, fos. 72r–81v; BL Additional MS 9069, fos. 43v–51v.

46. *CSP Spanish 1547–49*, p. 461; *Wriothesley's Chronicle* II, p. 29.

47. Ponet, *A shorte treatise of politike power*, sigs. I3r–I3v.

48. *Chronicle*, p. 26.

49. BL Additional MS 5464; LR I, pp. 173–205; MacCulloch, *Tudor Church Militant*, pp. 26–30.

50. Hume, pp. 190–92.

51. OL I, p. 395.

52. TRP I 352; OL I, p. 354.

53. *CSP Spanish 1547–49*, p. 446.

54. *Scudamore Letters*, pp. 93, 95.

55. 3&4 Edward VI c.5; Jordan, *The Threshold of Power*, pp. 37–8.

56. *CSP Spanish 1547–1549*, p. 468.

57. *Scudamore Letters*, p. 91.

58. *CSP Spanish 1547–49*, p. 476; BL Lansdowne MS 160, fos. 264–7, BL Additional MS 11042, fos. 53r, 53v.

59. OL I, p. 75.

60. *Scudamore Letters*, p. 104. Either Psalm 2 or 118.

61. 'Certayne Brife Notes', pp. 134–6.

62. *Chronicle*, p. 19; Scudamore, *Letters*, pp. 107–8.

63. *CSP Spanish 1550–52*, p. 47.

64. *CSP Foreign Edward VI*, 491; The preacher John Ponet thought that 'killed himself with sorrow in so much as he said he would not live in such misery if he might' since 'fearing lest he should come to some open shameful end, he either poisoned himself, or pined away for thought'; 'Certayne Brife Notes', p. 136.

65. *Scudamore Letters*, pp. 116–7.

66. BL Royal MS 17, A XVII.

8. Uncertain Times

1. On Candlemas Day, three Italians made a challenge at barriers against all comers, in a mock quarrel with 'the young gentlemen of the court' 'that Love should be hanged', with a lady 'richly apparelled set upon the midst of a ladder going up to the gallows'. Each time the challengers won a round, she was to take a step higher towards the gallows; if the defenders were successful, she took a step back. [HMC Rutland I]

2. *CSP Spanish 1550–1552*, p. 5.
3. *CSP Spanish 1550–1552*, p. 9.
4. *Scudamore Letters*, p. 116; APC III, p. 7; Hoak, *King's Council*, p. 271.
5. BL Cotton MS Caligula E IV, fo. 207.
6. *Scudamore Letters*, pp. 114–5; *Two London Chronicles*, p. 21.
7. On 12 February John Redhead, weaver, looking up at Kett's body was reported to have said: 'Oh Kett, God have mercy upon thy soul and I trust in God that the King's Majesty and his Counsel shall be informed once between this and Midsummer evening that of their own gentleness thou shalt be taken down by the grace of God and buried, and not hanged up for winter store, and set a quietness in the realm and that the ragged staff shall be taken down of their own gentleness from the gentlemen's gates in this city, and to have no more King's Arms but within the city under Christ but King Edward ...' Previously on 24 November one John Rooke had said 'before Christmas ye shall see as great a Camp upon Moushold as ever was. And if it be not then it shall be in the spring of the year, and they shall come out of the Lord Protector's Country to strike him': *Norwich Depositions*, pp. 20, 163; Beer, *Rebellion and Riot*, p. 203.
8. *Scudamore Letters*, pp. 125, 127. APC II, p. 425; III, pp. 40, 45.
9. PRO SP 10/10/2.
10. Stow, *Annales*, 602–3.
11. APC II, 384.
12. BL Lansdowne MS 160, fos. 264–7; Hoak, *King's Council*, pp. 96–7.
13. *CSP Spanish 1550–1552*, p. 43.
14. Hoak, *King's Council in the Reign of Edward VI*, Appendix.
15. *Scudamore Letters*, pp. 119–20.
16. *CSP Spanish 1550–1552*, p. 62.
17. *Scudamore Letters*, p. 130; *Chronicle*, pp. 24, 28.
18. O. Werdmueller, *A Spyrytuall and Moost Precyouse Pearle*, trans M. Coverdale (RSTC 25255, 1550).
19. *Chronicle*, p. 26.
20. APC III, 29–30.
21. *Antiquarian Repertory* IV, pp. 648–51.
22. OL I, p. 88.
23. BL Royal MS B XL, fos. 6r–7r. The tract was eventually presented to Mary during the following reign.
24. P.V., *Historical Narration of certain events that took place in the Kingdom of Great Britain in the month of July, in the year of our Lord, 1553,β* (London, 1865).
25. *CSP Venetian 1534–1554*, pp. 535–6; Foxe V, 699.
26. PRO E 315/221/131.
27. Ascham, *The Whole Works*, ed. Giles (3 vols. in 4, London 1864–1865), I ii, 226–8; Strype, *Ecclesiastical Memorials*, II i, 426–7.
28. Strype, *Life of Cheke*, p. 57; BL Cotton MS Nero C X.
29. *CSP Spanish 1550–1552*, p. 63.

30. *Scudamore Letters*, pp. 127–8.

31. LR I, cvi.

32. Hooper, *Early Writings*, 541, 558.

33. OL I, p. 82.

34. OL II, p. 561.

35. Hastings Robinson, *Zurich Letters* III (Parker Society, Cambridge, 1846), 548; For Constantine, see Bartholomew, Traheron to Bullinger, 12 June; *Zurich Letters* III, 324, 482; BL Harleian MS 419, fo. 123; printed LR I, clii.

36. Strype, *Ecclesiastical Memorials* I ii, p. 388; PRO E101/426/8.

37. BL Harleian MS 611, fo. 16r.

38. *CSP Venetian* V, p. 339.

39. *Chronicle*, pp. 31–2; *CSP Spanish 1550–1552*, p. 97.

40. *Chronicle*, pp. 36–7; *CSP Spanish 1550–1552*, p. 117.

41. Foxe VI, p. 352.

42. MacCulloch, *Tudor Church Militant*, pp. 31–5; Thompson, 'Order of the Garter'; LR II, pp. 511–538.

43. In fact her beliefs were more Socinian, believing that 'Christ did not take flesh from the Virgin Mary; He only passed through her body, as water through the pipe of a conduit, without participating anything of that body'. Heylyn, *History of the Reformation* (1661), p. 89; See Jordan, *Threshold of Power*, pp. 327–9, for the case.

44. Cox, *Memorials of Cranmer* II, p. 335.

45. *Chronicle*, p. 28.

46. *Chronicle*, p. 28. Scudamore reported that twelve persons had been arrested. (Scudamore, *Letters*, p. 131); MacCulloch, *Cranmer*, pp. 474–8; *Chronicle*, p. 28; Strype, *Memorials* II i, 343; APC II, 423, 425.

47. APC III, 6; J. C. Jeaffreson, *Middlesex County Records* (London 1887), 1:3.

48. James Scotter was overheard remarking that 'such as were slain and dead upon Mousehold in. the Commotion time were honest men'; *Norwich Depositions*, pp. 22, 19, 25,

49. *CSP Spanish 1550–1552*, p. 116; APC III, 35. At Sittingbourne, two ringleaders were pardoned, but a third who began 'to murmur and make certain speeches was incontinently seized and had his ears cut off'.

50. *CSP Spanish 1550–1552*, pp. 97, 116. For other instances of disorder and rebellious activity, see APC II, 385, 404, 421; III, 6–7, 18, 31, 42, 131, 198; PRO DL 5/8, fo. 292; R. C. Anderson (ed.), *Letters of the Fifteenth and Sixteenth Centuries from the Archives of Southampton* (Southampton 1921), pp. 78–9; *Chronicle* p. 37, Strype, *Memorials* II i, 343.

51. APC II, 421; Justices: APC II, 431; Informers: TRP I, 489–90; APC III, 31, 34, 50; TRP I, 489–90, 495, 498; *Chronicle*, pp. 20, 22, 24, 37.

52. *Chronicle*, pp. 41, 42; APC III, 50; *CSP Spanish 1550–1552*, p. 87.

53. *Chronicle*, pp. 32–3; *CSP Spanish 1550–1552*, p. 98.

54. BL Additional 48023, fo. 350r; *Scudamore Letters*, p. 134.

55. *Chronicle*, pp. 35–6.

56. Foxe VI, 80–85.
57. PRO SP 10/10/9, fos. 21r–21v.
58. *CSP Spanish 1550–1552*, pp. 82–3.
59. *CSP Spanish 1550–1552*, pp. 127–8; Prescott, *Mary Tudor*, pp. 130–32.
60. *CSP Spanish 1550–1552*, p. 47.
61. *CSP Spanish 1550–1552*, pp. 94, 111, 124–135; Prescott, *Mary Tudor*, pp. 132–43.
62. *CSP Spanish 1550–1552*, pp. 124–35.
63. *Chronicle*, p. 40; *CSP Spanish 1550–1552*, p. 152.
64. Foxe VI, pp. 4–7.
65. OL I, pp. 78–85.
66. MacCulloch, *Cranmer*, pp. 472–3.
67. *Chronicle*, p. 40.
68. *CSP Spanish 1550–1552*, p. 108.
69. Scudamore, *Letters*, p. 131.
70. *CSP Spanish 1550–52*, pp. 166, 168.
71. CLRO Journal 16, fo. 91r; Repertory 12, fo. 271v; Brigden, pp. 503–4; Hoak, *King's Council*, p.194.
72. *Chronicle*, pp. 45–7.
73. BL Royal MS 18 C XXIV; Jordan, *Threshold of Power*, p. 404. Edward's diary also falls curiously silent for November 1550.
74. APC II, 129.
75. *CSP Spanish 1550–1552*, p. 186.
76. Tytler I, p. 340.
77. PRO SP 10/10/46.
78. OL II, p. 734.
79. Cambridge University Library D IX 31, fo. 13.
80. *CSP Foreign: Edward VI*, no. 489.
81. Foxe, VI 5; Dickens, 'Parkyn's Narrative', pp. 72–3; J. Bale, *An Expostulation agaynste a Franticke Papyst of Hampshyre* (1552), sig. Bi.
82. *CSP Spanish 1550–1552*, pp. 205–9; 410–411; *Chronicle*, p. 50.
83. Foxe VI, 11–12; *CSP Spanish 1550–1552*, pp. 209–12.
84. *CSP Spanish 1550–1552*, pp. 205–9.

9. Hidden Conspiracies

1. *CSP Spanish 1550–1552*, p. 219.
2. *CSP Spanish 1550–1552*, p. 215.
3. Machyn, pp. 4–5.
4. *CSP Spanish 1550–1552*, pp. 258–60.
5. *Chronicle*, p. 55.
6. *Chronicle*, p. 56.
7. Psalms 78; this in fact took place on 16 March. MacCulloch, *Tudor Church Militant*, p. 228 no. 62.

8. BL Harleian MS 353, fos. 130–138v, printed LR I, pp. ccxxiv–ccxxxiv; Foxe V, pp. 700–701.

9. *Chronicle*, p. 56; APC III, 239.

10. Foxe VI, pp. 18–21. MacCulloch, *Cranmer*, pp. 495–6.

11. *CSP Spanish 1550–1552*, p. 249.

12. Edmund Ford of Sussex was sent to the Fleet for words against the council in January whilst Cranmer reported a clergyman for seditious preaching who, despite warning, had gone from 'evil to worse'. On 14 March a man and his sister were hanged at Smithfield for killing a gentleman, one Mr Arden of Faversham. Another woman was burned at Canterbury, one named 'Black Will' at Flushing and five more were hanged for the same offence; Machyn, p. 4.

13. BL Egerton MS 2623, fos. 9–9v.

14. APC III, 258–9, 260.

15. *CSP Spanish 1550–1552*, pp. 278–9.

16. OL I, p. 108.

17. *CSP Spanish 1550–1552*, p. 291; Machyn, pp. 3–4.

18. *Chronicle*, pp. 57, 58; *CSP Spanish 1550–1552*, p. 291.

19. PRO SP 68/6, fos. 213–14; *CSP Spanish 1550–1552*, p. 229. In late March Sir Ralph Vane, having switched from Warwick's affinity to Somerset's, threatened his possession of Postern Park in Kent with a force of between 160 and 180 men; he would raise a further four hundred if necessary. APC III, 215, 248, 391, 398. Sir Francis Leek, who had overheard the conversation, would only admit that he had 'prattled very much' and refused to back up Rutland's claim that he had replied to Whalley that he 'misliked much' his talk.

20. BL Cotton MS Titus B II, fos. 28–9v.

21. Bernard, *Early Tudor Nobility*, pp. 64–5.

22. OL I, p. 438; *CSP Spanish 1550–1552*, p. 279.

23. *CSP Spanish 1550–1552*, pp. 166, 168, 169, 262; APC III, 239.

24. APC III, 215, 256–7.

25. Brigden, *London and the Reformation*, p. 508.

26. APC III, 258–9, 260.

27. APC III, 262; CLRO Repertory 12, fos. 326v, 327r.

28. APC III, 272–4; APC III, 240.

29. *CSP Spanish 1550–1552*, pp. 280, 292.

30. *Chronicle*, p. 60; *CSP Spanish 1550–1552*, p. 285.

31. TRP, pp. 514–18, 522–3.

32. OL I, p. 438; BL Hatfield MS M485/39ii, 7–8; HMC Cecil I, no. 358.

33. *CSP Edward VI Foreign*, 370i, Francis Peto to Warwick, 6 June 1551.

34. *CSP Venetian* V, 339.

35. BL Cotton MS Titus B II, fos. 96–102, printed Strype, *Ecclesiastical Memorials*, II i, 156–165; OL II, 187; LR I, clxii–clxiii.

36. LR I, clxii–clxiii; *Tudor Studies*, p. 142.

37. *Chronicle*, pp. 159–67; xiv–xv.

38. *Chronicle*, xxv.

39. BL Royal MS VIII B VII.

40. BL Landsdowne 1236/14 (Latin): Translated by Haliwell, *Letters of the Kings of England*, pp. 42–4.

41. *Chronicle*, p. 54.

42. PRO E 101/426/8; Edward also gave £20 to one Barnardyne Granado 'for his relief in sickness'.

43. 'Mr Hoby's servant that played on a lute' was rewarded £10, and the 'Children of Paul's' £12 13s 4d.

44. BL Additional MS 10169, cited Loach, *Edward VI*, p. 155.

45. John Langridge's copy of *The mirror of the blessed life of Christ*, Trinity College MS B 15, 16, fo. 134, cited Jordan, *Threshold of Power*, p. 403.

46. *CSP Spanish 1550–1552*, p. 266; *Chronicle*, p. 57.

47. Machyn, p. 5.

48. *Chronicle*, p. 61.

49. *CSP Spanish 1550–1552*, pp. 293, 300; *CSP Venetian V*, 535. PRO E101/426/8.

50. PRO E101/426/8.

51. *A boke, or counseill against the disease commonly called the sweate*.

52. *Chronicle*, p. 71.

53. Edward wrote: 'There are some, I believe, who call consistency and seriousness – which we praise so much as hardness – just a lack of fun. For they think that those who do not mourn the death of a friend are empty of all human emotion and are bestowed with some degree of harshness. I, on the other hand, think that one must not mourn the death of a friend. For all grief seems to me to be necessary to be cursed, since it is a pointless act. For what can be more pointless than grief which, when it exists, brings about sadness and fills life with misery, and when it is made, there is no alleviation at all of suffering ... For when someone has been mourning the death of a friend what has he gained? Has he raised them from the dead? Not at all. Has he brought any profit to the dead man...? Not at all. So what has he achieved then? Certainly nothing, except at that present time he had brought upon himself great miseries and tortures of the mind. Further, grief is a certain effeminate emotion which does not befit a brave man in any way ... for to grieve is of a woman not a man, who tries to pursue the praise of bravery.

54. Machyn, p. 7–9; Other estimates placed the figure at 938, with eight hundred dead within the first week.

55. Holinshed, *Chronicles* II, p.506.

56. *CSP Spanish 1550–1552*, p. 332; OL I, p. 94; Cooper, *Chronicle*, p. 351; Grafton, *Chronicle* ii, p. 525; CLRO D L/C/3, fo.110r, cited in J. G. Davis, *Heresy and Reformation in the South-East of England, 1520–1559* (1983), p. 99.

57. Tawney and Power, *Tudor Economic Documents* ii, 187.

58. CPR IV 343.

59. *CSP Edward VI Foreign*, 381.
60. Scepeaux, *Memoires*, I 341.
61. *Chronicle*, p. 60.
62. *Chronicle*, p. 76.

10. The Destruction of the Duke

1. *CSP Spanish 1550–1552*, pp. 361–2.
2. Nichols, *Narratives*, pp. 79–80.
3. *Chronicle*, pp. 92–3.
4. BN Fonds Francais 15888, fos. 205–10.
5. OL II, p.636.
6. *CSP Spanish 1550–1552*, p. 384.
7. *CSP Spanish 1550–1552*, p. 377.
8. Bryson, 'The great men of this country' (thesis), p. 205.
9. *CSP Spanish 1550–1552*, p. 381.
10. *Chronicle*, pp. 88–9.
11. Sir Thomas Holcroft, John Bannister, George Vaughan and Sir Michael Stanhope. A list of prisoners, totalling 39 is in BL Harleian MS 249, fo. 42r, printed Tytler II, p. 37.
12. Lord Grey also called Northumberland 'the son of a notorious traitor'.
13. PRO SP 10/8/55; CPR IV, 113–14; *Chronicle*, p.101.
14. Fuller, *Church History* IV, pp. 80–82.
15. Alford, *Kingship and Politics*, p. 171.
16. *Chronicle*, p. 76.
17. APC III 411.
18. MacCulloch, *Cranmer*, p. 497; Hoak, *King's Council*, pp. 120–23, 154–5.
19. BL Royal MS 18 C XXIV, fo. 165v.
20. *Chronicle*, p. 84–5.
21. OL II, p. 652.
22. Brigden, p. 516; Machyn, p. 10; *Greyfriars Chronicle*, p. 71; *CSP Spanish 1550–1552*, pp. 390, 393.
23. Machyn, pp. 10–11.
24. *CSP Spanish 1550–1552*, p. 388.
25. *CSP Spanish 1550–1552*, p. 393.
26. *CSP Spanish 1550–1552*, p. 389; *Greyfriars Chronicle*, pp. 71–2.
27. APC III, 407.
28. APC III, 419; *Chronicle*, pp. 96, 98–9; PRO SP 10/13/64; PRO KB 8/19 mm. 6–8; LPL MS 3193, fo. 219; Bernard, *The Power of the Early Tudor Nobility*, p. 70; BL Harleian MS 523, fo. 26; CLRO Repertory 12, fo. 426r; Stow, *Annales*, 606–7; *Greyfriars Chronicle*, p. 72; *4th Deputy Keeper's Report*, App. II, p. 229.
29. *CSP Spanish 1550–1552*, p. 406.

30. *Chronicle*, pp. 98–9.
31. BL Harleian MS 2194, fo. 20v.
32. APC III, 462.
33. *Grafton's Chronicle* ii, p. 526.
34. Edward Coke, *The third part of the Institutes of the laws of England, etc.* (London, 1797), p. 13. See Jordan, *Threshold of Power*, pp. 92–8; Pollard, *England under Protector Somerset* (London, 1900), p. 284.
35. *CSP Spanish 1553*, pp. 185, 187; BN Fonds Francais 15888, fo. 212r.
36. *Chronicle*, p. 99.
37. *CSP Spanish 1550–1552*, pp. 407–9, 425.
38. *Greyfriars Chronicle*, pp. 72–3; *CSP Spanish 1550–1552*, p. 424; APC III, 462. Northumberland's interest in prophecy and alchemy is illustrated in PRO SP 15/2, fos. 156–9, and *Calendar of Carew Manuscripts* V, p. 243, which details how he once asked a spirit whether any man 'should overcome him by violence', the reply being that 'no man would'.
39. CLRO Repertory 12, fos. 434r, 437r, cited Brigden, *London and the Reformation*, p. 517; APC III, 465.
40. *CSP Spanish 1550–1552*, p. 396.
41. RL, p. 52; Machyn, pp. 12–3; *CSP Spanish 1550–1552*, p. 443.
42. Feuillerat, *Revels*, p. 47. The Imperial ambassador was not amused. 'Besides several witty and harmless pranks,' Scheyfve wrote, they 'played other quite outrageous ones ... They paraded through the Court, and carried, under an infamous tabernacle, a representation of the holy sacrament in its monstrance, which they wetted and perfumed in most strange fashion, with great ridicule of the ecclesiastical state. Not a few Englishmen were highly scandalized by this behaviour; and the French and Venetian ambassadors ... showed clearly enough that the spectacle was repugnant to them'. *CSP Spanish 1550–1552*, pp. 443–4.
43. Feuillerat, *Revels*, p. 47.
44. Grafton, *Chronicle* II, 526–7; *CSP Spanish 1550–1552*, pp. 436, 443; On 21 January Edward also watched horses being ridden, 'and like them very well as they were worthie'. Bodleian Rawlinson MS D 1087, fo. 55r.
45. APC III, 465.
46. *CSP Spanish 1550–1552*, p. 453.
47. Hume, p. 218; *CSP Spanish 1550–1552*, 12 February 1552; Rymer, *Foedera* XV, 295–6.
48. BL Stowe, MS 1066.
49. BL Cotton Charter iv, 17.
50. See also Machyn, p. 14; Wriothesley II, 65; Stow, *Annales*, 607.
51. BL Cotton Charter iv, 17.
52. Guaras, p. 84.
53. *CSP Spanish 1550–52*, pp. 452–3.
54. This account was once dismissed as mere fabrication on the part of the seventeenth-century historian John Hayward, Edward's first biographer, whose

work, *The Life and Reign of Edward VI*, was rather prone to lifting entire episodes from Tacitus' *Histories* and setting them in a Tudor context, the same story exists in manuscript at the British Library: Harleian MS 2194, fos. 19–20; Loach, pp. 102–104.

55. *Chronicle*, p. 108.
56. *Greyfriars Chronicle*, pp. 73–4; Machyn, p. 15.
57. LR II, 524; BL Stowe MS 595, fo. 41.
58. PRO SP10/14/53.
59. Cooper, *Chronicle*, p. 355; Bouterwek, K.W., 'Anna von Cleve, Gemahlin Heinrichs viii. Konigs von England', *Zeitschrift des Bergischen Geschichtsvereins* VI (1869), 140, cited in Jordan, *Threshold of Power*, p. 104.

11. An Emerging King

1. OL I, p. 438; *CSP Spanish 1550–1552*, p. 436. A letter of Northumberland's to Edward confirms this impression: 'I cannot enough (most gracious sovereign lord) lament and sorrow the miserable estate of my wretched and sick body, the which by occasion of many infirmities is so oft driven to the walls, and thereby drawn from the service of your highness, whereunto I acknowledge myself as much bound as any other your subjects.' Bod. MS. Smith 69, pp. 225–6.
2. Bibliotheque Nationale, MS. Ancien Saint-Germain Francais, 15888, fos. 214v–215v. Quoted from Hoak, *King's Council*, p. 123.
3. Nichols, *Legend of Nicholas Throgmorton*.
4. P. V., *Historical Narration*.
5. LR I, p. 70.
6. BL Cotton MS Vespasian F XIII, fos. 273r–v, printed LR II, pp. 489–90.
7. *Chronicle*, pp. 113–14, 116, 118–19, 74, 108, 128, 129; *CSP Spanish 1550–1552*, p. 493. Edward's surviving political papers attest his detailed attention to its business. He also prepared memoranda for bills passing through the latest session of Parliament, including a bill of his own that sought to curb the increasing fashion to wear sumptuous clothes above one's station. Certain clothes were to only be worn according to one's social class. No one beneath the rank of baron would be allowed cloth of silver and gold, whilst no man under the degree of a gentleman was to wear fur ('save lambs fur') or any 'silk points'. No husbandman was to wear dyed cloth or leather tanned or dressed out of the realm, and no man was to wear a chain that weighed less than ten ounces of gold. At the court, only Knights of the Garter were to be allowed to wear 'blue or crimson velvet' or any cloth made outside the realm; the privilege of wearing 'cloth of gold tinsel' was to be reserved only for dukes, whilst Edward insisted 'no man but of the blood royal [was] to wear cloth of gold or purple colour, or any other purple'. Edward also worked upon a

memorandum detailing reasons for establishing a mart in England which was discussed amongst the council. BL Cotton MS Vespasian F XIII, fos. 273r–v, printed LR II, pp. 489–90; Inner Temple Library Petyt MS 538/47, fo. 318, printed LR II, pp. 495–8. See also Hooper, W., 'The Tudor Sumptuary Laws' *EHR* XXX (1915), p. 436; BL Cotton MS Nero C X, fo. 85, printed *Chronicle*, pp. 168–73; *Chronicle*, p. 115.

8. BL Cotton MS Nero C X, fo. 79, printed LR II, 498–502; Alford, *Kingship and Politics*, pp. 162–5.

9. OL I, 79.

10. Duffy, *Stripping of the Altars*, p. 470; D. M. Loades, *The Oxford Martyrs* (London, 1970), p. 97.

11. Williams, *The Later Tudors: England 1547–1603*, p. 76.

12. MacCulloch, *Cranmer*, p. 512.

13. LR I, clxxxi–clxxxiv.

14. Loach, *Edward VI*, p. 100; P. Slack, 'Social Policy and the Constraints of Government, 1547–58', in J. Loach and R. Tittler, eds., *The Mid-Tudor Polity c. 1540–1560* (London and Basingstoke, 1980), pp. 110–11; Brigden, *London and the Reformation*, pp. 479–80.

15. *Journal*, p. 117; *CSP Spanish 1550–1552*, p. 504; LR I, pp. 79–80.

16. Elizabeth, *Complete Works: Letters*, pp. 36–7; original in the Houghton Library, Harvard University MS Typ 686.

17. Machyn, pp. 18–20; *CSP Spanish 1550–1552*, p. 507.

18. MacCulloch, *Tudor Church Militant*, p. 39; E 101/546/19; *Journal*, pp. 129–30.

19. BL Lansdowne MS 3/2, 27 September 1552.

20. LR I, p. 81.

21. Salisbury Borough Records Ledger B, fo. 309. Riding to the Earl of South-ampton's house at Titchfield on 10th, Edward lost a large pear–shaped pearl from his collar of gold (enamelled and set with 19 pearls and ten 'tablets' with thirty diamonds, 24 rubies and a 'very great and rich diamond, with a ruby enclosed in a flower'). It was eventually recovered by Sir John Gates. The same day he was presented with a dolphin captured in the Thames. Society of Antiquaries MS 129; Machyn, p. 22. Two others were sold in Fishstreet 'to them that would buy them'.

22. *CSP Spanish 1550–52*, pp. 565–6. An inventory of the Earl of Pembroke in the V&A (MSL 30/1982) gives a sense of this staggering wealth. His household plate totals 1,554 oz of gold, 12,283 oz of white plate and 15,898 oz of gilt plate; BL Royal MS 12 A XXXIII; *Reading Records: Diary of the Corporation*, Vol. I, ed. J. M. Guilding (Oxford, 1892), p. 228.

23. LR II, p.86.

24. PRO SP 10/15/1; SP 10/15/24, fo. 50.

25. Bodleian Ashmole MS 1730, fos. 166–167v.

26. Haynes, *State Papers*, p. 137.

27. PRO SP 10/15/66; printed Tytler II, 148–50.

28. CLRO Repertory 12 (2), fo. 521v.

29. BL Harleian MS 353, fo. 121, printed LR I, clxvi–clxviii. See also the investigation of a 'fond sermon' preached by James Bilney at Chigwell: APC IV, 136.

30. PRO SP 10/15/50. When another slanderer named Ford was arrested, the duke refused to hear the case, referring it to the council 'because the matter as it seems touches none other of the council but my brother and me', recalling that previously the man had been punished 'for such like matter, and yet I was then content freely to remit his offence towards me'; SP 10/15/39.

31. PRO SP 10/15/68, fo. 141.

32. J. A. Froude, *History of England from the Fall of Wolsey to the Defeat of the Spanish Armada* (1856–1870), V, 111.

33. PRO SP 10/15/11; SP 10/15/73.

34. *CSP Spanish 1550–1552*, p. 592.

35. *CSP Spanish 1550–1552*, pp. 572–3.

36. Foxe V 700; BL Egerton MS 2877, fos. 14v–15r.

37. Loach, *Edward VI*, p. 158; Perhaps Edward had studiously learnt the names of rivers from a book he owned, on 'the description of the whole land and a book covered with velvet embroidered with the king's arms declaring the same'; BL Harleian MS 1419A, fo. 238v; BL Egerton MS 2877, fos. 14v–15r; LR I cccxxv–cccxlii.

38. Foxe V, p. 702; Cardano, *Opera* (London, 1663) V, 503–8, quoted Burnet, *Reformation*, V 125–6; see also H. Morley, *Life of Geronimo Cardano* II, pp. 129–40.

39. BL Harleian MS 1419A, fo. 171r; Additional MS 46348, fo. 149v; BL Harleian MS 1419A, fo. 115v; on the quadrant, see LR I xxb–xxc; BL Royal MS 17 A XXXIII.

40. BL Additional MS 4724, fo. 104; printed LR I, 133–6. Edward argued that astrology was also indispensable for farmers tending their crops and merchants sailing upon the seas.

41. BL Harleian MS 1419A, fo. 171r; Levens, Peter, *The Pathway to Health* (1632), fo. 12, printed LR I, ccxv.

42. LR I, ccxv–ccxvi.

12. Promise Unfulfilled

1. PRO SP 10/18/2.

2. PRO SP 10/15/66; printed Tytler II, 148–50.

3. *The Report of the Royal Commission of 1552*, ed. W. C. Richardson (Morgantown, 1974).

4. *CSP Spanish 1553*, pp. 8–9, 10; Machyn, pp. 30–31. Further revels prepared for Candlemas Day (2 February), including 'a play of the State of Ireland' were also postponed 'by occasion that his grace was sick'.

5. Machyn, p. 32; College of Arms MS L 15, p. 130.

6. *CSP Spanish 1553*, p. 12; PRO SP 10/15/73.

7. BL Cotton MS Nero C X, fos. 86–9, printed Jordan, *Chronicle*, pp. 181–4; Petre's version is SP 10/1/, fos. 56–7. See Emmison, F. G., 'A Plan of Edward VI and Secretary Petre for Reorganizing the Privy Council's Work, 1552–3', BIHR XXXI (1958), 203–10; Hoak, *King's Council*, pp. 91–3, 118–22. Edward had also produced the detailed 'A Summary of Matters to be concluded' for the council on 13 October 1552; BL Lansdowne MS 1236, fos. 19–20.

8. *CSP Spanish 1553*, p. 3.

9. Petyt MS 538, vol. 46, fo. 9, printed L I, cxc.

10. BN Fonds Francais 15888, fos. 215r, 225r.

11. BL Royal 18 C XXIV fo.364.

12. BL Additional MS 70984.

13. Additions in italics, Inner Temple Library Petyt MS 538/47, fo. 317.

14. MacCulloch, *Tudor Church Militant*, p. 40; Alford, *Kingship and Politics*, p. 172; *CSP Spanish 1553*, p. 45

15. Bindoff, 'A Kingdom at Stake', *History Today* 3, 1953, p. 647.

16. PRO SP68/12, nos. 652, 684.

17. *CSP Spanish 1553*, p. 57.

18. D. McCulloch (ed), 'The Vitae Mariae Angliae Reginae of Robert Wingfield of Brantham'. [VM], pp. 247–8.

19. Montagu, pp. 4–6.

20. Royal MS 18 C XXIV, fo. 373v; Details of grants are as follows: 12 June Henry Gate was granted lands worth £102 12s 7d (CPR, p. 101), Francis, Earl of Huntingdon, lands worth £158 8s 5d yearly on 22 June (CPR, p. 228). Shrewsbury was granted the mansion of Coldharborrow in London and lands worth a yearly value of £66 13s 1½d. (CPR, p. 231; Royal MS 18 C XXIV fo. 368). On 23 June Henry Sidney was granted lands worth £160 6s 11½d (CPR, p. 61–2), and on 3 July he was granted the keepership of Sheen (BL Royal MS 18 XXIV, fo. 374v). On 29 June Bedford granted lands with yearly value £78 16s 7d (CPR, pp. 281–3), On 4 July Thomas Wroth was granted lands worth £87 3s 8¼d yearly (CPR, p. 240), Thomas Gresham £201 14s 9½d on 1 July (CPR, p. 240), Cheke was granted lands worth £100 on 22 May (CPR, pp. 92–3).

21. Petyt 538 xlvii, fo. 316; Burnet VI, pp. 307–8; Nichols, *Narratives of the Reformation*, p. 255.

22. MacCulloch, *Cranmer*, pp. 540–41.

23. *CSP Spanish 1553*, p. 70.

24. *CSP Spanish 1553*, p. 51; Harbison, p. 37–8; LR cxciii.

25. OL I, pp. 140–42.

26. OL I, p. 273.

27. *CSP Spanish 1553*, p. 53.

28. 'Look down with thy pitiful eyes upon thy servant Edward our King, and upon this realm of England professing thy word and holy name, as Thou didst most favourably deliver King Ezechias from extreme sickness, and

prolongest his life for the safeguard of thy people the Israelites, and defendest them and the city from the tyranny of the Assyrians, so we most entirely appeal to thy great mercies graciously to restore the health and strength again of thy servant Edward ... that as thou hast begun by him the rooting out of Error, Idolatry, and Superstition, and the planting of true Religion, true worshipping and verity: so it may please thy merciful goodness long to preserve him for the confirmation and establishment of the same ...'

29. Vertot II, 33–4, 48.
30. BL Royal 18 C XXIV, fo. 366v; *CSP Spanish 1553*, p. 66.
31. *CSP Spanish 1553*, p. 67; Machyn, p. 34.
32. Vertot II, 35–8.
33. Harbison, *Rival Ambassadors*, p. 43.
34. Haynes, *State Papers*, pp. 153–4.
35. BL Cotton MS Galba B XII, fo. 248v.
36. *CSP Spanish 1553*, pp. 60–65, 81, 101, 126–7.
37. Cooper, *Chronicle*, p. 356. Cited Brigden, *London and the Reformation*, p. 519.
38. *Greyfriars Chronicle*, p. 78.
39. *CSP Spanish 1553*, p. 70.
40. Foxe VI, p. 352
41. Vertot ii, 40; *CSP Spanish 1553*, p. 71; Machyn, p. 35.
42. *CSP Spanish 1553*, p. 72.
43. OL ii, p. 684.
44. Zurich Letters iii, p. 365; LR I ccxxxvii.
45. *CSP Spanish 1553*, p. 52.
46. 'Can you, being a Portugal born, so impudently defame our region with that horrible crime, without all likely or probable proof, now that twenty years be spent and gone, whereas no sober or discreet Englishman did ever conceive any such thought in his mind? The physicians reported that he died of a consumption; the same was affirmed by the grooms of his Privy Chamber, which did keep continual watch with the sick King. All his subjects did believe it for a confessed truth; neither could your slanderous fable have been blown abroad, but among tattling women, foolish children, and such malicious English losels like unto you'. *A Sight of the Portugal Pearle* [1565], LR I ccxxxvii.
47. *CSP Spanish 1553*, pp. 37, 70.
48. LR I, ccxxxviii.
49. LR I, ccxxiii. Therefore leaving open the question of whether Edward may have been poisoned.
50. *Chronicle*, p. 117.
51. For a contrary view see Loach, pp. 160–62.
52. Gorham, *Gleanings*, p. 300.
53. Foxe VI, p. 350.
54. See also Harleian Miscellany, vol. X (1813), pp. 252–3.

55. LR I, ccxxx–ccxxxi.

56. APC IV, 363, 367, 390, 263. See also APC IV 384.

57. APC V, 122.

58. BL Lansdowne MS 99, fo. 92; Cornford, M. E., 'A legend concerning Edward VI', *EHR* XXIII 1908, pp. 286–290; PRO Essex Assize file 35/29/H/33.

59. HMC, *Salisbury* IX, 167, 173.

13. Nemesis

1. BL Lansdowne MS.

2. Ellis, *Original Letters* iii 3, pp. 309–310.

3. *CSP Spanish 1553*, pp. 76, 79.

4. *Arch. Journal* 30 (1873), p. 276; HMC 7th Report, p. 609.

5. Robert Reyns – who had been notified by Nicholas Throckmorton, whose poetical autobiography later claimed:

> And, though I liked not the religion
> Which all her life Queen Mary had professed,
> Yet in my mind that wicked notion
> Right heirs for to displace I did detest . . .
> Wherfore from four of us the news was sent,
> How that her brother he was dead and gone;
> In post her goldsmith then from London went,
> By whom the message was dispatched anon . . .

6. VM, p. 252; On 8 July she further summoned her supporters, Sir George Somerset, Sir William Waldergrave and Clement Heigham, and letters to Sir Edward Hastings followed. BL Lansdowne MS 1236, fo. 29; Strype, *Ecclesiastical Memorials*, III ii, 1.

7. Together with lands worth £604 17s 1¾d. per annum, in recompense for Chiche St Osyths, CPR V, 176–7; BL Royal MS 18 C XXIV, fo. 364.

8. *CSP Venetian* V, p. 537.

9. *CSP Spanish 1553*, pp. 73–4, 75–80.

10. *Greyfriars Chronicle*, p. 79; *CSP Spanish 1553*, pp. 80, 106; Guaras, p. 88; P. V. *Historical Narration*. There were no cries of God save the Queen. Thousands of 'consenters' apparently heard the proclamation as it was read out at points across the city, one observer noted, 'yet durst they not once move their lips to speak'.

11. Foxe VI, 385.

12. *CSP Spanish 1553*, p. 81.

13. *CSP Spanish 1553*, p. 82.

14. Strype, *Annals* IV, 485; BL Lansdowne 3, fos. 48v–49.

15. VM, p. 262.

16. *Chronicle of Queen Jane and Mary*, p. 7.

17. Machyn, pp. 35–6; *CSP Spanish 1553*, p. 81.had 3000 horsemen and 30 pieces of cannon; p. 91. For the composition of Northumberland's army, see Braddock R.C., 'The Character and Composition of the Duke of Northumberland's Army', *Albion* 6 (1974), pp. 342–56; Tighe W. J., 'The Gentlemen Pensioners, the Duke of Northumberland, and the Attempted Coup of July 1553', *Albion* 19 (1987), pp. 1–11; Braddock R. C., 'The Duke of Northumberland's Army Reconsidered', *Albion* 19 (1987), pp. 13–17.

18. *CSP Spanish 1553*, p. 88.

19. BL Harleian MS 523, fo. 11v.

20. PRO REQ 2/25/190.

21. VM, p. 256.

22. Goldsmiths' Company, Court Book I, fo. 177r, cited Brigden, p. 521; CLRO Repertory 12, fo. 66r; Journal 16, fos. 255v, 257v, 258r, 261r.

23. F. Madden, 'The Narrative of Richard Troughton', *Archaeologia* XXIII (1831), p. 25. [Troughton]

24. CPR 1554–1555, pp. 42–43; Troughton, p. 41; the text of the sermon was appropriately taken from Joshua I 16–18: 'Whosoever he be that doth rebel against thy commandment, and will not hearken unto thy words in all that thou commandest him, he shall be put to death: only be strong and of a good courage'. Cooper, *Annals of Cambridge* II, p. 74.

25. VM, p. 254.

26. VM, p. 255.

27. VCH Warwickshire II, 442; HMC 12th Report App. IX, 466; BL Harleian MS 353, fos. 138–139v; *Narratives of the Reformation*, pp. 132–76.

28. BL Lansdowne MS 156.

29. Harbison, *Rival Ambassadors*, p. 45; Vertot II, 50–53.

30. Lodge I, 226–7.

31. *CSP Spanish 1553*, pp. 88, 94, 115.

32. Strype, *Annals* IV, 485.

33. *CSP Spanish 1553*, p. 173.

34. *CSP Spanish 1553*, p. 208.

35. Guaras, p. 86; Wriothesley II, 101; Harbison, p. 51, and Loach, J., 'A Close League with the King of France: Lady Jane Grey's proclamation in French and its part in a planned betrayal' *Proceedings of the Huguenot Society* XXV (3), 1991.

36. Led by Sir John Williams, Edmund Peckham and the sheriffs of Oxford and Northampton; BL Harleian MS 353, fos. 139–139v.

37. VM, p. 260.

38. Alsop, 'Succession Crisis', pp. 587–8.

39. For the fullest account of this episode, see Alsop, J.D., 'The Navy and the 1553 Succession Crisis', *Albion* 24 1992, pp. 577–90.

40. *Chronicle of Queen Jane and Mary*, pp. 8–9; VM, pp. 258–9; Guaras, p. 94.

41. HMC 7th Report, pp. 690–710.

42. *CSP Spanish 1553*, pp. 91–2.

43. Guaras, p. 92.
44. BL Lansdowne MS 3, fo. 50.
45. BL Additional MS 33230, fo. 21.
46. Arundel had married Katherine, second daughter of Thomas Grey, 2nd Marquess of Dorset (1477–1530), to whom his son and heir Henry, Lord Maltravers, was born.
47. Nichols, 'Life of the last FitzAlan, Earl of Arundel', *Gentleman's Magazine*, 1st ser., 103, ii (1833), pp. 118–20.
48. Guaras, p. 96.
49. BL Harleian 353, fo.139; *CSP Spanish 1553*, p. 108.
50. P.V., *Historical Narration*, sig. Diiir, cited in Brigden, p. 523.
51. Machyn, p. 37; Knox, *Admonition*, sig. Aiiiir, cited in Brigden, p. 526.
52. Cooper, *Annals of Cambridge*, II, p. 75.
53. *Chronicle of Queen Jane and Mary*, p. 10.
54. BL Lansdowne MS 3/26.
55. VM, p. 268.
56. *Chronicle of Queen Jane and Mary*, p. 10.
57. Troughton, p. 44; A. G. Dickens, *Reformation Studies* (London, 1982), p. 308; BL Harleian MS 353 fo. 139; printed *Chronicle Queen Jane & Mary*, p. 12; TRP II, 338; Bale, *Vocacyon*, pp. 56–8.
58. *CSP Spanish 1553*, pp. 92–3, 95–6, 105.
59. Harbison, *Rival Ambassadors*, p. 53.
60. Great Yarmouth Town Hall, MS Y/C19/1, fo. 85; cited in Tittler, p. 137.
61. VM, p. 269; Guaras, p. 66; Wriothesley, *Chronicle* II, pp. 91–2.
62. *CSP Spanish 1553*, pp. 116–17.
63. Every householder in the eastern wards of the city was 'in a readiness in harness'.
64. Machyn, p. 38; Guaras, p. 99.
65. VM, p. 268.
66. CLRO Repertory 13, fo. 67v, Journal 16, fo. 257r, cited Brigden, London.
67. BL Harleian MS 353, fos. 140–140v.
68. VM, p. 271; Machyn, pp. 38–9; BL Harleian MS 353, fo. 140. (10,000 horsemen estimated!)
69. M. A. Florio, *Historia de la vita de Giovannia Graia*, p. 38, cited Prescott, *Mary Tudor*, p. 190; *CSP Spanish 1553*, p. 209.
70. Machyn, pp. 39–40 provides an eyewitness account of the funeral.
71. Machyn, p. 39.
72. With 2056¼ yards of black cloth; with the mourners' blacks accounted for, 9376½ yards of black cloth were used, at a cost of £4,280 17s 7d: the entire spectacle cost £5,946 9s 9d. PRO LC2/41; printed *Archaeologia* xii, 334–96.
73. *CSP Spanish 1553*, pp. 129–35, 155–7.
74. MacCulloch, *Cranmer*, p. 547, citing Philpot, *Vera expositio*, fo. 30v.
75. Plans were still being fashioned for a memorial as late as 1573, but they came to nothing. The altar was later destroyed by Puritans in 1644 and all memory

lost of the whereabouts of the last Tudor king until it was rediscovered by workers in 1685, searching for a space to bury Charles II.

76. Grafton, *Chronicle* ii, p. 536.

77. *CSP Spanish 1553*, p. 204.

78. See Gunn, S. J., 'A Letter of Jane, Duchess of Northumberland, in 1553', EHR CXIV 459, 1999, pp. 1267–71.

79. The scaffold cost £120 13s 6¼d. In comparison, the stage for Somerset's trial had cost £64 0s 1¼d. PRO E 351/3326; Guaras, p. 101; BL Harleian MS 2194, fo. 21r.

80. BL Harleian MS 2194, fo. 21r; Guaras, p. 103.

81. BL Harleian MS 2194, fo. 21r; Wriothesley, *Chronicle* II, p. 99.

82. BL Harleian MS 353, fos. 141–141v; Wriothesley, *Chronicle*, pp. 99–100; BL Harleian MS 353, fo. 143.

83. Machyn, p. 42.

84. BL Harleian MS 353, fo. 142.

85. Ibid.

86. BL Harleian MS 787, fo. 61v.

87. *Chronicle of Queen Jane and Mary*, p. 21.

88. BL Harleian MS 353, fo. 142; see also Guaras, p. 106.

89. Psalm 130.

90. BL Harleian MS 353, fos. 142v–143; Froude VI, p. 74.

INDEX

Act against Revilers of the Sacrament and for the Communion in both kinds (1547), 81
Act of the Relief (1549), 112
Act of Six Articles (1539), 4, 82, 89, 116, 149
Act of Uniformity (1549), 132
Adwick le Street, Doncaster, 90
Aesop, 32, 36
Anabaptists, 167
Anne of Cleves, 2, 26, 29, 71, 74, 84, 226
Antwerp, 174, 175, 256
Aristotle, 161, 163
Arran, Earl of, 30
Arthur, Prince, 2, 10, 11, 251
Arundel, Henry Fitzalan, Earl of, xi: coronation of Edward VI, 59; Somerset consolidates power, 65; enclosure protests, 119; October 1549 coup, 136, 139; questions Somerset, 153; loses office, 154, 159; opposition to religious reforms, 177, 191; and Mary Tudor, 205; and coup against Somerset, 207; arrest, 210, 213, 214; escapes execution, 225; and Edward's 'Devise', 252–3; pardon, 252; objects to Edward's letters patent, 253; and Mary's rebellion, 274–6, 277; Mary proclaimed queen, 278, 279; arrests Northumberland, 279, 281–2, 287
Arundel, Sir Thomas, 148, 151, 154, 209–10, 224–5
Ascham, Roger, 31, 37, 162, 234, 280
Ashley, Katherine (Kat), xi, 73, 87–8, 99, 100, 104

Ashridge, 28, 36, 37
Askew, Anne, 69
Aucher, Sir Anthony, 134
Audley, Thomas, 25, 27
Ayscough, Anne, 167

Baldwin, William, 259, 260
Banister, John, 250
Barbaro, Daniel, 194
Barclay, Alexander, 187
Bath, Earl of, 271
Baynard's Castle, 275
Beaufort, Lady Margaret, 16
Beaulieu, Essex, 172
Becket, Thomas, 13
Becon, Thomas, 69
Bedford, Earl of *see* Russell, Lord
Bellin, Nicholas, 283
Belmain, Jean, 95, 149, 150, 194
Bennett of Ware, 191
Berteville, 218–19
Berwick, 77
Bewdley, 102
Bible, 162; translation into English, 3, 4; 'Bishop's Bible', 8; Act of Six Articles repealed, 89; Prayer Book rebellion, 116
Bisse, John, 81
Blackheath, 234
Blagge, George, 43–4
Blount, Sir Richard, 160
Bocher, Joan, 167–8
Body, William, 90, 114
Boisdauphin, xv
Boleyn, Anne, 1, 2, 12, 29, 251, 289

Bollani, Dominic, 94–5

Bonner, Edmund, Bishop of London, 80, 122, 283

Book of Common Prayer see Prayer Book

Borrough, John, 238

Boston, 281

Bosworth Field, Battle of (1485), 10

Boulogne, 30, 32, 35, 76, 126, 148, 160, 177

Bradford, John, 245

Braintree, 157

Brandon, Charles, Duke of Suffolk, 32

Brandon, Henry, Duke of Suffolk, 32, 164

Bridewell, 233

Bristol, 87, 113, 123, 236

Brook, Robert, 140

Browne, Sir Anthony, 45, 49, 57, 222, 235

Brussels, 256, 263, 268

Bryan, Lady Margaret, 22, 26, 27

Bucer, Martin, 163, 196–7, 231

Buckingham, Duke of, 215

Buckinghamshire: enclosure protests, 117, 119; and Mary's rebellion, 272, 282

Bullinger, Martin, 160, 258

Burcher, John, 258

Bury, 120–21, 270, 274

Butts, Dr William, 28

Caius, John, 199

Calais, 8, 30, 272

Calvin, John, 178, 212, 232, 260

Cambridge, 119, 126, 269, 274, 277

Cardano, Hieronymus, 240–42

Carew, Sir Peter, 114–15

Catholicism: Henry VIII breaks away from, 2–4; Pilgrimage of Grace, 3, 115; iconoclasm, 80; opposition to Reformation, 131–2; Princess Mary's right to religious freedom, 132, 151, 171, 179–82, 183, 184–8; Edward's views on papal supremacy, 149–50; books destroyed, 153, 175

Cato, 32, 36

Cavendish, Sir William, 91

Cecil, William, 133, 134, 178, 237, 246; Dudley's letters to, 94, 243, 244; Southwell breaks into his chamber, 131;

works for Somerset's release, 157; and Dudley's humiliation of Somerset, 189, 209; and Edward's illness and death, 247, 256, 263; and Mary's rebellion, 267, 272, 275; support for Lady Jane Grey, 280

Chantries Act (1547), 81–2

Charles V, Emperor, 76, 110; and Somerset's power, 66; and Mary's right to religious freedom, 132, 185, 186, 187–8; and the October 1549 coup, 139; plans for Mary's escape, 172, 173; Hapsburg–Valois conflict, 205; Dudley makes alliance with France against, 255; and Mary's claim to the Crown, 256, 265, 266, 268, 271, 272; Mary proclaimed queen, 280

Cheke, Sir John, xi, 167; and Edward's education, 31, 33, 95, 161–2, 187, 194, 212; Seymour consolidates power, 83, 85; The Hurt of Sedition, 121; and Edward's interest in astronomy, 241; and Edward's 'Devise', 248; and Edward's illness, 253, 254; and Mary's rebellion, 267, 272, 276

Chelmsford, 192

Cheyney, Lord Thomas, 177, 253, 276, 274

Chester-le-Street, 279

Chichester, 235

Chichester, Bishop of, 35

Christ Church, Canterbury, 80

Christ's Hospital, 233

Church of England see Prayer Book; Reformation

Cicero, 95, 161, 163

Clarencius, Mistress, 284

Cleves, Duke of, 26

Clifford, Lady Margaret, 249

Clinton, Lord, 147, 269

Clyst, 124

Cobham, Lord, 92, 147, 247

coinage, devaluation (1551), 200–1

Coke, Edward, 218

Colhurst, Matthew, 217

Company of Gentlemen Pensioners, 160

Constable, William, 261

Cooke, Sir Anthony, 161

Cooper, Thomas, 92

Cornwall, 114–16, 268

Cornwallis, Sir Thomas, 268–9

Cotton, Sir Richard, 235

Courtenay, Gertrude, Marchioness of
    Exeter, 15–16, 17

Coventry, 270

Coverdale, Miles, 98, 159

Cowdray House, Sussex, 57, 235

Cox, Richard, xi, 31, 32–3, 36–7, 39, 161,
    223, 284

Crane, William, 210, 214, 216

Cranmer, Thomas, Archbishop of
    Canterbury, xi, 238; and Henry VIII's
    reformation, 2; at Edward's christening,
    16, 17; and Edward's education, 35, 239;
    and Henry's death, 48; coronation of
    Edward VI, 56, 60–62, 63; reformation
    of Church continues, 68, 89; Homilies,
    90; Book of Common Prayer, 109;
    Prayer Book rebellion, 115–16; and
    Kett's rebellion, 121–2; and the October
    1549 coup, 144, 145, 146; and Dudley's
    advancement, 149; and Somerset's
    imprisonment, 150; and Edward's
    interest in religious affairs, 163; and Joan
    Bocher's execution, 167; and Mary's
    right to religious freedom, 186–7; and
    Somerset's execution, 225; 1552 Prayer
    Book, 232, 243; canon law reform, 245;
    and Edward's 'Devise', 252; Edward's
    funeral, 283; burnt at the stake, 8

Cromwell, Lord, 199

Cromwell, Thomas, Earl of Essex:
    dissolution of the monasteries, 3; and
    Anne Boleyn, 12; and Edward's birth,
    14–15; Jane Seymour's death, 19, 21–2;
    and Edward's childhood, 22, 23, 26–7;
    and Henry's marriage to Anne of
    Cleves, 26; Reformation continues, 70;
    enclosure problems, 91; execution, 2

Crowley, Robert, 91

Dalkeith, 77

Darcy, Sir Thomas, 149, 189

Dartmoor, 114

Day, George, Bishop of Chichester, 284

de Gye (French ambassador), 220–21

de la Rose, Margaret, 197

Denmark, 262

Denny, Sir Anthony, 48, 88

Deptford, 165

Derby, Earl of, 156, 190; October 1549
    coup, 140; opposition to religious
    reforms, 177, 190–91; Somerset attempts
    to topple Dudley, 192–3; and Mary
    Tudor, 205

Dethick, Gilbert, 176, 245

Devon, Prayer Book rebellion, 114–16,
    123–4

Diego, Don, 268

Doncaster, 90

Doria, Andrea, 177

Dormer, Jane, 28–9, 131–2

Dorset, 115, 118, 235

Dorset, Henry Grey, Marquess of see Grey,
    Henry

Dover, 33, 279

Drury, Sir William, 270

Dubois, Jehan, 172–4

Dudley, Sir Andrew, 149, 154, 249, 285,
    286

Dudley, Edmund, 11, 41, 237, 269

Dudley, Guildford, 249, 265, 268

Dudley, Sir Henry, 272

Dudley, Jane, Duchess of Northumberland,
    284

Dudley, John, Earl of Warwick and Duke
    of Northumberland, xi–xii; factionalism
    in Henry's court, 40–42; and Henry's
    last will and testament, 47; intrigues
    against Seymour brothers, 52–3;
    becomes Earl of Warwick, 56;
    coronation of Edward VI, 57, 60; rivalry
    with Somerset, 5, 64; and Hales'
    radicalism, 93–4; warns Seymour, 101;
    and Seymour's execution, 108; and
    enclosure protests, 113; Kett's rebellion,
    126–9, 130–31; October 1549 coup, 5,
    135–40, 143, 147; gains control of Privy
    Chamber, 149, 150–51; power grows,
    151, 152–5, 157–8; and Somerset's
    rehabilitation, 159; takes charge of
    Edward's education, 160–62; relations

Dudley, John, Earl of Warwick and Duke of Northumberland—*contd*
with Somerset, 169–71; joins reformers, 170–71; rivalry with Somerset increases, 178; Mary appears before regency council, 186; humiliates Somerset, 189–90; private army, 191–2; Somerset attempts to topple, 192–3; and devaluation of coinage, 201; attacks on Mary Tudor, 205–7; plans revenge on Somerset, 206–10; becomes Duke of Northumberland, 208; dominance of Edward, 5, 211–12, 227; interrogates Somerset, 214–15; and Somerset's trial, 216, 217–18, 219; and Somerset's execution, 220, 221, 224, 225–6, 228–9, 237–8; illness, 236–7, 243; foreign credit problems, 238–9, 245; grows weary of court, 243; and Edward's illness, 246, 255; unaware of Edward's 'Devise', 248, 249; and the line of succession, 249, 251; hopes for alliance with France, 253, 255; believed to have poisoned Edward, 258–9; and Mary's rebellion, 264, 265, 267–76, 277–8; imprisonment and trial, 279, 281–2, 284–5; 'conversion' to Catholicism, 286–7; execution, 5, 286, 287–8

Dudley, Lady Catherine, 249
Dudley, Robert, 270
Durham, 80
Durham Place, 249, 267
Dussindale, 128

economy: devaluation of coinage, 200–1; foreign credit problems, 238–9, 245
Edinburgh, 77
Edward V, King, 57, 69, 137
Edward VI, King: birth, 1–2, 14–15, 19–20; christening, 15–18; early childhood, 22–9; household, 23–4, 30–31; appearance, 25, 164–5, 203, 240; portraits of, 25–6, 29, 36, 203–4, 245; illness, 27–8, 177–8; proposed marriage to Mary Queen of Scots, 30, 76–7; education, 6–7, 31–3, 34–5, 36–7, 39, 95–6, 239–40, 253; friends, 32;

childhood possessions, 33–4, 35–6; love of music, 34, 197; relationship with Katherine Parr, 34, 51; relationship with Henry VIII, 35; early writings, 36–7; relationship with his sisters, 37–8; begins official duties, 38–9; Henry's last will and testament, 44–5; and Henry's death, 49, 55; Thomas Seymour attempts to become his Governor, 52–3, 54, 83, 85; coronation, 56–63; as 'second Josiah', 4, 7, 62, 163–4; Somerset consolidates power, 66–7; Thomas Seymour's influence over, 74–5, 78–80, 84–5; and Somerset's invasion of Scotland, 78, 79; Privy Chamber expenses, 84; generosity, 84, 197, 229; Thomas Seymour hopes to arrange marriage to Lady Jane Grey, 85, 100; and French attack on Scotland, 94; Thomas Seymour attempts to kidnap, 102–3; Thomas Seymour's trial, 104, 105; and the Prayer Book rebellion, 115; Kett's rebellion, 121; *Orationes*, 121; and siege of Exeter, 124; and Mary's opposition to the Reformation, 131–2; October 1549 coup, 137, 140–8; Dudley's power grows, 149, 150–51, 152, 158, 160–62; on papal supremacy, 149–50; security increased, 149, 159–61; and Somerset's imprisonment, 150, 209–10; diary, 162, 165, 230; interest in religious affairs, 162–4, 165–7; conflicting expectations of, 164; entertainments, 164–6, 197–9, 220; and Hooper's consecration, 176; summer progress, 176, 234–6; interest in foreign affairs, 177; and Mary's right to religious freedom, 180–82, 183, 184–8, 206; welcomes Elizabeth at court, 183–4; relations with regency council, 188; essays, 194–6; influence of Martin Bucer, 196–7; awarded Order of Saint-Michel, 202–3; betrothal to Princess Elizabeth of France, 202–4, 205, 220, 253; jewel collection, 203; Dudley's dominance of, 211–12, 227; fourteenth birthday, 211; and Somerset's trial, 216–19; on the gendarmery, 219; and

Edward VI, King—*contd*
  Somerset's execution, 221, 222, 224,
    228–9; letters to Barnaby Fitzpatrick,
    216, 217, 219, 220, 229–30, 235, 236;
    takes greater share of government,
    230–31, 234, 245–6; suffers 'measles and
    smallpox', 233–4, 260; interest in
    astronomy, 240, 241; eye problems, 241;
    horoscope, 242; last illness, 244–5,
    246–7, 249, 250–51, 254–7, 260;
    relations improve with Mary, 244;
    'Devise' (choice of successor), 7, 247–55,
    272; death, 4, 257–62, 263; believed to
    have been poisoned, 258–9; pretenders,
    261; funeral, 283–4; posthumous
    reputation, 4; achievements, 8–9
'Edward VI' schools, 82
Edward the Confessor, 15, 43, 58
Elizabeth, Princess (later Elizabeth I), xiv;
    birth, 1, 12; at Edward's christening,
    16–17; and Edward's childhood, 26, 27;
    restored to line of succession, 29;
    relationship with Edward, 37, 38; and
    Henry's last will and testament, 47; and
    Henry's death, 49; Thomas Seymour
    tries to seduce, 71, 87–8, 100–1, 104,
    178; and Thomas Seymour's marriage
    to Katherine Parr, 74; and Katherine
    Parr, 98, 99; Thomas Seymour
    encourages to conspire against Edward,
    104; and Thomas Seymour's execution,
    106; welcomed at court, 183–4; and
    Edward's illness, 233, 257; Edward
    refuses to choose as successor, 7, 248;
    and Mary's journey to London, 281,
    282; becomes queen, 8
Elizabeth, Princess of France (daughter of
    Henry II), 202–4, 205, 220, 253
Elizabeth of York, 11, 13
Empsom, Richard, 11
enclosures, protests against, 91–3, 112–14,
    116–19
Englefield, 205
Essex: enclosure protests, 117, 118, 119;
    insurrection foiled, 157, 169
Essex, Earl of *see* Cromwell, Thomas
Eton, 55

Euston Hall, Thetford, 263
Exeter: Prayer Book rebellion, 114,
    115–16; siege of (1549), 116, 123–4
Exeter, Lady, 284
Exeter, Marquess of, 215

The Family of Henry VIII (painting), 1, 29
Fayery, Robert, 23
Feckenham, John, 68
Ferdinand, King of Aragon, 10
Ferrers, George, Viscount Hereford, 155,
    157, 243
Fisher, Thomas, 136
Fitzalan, Henry *see* Arundel, Earl of
Fitzpatrick, Barnaby, xii, 32, 164, 216, 217,
    219, 220, 229–30, 235, 236
Flammock, Sir Andrew, 129, 136
Fleet Prison, 81, 162, 179, 187
Forest, John, 81
Forest, Friar William, 3
Forrest, William, 69
Fowler, John, 74–5, 79–80, 84, 102, 103
Foxe, John, 6, 111, 161, 163, 239–40,
    260–61
Framlingham, 264, 270, 271, 274, 278, 281
France: Henry VIII's expedition to, 30, 32,
    35, 37; after Henry VIII's death, 76–7;
    intervention in Scotland, 94; declares war
    on England, 126; peace treaty, 165;
    Edward awarded Order of Saint-Michel,
    202–3; Edward betrothed to Princess
    Elizabeth, 202–4, 205, 220, 253;
    Hapsburg–Valois conflict, 205;
    Northumberland hopes for alliance with,
    253, 255; and Mary's rebellion, 271–2
Francis I, King of France, 20, 66, 70, 76
Francis, William, 261–2
Frome, 113
Fuller, Thomas, 32, 211

Gardiner, Stephen, Bishop of Westminster,
    xii, 85, 111, 190; omitted from Henry's
    last will and testament, 45; and Henry's
    death and funeral, 52, 55; Somerset
    consolidates power, 65; and continued
    reformation of Church, 69; opposes
    iconoclasm, 80; imprisonment, 157,

Gardiner, Stephen, Bishop of Westminster—*contd*
170, 177; and Edward's interest in religious affairs, 162–3; Mary frees, 283

Gates, Sir John, xii; holds dry stamp of Edward's signature, 161, 212; Mary prevented from escaping, 175; promotion, 189; and Dudley's dominance of Edward, 227; and Edward's 'Devise', 248; trial and execution, 285, 286, 287, 288

gendarmery, 192, 219–20

George, St, 166

German mercenaries, 126

Gerrard, Philip, 160–61

Ginzam, Alexander, 197

Gloucester, 270

Goldsmith's Company, 269

Goodrich, Thomas, Bishop of Ely, 151–2, 153, 248

Gosnold, Judge John, 253

Grafton, Richard, 284

Grantham, 279

Gray, William, 179

The Great Edward (naval flagship), 95

Great Yarmouth, 280–81

Greenwich, 95, 136, 169, 176, 198, 234, 243, 246, 247, 257

Greenwich, Treaty of, 94

Gresham, Sir Thomas, 253

Grey, Henry, Marquess of Dorset and Duke of Suffolk, xii; Edward's coronation procession, 57; and Thomas Seymour's intrigues, 85–6; Thomas Seymour hopes to arrange marriage of Edward and Lady Jane Grey, 100; enclosure protests, 119; appointed to regency council, 152, 153; becomes Duke of Suffolk, 208; and Mary's claim to Crown, 267, 273; Mary proclaimed queen, 277; Jane decides to abdicate, 279–80

Grey, Lady Jane, xii; Thomas Seymour hopes to arrange marriage to Edward, 85, 100; marriage to Guildford Dudley, 248–9; Edward chooses as successor, 7,

249, 251–2; becomes queen, 5, 263, 265; coronation, 265–6; reactions to her accession, 265, 267, 268–9; and Mary's rebellion, 267, 270, 274–6; decision to abdicate, 279–80; supporters pardoned, 284; imprisonment, 286

Grey, Lady Catherine, 248–9, 275

Grey of Wilton, Lord, 119, 121, 124, 208, 210

Greyfriars Church, London, 80, 283

Greyhound (ship), 273

Grice, Gilbert, 273

Guaras, Antonio de, 223

Guildford, 176, 234

Guildford, Sir Edward, 41

Guildhall, London, 234

Guise family, 76–7

Guisnes, 272

Haddington, 94

Haddon, Walter, 33, 259

Hales, Sir James, 252

Hales, John, 92–4, 108, 112

Hall, Edward, 39, 161

Halnaker, 235

Hammes, 272

Hammond, Lawrence, 208, 209

Hampshire, 119, 168, 169, 235

Hampton Court, 15, 176, 199, 208; Edward's childhood at, 24; Edward's household at, 30–31; October 1549 coup, 136, 137, 138; sporting activities at, 198; French envoys at, 202

Hanseatic League, 2

Hapsburg–Valois conflict, 205

Harbottle, Margaret, 200

Harpsfield, Nicholas, 20

Harrington, Sir John, 270

Harrison, William, 249

Harwich, 172, 273

Hastings, Sir Edward, 272

Hastings, Lord, 249

Hatfield, 169

Havering, 27, 28

Hawkins (conspirator), 238

Hayward, John, 260

Helston, 90–91

Henry, Prince (first son of Henry VIII), 11

Henry II, King of France, 236; becomes king, 76; marriage contract with Mary Queen of Scots, 94, 202; declares war on England, 126; alliance with Northumberland, 253; and Mary's rebellion, 271, 272; Mary proclaimed queen, 280

Henry III, King, 140–41

Henry VI, King, 7, 57, 71

Henry VII, King, 10–11, 13, 41, 101, 237, 284

Henry VIII, King: portrait of, 1, 29; becomes king, 10, 11; marriage to Katherine of Aragon, 11–12; desire for an heir, 2, 11–15; and Anne Boleyn, 12, 29; reformation of the Church, 2–4, 40–41, 42–3, 59, 68, 70; marriage to Jane Seymour, 1, 12–14, 58; dissolution of monasteries, 3, 13, 38; and Edward's birth, 1, 14–15, 19–20; Edward's christening, 15–18; Jane Seymour's death, 18–22; and Edward's childhood, 23–4, 28, 29; appearance, 25; marries Anne of Cleves, 26; line of succession, 29; expedition to France, 30, 32, 35, 37, 91; proposes Edward should marry Mary Queen of Scots, 30; and Edward's education, 31; relationship with Edward, 35; marriage to Katherine Parr, 71–2; treason laws, 82; Privy Chamber expenses, 84; debases coinage, 91; Act of Six Articles, 149; Primer, 175; devaluation of coinage, 200; ill-health, 40; advisers, 41; last will and testament, 44–50, 65, 185–6, 191; Surrey's execution, 44; death, 2, 46–52, 68; funeral, 55

Herbert, Lord, 249

Herbert, William, Earl of Pembroke, xii, 139, 168; enclosure protests, 113; and the Prayer Book rebellion, 124; October 1549 coup, 136–7, 142, 143, 145; becomes Earl of Pembroke, 208; and coup against Somerset, 209; and Somerset's trial, 216–17; entertains Edward at Wilton, 235–6; imprisoned in Tower, 274; and Mary's rebellion, 275, 276, 277

Hereford, Viscount see Ferrers, George

Herne, Isaac, 201

Hertford, 81

Hertford, Earl of (son of Duke of Somerset), 198

Hertford, Edward Seymour, Earl of see Seymour, Edward

Heywood, John, 201

Hoby, Sir Philip, 145–6, 197, 256, 263, 268

Holbein, Hans the Younger, 13, 25–6

Holcroft, Thomas, 215

Holinshed, Oliver, 241

Holland, Thomas, 220

Holt Castle, Denbighshire, 86–7, 102

Holy Roman Empire, 3–4; see also Charles V, Emperor

Honnings, William, 157

Hooker, Richard, 4

Hooper, John, 69, 153, 154, 160, 163, 176, 189, 200, 231

Howard, Sir George, 243

Howard, Henry, Earl of Surrey, xiv, 40–42, 43–4, 53, 65

Howard, Katherine, 2, 29, 289

Howard, Thomas, Duke of Norfolk: at Edward's christening, 16, 17; Jane Seymour's death, 19, 21; factionalism in Henry's court, 40–42; imprisonment, 44; Mary frees, 283; Northumberland's trial, 284–5

Huddleston, John, 270

Huggarde, Miles, 89

Huggons, Elizabeth, 237–8

Hull, 90

Hunsdon, 27, 28, 257, 263

Huntingdon, Earl of, 119, 272

Hurlock (master of the Greyhound), 273

Ipswich, 268–9, 281

Ireland, 272

Isabella, Queen of Castile, 10

Isle of Wight, 213, 215

Isocrates, 95, 212

James V, King of Scotland, 30, 76, 211

Jerningham, Sir Henry, 273
Jersey, 109
Joseph, John, 122
Josiah, King of Judah, 4, 7, 62, 163–4

Katherine of Aragon, 1, 2, 10, 11–12, 29, 251
Kenninghall, Norfolk, 43, 132, 133, 263, 269–70
Kent, 110; enclosure protests, 113, 118, 119
Kett, Richard, 131
Kett, Robert, xiii, 119–20, 125, 127–31, 134, 157, 168
Kett, William, 129–30
Kett's rebellion (1549), 119–23, 124–31, 134, 152, 168
Kilkenny, 279
King's Bench, 251
King's Lynn, 280
Kingston, Sir Anthony, 124
Kingsweston, 124
Knox, John, 243–4, 276–7, 282
Knyvett, Sir Edmund, 130, 131

Latimer, Hugh, Bishop of Worcester, xiii, 69, 91; and Edward's birth, 18; and Seymour's execution, 106–7; sermons at court, 111; 1549 rebellions, 112; pardon, 134; and Edward's interest in religious affairs, 163; advises Edward, 164; condemns devaluation of coinage, 201
Latimer, Lord, 72
Leghe, Nicholas, 59–60
Leith, 77, 94
Leland, John, 26, 33
Leti, Gregorio, 71
Lever, Thomas, 82, 164
Liber Regalis, 60
Lincolnshire, 269, 270
Lionell (Princess Mary's servant), 133
Lisle, Lord, 169
London: population growth, 91; Kett's rebellion, 121–2, 125, 134; October 1549 coup, 137–8, 139–42, 148; price inflation, 168; security increased, 169, 177, 212–13, 255; Ridley orders removal of altars, 175–6; Mary's procession

enters, 184; May Day conspiracy, 192; sweating sickness outbreak, 199–200; hospitals, 233; and Jane's accession, 269; Mary proclaimed queen, 276–7, 278; Mary's entrance into as queen, 281, 282–3; Northumberland's imprisonment, 281–2
Lowe, William, 237
Lowestoft Road, 273
Luttrell, Sir John, 199
Lydgate, John, 57

MacCulloch, Diarmaid, 8
Machyn, Henry, 258
Maldon, 171, 172
Mallet (Mary's chaplain), 187
Mantell (pretender), 261
Marney, Lady, 231
Marshalsea prison, 261
Mary, Princess (later Mary I), xiv–xv; birth, 1, 11; as Edward's godmother, 16, 17; at Jane Seymour's funeral, 21; and Edward's childhood, 24–5, 26, 27; restored to line of succession, 29; relationship with Edward, 37–8; and Henry VIII's death, 51; Thomas Seymour considers marriage to, 71; and Thomas Seymour's marriage to Katherine Parr, 74; and Katherine Parr, 97–8; Thomas Seymour encourages to conspire against Edward, 104; opposition to Reformation, 131–2; and the Prayer Book rebellion, 131, 133; right to religious freedom, 132, 151, 171, 179–82, 183, 184–8; and the October 1549 coup, 137, 138–9; opinion of Dudley, 156; refuses to visit court at Christmas, 156; escape plan fails, 171–5; Dudley attacks, 205–7; ordered to give up mass, 205–6; relations improve with Edward, 244; and Edward's illness, 246–7; Edward refuses to choose as successor, 7, 248, 251; Charles V's support for succession of, 256; flees Hunsdon, 257, 263; and Edward's death, 259, 263–4, 266; claims Crown, 264–5, 266–8, 269–76; proclaimed queen, 7–8,

Mary, Princess (later Mary I)—*contd*
276–81; Northumberland arrested, 279;
entrance into London, 281, 282–3; and
Edward's funeral, 283, 284; issues
pardons to Jane's supporters, 284
Mary, Princess (daughter of Henry VII),
248
Mary Queen of Scots: becomes queen, 30;
proposed marriage to Edward, 30, 76–7;
and Henry's last will and testament, 47;
marriage contract with Henry II of
France, 94, 202
Mary of Guise, 76–7, 210
Mary of Hungary, 172, 207
Mason, Sir John, 159, 178, 276
Mediterranean, 177
Melton, 120–21
Mercers Company, 212–13
Micronius, Martin, 163
Midlands, enclosure protests, 118
monasteries, dissolution of, 3, 13, 38, 81
Mordaunt, Sir John, 270
More, Sir Thomas, 3, 91
Morgan, Thomas, 270
Morison, Sir Richard, xiii, 25–6, 179, 268;
on Edward's birth, 1; and Jane
Seymour's death, 20–21; on Dudley, 53;
on Wriothesley, 154–5; on Edward's
relations with regency council, 188; and
Dudley's humiliation of Somerset, 189;
on Edward's illness and death, 250–51,
261
Morley, Lord *see* Parker, Henry
Moronelli, Francesco, 183
Mousehold Heath, 120, 125, 127, 128, 168
Much Wenlock, 80

navy: and Somerset's invasion of Scotland,
77, 87; support for Seymour, 87;
flagship, 95
Netherlands, 262
Newcastle, 191
Newdigate, Francis, 209, 215
Newgate prison, 125, 129
Newhall, 183, 281
Newport, John, 81

Noailles (French ambassador), 254–6, 258,
271, 280
Norfolk, 110; Kett's rebellion, 119–23,
124–31, 168; opposition to
Reformation, 131
Norfolk, Thomas Howard, Duke of *see*
Howard, Thomas
Northampton, 279, 282
Northampton, William Parr, Marquess of
see Parr, William
Northumberland, Duchess of, 266–7
Northumberland, John Dudley, Duke of
see Dudley, John
Norwich: Kett's rebellion, 119–20,
124–31, 157; and Mary's rebellion, 270

Oatlands, Surrey, 176
Ochino, Bernardino, 149
Oldman, John, 168
Order of the Garter, 56, 166, 189, 192, 204,
225, 234, 246
Orwell, 273
Osorius, Bishop of Sylves, 259
Owen, Dr George, 257, 259
Owen Tudor, 283
Oxford, Earl of, 52, 59, 274
Oxfordshire, 169: enclosure protests, 117,
119; and Mary's rebellion, 272, 282

Page, Sir Richard, 79
Paget, Lady Anne, 73, 225, 284
Paget, Lord, 214
Paget, Sir William, xiii, 39; factionalism in
Henry's court, 40–43; and Henry's last
will and testament, 44, 45, 47, 48, 49;
and Henry's death, 49; and resumption
of war with France, 76; on Somerset, 92;
and Thomas Seymour's arrest, 103;
warns Somerset, 109–11, 117–18, 135;
1549 rebellions, 112, 133; October 1549
coup, 141, 144–7; Dudley's power
grows, 152; 'Advice to the King's
Council', 158; and Mary's right to
religious freedom, 183; imprisonment,
210; trial, 225; Mary proclaimed queen,
277, 278

Palmer, Sir Thomas, xiii, 207–10, 216, 224, 285, 286, 287–8

Parker, Henry, Lord Morley, 138

Parkhurst, Dr, 98–9

Parkyn, Robert, 90, 179, 258, 279

Parliament: and Henry VIII's death, 50; religious reforms, 81, 175; Somerset consolidates power, 82–3; Thomas Seymour's trial, 105; rejects Hales' social legislation, 112; legislation after Somerset's fall, 152; 'still Parliament', 152; and Edward's illness, 245; and Edward's 'Devise', 248

Parr, Anne, 73

Parr, Katherine, xiii, 29, 30, 31, 284; marriage to Henry VIII, 71–2; relationship with Edward, 34, 51; Edward asks her to protect Mary, 38; plot against, 40; loses regency, 45, 76; and Henry VIII's death, 50; marriage to Thomas Seymour, 71–5, 79; rivalry with Anne Stanhope, 75–6; Somerset's treatment of, 76; pregnancy, 88, 97–8; Thomas Seymour tries to seduce Elizabeth, 88; death, 98–9

Parr, William, Marquess of Northampton, xiii, 156, 160, 214; becomes Marquess of Northampton, 56; Thomas Seymour looks for support from, 86; Kett's rebellion, 122, 124–5, 126, 130; and Dudley's advancement, 149; becomes Lord Great Chamberlain, 155; and possible alliance with France, 202; assassination plan, 207; and Somerset's trial, 216–17; trial and execution, 284, 286

Parry, Thomas, 100, 104

Partridge, Sir Miles, 207–8, 215, 224–5

Pattison, Matthew, 260

Paulet, William, Earl of Wiltshire and Marquess of Winchester, 166, 230, 235; October 1549 coup, 136, 139, 147; questions Somerset, 153; Wriothesley conspires against Dudley, 153–4; becomes Earl of Wiltshire, 155, 158; becomes Marquess of Winchester, 208; and Somerset's trial, 215; objects to Edward's letters patent, 253; and Mary's

rebellion, 272; imprisoned in Tower, 274

Peasants' Revolt (1381), 5, 133

Peckham, Sir Edmund, 272

Peers, John, 209

Pembroke, William Herbert, Earl of see Herbert, William

Penne, Sibyl, 22, 26–7

Peter Martyr, 258

Petre, Sir William, 133, 141, 246

Petworth, Sussex, 234

Pickering, William, 230

Pilgrimage of Grace (1536), 3, 115

Pinkie, Battle of (1547), 77–8

Pliny, 95

Poley, Thomas, 133, 269

Ponet, John, 92, 148, 149

Poole, 215, 236

Pooley (Mary's servant), 273

Portsmouth, 235

Potter, Gilbert, 266, 281

Powis, Lord, 199

Prayer Book: Book of Common Prayer (1549), 8–9, 109, 110, 112, 231; Prayer Book rebellion (1549), 114–16, 123–4, 133; Kett's rebellion and, 120; Mary's opposition to, 132; and Edward's beliefs, 167; second Book of Common Prayer (1552), 8, 231–2, 243; Elizabethan Prayer Book, 232

Privy Chamber: Holbein fresco, 13–14; Henry VIII's death, 51; Edward's expenses, 84; Edward's security increased, 107, 149, 159–61; Dudley's power grows, 157–8; Somerset's rehabilitation, 159; Dudley's dominance of Edward, 227; Edward takes greater share of government, 231

Privy Council, 13, 157; Somerset consolidates power, 65–6; October 1549 coup, 136; legislation after Somerset's fall, 152; and Edward's illness, 177; Edward takes greater share of government, 230–31, 246; and Edward's 'Devise', 252; and Edward's death, 261

Puttenham, Robert, 60

Quinones, Cardinal, 109

Radcliffe, Henry, 270
Reading, 169, 236, 247
Red Cap, Captain, 168
Reformation: Henry VIII's reformation,
    2–4; continues after Henry's death, 4–5,
    6, 8, 68–70, 88–91; iconoclasm, 80–81,
    89–90; congregation becomes active
    participant in services, 89–90; Mary's
    opposition to, 131–2; continues after
    Somerset's fall, 151; Dudley's power
    grows, 153; Edward's interest in
    religious affairs, 162–4, 165–7;
    destruction of altars, 175–6, 179;
    legislation, 175; forty-two articles of
    faith, 232; see also Prayer Book
regency council: Henry VIII's last will and
    testament, 44–50; tries to restrain
    iconoclasm, 80–81; religious reforms,
    89; and Mary's opposition to the
    Reformation, 132; Dudley's power
    grows, 152–3, 158; evangelicals hold
    majority on, 152; Paget's reforms, 158;
    Somerset's rehabilitation, 159; and
    Mary's right to religious freedom,
    180–81, 183, 185–8; Edward's relations
    with, 188; gendarmery, 192, 219–20; and
    Somerset's attempt to topple Dudley,
    193; orders Mary to give up mass, 205–6;
    Dudley takes control of, 211–12;
    Edward takes greater share of
    government, 230–31, 245–6; and
    Edward's illness and death, 247, 254,
    265; and Mary's rebellion, 266–8, 270,
    273–4; Mary proclaimed queen, 278;
    Mary distrusts, 282; and
    Northumberland's execution, 286
Renaissance, 9, 25
Renard, Simon, xv, 188, 193, 256, 271–2,
    280
Rich, Sir Richard: peerage, 56; enclosure
    protests, 112; October 1549 coup, 140;
    appointed to regency council, 152;
    insurrection foiled, 157; orders Mary to
    give up mass, 205, 207; and coup against
    Somerset, 210–11; and Mary's rebellion,
    274
Richard III, King, 10, 69, 137

Richmond, 176, 202, 205
Ridley, Nicholas, Bishop of London:
    denounces images of saints, 69; takes
    mass in English, 81; orders removal of
    altars, 175–6; and Mary's right to
    religious freedom, 186–7; and
    Somerset's execution, 225–6; sermon
    on charity, 232–3; denounces Mary and
    Elizabeth, 257
Roberts, Anthony, 125
Robotham, Robert, 261
Rochester, Robert, 172–4, 205, 264
Rogers, Sir Edward, 149, 154
Romford, 122, 169
Romney Marsh, 247
Rosso, Giulio Raviglio, 259
Royal Library, 33
Russell, Lord, Earl of Bedford, 168, 177;
    and Thomas Seymour's advances to
    Elizabeth, 100–1; and Prayer Book
    rebellion, 115, 117; Kett's rebellion,
    122, 123; ends siege of Exeter, 123–4;
    October 1549 coup, 136, 142, 143, 145;
    peerage, 155; ordered to prevent Mary's
    escape, 175; objects to Edward's letters
    patent, 253; and Mary's rebellion, 272
Rutland, Earl of, 86, 99, 156, 190, 282
Ryan, John, 23

Sadler, Sir Ralph, 30
St Albans, 117
Saint-André, Jacques d'Albon, Marshal de,
    xv, 202
St James's Palace, London, 79, 107
St Magnus Church, London, 70
St Martin Ludgate, London, 68, 200
St Paul's Cathedral, London, 122, 213; and
    Edward's birth, 14; Jane Seymour's
    death, 21; dirge for Francis I's death, 70;
    celebration of Battle of Pinkie, 78;
    iconoclasm, 80, 81; altars removed, 176;
    Mary proclaimed queen, 277
St Paul's Cross, London, 219, 285–6
Salisbury, 235
Salmon, Christopher, 257
Sampford Courtenay, 114–15, 124, 133
Sanders, Nicholas, 20

Scepeaux, Francois de, Marechal de
    Vieilleville, xv
Schepperus, Cornelius, 172, 173, 174, 175
Scheyfve, Jehan (Imperial ambassador), xv,
    172, 177, 187, 265; reports on Edward,
    165, 198, 239; on rivalry between
    Dudley and Somerset, 178, 189; and
    Mary's right to religious freedom, 183,
    206; on opposition to religious reforms,
    191; on May Day conspiracy, 192; on
    accusations against Somerset, 208, 210,
    213; on increased security in London,
    213; on Somerset's trial and execution,
    216–21; on the gendarmery, 219; on
    Edward's illness and death, 244–5, 247,
    250, 254, 257, 258, 259; on Edward's
    letters patent, 253; on Mary's claim to
    the Crown, 266, 268; Mary proclaimed
    queen, 277; on Edward's funeral, 284
Scotland: proposed marriage of Edward VI
    and Mary Queen of Scots, 30, 76–7;
    'rough wooing', 30, 94; English
    garrisons, 77, 82, 94; Somerset invades,
    77–8, 79; costs of campaign against, 109
Scrots, William, 203
Selve, Odet de, xv, 67
Seymour, Alexander, 208
Seymour, Anne (Somerset's daughter), 169
Seymour, Davy, 209
Seymour, Edward, Earl of Hertford and
    Duke of Somerset, xiii-xiv; at Edward's
    christening, 17; becomes Earl of
    Hertford, 18; factionalism in Henry's
    court, 40–43; and Henry VIII's last will
    and testament, 47–50, 65; becomes Lord
    Protector, 48, 49–50, 52–4, 56; and
    Henry VIII's death, 49–50; Dudley
    intrigues against, 53; becomes Duke of
    Somerset, 56; coronation of Edward VI,
    57, 62, 63; consolidates power, 63–7, 71,
    82–3; rivalry with Dudley, 5, 64; and
    continued reformation of Church, 69,
    70; religious affiliation, 69; feud with his
    brother, 71, 78–9, 83, 97; and his
    brother's marriage to Katherine Parr,
    75, 79; treatment of Katherine Parr, 76;
    invasion of Scotland, 77–8, 79, 82, 94,

109; religious reforms, 81; repeals
    treason laws, 82; concern for social
    justice, 91–3, 108; Thomas Seymour's
    trial and execution, 104–5, 106, 107–8;
    Somerset House, 108–9; Paget warns,
    109–11, 135; and enclosure protests,
    112–14, 116–19, 134; and the Prayer
    Book rebellion, 115; Kett's rebellion,
    121, 122–3, 125–6, 134; ends siege of
    Exeter, 123–4; and Mary's religious
    freedom, 132, 206–7; October 1549
    coup, 5, 135–48; arrest and
    imprisonment, 147–8, 150, 153–4, 157;
    rehabilitation, 159; relations with
    Dudley, 169–71, 178; ordered to prevent
    Mary's escape, 175; turns towards
    conservatives, 178–9, 190–91; Dudley
    humiliates, 189–90; attempts to topple
    Dudley, 192–3; supports Mary, 205;
    Dudley plans revenge, 206–10;
    imprisoned in Tower again, 209–10, 213;
    accusations against, 213, 214–15, 218;
    trial, 215–19; execution, 5, 220–24,
    225–6, 228–9, 237–8, 245
Seymour, Jane, 24, 29, 33, 71; marriage to
    Henry VIII, 12–14, 58; Edward's birth,
    1, 14, 19–20; at Edward's christening,
    16, 18; death, 18–22
Seymour, Jane (daughter of Duke of
    Somerset), 206, 218
Seymour, John, 209
Seymour, Lady Marjorie, 99
Seymour, Mary, 98, 99, 106
Seymour, Thomas, 1st Baron, xiv; on
    regency council, 47, 64; attempts to
    become Edward's Governor, 52–3, 83,
    85; Dudley intrigues against, 52–3;
    peerage, 56; becomes Lord Admiral, 56;
    coronation of Edward VI, 60, 63;
    Somerset consolidates power, 65; feud
    with his brother, 71, 78–9, 83, 97;
    marriage to Katherine Parr, 71–5, 79;
    influence over Edward, 74–5, 78–80;
    finances Edward, 79–80, 84–5; hopes to
    arrange marriage of Edward and Lady
    Jane Grey, 85, 100; builds power base,
    85–7; tries to seduce Elizabeth, 87–8,

Seymour, Thomas, 1st Baron—*contd*
100–1, 104, 178; and Katherine's
pregnancy, 97; and Katherine's death,
98; warned about his behaviour, 100–1;
hopes for support from Edward, 101–2;
attempts to kidnap Edward, 5, 102–3;
arrest and trial, 102–5; execution, 105–8
Sharington, Sir William, 87, 102
Sheen, 169
sheep: enclosures, 91; taxation, 112, 114
Sheffield, Lord, 56, 125
Shrewsbury, 80, 199
Shrewsbury, Earl of, 190, 215; coronation
of Edward VI, 59, 60, 62; enclosure
protests, 119; Kett's rebellion, 125;
October 1549 coup, 140; opposition to
religious reforms, 177, 191; Somerset
attempts to topple Dudley, 192–3;
supports Mary, 205, 276; objects to
Edward's letters patent, 253
Sidney, Sir Henry, 227, 257, 258
Sidney, Sir William, 28
Sittingbourne, 168
Smeaton, Mark, 12
Smith, Dr, 70
Smith, Sir Thomas, 93, 133, 135, 144, 145,
146, 147, 155
Solomon, King of Israel, 4, 58–9
Solway Moss, Battle of (1542), 30
Somerset, 115, 124
Somerset, Anne Stanhope, Duchess of *see*
Stanhope, Anne
Somerset, Edward Seymour, Duke of *see*
Seymour, Edward
Somerset House, London, 108–9, 139, 214
Sommer, William, 197
Southampton, 235
Southampton, Thomas Wriothesley, Earl
of *see* Wriothesley, Thomas
Southwell, Sir Richard, 43, 91, 130–31,
133, 148, 154, 270
Spain, 262
Speke, Sir Thomas, 199
Stanford in the Vale, 90
Stanhope, Anne, Duchess of Somerset, xiv,
178, 214, 237; religious beliefs, 69;
rivalry with Katherine Parr, 75–6; and

the October 1549 coup, 141, 144; and
her husband's imprisonment, 150, 153;
arrested, 210; Mary frees, 283
Stanhope, Sir Michael, xiv, 66, 214, 215,
224–5
Stansgate, 172
Sternhold, Thomas, 34
Strange, Lord, 191, 206, 241
Stranger Church, London, 163
Succession Act (1536), 44–5
Sudeley Castle, Gloucestershire, 86, 97
Suffolk: enclosure protests, 110, 117, 119;
Kett's rebellion, 119, 120–1, 125, 133
Suffolk, Frances, Duchess of, 248, 265,
266–7
Suffolk, Henry Grey, Duke of *see* Grey,
Henry
Suffolk, Catherine, Duchess of, 157, 178
Surrey, 113, 119
Surrey, Henry Howard, Earl of *see* Howard,
Henry
Sussex, 169; enclosure protests, 110, 113,
117; Mary proclaimed queen, 274
Sussex, Earl of, 270, 271
Swannington, 129
Swanston Hall, Cambridgeshire, 257, 263,
269
sweating sickness, 199–200, 236
Swiss mercenaries, 127, 128
Syon, 55, 157

Terentianus, Julius, 258–9
Thames, River, 165, 215, 245, 255, 263
Thirlby, Thomas, Bishop of Westminster
and Bishop of Norwich, 45, 96
Thomas, William, xiv, 95, 194, 227–8
Thompson, William, 219
Throckmorton, Sir Nicholas, 107, 179,
228–9, 279
Thynne, Sir John, 124
Titchfield, Hampshire, 139
Tower of London, 14, 56; October 1549
coup, 141; Somerset imprisoned in, 147,
209–10; Lady Jane Grey's coronation, 265;
Northumberland imprisoned in, 281
Tracy, Richard, 192
Treason Act (1534), 82

Tree of Reformation, Mousehold Heath, 120

Tresham, Sir Thomas, 279

Troughton, Richard, 269, 270, 279

Tunstall, Cuthbert, Bishop of Durham, 21, 60

Turner, William, 69, 89

Tyndale, William, 3

Tyrwhitt, Lady, 104

Tyrwhitt, Robert, 104

Underhill, Edward, 271

Underhill, Guildford, 271

Van der Delft (Imperial ambassador), xv, 68–9, 71, 103, 135; and Edward's coronation, 56, 63; predicts rivalry between Somerset and Dudley, 64; on Somerset's power, 66; and Charles V's demands for Mary's religious freedom, 132; and the October 1549 coup, 140, 141, 148–9; on Wriothesley's ill-health, 152, 154; on religious divisions in government, 156–7; on Dudley, 158; on Somerset's rehabilitation, 159; plans for Mary's escape, 171–2; death, 183

Vane, Sir Ralph, 207, 209–10, 224–5

Vendome, Francois de, Vidame of Chartres, 165, 169

Vives, Ludovico, 36

Waldegrave, 205

Wales, 126, 168

Waltham, 235

Wanstead, 281

Warblington, 235

Ware, 269

Wars of the Roses, 10

Warwick, John Dudley, Earl of see Dudley, John

Warwickshire, 118

Watson, Dr, 285–6

Wells, 124

Welsh, Robert, 124

Wendy, Dr Thomas, 257, 259

Wentworth, Thomas, Lord, 121, 155, 189, 271

Werdmueller, Otto, 159

Westminster, 40, 209

Westminster Abbey, 59, 60, 189, 283–4

Westminster Hall, 62–3, 217, 284

Westminster Park, 246

Westmorland, Earl of, 191

Whalley, Richard, 170, 171, 190

White, John, 168

Whitehall, 29, 60, 63, 198, 283

Wilder, Philip van, 34, 197

Willoughby, Sir William, 56

Wilton, Wiltshire, 113, 235–6

Wiltshire, 115, 169; protests against enclosures, 113; Edward's progress through, 235–6

Wiltshire, Earl of see Paulet, William

Winchester, 179, 236

Winchester, Marquess of see Paulet, William

Windsor, 55, 120, 176, 197

Windsor Castle, 117, 141, 145–7, 236, 247, 272

Wingfield, Sir Anthony, 121, 147, 155

Wingfield, James, 210

Woking, 176

Wolf, Sir Edward, 141

Wolsey, Cardinal, 12, 35, 91

Woodham Walter, Essex, 171, 172, 174

Wotton, Nicholas, 187

Wriothesley, Thomas, Earl of Southampton, xv; joins evangelical faction, 43; and Henry VIII's death, 50; on regency council, 53–4; becomes Earl of Southampton, 54, 56; arrest and trial, 64–5; and Thomas Seymour's intrigues, 86, 100; October 1549 coup, 139, 148; Princess Mary allowed mass, 151; ill-health, 152; conspires against Dudley, 153–5; questions Somerset, 153; arrest, 154; death, 154–5, 159

Wroth, Sir Thomas, 149, 164, 257

Wymondham, 119, 130

Yarmouth, 273

Yeomen of the Guard, 159

York, John, 140

Yorkshire, 123

WEST END